The German Military Elite of the Battle for Budapest, 1944–1945

KRISZTIÁN UNGVÁRY

THE GERMAN MILITARY ELITE OF THE BATTLE FOR BUDAPEST, 1944–1945

peko
PUBLISHING

First English edition

ISBN 978 615 5583 93 3

The original Hungarian edition of this book was published
as Ungváry Krisztián: *Hősök?*
A budapesti csata német katonai elitje.
Budapest, Jaffa Kiadó, 2019

Translated by Blanka Bíró

Published by
PeKo Publishing
Keszthely, Hungary
www.pekobooks.com

TABLE OF CONTENTS

INTRODUCTION

FOREWORD

The history of the siege of Budapest is attracting more and more interest among the general reading public – and not only in Hungary. Among other factors, the continued interest in the author's work, *The Siege of Budapest* (*Budapest ostroma*), which has been published in 18 editions in seven countries, vouches for the ongoing attention paid to these events. We witnessed an increasing number of spontaneous remembrances, erecting statues, organized memorial tours, and the creation of monuments. This verifies that the siege of Budapest that occurred more than 70 years ago is still a significant focal point in our collective memory. In other words, these events can still be considered "living history."

The French historian Pierre Nora formulated the theory of collective memory, which states that the memory of specific social groupings (in his case, the French nation) becomes clearly and exactly manifested at specific geographical locations. It increasingly seems that in the case of Hungary, the siege of Budapest corresponds with Nora's theory. At the same time, however, in terms of German national identity, the siege of Budapest during 1944–1945 does not bear any exceptional significance. It is considered to be merely a marginal event in the long line of catastrophes that are collectively called the Second World War, and even the most brutal chapter of the siege itself, the breakout attempt, is overshadowed by the bombing of Dresden on 13 February 1945. Considering the number of German casualties in the Second World War, it undoubtedly cannot be expected that the role and importance of the siege of Budapest would have greatly increased in Germany. The situation is very similar in terms of the Russian collective memory. However, as far as the Hungarian remembrance culture is concerned, the siege of Budapest during the Second World War is gradually becoming an event of increasing significance. Until 1990, the national collective memory could not elaborate on this topic in any way. The author still remembers the school ceremonies where *úttörők* (little pioneers) and *kisdobosok* (little drummers) read out the compulsory tales of the caring humanism of the Soviet soldiers and the barbaric acts of the "villainous German fascists."

The residents of Budapest who survived the siege have extremely conflicting memories of the event and its consequences. Those whose lives had been saved by Soviet soldiers will obviously consider 1945 as a time of liberation. However, those who did not belong to this group have used, according to their temperament, various expressions to describe the events, including "being freed," "occupation," or "Bolshevist terrorism." It was not until 1990 that they could openly express and discuss their views in public.

Interestingly, the situation remained unchanged for a considerable time, even after the so-called *rendszerváltás* (change of the system). Every political party continued to commemorate the so-called "liberation" of Budapest in 1945; differences could only be discerned in that the liberals and the Magyar Demokrata Fórum (MDF, Hungarian Democratic Forum) had taken time to openly talk about the consequences of the Soviet occupation, while no other political party was willing to represent themselves at the commemorative events of the Szocialista Párt (Socialist Party) in the Gesztenyéskert.

A few years later, however, the denial of the concept of the liberation of Budapest no longer invoked extreme sentiments. When the author's work *Budapest ostroma* (*The Siege of Budapest*) was published in 1998, the whole range of the Hungarian media, from the right-wing magazine *Magyar Demokrata* to the now defunct left-wing daily *Népszabadság*, eagerly spoke appreciatively of the work. It is true, however, that all have acknowledged different sections of it. At the same time, one year before the publication of the author's work, a new, extreme right-wing inclined interpretation also surfaced, which, at that time, had not gained particular public attention. The organization called Magyar Nemzeti Front (Hungarian National Front) organized the event called Day of Honour for the first time that year, with a couple of dozen people in attendance. According to their interpretation, the breakout attempt was a heroic deed, upon which they looked as an example of anti-communism and a showcase of military virtues fulfilling the SS motto *Meine Ehre heißt Treue* (My honour is loyalty). The participants chose the Kapisztrán statue in front of the Hungarian Military History Museum as their location obviously because they also wished to underline the interpretation that Hungary is "the bulwark of the West against Bolshevism". However, it might not be entirely coincidental that the statue as a symbol bears another trait of significance as well. János Kapisztrán (John of Capistrano) was not only a hero of the Battle of Nándorfehérvár against the Turks (it might be worth noting too that his actions seriously jeopardized the success of the Hungarian army), but preceding this campaign, he, as a notorious antisemitic inquisitor, contributed to the burning of hundreds of Jews at stake in Breslau (present-day Wrocław). The choice of the statue of Kapisztrán was not a coincidence, which is further reinforced by the fact that there are a number of other locations that would have been more suitable for memorial locations for anti-communist organizations. These include the Vienna Gate (Bécsi kapu, or Wiener Tor), which was one of the assembly points of the breakout attempt; the exit point of the Devil's Ditch (Ördögárok) and the Vérmező (today a large communal park under Buda Castle) which, as a former German military airfield, would have been a better suited, and historically a more authentic location than the open ground in front of the Hungarian Military History Museum where nothing of importance happened during the siege.

In the meantime, however, everything seemed to indicate that the political parties could not properly deal with the memory of the siege of Budapest. The Socialists adhered to the anti-fascist tradition and had been trying to avoid acknowledging the fact that, in a political sense, the events could not be classified as liberation. Fidesz (the Federation of Young Democrats), based on the *"egy a tábor, egy a zászló"* ("one side, one flag") notion, did not want to present their own clear-cut message or interpretation as this would have severely jeopardized the increase in their voter base. In order to achieve this, several of their media representations, for example, the weekly magazine *Magyar Demokrata*, tried to knock the wind out of the far-right sails when they themselves started to promote and facilitate far-right ideology and memorial culture. An example of this is the issue of the *Magyar Demokrata* in February 2004, on the cover of which was stated, "They were the heroes of Europe." The "heroes," according to the magazine, were, besides the soldiers of the Royal Hungarian Army (*Magyar Királyi Honvédség*), the soldiers of the Wehrmacht and the Waffen-SS as well. The question of whether the members of the *Nyilaskeresztes Párt* (Arrow Cross Party) should be included in this group was deliberately left unanswered. Similarly, no mention was made of the mass murders perpetrated by Hungarians in the city. At the same time, however, the magazine deemed it essential to describe in detail the barbaric acts committed by Soviet soldiers. This kind of approach has not changed in the Fidesz media to this day.[1]

In connection with the siege of Budapest and the breakout attempt, it is necessary to mention a few other aspects as well, most importantly one pertaining to the combat morale of the German army. Strictly from the perspective of military science, the accomplishments of the German army during the Second World War have been acknowledged and recognized by all observers. It is a fact that the Wehrmacht was able to stand its ground for almost six years against vastly superior numbers. This could only have been achieved with the excellent performance they showed in terms of military professionalism. After the Vietnam fiasco of the USA, the Pentagon launched serious research in order to find out how the internal cohesion of their army could be increased and how their combat efficiency could be raised. Among the results of these research activities was the work of Israeli military historian Martin van Creveld, published for the first time in 1982, which named the Wehrmacht the best army of the Second World War by considering the factors of combat morale, internal drive, motivation, flexibility and group cohesion. The author stated that neither of the opposing forces were comparable to the Wehrmacht.[2] According to his calculations, the efficiency of the German soldiers was at least 30 percent higher than that of British or American soldiers, and this advantage remained the same throughout the entire war. Creveld has also not shied away from the statement that in terms of technical background, strategy, organization, doctrine, and the cooperation of the military branches, no other army would be closer to the Wehrmacht than the Israeli.[3] As the author notes: "The common German soldier in the Second World War was not prone to psychosis. They were not fighting to achieve social prestige, at least not after the winter of 1941. In general, they were not driven by their belief in Nazi ideology – in fact, quite the opposite was often true. They were fighting for reasons that have always dictated the fighting spirit of men: they were fighting because they could feel themselves part of a unified and professionally led group, the organization, operations, and leadership of which felt correct and justified to them despite the inevitable presence of slackers and 'ribbon happy' people."[4]

It has to be noted, however, that incredible combat morale cannot be considered independent from the high level of efficiency of the German military judiciary system and the related motivational value. Within the Wehrmacht during the war, more than one-and-a-half million convictions had been pronounced as opposed to a mere 25,000 acquittals. On a quarterly average, around 25,000 convictions were pronounced during 1941/1942; this means that, on average, one in every two hundred soldiers had been convicted in just a quarter of a year. At least the same number of cases were concerned with disciplinary matters and ended with convictions. Considering all of the combatant armies, the largest number of death penalties were imposed in the Wehrmacht (not considering the Soviet Union, where these legal procedures – altogether 150,000 execution sentences – could hardly be differentiated from politically biased show trials). In the German army, there were 30,000 convictions pronounced, which were punishable by death, and around 23,000 such death penalties were carried out. At the same time, in the United States military, one death penalty was carried out, 140 in the French and 40 in the British.[5] The austerity of the military tribunals can be demonstrated not only by the death penalties issued and executed en masse. The case of *Gefreiter* Hans Heller is a striking example of the severity of the sentences for other offences: he first stole 120 cigarettes. He was sentenced to six months in prison and served two months immediately. Soon after this, he was sentenced to three years in prison and lost his rank because he had eaten the food rations of one of his fellow cellmates, which was entrusted to him by the father of the inmate. Moreover, the sentence was made executable immediately.[6] Comparing the workings of the German military discipline apparatus to the operations of the Hungarian military tribunals, the austerity of the former seems especially draconic.[7] This is also underlined by the fact that the biographies published in the present work contain numerous references to the proceedings of German military tribunals – even if most of these cases concluded with acquittal.

There is yet another factor apart from the strict military discipline that would explain the almost completely irrational perseverance of the German soldier right until the very last minute: that is, the ideological war on the Eastern Front. The majority of German soldiers were convinced that being a prisoner of war would mean certain death. They were not entirely wrong since the massacre of prisoners of war was a well-established practice of the Red Army. This is verified by a report of Miklós Steinmetz, whose death later on the outskirts of Budapest was a tragic coincidence. In 1944, Steinmetz was assigned to the political department of the Soviet 317th Rifle Division and was responsible for the interrogation of German and Hungarian officers (he spoke German fluently). In a report to Mihály Farkas at the beginning of October 1944, he complained that the leader of the political department "does not actively oppose the strongly held belief of the division commander and the deputy leader of the political department that prisoners of war, especially officers, and especially the German officers, should be summarily executed even before they could be interrogated at the division".[8]

The number of Hungarian soldiers taking part in the breakout attempt was small. There are no exact data available; however, it is known that approximately 2 percent (13 persons) of the escapees who succeeded in reaching the German lines were Hungarian. The mass graves opened after the breakout attempt contained few Hungarian remains. The considerable number of available witness accounts confirm that during the siege, most Hungarian participants ceased resisting within the city's administrative boundaries. However, this data is also misleading as the vast majority of Hungarian soldiers could hardly be deemed participants at all. There is ample evidence to suggest that many of the Hungarian soldiers switched to civilian clothing weeks or even months before the breakout attempt or stayed inactive in their uniform. At least 90 percent of them were not participants in the combat actions in any way by February 1945, and those who still took up arms were mostly on the Soviet side. Therefore, there is an almost grotesque development in the remembrance culture evolving in connection with the breakout attempt – the Hungarian commemorators consider such soldiers as "their" soldiers who were not even members of the Hungarian nation (not including, of course, persons belonging to the German ethnic minority living in Hungary who were forcefully enlisted and whose classification is a very complicated issue in this case). The silent majority of Hungarian soldiers did not behave the way that those who commemorate this event would like us to remember: most of them surrendered without combat or resistance. Some of them even volunteered to fight against those attempting to break out in order to avoid being taken prisoners of war.

Interestingly, an attempt to reach a consensus regarding this matter originated from the few Jewish survivors of the siege of Budapest who wish to install a memorial plaque in Széna Square dedicated to *Generalmajor* Gerhard Schmidhuber, the saviour of the Jewish ghetto, who died during the breakout attempt. A high-ranking German officer, who distanced himself from Nazi ideology, and who perished amongst unworthy conditions with many of his comrades at one of the most contested points of the city would certainly be an appropriate person whose grave could serve as a place of remembrance for anyone, regardless of their conflicting notions. Interestingly, the proposal – although Yad Vashem, The World Holocaust Remembrance Centre does not challenge the underlying facts – was not endorsed by any of the political parties despite numerous civilian initiatives being launched in the last fourteen years.

At the same time, there are smaller-scale local initiatives and commemorations. However, for the only ones that have been realised (and in every sense worthy) nationwide commemoration, Tamás Cseh and Géza Bereményi should be credited. The song *Széna tér* on their 1997 album commemorates the nameless German and Hungarian victims of the siege of Budapest. However, there is still no appropriate physical memorial place that would allow their remembrance in dignified circumstances.

In a war, there are no idealised heroes, only very fallible humans. Some people commit heroic deeds but, in the meantime, perpetrate horrible acts of barbarism; notions of military professionalism can be ascribed to others; and there are some who do nothing of particular importance, and yet *they* are decorated. What is common to all these people is their uniform and the physically visible marks of recognition. Those differences, which are apparent in their moral conduct, ethical views and military professionalism, would remain invisible if we restrict our research only to sources that support the justification of military awards and decorations. There is yet another aspect that brings the decorated personnel closer together: most of them did not survive the war, and their gravesites are unknown. In the majority of cases, we can only suggest hypotheses about the circumstances of their death. At the same time, despite the small amount of information we have, we can assemble a fairly certain picture of the events that took place during the last few days. Anybody who approaches this topic with an academic mindset would, by all means, refrain from shedding a heroic light on these very last moments.

The most often quoted sentence of the American philosopher George Santayana is, "Those who cannot remember the past are condemned to repeat it." This thought can be supplemented with the notion that tragedy, when repeated without being reflected upon, will transform into comedy in history. Therefore, repetition without reflection also does not do justice to those who are the actual subjects of remembrance.

My work formally focuses on "heroes," but in reality, these were very real, everyday people. Their virtues and vices may only be understood in relation to each other. Their stories reveal not only their own personal histories but also the harsh realities of war itself. This means the death of around seventy million people in the Second World War.

My work wishes to contribute to the commemoration of the victims of the war.

NOTES ON HISTORIOGRAPHY AND METHODOLOGY

Works published on military leaders are a popular but not unproblematic genre in historiography. The genre is not exempt from certain problems and difficulties. There are many examples of this, before and after the change of the system here and beyond the Iron Curtain.

Firstly, it is necessary to discuss the genre itself in detail. The archontologies (databases of government and administrative officials) are important auxiliaries of history itself, and prosopographies (collective biographies of defined person groups) can also reveal such correlations in a historical context that would otherwise remain hidden in a single source. As a consequence, both of these genres are of essential importance, although the latter only became prominent with the emergence of social history research in the 1970s.

Due to historical and political reasons, the path on which similar works that deal with leading figures of the 20th century can function and progress is very narrow. This is a consequence of the political and general public's demand for the glorification, or conversely, the shaming of those persons in question without the effort of examining their personality, nature and extent of involvement in the historical events.

In 1981 Zrínyi Publishing House published a book titled *Hősök* (Heroes) about the Soviet soldiers who were awarded the Hero of the Soviet Union on the territory of Hungary in the Second World War.[9] Unsurprisingly, the work was utterly devoid of source criticism and more profound analysis, and the readers were presented with the award recommendations that the Stalinist regime had prepared. It was possible to receive such an award for a wide variety of activities. Ramón Mercader is a good example of this: he spent 20 years in prison for assassinating Leon Trotsky, and after he was released, he received this award – for committing the murder.

After the change of the system in Hungary in 1990, a number of detailed and scientifically grounded military databases were published, mostly written by Sándor Szakály. Szakály published the statistical research of biographies of 414 generals and other officers of the Hungarian high command for the first time in 1987. This work was deemed revolutionary in its own time, as Szakály's research results did not reflect the official memorial culture of the day, which wished to show the "elite of Horthy's regime" in a damning light as an oppressive group of the ruling social class. In 2001, Szakály also published his research results in the form of "lexicon and database".[10] He also researched the biographies of the heads of the 2nd Department of the General Staff of the Royal Hungarian Army).[11] These works, however, do not present the subjects' personal professional qualifications and assessments[12] nor detail the reasons for awarding them with awards and decorations.[13] Furthermore, they do not interpret and evaluate their relationships with the parties of the far right[14] or whether they committed war crimes. Nor do they mention the judicial proceedings to which the biographical subjects were subjected. Also, in the case of trials at the peoples' courts after 1945, it is unclear if the proceedings were show trials or were based on facts and the sentences handed down were fair and reasonable (examples can be found for both cases). How, then, would a reader of Szakály's work know if a subject of his research was a war criminal or a victim of an unfair show trial?

Therefore, Szakály's assertion that "these biographies speak for themselves",[15] is a serious conceptual misapprehension, as this statement of the author is entirely not true in the case of the biographies, which, apart from the formal data regarding the given person, do not contain any further details from which we could draw conclusions regarding the given person's capabilities and responsibility. The fact that gathering relevant data is a complex, labour-intensive task that cannot be fully realised in every single case, although true, cannot be an excuse.

The history of the decorated personnel of the Royal Hungarian Army is discussed in a number of works and publications. Roland Maruzs has published two works on the posthumously decorated personnel,[16] as well as an album of the officers decorated with Hungarian Gold Medal of Bravery for Officers.[17] The previously mentioned works do not discuss the biographical details of those concerned apart from their decorations and military career – a more comprehensive discussion would have been impossible due to length restrictions in a work featuring 884 officers posthumously awarded with the Hungarian Order of Merit.

The most excellent work in this regard is the publication of Csaba B. Stenge titled *Elfelejtett hősök* (*Forgotten Heroes*).[18] The work lists the biographies of the aces of the Royal Hungarian Air Force. It discusses in unparalleled detail the relevant actions of these soldiers, as well as striving in every case to introduce the given events from at least two viewpoints. This is made possible by surviving documentary sources as the Air Force kept a piece-by-piece inventory of their military equipment, and the relevant Western sources are openly researchable. Besides, the author has emphasised his efforts to introduce his heroes as real flesh and blood persons and provides detailed accounts of their lives apart from their military careers. It has to be noted that the publication concerned with the aces of the Air Force faced an easier investigative situation as the combat events in these cases are more easily definable, and the sources supporting and confirming the latter are available, and in each case, the military actions require personal bravery. Due to this, the existence of recommendations and petitions that are fictitious is less plausible, and, in the case of the members of the Royal Hungarian Air Force, no war crimes, antisemitism or extreme right-wing behaviour can be detected.

This is, however, not the case for the military personnel discussed in the present work. There is yet another publication that needs to be mentioned, which, apart from Csaba B. Stenge's work, stands out with its critical research approach. In 2018 János Rainer M. published a collective biography of 160 officers who had been inaugurated on 15 January 1939.[19] The work titled *Századosok* (*Captains*) offers an admittedly sociological analysis, but it provides much more than that. The readers are familiarised through the life stories of the officers with typical family histories of the 20th century in Hungary; at the same time, the work provides a brilliantly written, literary-level summary of the history and social history of the country. Besides detailing the events of military history, the author has researched the biographies of the relevant officers before and after the war and included their wives and children in his research. Thus, the work is a minutely detailed summary of those attempts at holding on to and starting life over and over again, which was an all too familiar experience for the Eastern European elite in the 20th century. The last chapter of Rainer M.'s work bears the title "What remains of a man". Given that the personnel examined in the book were born between 1913 and 1918, today's readers might surmise that these officers and their possessions belong to the "distant past" and have little to do with their everyday lives. Accordingly, one can imagine the author's immense surprise when he accidentally found a video footage of the inheritance proceedings of the recently deceased Captain Ottmár Récsey. The last member of the examined group died in 2017 – as readers will see, the situation is very similar to the cases of personnel included in the present work. A similarly excellent example is the study titled *Utak a kommünhöz* (*Roads to the Commune*) by Ignác Romsics, which is concerned with the research of the biographies of the people's commissars during the Hungarian Soviet Republic (1919) period.[20]

In relation to the research of the elite, the databases of the political or secret service elite after 1945 are also worth mentioning. Some of these also contain the information referred to above,[21] but most are of the "database" type that, similarly to Szakály's work, lack the data essential for assessment (for example, decorations, crimes committed, evaluations, role in significant events).[22] Yet another group of these works have been compiled based on direct political commission,[23] and these, too, lack the criteria of the scientific approach.[24]

The literature of the research concerned with the German military elite is disproportionate: on the one hand, a large number of works are preoccupied with the personnel decorated with the *Ritterkreuz des Eisernen Kreuzes* (Knight's Cross of the Iron Cross), but on the other hand, these publications rarely differ from the style of the award documentations in terms of the information provided.[25] The biographies of Waffen-SS personnel decorated with the *Ritterkreuz des Eisernen Kreuzes* have been published in a separate work.[26] The decorated personnel of the *Wehrmacht/Heer*, *Kriegsmarine* and *Luftwaffe* have been commemorated in separate publications. However, the monumental effort concerning the *Infanterie* and the *Panzergrenadiere* was not completed.[27] The portraits of the personnel decorated with the *Eichenlaub* (Oak Leaves) have been published in nine volumes.[28] There are monographs preoccupied with the decorated personnel of certain German states. In order to be able to filter out the personnel awarded with "politically inclined" decorations, Florian Berger has published a separate volume for those 98 persons who were decorated with the *Nahkampfspange in Gold* (Close Combat Clasp in Gold) besides having been decorated with the *Ritterkreuz des Eisernen Kreuzes*. According to his own account, his selection was based on the assumption that the combat actions associated with close combat essentially contain all those elements and criteria we usually identify with "heroism".[29] The *Nahkampfspange in Gold* was a considerably less frequently awarded decoration than the *Ritterkreuz des Eisernen Kreuzes*: of the latter, approximately 7,145 were awarded. In contrast, the former was awarded in only 631 cases. Jürgen Huss and Heinz-Werner Sondermann probably had similar considerations when they included only enlisted personnel (252 persons) in their research.[30] Mark C.

Yerger published the biographies of the recipients of the *Deutsches Kreuz in Gold* (German Cross in Gold) regarding the Waffen-SS in distribution per combat arms,[31] however, a number of personnel are not mentioned in his publication. Horst Scheibert researched and published every single award of the *Deutsches Kreuz in Gold* (altogether more than 26,000 awards). However, his work provides only the name, relevant unit, and the date of the award for those contained in his work.[32] It is remarkable that, more than seventy years after the war ended, Veit Scherzer is the only author who displayed interest in the topic of source criticism and the victim-offender problem cycle in his works of patristics concerning the *Ritterkreuz des Eisernen Kreuzes*.[33] Scherzer's work revealed that more than 200 persons have unlawfully deemed themselves to be recipients of the decoration after 1945. Furthermore, the *Ordensgemeinschaft der Ritterkreuzträger* (*OdR*), Association of Knight's Cross Recipients that was active in West Germany and, from 1990, continued working in the reunified Germany, actively assisted in this – what is more, in some cases by stepping in as the "awarding authority". "Awards" of this type were generally related to the period before the 1970s. However, the *OdR* has never acknowledged assisting in awarding unlawful decorations. As will be revealed in the subsequent chapters, one such award is connected to the siege of Budapest.

Discussing decorations awarded to military personnel within a political system actively involved in mass genocide is a difficult task. This also applies to the German military elite in Budapest. There are known cases when, due to relocations, personnel arrived in Budapest having earlier served in concentration camps. It is less well known that certain German units eradicated during the siege of Budapest had earlier committed a series of mass murders. In connection with this, two unit types need to be mentioned.

The two *SS-Reiter-Regiments* from which later the 8th SS Cavalry Division and 22nd SS Cavalry Division was formed, had received an order from Heinrich Himmler in the summer of 1941 stating that "members of the male population who are either deemed hostile from a national point of view or those who are of the lower category in terms of race or humanity [*sic!*] are to be shot down." Regarding Jews, the order issued advised: "They should be dealt with as is usually done with marauders." Heinrich Himmler was not satisfied with the speed and efficiency of the execution of his orders; therefore, on 1 August 1941, he issued another order via radio: "All Jews have to be shot down, the Jewish women have to be chased deep into the marshland."[34] The *SS-Reiter-Regiments* combing through the small villages and towns of Polesia reported gunning down 13,788 Jews in twelve days while their own losses amounted to two persons who died in a mine explosion. The mass murders resumed at the end of August 1941 and claimed many more thousands of lives.[35] Due to the very high number of victims and the large scale of the territorial operations, it is inconceivable that these actions could have been undertaken by a mere handful of *SS-Kavallerie* personnel. Even the most cautious researcher would have to concede that whoever had served in the SS Cavalry Brigade in 1941 must have seen, heard or experienced otherwise the consequences of these murders. During the summer of 1943, the SS Cavalry Division was also deployed against partisans, partly in the same area, during which actions they also murdered significant numbers of civilians. In the 1960s, the prosecution boards of West Germany continued their detailed investigations into this matter. However, this investigation was characteristically launched due to a mistake. In the lawsuit against *SS-Obergruppenführer* Erich von dem Bach-Zelewski,[36] one of the witnesses, *SS-Sturmbannführer* Franz Magill, accidentally let slip information about what his units had committed during the summer of 1941.

On 20 April 1964, the jury of Braunschweig at last sentenced four persons for their role in mass murders to four and five years imprisonment. *SS-Hauptsturmführer* Kurt Wegener, who was among the convicted criminals, had also been in combat in Budapest and had successfully survived the breakout attempt. The small number of convicted personnel is misleading: originally, in the trial before the West German prosecution case, there had been more defendants, but only officers were accused (230 witnesses had confessed, most of whom were enlisted personnel who acknowledged their role in the mass murders). Due to the length of time that had elapsed since the committed deeds and defendants coming to agreements among themselves about their evidence, such trials produced few convictions. Furthermore, many potential suspects had already fallen in combat.

Certain *SS-Polizei* units (primarily *SS-Polizei-Regiment 1*) which had been relocated to Hungary also had connections to mass murders. The battalions of *SS-Polizei-Regiment 1* had partly been formed from the strength of *Polizei-Bataillons* whose main occupation had been to exterminate the Jewish population in the Soviet Union and elsewhere. A somewhat less serious example of involvement might be that the II Battalion of the *SS-Polizei-Regiment 12*, had earlier taken an active part in anti-Polish and anti-Jewish actions in the area of the *Generalgouvernement* (Governorate for the Occupied Polish Region). From the summer of 1944, the same unit had been assigned to stand guard over the deportation trains used to transport Hungarian Jewish people from Košice (Kassa) to Auschwitz.[37]

Between 1941 and 1944, the actual numerical strength of these units underwent large-scale fluctuation. However, it is clear from the author's present work that this was by no means full-scale. In this statistical regard, the German officers in combat in Budapest may be deemed representative of the entire German military apparatus. Although it is not possible to talk about collective responsibility, it does need to be mentioned that a small, but in no way negligible, fraction of German officers in Budapest had previously participated in committing war crimes.

Naturally, military heroism exists independent of all systems and political affiliations. Nevertheless, the author hopes that the above-mentioned factors and viewpoints make it clear that the idealisation and glorification of such heroism are extremely problematic, as they would remove the historical event from its larger context.

Apart from the above, other problems, primarily arising from the genre of the research itself, are present. Source criticism would be the first and foremost task of work focused on such topics and is especially essential in connection with award recommendations. It is not rare to see that those who recommended individuals for awards had a kind of partiality towards certain people, and even in the case of military awards, these recommendations often had a political background. Even more frequently, the individual receiving the award was chosen because of his relationship with the person in charge of making recommendations (or certain other factors), and military achievements were only partly, if at all, considered when formulating the recommendation.[38] These factors would probably be statistically noticeable if one were to examine, for example, why military personnel in adjutant positions received awards and decorations more often than others. One possible explanation could be that these personnel were more frequently present in situations where award recommendations were being considered. Another repeatedly occurring case was that officers who had fallen in combat received decorations posthumously as a certain kind of compensation. There are also cases where posthumously awarded decorations were meant to gloss over the unnecessary death of the applicant. In yet other cases, disagreeable or simply horrific actions were stylised into military achievements and heroic deeds by awarding decorations (Hungarian officers had been decorated with Iron Cross 1st or 2nd Class or Signum Laudis for massacring Jewish people on the Eastern Front.[39] For example, almost all of the officers taking part in the notorious raid in southern Bačka/Bácska (*"délvidéki vérengzés"*, "massacre in the Southern Territory") received some kind of visible decoration during the course of 1942. However, this kind of award was most prevalent in the Soviet army. In November 1941, for example, 28 soldiers of the 316th Rifle Division of Major General Panfilov were posthumously awarded the Hero of the Soviet Union for stopping a German armoured assault. The story was widely publicised and had become the ideal of self-sacrifice of true patriots.[40] However, in 1948, an internal investigation revealed that not a word of this widely circulated story was true. One problem that emerged was that a number of supposedly dead soldiers came forward to request the award for themselves. There were others among the decorated soldiers who had been arrested by the People's Commissariat for Internal Affairs (*NKVD*) for also fighting on German side during the war. Although such falsifications did not occur in the German army, the number of decorations awarded for political rather than military reasons was considerable.

In connection with this topic, it is equally interesting to investigate those who did not receive decorations, although they clearly should have. The Budapest breakout attempt is a helpful example here. Based on the author's research work so far, none (!) of the German officers participating in the breakout attempt received decorations recognising *solely this* event, although this was probably their most extraordinary ordeal. Those who had been in charge of leading the larger combat groups would definitely have deserved some kind of visible acknowledgement besides counting the day of the breakout attempt among their "close combat days" (*Nahkampftage*) that would contribute to the award of the relevant level of *Nahkampfspange*. Although three Waffen-SS officers and one officer serving in the Wehrmacht (Boosfeld, Maringgele, Phoenix and Wolff respectively) were decorated with the *Ritterkreuz des Eisernen Kreuzes*, these acknowledgements were not based purely on the breakout attempt but had been almost solely the spontaneous personal decision of Adolf Hitler and as such are regarded as out of the ordinary. Of the 53 officers who made it through to the other side of the siege, 49 did not received any kind of decoration or acknowledgement at all if one does not consider the relevant classes of the Wound Badge and Close Combat Clasp.

Missing out on decorations was also true for the majority of soldiers as well. Only in the case of Waffen-SS personnel can it be proven that anyone who survived the breakout attempt received at least an *Eisernes Kreuz II. Klasse* (Iron Cross 2nd Class) – unless they had already been awarded this decoration. Those who had received the aforementioned decoration earlier remained without any acknowledgements.[41] The above-mentioned facts clearly show that it would lead to the misinterpretation of the events in drawing conclusions regarding the intensity of combat from the number of decorations awarded.

At the same time, it would be a similar mistake to conclude that nothing can be discerned about the actual events from the award recommendations. Although distorted, biased, and at times deliberately deceitful, these documents sometimes reveal much more than at first seems apparent. This is because the decorations not only characterise the person who was acknowledged but also the person who awarded the decoration, and research of the actual process can reveal a number of interesting details.

Similar source criticism concerns must be voiced in connection with the assessment documents researched during the collection of biographies. In these documents, a number of references are made to the positive attitude towards or direct connections of the given person to National Socialism. Based on these notes, it would be easy to label these personnel as zealous Nazis. In reality, however, the vast majority of such notes refer not to facts but to the goodwill of the superior officers. This is due to the fact that, with the progress of the war, the correct ideological pedigree of the person recommended for decoration came to be an increasingly important formal prerequisite. The superficial nature of this factor is further proven by the fact that the author has never encountered a negative assessment in this regard among hundreds of documents researched. The majority of the officers deemed to be ardent followers of National Socialism had not even been members of the *NSDAP* (*Nationalsozialistische Deutsche Arbeiterpartei*, National Socialist German Workers' Party). Furthermore, it also needs to be noted that, in contrast to the communist militaries, where systematic ideological indoctrination was an everyday practice for everyone, this was not so in the Wehrmacht. Neither party membership nor knowledge of the *NSDAP* brochures was a prerequisite. Therefore, even the comparison with post-1948 cadre materials of Communist Hungary does not hold up: the latter also contain references to political views, but these could at least in reality be based on the fact that assessed personnel, in principle, must have been members of party organisations and had to do some work in them. In contrast, in the army, not even the *NSDAP* members conducted any party work; besides this, *NSDAP* never had any dedicated organisations within the army.

In order to increase the ideological preparedness of army personnel, on 22 December 1943, by special order of Adolf Hitler, the organisation of National Socialist Leadership Officers (*Nationalsozialistische Führungsoffizier*, *NSFO*) was created. This was obviously motivated by the presence of Stalinist political officers in the Red Army, but the execution of Hitler's order resulted in political officers whose function in no way resembled that of their equivalents in the Red Army. In fact, it can be said that they were little more than caricatures of them. Only around 1,100 independent *NSFO* posts were created within the whole of the Wehrmacht, and the *NSFO* duties at the regiment and battalion levels had to be carried out by persons assigned to this task by the commanders. The fact that theologians were sometimes appointed to this role clearly shows the lack of seriousness with which this position was treated as a religious worldview was most definitely not reconcilable with National Socialism. The *NSFO* never had precedence over the unit commander; furthermore, he did not even have the right of agreement in connection with military affairs. (As opposed to this, in the communist regime, the role of the political officer was far more extensive:

he was independent of the unit commander, had the right to override the commander's decisions in certain situations and had the right to approve military actions.) This meant that it was of no great consequence if somebody was appointed as an *NSFO* below the division level – however, it has to be noted that, according to the author's recent research, none of the focus group members served in this role (otherwise the officer's qualifications would have contained a reference to this fact if he had been appointed to the post).

Consequently, I could have gotten closer to the question of commitment to Nazi ideology if I had simply disregarded the sections of the contemporary assessment documents related to this question. However, I did not do this for two reasons. Firstly, I wished to avoid even the semblance that I was manipulating the sources in any way, and secondly, during the compilation of the biographies, involving other sources, I made a considerable effort to uncover the relationships of the relevant personnel to Nazi ideology. This in a certain regard was not a particularly difficult task as the date of joining the *NSDAP* or SA was already telling but, besides this, there were countless other opportunities open to anyone who wished to be seen as an ardent Nazi: one could have joined the *Allgemeine SS* (General SS), or perhaps the *Lebensborn* movement, or have been a member of the *Sicherheitsdienst* (SD, Security Service), or have resigned from a church congregation. The subsequent biographies provide examples of such instances. In the case of Waffen-SS officers, their political motivations were traceable in all cases. However, in the case of Wehrmacht officers, I could only gather all the relevant information if the personal files of the officers in question were available. The author hopes that readers will be able to interpret correctly when a biography contains the expression "ardent national socialist" without any accompanying information.

According to a *bon mot* there is no difference between an enemy shell or decoration, as both fall on the innocent. The author wishes to state that the intention of the present work is to reflect on the bias present in other works published on this topic by examining personal stories in which the fates and responsibilities of individuals are reflected in order to provide insight into the temptations, sins, tragedies and heroic deeds which were very much indicative of the Second World War.

THE GERMAN SYSTEM OF AWARDING MEDALS AND DECORATIONS, AND THE GERMAN MILITARY ELITE

In this work, the author introduces three categories of personnel that can be regarded as members of the German "military elite". The first category includes personnel awarded the *Ritterkreuz des Eisernen Kreuzes* (or higher levels of the same decoration) during the Second World War or those who had taken part in the siege of Budapest while holding an important high position, or fulfilled other significant roles. In the strictest sense, these were the German "military elite". The author has included personnel to whom the decoration award is contested. Based on these criteria, 48 persons have been classified in this work as belonging to the "military elite" at the beginning of the siege of Budapest.

In order to allow readers to gain more extensive insight into the lives of the German "military elite", the author provides a separate chapter for the introduction of personnel who, regardless of rank, received the German Cross in Gold (*Deutsches Kreuz in Gold*) during the siege of Budapest or during the autumn of 1944 for combat actions in Transylvania. There are altogether 71 recipients in this group. In these cases, the decoration was not awarded for singular combat actions or heroic deeds; to earn it, at least five to seven such deeds were necessary, which would, individually, have earned the person the Iron Cross 1st Class (*Eisernes Kreuz I. Klasse*). Consequently, the relevant combat actions could have spanned the course of one or more years. On the other hand, the actual award process for the decoration could take two or three months (which, it has to be noted, is far less than in the case of Hungarian decorations). Consequently, it cannot be established in every case whether the associated deeds are connected to Budapest or not. All of the decorations awarded during 1945 lack accompanying recommendation documents. However, if the award recipient lived through the siege in Budapest, it could be fairly concluded that at least a few of his combat actions could be linked to the siege itself. The author has excluded personnel from this category when it can be safely established that none of their combat deeds were linked to Budapest.

Apart from the above-mentioned two categories, the author also included four more decorated persons who received considerably rarer military decorations during the siege of Budapest. This work, therefore, contains altogether the biographies of 123 personnel. During the discussion of the biographies, the author presents, in the first place, the figure at the centre of the actual historical events, Karl Pfeffer-Wildenbruch, the commander of the German troops during the siege of Budapest. After that, the remaining personnel's biographies are discussed alphabetically within their respective groups. Although the German "military elite" and the leaders of the German security police (*Sicherheitsdienst/SD* and the *Gestapo*) comprise two separate groups, there are notable overlaps. The author did not include among the biographies that of *SS-Obergruppenführer* Otto Winkelmann as he was *Stadtkommandant* in Budapest only for five days (1–5 December 1944) and did not take part in actual combat operations. In addition, his previous high-ranking SS and police positions are not connected to the siege of the city in any way. (Notably, he was discharged from the position of *Stadtkommandant* because he advised the surrender of the Pest side of the city.) On the contrary, however, the author has included Winkelmann's direct subordinate, Hans-Ulrich Geschke, as he remained in Budapest until 23 December 1944 and had a significant role in securing the rear areas for the occupying German forces.

The author's work has not been written with the intention of producing a thorough and comprehensive socio-historical presentation of the award recipients and their circumstances; this would have been practically impossible due to the scarcity of the sources available. The author's approach is primarily phaleristic but also takes into consideration notable viewpoints relating to local and military history. At the same time, the author deemed it essential to undertake research that would enable him to present the person behind the supposed or real military actions. It must be noted that this should be self-evident in a century so profoundly influenced by the Nazi and communist dictatorships. Apart from the above-mentioned factors, the author also focused on uncovering facts about the capital city. In this regard, the history of the Jewish ghetto and the pogroms against Jewish civilians could not be overlooked, as at least five different persons from the group discussed in the present work were involved in these events.

The author has striven to introduce the whole personality of the selected personnel in their respective biographies. The acquisition and research of the relevant data required minutely detailed research work. However, a large amount of data had been impossible to recover. Therefore, the author only hopes it will be possible to revise and extend the present work at some point in the future. As the relevance of the introduced personnel and the amount of data available about them vary, their biographies also vary in length. However, certain biographies are also interconnected with each other. This is completely intentional. The author firmly believes that a compilation such as the present work can offer invaluable insights into not only the biographical subjects' lives but also the specific age and time in which they lived. For example, in the case of the biographies of Schmidhuber, Pfeffer-Wildenbruch or Remlinger, it would have been a mistake not to exploit the relative wealth of the sources available or to exclude the interpretation of military and political questions relevant to them, the consequences of which reached far beyond the siege of Budapest. Other biographies, for example, that of Joachim Rumohr, can demonstrate the limits of the possibilities of historical knowledge.

After the biographies, a separate list contains the decorations of the relevant personnel; this includes SS decorations but excludes service and memorial-type decorations. In the case of those who had already received any class of the *Eisernes Kreuz* (Iron Cross) during the First World War, the relevant date is shown in brackets (1914). There are cases where the date of the award of some of the decorations is not, or only partially, known – the absence of information in this regard in the biographies is due to the lack of sources. The higher classes of the Close Combat Clasp or the Wound Badge were only awarded if the recipient had already received the lower classes of the given decoration based, respectively, on the number of days of his service or wounds suffered. In principle, the present work mentions only the highest level of a given decoration. In a separate list, the promotions of the relevant person are also listed. (The Waffen-SS ranks and relative Wehrmacht equivalents are given at the end of the present work accompanied, where applicable, by the approximate British equivalents). In addition, the lists of promotions include the ranks of the SA and the *Allgemeine SS* in cases where the author has found any piece of verifiable data. The database introduced here may be deemed complete regarding the relevant names, but the amount of data provided for each person varies. It is fairly certain that there are no further uncoverable elements in the list of decorations for each relevant person. Non-German decorations are only mentioned occasionally in the surviving archival files of the personnel included in the present work, although it is almost certain that the majority of them had received some kind of Hungarian decoration as well (several surviving contemporary documents attest to this). In cases where the author had more data available, separate lists following the biographies show the decorations awarded to the relevant person *other* than the German awards. In the present work, the award dates of decorations and the dates of promotions in some instances differ from those provided in other literature dealing with this subject. This is because, in some cases, the promotion documents contain two dates that are interchangeable, signifying that certain promotions were granted posthumously.

The articulated and complex system of German decorations and awards was not introduced as a whole in 1939 but developed continually during the war and achieved its final form only in the first half of 1944. Additionally, some explanatory notes regarding Waffen-SS decorations may be useful to the reader. For example, the *Julleuchter* was a clay candleholder adorned with Germanic symbols and runic writing and was awarded as a decoration. At the same time, the *Julleuchter* served as a symbolic expression of Himmler's pagan-Germanic substitute religion. Altogether around 70,000 pieces of *Julleuchter* were awarded. The *Ehrendegen RFSS* (*Ehrendegen Reichsführer-SS,* ceremonial short sword of the Reich Leader) was a personal gift of Heinrich Himmler, which was not automatically awarded during the officer's inauguration. The *SS-Ehrenring* (SS Honour Ring) was also presented as a personal gift from Heinrich Himmler to officers, and approximately 16,000 were awarded. The *Ehrenwinkel der alten Kämpfer* (Honour Chevron for the Old Guard) was a 10-mm wide, V-shaped chevron worn on the upper sleeve of the right arm (similar to the *SS-Sturmmann* sign). It was awarded to those who had distinguished themselves in the National Socialist movement, or had joined the *NSDAP* before 1933 or had been an activist in any kind of National Socialist movement before 1933.

The award of the *Ritterkreuz des Eisernen Kreuzes* (Knight's Cross of the Iron Cross) was, in theory, governed by strict quality assurance policies. Recommendations had to pass through no less than six forums before final consent was given (the superior officer of the nominated person handed in the recommendation, which then was considered by the personnel department of the army, the department leader in charge of decoration-related matters, the deputy head of office, the chief adjutant and then the *Reichskanzlei*). The usual stages of the decoration award process could take three months to complete, and a significant percentage of submissions were rejected. Those who had not been awarded with this decoration, in certain cases, received as recompense other decorations that were not wearable.

The *Anerkennungsurkunde des Oberbefehlshabers des Heeres für hervorragende Leistungen auf dem Schlachtfeld* (a certificate presented for outstanding conduct on the battlefield, "Appreciation Document of the Commander in Chief of the Land Army for excellence on the battlefield") was among these decorations. Altogether, 1,322 such documents were awarded, but, according to the author's research, only one is connected to Budapest.[42] In cases where a nominee had already received the *Ritterkreuz des Eisernen Kreuzes,* but the decision-makers did not want to award in addition to it the *Eichenlaub* (Oak Leaves), or a nominee had not yet been awarded the *Ritterkreuz* and his actions were deemed exceptional but not sufficient for the award of that decoration, then he could have been eligible for the mentioning in the Honour Roll of the German Land Army (*Nennung im Ehrenblatt des Deutschen Heeres*). There were 4547 cases of this mentioning. A similar decoration was brought into service by the *Luftwaffe* and *Kriegsmarine,* but according to current research, no decorations of this kind were awarded in connection with Budapest. From the beginning of 1944, a visible signage was designed for this decoration – a golden wreath was attached to an *Eisernes Kreuz II. Klasse* ribbon. This decoration was called *Ehrenblattspange des Deutschen Heeres* (Honour Roll Clasp of the German Land Army) and was awarded in altogether 3,899 cases. In cases concerning the lower classes of the *Eisernes Kreuz*, we have data for awarding this decoration only until 28 February 1945. According to the available sources, the Wehrmacht, Waffen-SS and *Polizei* received 2,277,729 Eisernes Kreuz II altogether, 33,370 bars to denote the repeated award of the *Eisernes Kreuz II. Klasse* originally had earned in the First World War, and 264,567 *Eisernes Kreuz I. Klasse,* and 5,929 with bars to denote the repeated award of the *Eisernes Kreuz I. Klasse* originally had earned in the First World War.[43] The above-mentioned numbers, however, do not include the relevant data of the *Kriegsmarine* and the *Luftwaffe*. The total number of awards of the *Eisernes Kreuz II. Klasse* was over four million.

In the case of politically motivated awards, and in extraordinary circumstances, too, the award processing time could be considerably shortened. The award of the decorations in such cases was carried out due to the propaganda value of the event itself: the morale of the troops, it was hoped, would be strengthened and lifted by these awards and would give meaning to their military perseverance. Adolf Hitler also awarded the *Ritterkreuz des Eisernen Kreuzes* in spontaneous acts without reference to any other authority. Heinrich Himmler, Ernst Kaltenbrunner, and Wilhelm Keitel had, on many occasions, handed in personal recommendations, and there are several examples of that in connection with the siege of Budapest. Consequently, in many cases, the decoration could already have been awarded just one or two weeks after the presumed or real military deed.

In almost all cases, the previously mentioned extraordinary situations concerned encircled troops. In such cases, the recommendations were submitted via radio telegram, and based on this, a decision could have been reached in Berlin overnight. In Stalingrad, for example, *Oberstleutnant* Richard Eichler was recommended for decoration by the command of the 6th Army via telegram on 29 January 1945 at 0800 hours for exemplary deeds committed on 28 January 1945, and Hitler signed the necessary papers on the same day. In these cases, detailed descriptions of the military deeds that prompted the recommendations are not available, so it is not easy to establish exactly what kind of military deed had been performed. However, the lower the rank of the soldier receiving the award, the more likely it can be concluded that the decoration was awarded for real combat actions and not due to the soldier's rank or role.

At the beginning of the war, for a while, the *Ritterkreuz des Eisernen Kreuzes* was awarded personally by Hitler. However, due to the rapid progress of events and the ever-growing number of recipients, Hitler started personally presenting only the *Eichenlaub* award and higher decorations. The decoration was accompanied by the award document bound in a book, but from 1944 onwards, this was not given to the recipients but retained at the *Reichskanzlei*. Postcards featuring decorated personnel were also issued, and according to the plans, holders of the *Ritterkreuz des Eisernen Kreuzes* would have been exempt from paying taxes after the war.

While the award of the *Ritterkreuz des Eisernen Kreuzes* had to be approved by Hitler, the *Eisernes Kreuz I. Klasse* and *II. Klasse* could be awarded by army, corps and division commanders. In the case of encircled troops, even personnel in lesser ranks in conferred roles could, in extraordinary cases, decide to award these medals. In the case of foreign nationals, these recommendations had to be approved by the higher commands due to the potential for implied political overtones. In the case of Budapest, we know of a telegram in which the high command of the *IX. Waffen-Gebirgskorps der SS* had, on 29 December 1944, requested from the *Operationsabteilung* of *Armeegruppe Balck* to confer the right to award "Hungarian personnel prominently distinguished itself".[44] The response to this request is unknown. It is, however, a fact that, according to a surviving award document, at the end of January 1945, the 13th Panzer Division was already awarding *Eisernes Kreuz II. Klasse* decorations to Hungarian soldiers. The fact that the document survived is also of interest. Staff Captain Győző Benyovszky – who received the decoration due to his official rank as the last Chief of Staff of the Hungarian 10th Infantry Division – tore the A5-sized document in two before the capitulation, rolled up each part and secured them with black and white yarn, hoping that he would be able to keep them safe during his captivity. One of the rolls was lost eventually, but the staff captain was able to bring the other one home. (The image of this roll has been attached to the Schmidhuber biography.) It is worth considering that an *Eisernes Kreuz* decoration was held in such high esteem even by an undeniably non-Nazi officer.[45]

It is also worth noting that, due to the relevant regulations, the *Ritterkreuz des Eisernen Kreuzes* could not be awarded to personnel assumed to have fallen into captivity. This means that recommendations relating to Budapest presented after the middle of January 1945 were not even considered or assessed in the majority of the cases. In the case of Budapest, for officers who had not taken part in the breakout attempt and so did not succeed in reaching the German lines, the latest award of the *Ritterkreuz des Eisernen Kreuzes* took place on 14 February (Heinz Hamel and Rudolf Weber were decorated). It is highly probable that they received the decoration because, due to the slow processes of the bureaucratic system, the relevant authorities had simply forgotten to stop the awarding procedure. It is certain that at least a dozen recommendations for the *Ritterkreuz des Eisernen Kreuz* had been left unassessed.[46] In consequence, the list of *Ritterkreuz des Eisernen Kreuze* recipients does not contain the names of some of those found worthy and brave enough by their superiors to receive this decoration but only those who actually received the decoration, in all probability due to an earlier date of recommendation, are listed.

The composition of the German military elite shows considerable differences when compared to the Hungarian military elite. In Hungary, an officer could not reach the rank of major, let alone that of general, without completing study at the military academy. Reserve officers born after 1900 rarely achieved staff officer ranks. Almost none of the enlisted personnel had been taken over to the commissioned personnel, and reserve officers were only assigned to units up to battalion strength – and even then, very rarely and only temporarily. At the same time, however, a considerable percentage of the German officers featured in the present work had been promoted from the enlisted personnel. Most of them had been reserve officers. The caste system that prescribed and restricted the promotion of Hungarian commissioned personnel was virtually non-existent in the Wehrmacht and the Waffen-SS. Franz Bäke is a good example of this; he was born in 1898 and finished the First World War as a reserve non-commissioned officer. After the war, he ran a dental practice. At the beginning of the Second World War, he was promoted to *Zugführer* of the *Werkstatt-Zug/Panzer-Abteilung 65*, which at that time was not considered a highly favoured service position. Bäke, however, was in combat in the front line in the French campaign and was wounded three times in five weeks. He ended the war with the rank of *Generalmajor* and was the commander of Panzer Division *Feldherrnhalle 2*. His list of decorations is impressive – *Ritterkreuz des Eisernen Kreuzes mit Eichenlaub und Schwertern* (Knight's Cross of the Iron Cross with Oak Leaves and Swords), the *Verwundetenabzeichen in Gold* (Wound Badge in Gold) and the *Panzerkampfabzeichen mit Einsatzzahl 100,* denoting 100 armoured deployments. It also needs to be mentioned that in 1944, he, as an *Oberstleutnant*, knocked out three tanks using *Panzerfäuste*. After returning from internment, he resumed his dental practice – we can only assume that his work in this profession reached the standard of excellence he demonstrated when commanding his armoured troops. Similar progress in a military career, based solely on personal professionalism, was considered impossible to achieve in the Russian, British or Hungarian armies.

RESEARCH OF THE ELITE AND THE HISTORICAL FACT

Several factors are hindering the research of the German military elite taking part in the siege of Budapest and the decorations awarded during the siege itself. Primary archival sources contemporary to the siege are almost non-existent. Apart from a few fragments, the archival files of those besieged were destroyed or are still missing. The majority of the personal files of the relevant personnel were also destroyed and, in the majority of cases, the original recommendation documents are unavailable. Nevertheless, criticism of these rare sources is still deemed possible – deliberate and unintentional distortions in the data can be typified and the reasons for it researched. This research alone can help the reader get more closely attuned to the reality of the time in question.

However, despite the apparent lack of sources, the research by the author in the present work was still based on contemporary archival documents. This was made possible by, for example, using the casualty reports and the database of the German Red Cross, which listed the personnel missing in action. This helped uncover and reconstruct several actual events. It has to be noted, however, that this research was only possible by processing large amounts of data and by utilising many sources and fields of study. The author deemed it essential in each case to directly research original personal files wherever possible, paying special attention to the political activity of the relevant person and ascertaining whether or not he committed war crimes. Beyond these data, the author has paid special attention to the research and introduction of the activities of the relevant personnel in relation to Budapest. Luckily, the German information office handling the documents relating to Wehrmacht casualties (*Deutsche Dienststelle für die Benachrichtigung der nächsten Angehörigen von Gefallenen der ehemaligen deutschen* Wehrmacht, earlier known as the *Wehrmacht-Auskunftststelle* or, in abbreviated form, *WASt*) still keeps today the files of those who had been treated in hospital at least once during the war, as well as the files of those in connection with whom the legal process of presumption of death was initiated after 1945. These files have proved to be invaluable sources of information as they contain details of when, where and by whom the relevant person was last seen alive. They also contain information about who had been looking for the missing person after 1945. The above-mentioned organisation also retains the summarised casualty reports of the units (provided that these reports had been created at all and had not been destroyed during the war), the personal casualty report forms and the drafts pertaining to it, the source materials for identification and also a number of other very useful documents.

In connection with the determination of losses and identification of the fate of those lost in the war, the tracing service of the German Red Cross (*Suchdienste des Deutschen Rotes Kreuz*) interviewed everyone returning home from internment to learn what they could recall regarding their fellow prisoners of war. Apart from these questionnaires, family members made contact with *WASt* in order to try to establish contact with former personnel serving in the same unit as their relatives. This produced millions of pages of eyewitness accounts.

Unfortunately, however, during this time, the contemporary authorities in Hungary completely ignored such attempts and actively sought to destroy documents related to this problem. Consequently, searching for personnel missing in action was almost impossible.

During the research of the archival sources, the author actively sought to establish contact with the relevant persons or their descendants. This alone required a certain amount of investigative work that, without the use of the Internet, would not have been possible in most cases. Luckily, a number of former personnel responded and kindly helped the author with his research. At the same time, there was interest from the other side as well, which greatly helped the investigation: after the author's book on the siege of Budapest was published in Germany, many relatives sought contact with the author in the hope of receiving information about the fate of their relatives. Regardless of the origin of these contacts, based on the author's experience, they benefited all parties.

It is not unusual for different witnesses to a given event to report dissimilar recollections. This is the case in relation to the siege of Budapest and to those who fell or went missing during the breakout attempt. In a number of cases, there are four or five different narrations relating to the fate of an individual. In all probability, it will never be known for certain which of these stories stand closest to "reality". However, during the research of archival documents, the author realised that so-called "historical facts" – the reconstruction of which seems to be the most important task of positivist historical science – are not always as interesting as the various interpretations that can be attributed to a particular historical event. In that sense, the author, with his present work, wishes to build a bridge towards the achievements of postmodern history.

From the facts of where and when an officer died, one can conclude a few important details. However, the scope of a historical interpretation can be much wider if one also receives information from eyewitnesses who lived through a particular event or from the relevant person himself who, for example, might have penned a last letter about his experiences. What is more, such events rarely have just a single eyewitness. During the siege of Budapest, death itself was a process; total annihilation was reached through several stages. The relevant personnel in the present work were soldiers who found themselves in enormously vulnerable positions and who underwent extreme physical and psychological stress. The same can be said about those who provided information about the personnel in question. Their commentaries rarely consist only of dry observations and often include a number of small details, minute facts which reveal as much about the circumstances, and to a certain degree about the eyewitnesses themselves, as about the given historical event.

All of this raises what is perhaps the most fundamental question in historical research: what is to be classified as a piece of factual evidence, and what is just a matter of mere interpretation, or in other words, opinion? This decision is not easy to make, and in many cases, regarding the deaths of personnel introduced in the present work, it is not at all clear-cut. This is due to the fact that when there are a number of reports referring to the death of a relevant person, they are often contradictory and even conflicting (for example, in the case of Joachim Rumohr). The unreliability of memory can best be demonstrated by the eyewitness accounts of Hitler's death. It is a fact that the death of Adolf Hitler was an event of international importance, and the details of the circumstances of his death are, therefore, also of the utmost concern. Of those who resided in the *Führerbunker,* only a few saw the bodies of Hitler and his wife. Hitler's personal steward Heinz Linge, Hitler's adjutant *SS-Surmbannführer* Otto Günsche and telephone operator Rochus Misch each had different recollections of how and by whom the suicide was discovered, where Hitler's body had been lying and where bloodstains were seen. The inconsistencies in their eyewitness accounts resulted in lengthy and intensive torture sessions as their interrogators were under orders from Stalin to reconstruct the actual events, although, by then, it was an uncontested fact that Adolf Hitler was dead. Their eyewitness accounts were, however, impossible to match. Hitler's driver, Erich Kempka, managed to evade Soviet captivity, and in his book published in 1950, titled *Ich habe Adolf Hitler verbrannt*, he introduced a fourth version of the events, meanwhile, the three other principal witnesses were still in captivity in the Soviet Union. It is undoubtedly true that Adolf Hitler committed suicide around 1530 hours on 30 April 1945 together with Eva Braun in his bedroom in the *Führerbunker*. However, many of the details surrounding their deaths are still unknown: who died first, what were the exact positions of the bodies when found, who had gunshot wounds and where were they located? These details might seem to be of minor importance, but given that the person in question is an extremely important historical figure and that eyewitness statements had been documented within one or two years of Hitler's death, it suddenly becomes disturbingly clear how unreliable data based on memories can be. From this, we can also conclude that in the case of the deaths of German officers in Budapest, who were historically much less important figures than Hitler, the recollections of witnesses are unlikely to reflect the facts fully, particularly so because of the much wider time frames involved.

Eyewitnesses usually reported about different stages of the process leading to the death of a given person. There had been soldiers and officers that eyewitness reports suggested had been in a more or less stable, good condition in the last moments before the breakout attempt. Others, as witnesses reported, had been already seriously wounded when still within the city, or in the forests, or just before reaching the last Soviet positions. In some instances, according to eyewitness reports, the officer in question had asked for a handgun to commit suicide, while other reports even stated that the suicide had already been committed. There were personnel who had been seen on the roadside, presumably dead, and others were seen in captivity. Lastly, there were those who vanished into nothingness; nobody ever asked for them, and nobody looked for them after the end of the war. Luckily, however, the majority of personnel were indeed sought and looked for. But those who had been maimed by tanks or whose remains were discarded by grave robbers will never be identified.

The author has made every effort to describe in as much detail as possible the relevant persons' connections to Hungary, particularly regarding their role in the siege of Budapest, their movement within the city, the events they participated in, and the parts they played in the breakout attempt. Apart from this, the author has included in his research the relevant Russian-language literature published after 1945. These literary sources were carefully compared with accounts and descriptions of the siege of Budapest that were already widely known. By applying this method, a large number of events can be shown to be no more than legends.

A good example of the latter is Gyula Elischer's recollections, which were written around the period of the change of the system in Hungary. He remembered a briefing that took place on 28 December 1944, on the corner of Törökvészi Street and Nagybányai Street: "...the commander of the German unit to be relieved was a young Waffen-SS officer. He was wearing a long coat, open at the front, and his *Ritterkreuz des Eisernen Kreuzes*. A submachine gun was hanging around his neck on a strap. [...] He said he was a high school teacher. He spoke nice German, and he was very likeable."[47] We can readily believe that Elischer found the German officer likeable; however, by closely scrutinising the *Ritterkreuz des Eisernen Kreuzes* recipients list, it is clear that the person he spoke to could not possibly have worn a *Ritterkreuz des Eisernen Kreuzes*. At the time specified, only units of the 8th SS Cavalry Division were present in the designated area and, from that *Division*, only Joachim Rumohr, Hans von Charpentier, Albert Klett and Walter Drexler had received that decoration – and none of them had been a high school teacher. Due to their social status, family background and general education, it is quite likely that neither Klett nor Drexler spoke literary German; at the same time, Charpentier and Rumohr were too highly ranked to be relieved by a Hungarian reserve lieutenant. Elischer's recollections are, therefore, erroneous.

Similarly, it can be classified as a fictional detail when Dénes Vass recalled how, in their shared shelter with the Germans, *SS-Untersturmführer* Hermann Maringgele gave them a lecture about how he had already got out of Stalingrad, so he would also get out of Budapest. Dénes Vass gave precise and exact information in the majority of cases, but it is evident that his memories were somewhat distorted by his sympathies and the books he read later. On the one hand, Maringgele was only a non-commissioned officer in the designated time frame (he was promoted to *SS-Untersturmführer* in January 1945) and, on the other hand, he had never been in, or even near Stalingrad. It was indeed possible for a soldier to get out of the Stalingrad pocket, but only if he was seriously wounded and so airlifted out of the encircled city – no breakout attempt was recorded there. The two persons could possibly have been together in the same cover, and it is also possible that the officer was not Maringgele but somebody who had indeed been in combat at Stalingrad. What is certain, however, is that the story is, at least to some extent, the creation of Vass' imagination.[48] It is possible that he read about Maringgele later and matched this information unintentionally with what he had heard in the shared shelter; however, it is also possible that the entire discussion had never happened. What can clearly be seen from this account is that Dénes Vass was sympathising with his former German allies at the time of the writing of his book (in 1995). From various other events, we can also assume that his opinion was no different during the siege.[49]

As the author has already mentioned, the success of this research would not have been possible without the documents and files retained by the *WASt*. It needs to be noted that the survival of these documents was never self-evident. In Berlin, the Allies initially wanted to destroy all the archival documents, reasoning that they only contained information that was useless or worthless to them, and they were also concerned that these documents might help Germany in the course of possible rearmament and revenge. Therefore, the Allied Control Council issued a decree in October 1945 regarding the destruction of the documents. However, the American Major Henry Sternweiler and the Alsatian French Captain Armand Klein decided to make a bold move: they recognised the importance and relevance of the documents while also being aware that without them, millions would be unable to search for their relatives – therefore, they did not obey the decree. They both appealed to their superiors on the grounds that it would be inhumane to execute the order. Thanks to these two officers, an unprecedented event happened: the Allied Control Council revoked their order.[50] It is worth reflecting on how much courage it took in 1945 for two officers of not even a significant rank to sabotage the decision of the Allied Control Council and to persuade Eisenhower and General Marie-Pierre Koenig, the commander of the French occupation zone, to change their minds. What is more, they risked their careers in a case which, if successful, would not have positively impacted their military careers nor conferred any benefit on their countries. In the event that their appeal to save the records failed, their jobs and future careers might well have been at risk. According to the author's personal opinion, this act stemmed from a higher level of courage than a number of wartime heroic deeds.

Thanks to the two officers – and the documents they helped save – the cataloguing and preservation work continued after 1945, and this might have been the most intensive and fruitful period of this essential work. This is not surprising if we consider that, at the end of the war, three million persons were recorded as missing in action. Based on *Feldpostnummern* (military postcodes), the German Red Cross published a compendium of the missing persons with photos in several subsequent volumes. In the three decades after the war, the fate of more than one million persons was successfully established. The author wishes the present work may also contribute to this effort.

ACKNOWLEDGEMENTS

The writing of this book has a long history. The author has been asked on several occasions to organise themed walking tours in Budapest that are related to the siege of the city. In order to be able to give more, and possibly new, information to the participants of these walks, the author, during 2013–2014, reviewed the extensive correspondence he had conducted in connection with the Hungarian, German and English publication of his book on the siege of Budapest. This led to the realisation that an entirely new book might be written without repeating any of the earlier published facts.

It was a lucky coincidence that the author regularly travelled to Berlin every year due to his work. These visits were connected to research periods in the archives. In five years, the days spent in this way added up to at least half a year of intensive research work. The author wishes to express his gratitude to János Rainer M., who was the director of the 1956 Institute (*1956-os Intézet*), which was disbanded in 2019. The institute, as a workplace, was an extraordinary island of freedom for decades.

The collection of personal stories was slow and cumbersome. In this task, the author received the invaluable help of Ludwig Norz from the Berlin *WASt*, who kindly provided accommodation as well. From the *Volksbund Deutsche Kriegsgräberfürsorge e. V.* (German War Graves Commission), Margarethe Stefaniak provided answers to the detailed questions regarding burials. From the several related forums and sites on the internet, the author wishes to acknowledge the immense help provided by the editors of the *Lexikon der Wehrmacht* and Roland Pfeiffer in particular. Thanks to the latter, the author received highly detailed responses to questions of organisational history. Ingo Möbius, who compiled the biographies of the Saxonian recipients of the *Ritterkreuz des Eisernen Kreuzes*, provided the author with several small but important details. József Meruk offered professional help in uncovering important Russian-language sources, and he was a trusted help in revising the text of the work in its creation. Jury Frolov and Danyl Holkov from Moscow were of great help. Peter Zwack, Mirko Bayerl, Jürgen Fritsche, Veit Scherzer, Robert Balsam, Zoltán Weimper, Florian Berger and Karl-Heinz Sondermann selflessly provided photographs from their own collections. Károly Baintner offered financial help for a number of the research trips to Berlin. In Freiburg, Maria and Werner Krempels provided not only accommodation but a second home for the author while he was working on the research. László Halasi contacted the author following the publication of the Hungarian-language version to correct and amend the biographies with a number of details.

Finding the relatives was not an easy task, and in a number of cases, it was impossible to do so. The various Internet forums and online phonebooks were of invaluable help during the research. The moments when children and grandchildren of those personnel mentioned in this book contacted the author, or when the author himself was able to provide information to the relatives, were moving and irreplaceable. Often, the author was the person who could provide the last account of their beloved. Without Hartmut Müller, Otto von Mitzlaff, Tibor Sugár, Heide Scharfe, Hans-Jürgen Wolff, Daniela Burger, Jürgen and Christine Flügel, the present work would only have been unfinished research. Of the personnel included in this work, the author corresponded with Helmut Friedrich and Johannes Finger regularly during the 1990s. Their openness and honesty are well described by the fact that they welcomed the then-unknown Hungarian university student into their homes. It is a long-held regret of the author that he did not ask for more detailed descriptions from these persons. Those whom the author mentions above deserve gratitude not only because of the information they provided for the present work. The author's research had three aims from the beginning: the compilation of the biographies of the "heroes", uncovering formerly unknown Soviet sources and the publication of recollections relating to the breakout attempt itself. The first, in the form of the present work, is now complete. The author wishes to work on the other two topics so that they, too, can be published soon.

1.

THE GERMAN MILITARY ELITE OF THE BATTLE FOR BUDAPEST

1937–1941

1943–1944

1945

PFEFFER-WILDENBRUCH, KARL

Karl Pfeffer was born in 1888 in the small village of Kalkberge near Berlin. His father was a doctor. The family was originally from Salzburg, from where they were forced to flee in the 18th century because of their protestant religion, to Prussia, a country of religious tolerance. He began his military service in 1907 as an officer candidate in *Feldartillerie-Regiment Nr. 22* (2nd Westphalian Field Artillery Regiment No. 22). Between 1911 and 1914 he studied at the *Militärtechnische Akademie* in Berlin-Charlottenburg. He served with Field Artillery Regiment No. 22 on the Western Front until 1915 before being transferred to Field Artillery Regiment No. 237, which was deployed to serve on the Russian Front. He served as the regimental adjutant here. Thereafter he was assigned to the Persian military mission of *Generalfeldmarschall* Wilhelm Leopold Colmar von der Goltz in a staff position. Von der Goltz had commanded the Turkish 1st Army, based in Baghdad. After the death of von der Goltz, Pfeffer was reassigned to the Constantinople (Istanbul) German military mission, the commander of which was *General der Kavallerie* Otto Liman von Sanders, who was partly of Jewish origin. Pfeffer served as head of the operations department. In this position, he must have gained information about the Armenian genocide, even more so because von Sanders was the only high-ranking German officer who actively opposed the mass murder and prevented several genocidal acts in the region of Smyrna (Izmir). The related actions and orders were partly coordinated and issued by Pfeffer. During his stay in Turkey, he learned to speak Turkish and Persian, as well as English and French.[51]

At the beginning of 1918, he was reassigned to the Western Front, where he served in staff positions (11th *Division* and *XXIV. Reserve-Korps*). In 1919, he

Karl Pfeffer-Wildenbruch as *General der Polizei* between 1937–1943

joined the newly founded *Schutzpolizei*. In the same year, he married Dorothea Nierhoff. He adopted the name Wildenbruch on 10 September 1924 (a number of his biographers also add the forename "von"; however, this is unfounded). Between 1928 and 1930, he acted as a training officer and inspector of the *Carabineros de Chile* (Chilean police force) together with Ernst Röhm, the commander of the SA (*Sturmabteilung*), who was subsequently murdered. During this period, he also learned to speak Spanish and, after just a few months, gave lectures in Spanish. After his return to Germany on 28 July 1932, he joined the *NSDAP*; his membership number was 1,364,387. On March 3 1933, he stopped paying his membership fee to the organisation. In the spring of 1933, he took over the police command of the Kassel–Frankfurt region (in reality, this was an undercover military position and later corresponded to the command of the 81st Infantry Regiment). In 1936, he was promoted to the rank of *Generalinspekteur der Polizeischulen* (Inspector General of the Police Schools). On 12 March 1938, he joined the ranks of the *Allgemeinen SS* (with membership number 292,713) as *Oberführer*. At the same time, he was transferred to the *Führungsstab* of the *Reichsführer SS* (Heinrich Himmler). This must have reminded him to try and settle the question of his party membership. So, he requested, in writing, the relevant party office to allow him the possibility to settle his arrears of unpaid party membership fees in one payment. He then claimed that his membership status had "fizzled out" (!) after being reassigned. The relevant authorities did not want to accept this explanation, and they offered Pfeffer-Wildenbruch a new party membership number, but later, he somehow managed to keep his old number.

From 1 October 1939, he became the first commander of the newly founded *Polizei-Division*. In the French Campaign of 1940, the unit was initially in defence in the "Westwall" fortified line on the French-German border before they advanced via Verdun to the Swiss border. Pfeffer-Wildenbruch was a pedant bureaucrat who demanded the strict observation of rules and regulations; in 1940, for example, he sentenced a soldier to 10 days of confinement for taking half a kilogram of coffee from an empty house in occupied France.

After the French Campaign, he served in the *Stab* of the *Reichssicherheitshauptamt* (*RSHA,* Reich Main Security Office) and in the *Führungsstab* of the *Reichsführer-SS* as *Chef des Kolonial-Polizeiamtes im Reichsministerium* (chief of the colonial police service). On 27 August 1943, after the colonial police had lost its importance, he was appointed commander of the *VI. SS-Freiwilligen-Armeekorps* (Latvian): he served as the commander of this unit until 11 June 1944 on the relatively calm frontline of *Heeresgruppe Nord.*

Soon after that, according to his personal files, he found himself in a peculiar situation. While Pfeffer-Wildenbruch was on leave, he received an invitation from the *Stab* of the *Oberkommando des Heeres* (*OKH*) – or more precisely, he made them invite him to the generals' conference organised by Heinrich Himmler that was held in the *Adolf-Hitler-Schule* (*AHS*) in Sonthofen between 19 and 22 June 1944. At this event, the main topic was the presentation of ideological lectures by *Generalfeldmarschall* Wilhelm Keitel. The narrow-minded views of Himmler are demonstrated by the letter he sent on 27 June 1944 to *SS-Gruppenführer und Generalleutnant der* Waffen-SS Hans Jüttner, commander of the *SS-Führungshauptamt,* and *SS-Obergruppenführer und General der Waffen-SS* Maximilian von Herff, commander of the *SS-Personalhauptamt.* He complained to them about the invitation of Pfeffer-Wildenbruch because the invitation was originally only meant for high-ranking Wehrmacht officers. Pfeffer-Wildenbruch allegedly got himself invited so that he could meet Himmler in person. Unfortunately, we are not familiar with the subject of their discussion. Himmler, however, did not take this case lightly and sent a damning letter to the organisers of the conference, stating that:

> I do not want to see SS leaders [among those invited], as this would make other invitees feel they were being observed or, worse still, reported. This way is certainly much better psychologically. On the other hand, anybody can be sent to me individually if I want to meet that person myself. This is because I, like the rest of you, must allocate my time wisely.[52]

It seems grotesque that the *Reichsführer-SS* showed himself to be this sensitive to informants – a month later, after the assassination attempt on Hitler, he surely no longer had such reservations.

Pfeffer-Wildenbruch was assigned to Budapest on 1 September 1944 to take part in the prevention of the armistice attempt by Miklós Horthy and also to lead and oversee the organisation of new Waffen-SS units (18th SS Panzergren-

Karl Pfeffer-Wildenbruch as *SS-Obergruppenführer* in September 1943

adier Division, 22nd SS Cavalry Division, and the 31st SS Grenadier Division). His promotion was mainly due to his experience in police matters – on the other hand, he had almost no battlefield experience. His seat was in the Erdődy–Hatvany-Palace in the Castle District, under Nr. 7 Werbőczy (today: Táncsics) Street; this was the location where Ferenc Szálasi was being hidden during this time. The swift prevention of the armistice attempt (in which he personally did not take part) and the internal political processes which were favourable for the Germans would not have lent him a significant role in the events had the Soviet units not arrived at the foreground of the capital two weeks later.

At the time of Pfeffer-Wildenbruch's arrival, he could only expect support from the commands of the Waffen-SS, which were headquartered in Budapest. When the Soviet units reached Budapest, he was appointed as the commander of the hastily assembled *Korpsgruppe Budapest* (Budapest Corps Group), which in practice meant that he became the superior commander of the Hungarian I Army Corps and the Hungarian VI Army Corps which was incorporated into the former unit. At the same time, however, he did not have any significant units at his disposal. This was in itself extremely humiliating for Iván Hindy, the commander of the Hungarian I Army Corps, who would have had authority over much larger Hungarian resources had he not been placed under the command of Pfeffer-Wildenbruch. That is, the command authority of the latter was limited only to the rear areas, whereas the *III. Panzerkorps* bore the sole responsibility for the combat command on the frontline. Pfeffer-Wildenbruch could count on the *SS-Polizei-Regiment 1*, four German *Alarm-Bataillons*, the alarm unit of the *Sicherheitdienst*, half of a *Waffen-SS-Wachbataillon* and the Hungarian units. However, when these units found themselves in the first line, they were no longer under Pfeffer-Wildenbruch's command.

IX. Waffen-Gebirgskorps der SS, which took over the tasks of *Korpsgruppe Budapest*, had only arrived in Budapest from Croatia on 18 November 1944 and was considered only partially organised.[53] Theoretically, the *IX. Waffen-Gebirgskorps* must have had a number of corps units, that is: *Nachrichten* (signals), *Pionier*, *Aufklärung* (reconnaissance), *Panzerjäger* (anti-tank), *Flak* (anti-aircraft) and *Artillerie Abteilungen* as well as a *Feldpostamt* (military postal service), transport battalion, field pharmacy, *Sicherungs-Kompanie* (security company), field police units and several *Abteilungen* comprising the *Korpsstab* (corps staff) itself. These would have included operational, logistics, intelligence and counterintelligence units as well as personnel department, corps court martial, intendance, medical and veterinarian offices – altogether more than 5,000 personnel. Nevertheless, the *IX. Waffen-Gebirgskorps* did not have the structural units that would have been minimally essential to function effectively. Probably only a couple of hundred personnel arrived in Budapest to be placed under the command of Pfeffer-Wildenbruch, some part of whom had been served in the Bosnian 13th *Waffen-Gebirgs-Division der SS "Handschar"*. This is because the majority of the *Stab* and the *Korps* units of the *IX. Waffen-Gebirgskorps* were mainly established with the help of the auxiliary units of the 13th *Waffen-Gebirgs-Division*. From November 1944 the functioning of the *IX. Waffen-Gebirgskorps* was, therefore, only possible if officers from the subordinated German troops had been transferred to the key positions in the *Korps*. Consequently, many of the personnel did not even belong to the Waffen-SS, and many had been reassigned there as a temporary transfer, mainly from the 8th SS Cavalry Division. According to the report of the 6th Army issued on 18 November 1944, the arrival of the units of the *IX. Waffen-Gebirgskorps* was due in four days. However, it was estimated that it would be only possible to organise the *SS-Korps-Nachrichten-Abteilung* at the end of December. Therefore, only administrative tasks were assigned to the command.[54]

At the end of December 1944 or at the beginning of January 1945, the German commander of Budapest transferred his headquarters to the Governor's shelter located in the *Buda Castle Tunnel*, where he occupied the upper floor rooms. The lower floor rooms had already been occupied by the high command of the Hungarian I Army Corps because the Sándor-palace had been hit a number of times and was considerably damaged. It is characteristic that there was almost no formal or informal contact between the German and Hungarian High Commands. Pfeffer-Wildenbruch offered virtually no information or guidance to the commander of the Hungarian I Army Corps, Lieutenant General Iván Hindy, whose head of the operations department, Staff Captain Ferenc X. Kovács, recalled that if they wanted to gather information on any matter he, or his superior, Colonel Sándor Horváth, had to practically "force their German colleagues to confess", as they had disclosed almost nothing of their plans. It is especially telling of the personal conduct of Pfeffer-Wildenbruch that earlier in December, instead of providing direct contact, he had sent Hungarian officers who came for information to *Obertsleutnant →Leopold von Münchow*, commander of *Korück 593 (Kommandant rückwärtigen Armeegebiets 593).*[55] However, he was only competent in the issues of the rear areas and had no authority over the frontline matters.[56]

While he denied his Hungarian colleagues even minimal information, he regularly bombarded the high command of the 6th Army with telegrams asking for information. On 3 January 1945, he even requested that an officer able to inform him about the general situation be flown on a Junkers into the encirclement.[57] Pfeffer-Wildenbruch strictly retained his meticulous pedantry in the command shelter and never left it during the siege at all; also, he did not trust his own officers and monitored them continuously. →*Generalmajor Gerhard Schmidhuber*, commander of the 13th Panzer Division was seriously reprimanded because, on 30 December, he had chosen (on the basis of social background considerations) an officer to whom he entrusted the war logs and other files of the *Division* and airlifted him out of the encirclement. According to Pfeffer-Wildenbruch this act "decreased the combat strength". It is characteristic that, as a punishment, he ordered the *Divisionsstab* to transfer one more officer to the city command.[58] Pfeffer-Wildenbruch also continuously complained about significant differences between the combat strength of the 13th Panzer Division and its provisioning numbers and refused to accept the results of the initiated investigation despite the division providing a detailed account of all of their units. → *Major i. G. Sven von Mitzlaff*, *Stabschef* of the 8th SS Cavalry Division, described his impressions of Pfeffer-Wildenbruch after the breakout attempt as follows:

> Pfeffer-Wildenbruch is a particularly noble person. But he is not a unit commander, and it is really a novelty that an acting general would not leave the tunnel for eight weeks. This has become a characteristic of his staff officers as well, who visited the troops pro forma only after they had been awarded the *Ritterkreuz*. Particularly harsh criticism was directed towards the *Generalstabschef*, Major Lindenau. He did not handle the given situations with due seriousness. Due to his complete lack of overview of the situation, he always remained calm and hopeful, which, on the other hand, had its positive aspects as well. Regardless of all this, the fact that none of the members of the *Stab* [of the *Korps*] had been able to escape the siege encirclement was most probably due to them considering the breakout attempt as nothing more than a bad joke…[59]

All evidence leads to the assumption that via Otto Winkelman Pfeffer-Wildenbruch also reported *Generalleutnant* Hermann Breith, commander of the *III. Panzerkorps* to *Armeegruppe Süd.* Namely, Winkelmann called upon Breith for clarification regarding how he had handed over the documents relating to the combat situation in Budapest to the *IX. Waffen-Gebirgskorps.* The response from Breith was as follows:

> The orders of the *Kampfkommandant Budapest* issued by the 6th Army had been handed over by the *Erster Generalstabsoffizier* of the *III. Panzerkorps* on 7 December 1944 with No. 171/44. to the first adjutant of the *IX. Waffen-Gebirgskorps, SS-Hauptsturmführer* Lösch. The receipt is available for inspection. Apart from this, the *III. Panzerkorps* and the *IX. Waffen-Gebirgskorps* had, in the presence of both of the *Generalstabschefs*, organised a detailed discussion on 12 December 1944. On this occasion, all relevant questions and aspects of the defence of Budapest had been discussed. Duration: two hours. Furthermore, after the handover of the information and documents, the *Korpskommando* assigned from all *Abteilungen* an officer familiar with the current issues to remain for 4-6 days so that all potentially surfacing details and questions can be reassuringly settled. I report that during the war, I never took over or handed over issues and tasks in such or even a similarly prepared manner.[60]

Pfeffer-Wildenbruch's personality evoked mixed feelings in his other subordinates as well. For example, the seriously wounded *Oberstleutnant →Helmut Wolff* remembers him bitterly:

> We received only dirty and arrogant responses to all of our helpful commentaries and ideas. Pfeffer-Wildenbruch was always lying, even in his reports. For example, the Keleti Railway Station was occupied two days later than was originally reported.[61] All of his reports contained such a magnitude of exaggerations that even his adjutant[62] commented disapprovingly that he would not have dared write down such things.[63]

General der Panzertruppe Hermann Balck had a similarly disapproving opinion about him:

> Budapest was led by a civilian or a political officer at best. […] He and his *Generalstabschef* could not cope with the situation. After a few days, we had this impression.[64]

Although Balck had a prejudice against all SS generals (later, during *Operation Frühlingserwachsen,* this led to heated arguments), one still cannot dismiss this criticism as being without any foundation.

Based on this information, it is no surprise that he found himself in an even worse relationship with his Hungarian colleague, Iván Hindy. This is especially remarkable because no one could doubt the ardent devotion of Hindy towards the Germans – he deemed the continuation of the war to be so crucial that the otherwise apolitical officer even dared to arrest his own commander on 15 October 1944. In a few months, however, Pfeffer-Wildenbruch made Hindy an embittered and disillusioned man who wrote a telegram on 6 February 1945 to the Chief of the General Staff of the Hungarian Army stating that because of the Germans, the civilians were waiting for the Russians and were considering them as liberators.[65] He could not possibly draw a more damning picture of his German colleague, especially if we take into consideration the fact that earlier, Hindy himself had issued posters demanding that "Anyone who despairs shall be hanged!" According to the recollections of József Paulits, who served at the headquarters of the Hungarian I Army Corps, Pfeffer-Wildenbruch "took a bath every day in a bathtub of water while the Hungarian commander of the corps and his close subordinates only received 6 litres of water per day."[66]

The most peculiar aspects of Pfeffer-Wildenbruch's role can be linked to the fate of the Jewish residents in Budapest. It must be noted beforehand that no surviving contemporary documents are available to confirm how the German commander of Budapest related to this issue. There are no reports by diplomats or other eyewitnesses confirming that Pfeffer-Wildenbruch had executed any orders or would have taken any actions relating to the Budapest ghetto. It has to be noted, however, that until the encirclement of the capital, such matters belonged primarily to *Generalmajor →Heinrich Remlinger*, the German administrative commander of the city, and that the Germans had assigned all issues relating to Jews to the competence of the Arrow Cross authorities. This, however, does not mean that no conclusions could be drawn from the statements Pfeffer-Wildenbruch made after the war.

In connection with the German commanders of Budapest, the question of responsibility is relevant in this case, that is to say, did they do everything in their capacity to reduce the level of atrocities as much as possible? In the case of a number of German officers, such actions have been documented. However, in the case of Pfeffer-Wildenbruch, only his own confession is available. This confession was obtained by a Swiss diplomat, Carl Lutz, who contacted Pfeffer-Wildenbruch at the beginning of 1956. Even the establishment of this contact is mysterious because these two persons had never previously met and had obviously not worked towards the same goal before. Lutz, however, behaved almost as if Pfeffer-Wildenbruch could have been his superior. After continuous correspondence and several personal meetings, on 6 March 1957 Lutz sent Pfeffer-Wildenbruch an article about Raoul Wallenberg with references to the effect that the Swedish diplomat had also contacted him. Pfeffer-Wildenbruch responded on 31 March 1957. He denied the validity of the establishment of contact with Wallenberg but, at the same time, wrote the following:

> Shortly before Christmas of 1944, an order was issued about the defence of Budapest. I strictly ordered the commander of the *Gestapo* group that remained in Budapest and, therefore, after the encirclement, came under my authority to ensure the safety of the Jewish population. After this, he ordered the closure of the so-called Pest ghetto and ordered his own men, and those that I had assigned under his command, to protect the area, and with guards and patrols, he managed to prevent the Arrow Cross Party members or other radical elements from entering the area and causing a catastrophe. The last remaining members of the rear guard had been taken to safety via hidden passages by the Jewish people themselves when this became necessary due to the advance of the Russians on the night of 15 January, and our own evacuation plans were underway.[67]

After this section, Pfeffer-Wildenbruch refers to a 1947 letter from one of his German acquaintances in which the person in question describes his astonishment at the fact that during his stay in Budapest, the local Jewish population was saved by the intervention of the SS.

This interpretation requires further explanation. On the one hand, if the situation had been this harmonious, then it seems incomprehensible that the grateful Jews did not follow their saviours whom they had brought to safety earlier through secret passages from the Soviets. More importantly, however, the facts contradict entirely Pfeffer-Wildenbruch's story. It is true that in certain cases SS soldiers had protected houses designated with yellow stars (one such case is documented), but until 12 January, the ghetto was exclusively guarded by the Hungarian police and armed Arrow Cross Party members. Outside the ghetto walls, the mass murders were ongoing. The commander of the *Sicherheitspolizei* and the SD in Budapest (so not of the *Gestapo*) was →*Reiner Gottstein* during the period in question. Of him, it is known that at the beginning of January 1945, he took part in planning mass murders aimed at the ghetto inhabitants, a plan prevented not by Pfeffer-Wildenbruch but by *Generalmajor* Gerhard Schmidhuber acting independently of Pfeffer-Wildenbruch. On 2 February 1945, Schmidhuber tried to convince Pfeffer-Wildenbruch during a long argument to act independently on its own authority, but his reasons went unnoticed.[68] Similar attempts at convincing Pfeffer-Wildenbruch happened earlier as well. On 26 January 1945, when the Germans stopped *Operation Konrad III*, aimed at relieving Budapest, Pfeffer-Wildenbruch called all *Regimentskommandeurs* to a briefing. It is no surprise that perhaps all the officers present realised the same truth: that, most probably, this was the last time when a successful breakout might be attempted. Pfeffer-Wildenbruch, however, had strictly prohibited all such endeavours on the grounds of Hitler's orders. Despite this, the commander of the 13th Panzer Division informed those present of a plan codenamed *"Glücksspiel"*, which detailed a breakout attempt towards the southwest. The German commander-in-chief reacted only with a short statement: "We shall wait for the Führer's orders".[69]

On 3 February 1945, he was visited in the bunker by the Apostolic Nuncio Angelo Rotta, who, as the doyen of the Christian diplomatic college, demanded that he take heed of the sufferings of civilians. Pfeffer-Wildenbruch answered that this was outside his capacity, but he promised to turn to the *OKH*. And he did this. However, the next day Heinz Guderian, *Generalstabschef* of the *OKH*, informed him that Adolf Hitler's orders had not changed; the Hungarian capital was to be held at all costs. Despite this, he repeated his request regarding a breakout on 5 February but received a dismissive response again.

On 11 February 1945, the German commander of Budapest left his Castle bunker for the first time in weeks. From one of the houses on Horváth Garden (Horváth-kert), in the vicinity of Buda Castle, through an opening, he clambered down into the ditch of the Ördögárok (a partly covered ditch of a seasonal small stream coming from the Buda Hills and going through the densely built parts of Buda) with a small group of soldiers belonging to his *Korps*. Peculiarly, he put on a common soldier's uniform for this action. (Péter Gosztonyi comments that Pfeffer-Wildenbruch tore off the rank insignia from his uniform right before being taken prisoner,[70] but Soviet photographs taken of him that day show no sign of this, and Soviet eyewitness accounts also contradict this description.) Experiencing the situation around Bolyai Academy on Hidegkúti Street, he turned back. From a side tunnel with its other end in Budenz Street, he climbed up to the surface in the early morning hours and took refuge in the next possible building. This building was still under construction. The Soviets discovered them a few hours later that morning. The events during which he and his group were taken as prisoners are described differently in several Soviet sources. According to the political commissar of the 297th Rifle Division, the following happened:

> During the combat for the building,[71] we sent a Hungarian civilian who spoke German to the enemy to relay the message to them to surrender. To lend weight to our demand, we pointed towards the house our 45mm gun commanded by 1st Lieutenant M. U. Zagoryan. From the house came the answer that they would surrender on the following conditions: (a) that we made sure their life was not in danger and (b) that a Soviet soldier with the rank of at least Major took them as prisoners. Major Skripkin, commander of the chemical unit of the division, inked his own finger [sic!] and wrote on a scrap of paper that he was a major of the Red Army and was ready to take them over.[72]

N. V. Komissarov, in his work *Battle for Budapest* describes what happened similarly:

> Major Skripkin ordered the soldiers to hang out a poster with the following inscription: "Surrender yourselves, we will not shoot at you. [...] Otherwise, we will begin the siege of the building in five minutes." [...] After some time was spent, a white flag appeared in the window of the cellar of the house. We ordered the Hitlerites to leave their weapons in the building, come forth and line up on the street. There were 118 of them there.[73]

The monograph concentrating on the Soviet border troops during the Second World War, based on the contemporary recommendations for decorations, describes the same situation as follows:

> The 1st Battalion of the 134th Ruschuk[74] Regiment was guarding this area [Budakeszi Street–Zugligeti Street] under the command of Captain Zhukov, and faced considerable enemy forces that numbered up to around 1,000 soldiers who were preparing to break through towards the frontline. The patrols by the 1st Battalion of the 134th Ruschuk Border Control Regiment stormed the Germans and, with their swift and determined action, took 151 German soldiers and officers as prisoners, among them General Pfeffer-Wildenbruch, the commander of the German troops in Budapest and his chief of staff, colonel Lindenau.[75] During this battle and afterwards, in the capture of the Germans, the following soldiers distinguished themselves with outstanding performance: battalion commander Captain Zhukov, patrol leader 2nd Lieutenant Prihodchenko, lance sergeant Stolnichenko and soldier Ognev. All four of them were awarded the Order of the Red Banner.[76]

This version is supported by another eyewitness account:

> Chadaikin led a large group of prisoners to the staff. At the same time, another group of prisoners was led by patrol leader 2nd Lieutenant Prihodchenko. He, with his soldiers, had captured the whole staff of the German commander of Budapest.[77]

A former news agency correspondent, Yuri Baranov, offered a third version of the events surrounding the taking of the prisoners. According to his words, at first an *NKVD* unit subordinated to the 3rd Ukrainian Front had taken Pfeffer-Wildenbruch prisoner. Soon thereafter, however, an officer of a higher rank from the 297th Rifle Division subordinated to the 2nd Ukrainian Front, arrived at the scene and "kidnapped" the German officer from the border patrol unit to gain recognition for the capture of the German commander.[78] In this action, he was aided by the political commissar of the division, the military prosecutor and the leader of the counterintelligence unit, who gave "proper weight" to his "request". The border patrol unit handed over their prisoners begrudgingly after receiving a receipt.[79]

The text of the contemporary recommendations for decorations also reveals that together with Pfeffer-Wildenbruch, his adjutant, *SS-Sturmbannführer* Ulrich von der Damerau-Dambrowski,[80] was also captured, as well as *SS-Sturmbannführer →Karl-Heinz Sobotta*, *Korps-Pionier-Führer* of the *IX. Waffen-Gebirgskorps*, and *Oberstleutnant →Daniel Lindenau*, *Generalstabschef* of the *IX. Waffen-Gebirgskorps*. However, in an account given to Péter Gosztonyi by Lindenau, he stated that he was separated from his commander and left the ditch somewhere near the area of today's Körszálló and then wounded.[81] It is probable, however, that Gosztonyi is not a reliable source here either. It is certain that Nikolai Vladimirovich Novikov, a doctor of philology, was present during the first interrogation of Pfeffer-Wildenbruch, as was Lindenau – this makes it extremely unlikely that Lindenau was captured separately. Novikov described most probably the same interrogation in his *Battle for Budapest* as follows:

> On the morning of 12 February, apart from taking part, with the guidance of Galperin, in the mass takeover of the prisoners, their confinement, temporary accommodation and controlling their transport to the rear areas, I had the opportunity to be present at the reconnaissance department of the division where they conducted the preliminary interrogation of General von Pfeffer-Wildenbruch, the commander of the German troops in Budapest. [...] The reconnaissance department occupied a considerably spa-

cious room. Stepping through the door, I saw the following: directly left of the entrance door, chairs were arranged in multiple rows on which the group of captured officers and non-commissioned officers from Pfeffer-Wildenbruch's staff were seated, and another group was standing in the entrance behind the last row of chairs. It is hard to say how many of them were there, but no less than a hundred. At the front, in one of the corners, the Soviet officers were seated around a table in a half circle, among them Colonel Galperin, and at the other end of the table, slightly askew to Galperin, and with his back slightly towards the prisoners, sat General Pfeffer with Chief of Staff Lieutenant Colonel Lindenau, who we initially thought was a political commissar. He was a particularly silent man who did not say a word during the interrogation.

Pfeffer was advanced in age. His face was worn and wrinkled. Outwardly, he was very calm. His clothes consisted of a very worn soldier's uniform, left unbuttoned and smeared with something white, on his feet, not too fresh footrags, shoes, and his cap was in front of him on the edge of the table. To start the conversation, Galperin opened a pack of *papirosy* [a type of Russian cigarette] and offered it to Pfeffer to light one; then, he offered it to his colleague next to him. After waiting for some moments, the former took the opportunity and lit one; the other did not want it.

Galperin asked what the situation was like among the German troops in Buda in the last few days (the conversation was going on with the help of an interpreter), Pfeffer responded by saying that it was catastrophic and beyond hope: food ran out and the ammunition airdropped from transport aircraft was miserable and in mostly landed in the Soviet positions anyway. There was no hope of relief from anywhere. This was the situation when the command took the risk and gave the orders to the troops of the garrison to try to break out from the encirclement, everybody as best they could. Pfeffer himself was dressed as a common soldier [that is, he did not tear off the rank insignia from his own uniform!] and, together with his officers, started off from the tunnels of the Horthy palace. Then at the exit of the tunnel, they were stopped and captured. [...] Henceforth, the conversation was going on about the immediate necessity to eliminate the largest enemy fire pocket around the local hospital.[82] The sound of rifles and machine guns was often heard from that direction, sometimes even silenced by the rumble of cannons. Galperin turned to Pfeffer and said: "General, I believe you agree that the resistance your troops show around the hospital area is hopeless. In order to avoid further unnecessary bloodshed, the Soviet high command offers you personally

> the opportunity to give an order to your troops to end the meaningless resistance and surrender themselves without conditions." The general was silent. He bowed his head down. After a considerably long silence, an air force officer[83] stood up among the captured officers and said that he was ready to go to "their" troops at the hospital and persuade them to surrender, on the condition that the commander consents to this. Upon this, somebody among the Soviet officers shouted that "being captured frees you from your subordination to your commanders!". However, the officer was adamant in his decision. At last, the consent was given, and Pfeffer scribbled the order that was demanded of him on a scrap of paper. After that, a four-member delegation was formed. The members were, apart from the aforementioned air force officer, one captured German first lieutenant, a first lieutenant from our troops (I cannot recall his name) and the writer of these words.
>
> Firstly, we gave the Germans assigned to our group something to eat, then they were given white armbands, and we started off towards the hospital. We went on a long, straight, wide road which was lined with trees, and everywhere we could see the marks of the combat throughout the night: spent bullet casings everywhere, on the roadside too, German helmets, gasmasks, other equipment, dead German soldiers. Our little delegation was surely an extraordinary sight to anyone who saw us. It is true that all our soldiers, who were coming from the opposite direction, stopped at us and marvelled at our group. They could not believe that it was possible for German and Soviet officers to go together peacefully. And to where? Towards the frontline. The short, black-haired, almost hopping aircraft officer, whose uniform was gleaming with a lot of Hitlerite awards and medals, was especially in the centre of interest. Our group was halfway to the hospital when we noticed that the noise of the combat started to decrease. First, the gunshots stopped, and then the rifle and machine gun sounds were attenuated. Then, we heard the sound of one single shot from the distance. We learned from our soldiers coming from the opposite direction that the last pocket of German resistance in the city had fallen.[84]

Lieutenant General I. M. Managarov, commander of the Budapest Operational Group, wrote in his memoirs that Pfeffer-Wildenbruch, on his interrogation a day later, was "dirty and unkempt, was in an irresponsible state of mind, and answered any questions directed to him with: 'Hitler knows.'" Although the "dirty looks" was probably not true, the description of Pfeffer-Wildenbruch as uncommunicative is consistent with other sources about his personality.[85] However, the question of the capture of Pfeffer-Wildenbruch sparked debates not only among the officers of lesser ranks, as is demonstrated by the following excerpt:

> The commander of the 17th Air Army, Marshall Sudets remembered that during the elimination of the German troops in Budapest, an incident happened in which Marshall F. I. Tolbukhin and Marshall R. Y. Malinovsky were quarrelling. On 13 February 1945, Malinovsky reported to the Stavka [Headquarters of the Supreme High Command of the Armed Forces of the USSR] that Budapest had been taken. But he added that within the city, there were still around 16,000 to 20,000 German and Hungarian soldiers maintaining their resistance.
>
> The next day, the commander of an anti-aircraft regiment of the 17th Air Army, whose unit was assigned here to combat the encircled pockets of German resistance, called the commander of the air army via phone and reported to him:
>
> "Comrade commander, we have eliminated a considerable fascist unit. We took a lieutenant general prisoner and a number of other generals and other officers. What is the order, what should we do with them? Where to take them?" Sudets was there together with Tolbukhin and Nedelin, and relayed this message to them. Tolbukhin ordered that the German high-ranking officers be taken immediately to the front command. But the captured officers never reached Tolbukhin. In the evening, the *Sovinformburo* reported at last that on 15 February, units of the 2nd Ukrainian Front had eliminated the encircled pockets of enemy resistance in the Budapest area, capturing their commander and two of their generals. Tolbukhin demanded an explanation from Sudets, but he could only tell the exact date when the anti-aircraft regimental commander started off with the German officers from the location where they were captured. Upon request of the marshall, Sudets called Malinovsky via phone and asked him to tell Moscow what happened in reality. "What has happened has already happened; what is the point talking about it again?" replied the irritated Malinovsky.
>
> After that Tolbukhin called Stalin and reported to him who were actually responsible for capturing the German generals in Budapest. The high commander – according to the words of Sudets – decided the following: "We will not issue a correction of these events, but we will take it as this: that the final victory over the enemy in Budapest was gained exactly by your 3rd Ukrainian Front."
>
> When at last, the commander of the anti-aircraft regiment of the 17th Air

> Army arrived at the headquarters of the 3rd Ukrainian Front, he explained to us that upon orders of his own high commander, the German officers had been transported under reinforced guard, with two cars, and that along the road they were stopped by members of the Special Department of the 2nd Ukrainian Front who ordered the captives to be transported to Malinovsky's command post. So, this is how the marshals were dividing the honours of gaining victory over Budapest two months before Zhukov and Koniev were quarrelling over who took Berlin.[86]

In the extremely short memoirs of Pfeffer-Wildenbruch, there are no details of the circumstances in which he was captured, and neither is the quarrelling over his person mentioned. There is a note in a Russian account stating that "Pfeffer asked Battalion Commander A. M. Zhukov,[87] to whom he was assigned, to give him back his sabre adorned with precious stones which he inherited from his warrior ancestors; with this weapon, the Hitlerite campaigner marched through Europe in a triumphant march."[88] Considering that the ancestors of Pfeffer-Wildenbruch were not professional soldiers, and it is highly unlikely that he would have taken a ceremonial weapon with him in his common soldier's uniform to the Devil's Ditch, the text seems to be more of a Soviet propaganda snippet than a description of the actual facts.

After he was captured, the German commander of Budapest was taken to Budakeszi, to the house at 19 Kossuth Lajos Street. Although in certain writings it is mentioned that he was wounded during the breakout attempt,[89] there is no evidence of this either in his own memoirs or in other contemporary documents, and the circumstances of his capture do not make this feasible. The contemporary Soviet propaganda was making fun of him getting dirty during the escape, quoting that his wet, damp clothes were extremely putrid, so at first, he had to be asked to bathe before new clothes were given to him.[90] The reference to the putrid smell seems to be an over-exaggeration. However, it is correct that in the contemporary Soviet newsreels, his cloak seems to be surprisingly clean. Therefore, he must have been given a new one.

A caricature of Pfeffer-Wildenbruch in the *Krasnaya Zvezda* newspaper

During his time in imprisonment, on 10 August 1949, he was sentenced by the court martial of the Latvian Soviet Socialist Republic as a war criminal to the heaviest penalty that was applicable at that time: 25 years of correctional labour. He was among the last to be released from captivity in 1955. He died in West Germany in 1971 after tripping on the stairs of his own home and fracturing his skull.[91]

He was decorated with the *Ritterkreuz des Eisernen Kreuzes* on 11 January 1945 and received the *Eichenlaub* on 1 February. The decoration itself was most probably physically transferred to him only in the first case. This is what a note written by *Oberleutnant* Ernst Schweitzer in 1955 implies. In it, he states the following:

> …since the battle in the encirclement, a virtual rain of decorations is showering on us from the high command. *Ritterkreuz des Eisernen Kreuzes, Eichenlaubs*, even with *Schwertern* for Dörner, to reinforce the fighting spirit of the defenders. During this the performance of the SS compared to that of the 13th Panzer Division is honoured in a ratio of 4:1. It is almost moving as the few liaison aircraft that could land on the small airfield beyond the Castle bring the decorations in order.[92]

The details of the award of these decorations are telling. Regarding the *Ritterkreuz des Eisernen Kreuzes*, it is known that formally it was given upon a proposal from *Generalfeldmarschall* Keitel, and the recommendation – most probably upon initiation by Keitel – was handed in by *Generaloberst* Hermann Balck, supported by *Heeresgruppe Süd*. This can be interpreted as a formal recognition of the fact that Hitler had sacrificed the German and Hungarian defenders of Budapest. And the same can be said in the case of the award of the *Eichenlaub*.

In the first days of January 1945, the German commander of Budapest constantly bombarded his superiors with telegrams claiming that the food and ammunition supplies of his troops would run out in one or two days (which was certainly incorrect, in the light of the events) and, referring to this situation, he appealed for formal consent to the initiation of the breakout attempt. However, this appeal was rejected every single time. According to the war diary of *Heeresgruppe Süd*, on 10 January 1945 at 0220 hours

> The *Generalstabschef* of the *Heer* called the *Chef des Führungsstabes im Generalstab* [Chief of the Command Department of General Staff of the Army] from the *Führerbunker*, and relayed the information that he had fought for the decision for two hours [that is, to convince Hitler to con-

> sent to the breakout attempt], but had achieved the same result as *Generaloberst* Guderian did [earlier] via phone. The only thing he could force out [of Hitler] was the award of the *Ritterkreuz des Eisernen Kreuzes* to Pfeffer-Wildenbruch.[93]

This clearly depicts the practice of "sugaring the pill" with decorations. After Pfeffer-Wildenbruch returned home from internment, he ordered a version of the *Eichenlaub* that could be worn in his buttonhole and, on more than one occasion, he had worn it.[94] The recommendations for the decorations and the warrants for their award did not survive the war; therefore, we are only familiar with the short text issued in the contemporary media about the events. In Pfeffer-Wildenbruch's case, the decoration was awarded clearly with political and propagandistic intentions. It was predictable that the days of *"Festung Budapest"* (Fortress Budapest) were numbered, therefore Pfeffer-Wildenbruch could not have remained without being decorated. Naturally, he received Hungarian decorations as well: Ferenc Szálasi (the "Leader of the Nation" after 15 October 1944) decorated him on 18 December 1944 with the Commander's Cross of the Order of Merit of the Kingdom of Hungary with War Decorations and Swords, and on 15 February with the Grand Cross of the Order of Merit of the Kingdom of Hungary with War Decorations and Swords.[95] Neither of the relevant recommendation documents has survived; in both cases, the decorations were awarded for clearly political reasons.

Pfeffer-Wildenbruch had two sons. His firstborn son, Günther, was serving in an artillery regiment when, on 25 June 1941, he was seriously wounded near Tobruk in Libya and died five days later. His second son, *Leutnant der Reserve* Edgar, died in France on 24 August 1944 as an adjutant serving in the 26/III Battalion of the 12th SS Panzer Division.

DECORATIONS	RANKS
• *Eisernes Kreuz II. Klasse* 1914 • *Eisernes Kreuz I. Klasse* 14 September 1917	• *Unteroffizier* 1907 • *Fähnrich* 18 November 1907 • *Leutnant* 18 August 1908

DECORATIONS	RANKS
• Bar to denote the subsequent award of the *Eisernes Kreuz II. Klasse* 20 June 1940 • Bar to denote the subsequent award of the *Eisernes Kreuz I. Klasse* 22 June 1940 • *Ritterkreuz des Eisernen Kreuzes* 11 January 1945 • *Eichenlaub* for the *Ritterkreuz des Eisernen Kreuzes* 1 February 1945 • Mecklenburg-Schwerin's Military Merit Cross 2nd Class • German Olympic Decoration 3rd Class • Ottoman War Medal (Turkish Iron Half-Moon) • Turkish Liyakat Medal • Military Merit Cross 3rd Class with War Decorations and Swords (Austria–Hungary • *SS-Ehrenring* • *Ehrendegen RFSS* 1938 • *Julleuchter der SS* 1938 • *Kreuz des Südens* (*Traditionsabzeichen*)[96] • *Hanseatenkreuz*	• *Oberleutnant* 28 November 1914 • *Hauptmann* (*Polizei*) 18 April 1919 • *Major* (*Polizei*) 6 July 1920 • *Oberstleutnant* (*Polizei*) 21 March 1921 • *Oberst* (*Polizei*) 10 April 1934 • Honorary *Generalmajor der Schutzpolizei* 21 October 1936 • *Generalmajor der Polizei* 13 August 1937 • *SS-Oberführer* 12 March 1938 • Honorary *Generalleutnant der Polizei* 20 April 1939 • *SS-Brigadeführer* 19 May 1939 • *Generalleutnant der Polizei* 15 November 1939 • *SS-Gruppenführer* 21 June 1940 • *SS-Obergruppenführer* 27 September 1943 • *Waffen-SS Obergruppenführer* and *Generaloberst der Polizei* 18 November 1943

1939–1942

BARTSCH, KURT

Kurt Bartsch was born on 29 November 1910 in Posen (today Poznań, Poland). He started his career as a non-commissioned officer; he married in 1935 and was promoted to *Leutnant der Polizei* on 6 September 1938. He spoke English and French as well. In 1940, as a member of the *Polizei-Division* (later 4th SS Panzergrenadier Division) serving in an unknown position, he participated in the French campaign.[97] On 9 December 1939, he was promoted to *Oberleutnant der Polizei*, and on 1 January 1942, he was promoted to *Hauptmann der Polizei*. In April 1942, he joined the ranks of the SS, and at the same time, he was transferred to the Waffen-SS, where he served in the SS Cavalry Brigade. On 30 November 1942, he was lightly wounded near Knyaske. Due to unknown reasons, he was discharged on 15 April 1943. However, he was readmitted on 31 July 1944. At that time, he was transferred to the reserves of the 8th SS Cavalry Division stationed in Warsaw, and on 15 September 1944, he was assigned as the appointed commander of the 53rd SS Cavalry Regiment of the 22nd SS Cavalry Division – an unusually high position compared to his rank of *Hauptmann*. This can only be explained by the severe lack of high-ranking officers. His new unit saw its first combat action on 15 October 1944. A photograph of him, taken by one of his soldiers at the entrance of Pasaréti Street, attests to this combat action. At the same time, this also proves that Bartsch's unit had a central role in the prevention of the armistice attempt: his soldiers can be seen in a different photograph (not published in the present work) which depicts the mansion under 10 Pasaréti Street that was used as an undercover weapons depot.

Bartsch with Sándor Csia (on the left), an Arrow Cross Party leader, and an unidentified person on 15 October 1944 at the junction of Pasaréti Street and Olasz Boulevard (today Szilágyi Erzsébet fasor).

His decorations were awarded almost exclusively for his actions in Budapest. On his personal files, a note can be seen on the date 30 January 1945 about the award of the *Ritterkreuz des Eisernen Kreuzes*, but there are no further signs of the actual registration of the award apart from a statement which is mentioned in the biography of →*Alfred Heuer*. On 5 February 1945, he was awarded *Ehrenblattspange des Deutschen Heeres* (Honour Roll Clasp of the Land Army) and received the *Deutsches Kreuz in Gold* (German Cross in Gold) the following day. The reason for the award in the second case is unknown; the first was awarded for his combat command actions in the area of Pestszentimre between 4 and 10 November 1944. On 13 January 1945, he also received a Hungarian decoration, namely the Knight's Cross of the Order of the Holy Crown of Hungary with Swords – most probably for the same reasons.[98]

His last letter from Budapest was sent on 30 December 1945. His *Regiment* was deployed on the southwestern side of the Pest bridgehead until 18 January, this is also proven by the manuscript of →*Wilhelm Schöning*, according to which he was subordinated to him for a short period of time on 3 January 1945 in Kispest. There is only one piece of data about his deployment in Buda: according to Gyula Litteráti-Loótz, he relieved *SS-Sturmbannführer* →*Karl Waller* from 24 January 1945 on Margaret Island (*Margit-sziget*).[99]

He was last seen on the day of the breakout attempt. A person who returned from Soviet internment stated that he had seen Bartsch near Kiev working on a building site. However, three other persons stated (based upon hearsay) that he had fallen in Budapest. In a Hungarian publication, although without relevant source information, it is noted that he shot himself in the head.[100]

DECORATIONS	RANKS
• *Eisernes Kreuz II. Klasse* • *Eisernes Kreuz I. Klasse* • *Verwundetenabzeichen in Schwarz* • *Ritterkreuz des Eisernen Kreuzes* 30 January 1945 • *Ehrenblattspange des Deutschen Heeres* 5 February 1945 • *Deutsches Kreuz in Gold* 6 February 1945 • Knight's Cross of the Order of the Holy Crown of Hungary with Swords 13 January 1945	• *Leutnant der Polizei* 8 September 1938 • *Oberleutnant der Polizei* 22 September 1939 • *Hauptmann der Polizei* 1 January 1942 • *SS-Hauptsturmführer* 1 April 1942 • *SS-Sturmbannführer* 21 December 1944

1945

around 1968

2003

BOOSFELD, JOACHIM

Joachim Boosfeld was born on 1 June 1922 in Aachen in a middle-class civic family. In 1937, he left the church, which might be connected to the fact that between 1934 and 1939 he was a student of the *Nationalpolitisches Erziehungsanstalten* (NAPOLA, National Political Institutes of Education) in Oranienstein. These institutions were considered a mixture of cadet schools and institutions for National Socialist elite education, and the students of these schools were supposed to be ardent National Socialists. It is not surprising, therefore, that in 1939, after his maturity exams, Boosfeld joined the SS. Originally, he was trained as a tank driver and was sent to the SS school for non-commissioned officers. In May 1941 he became a student at the *SS-Junkerschule* founded by the SS in Bad Tölz, which he finished on 15 September 1941. Boosfeld was assigned to the 1st SS Cavalry Regiment of the SS Cavalry Brigade, initially as platoon commander and later as battalion adjutant. In the occupied territories of the Soviet Union, during the autumn, the unit committed a number of mass murders labelled as "partisan hunts", although Boosfeld's role in these events is unknown. From December 1941, he, together with his unit, was deployed on the frontline in the Rzhev area for five months, during which his unit lost 80 percent of its strength. Boosfeld earned the *Eisernes Kreuz II. Klasse* and the *Eisernes Kreuz I. Klasse* in these combat actions. In May 1942, he was assigned to the *SS-Junkerschule* in Braunschweig as a trainer. Parallel to this, he enrolled in the local polytechnic, where he studied history, philosophy and ethnography. On 21 November 1943, he was promoted to *Schwadron-Chef* of the 4th *Schwadron* of the 16th SS Cavalry Regiment. In the summer of 1944, his unit was replenished with forcefully conscripted ethnic Germans living in Hungary; approximately 25 Russian volunteers also belonged to his unit. After the occupation of Hungary, they were assigned to the area around Szekszárd.

For his courageous and initiative actions performed in Transylvania between 9 and 22 October 1944, he was decorated with the *Deutsches Kreuz in Gold*. He was positioned with his *Schwadron* around Vecsés from November until 24 December. On 25 December, he was directed to the Farkasréti Cemetery (Farkasréti temető), where he celebrated Christmas with an engineer and his family in their villa. On 20 February 1945, Adolf Hitler personally decorated him with the *Ritterkreuz des Eisernen Kreuzes*. According to the recommendation, "It was due to his merit that the Vérmező, essentially important for reinforcements, could be held for such a long time. He was wounded, and despite this, he went into action with his unit, clearing incursions, making it possible for glider aircraft to land on the Vérmező."[101]

At the same time, in an interview with Peter Zwack Jr. in the 1980s, Boosfeld took an entirely different view of these events. In this interview, Boosfeld did not mention the defence of the airfield at all, an event in which he could not have taken part because he was wounded before the Soviet forces could even threaten the Vérmező area. In all probability, his recommendation was either mixed up with somebody else's or prepared based on incorrect data.

According to the Zwack interview, his first area of action was in Buda, in the area of Ágnes Street. However, a Soviet attack drove them out of this position on 29 December (*"we were thrown out"*), and they could only gain a foothold again in the line of Németvölgyi Street – Farkasréti Cemetery, where they were supported by a few Hetzer tank destroyers of the division. With his *Schwadron* they were to hold an approximately 300-400 metre-long frontline. During his time in Buda, he was astonished to see the unsuspecting behaviour of the civilians: for example, an elegant old lady, who always wore an expensive fur coat, went for walks with her dog in the Farkasréti Cemetery every day until the beginning of January when the frontline was only 200 metres away, and snipers had been active in the area. Boosfeld's command post was on the corner of Érdi Street and Németvölgyi Street, around 200 metres from the cemetery. The mansion that stood there most probably belonged to a wealthy restaurant owner because, besides the cellars, in a separate shelter, soldiers found food and wines stashed in perfect condition. Even after fifty years, Boosfeld remembered the French red wine of 1922 vintage, that he consumed in that house. It is characteristic of the amount of alcoholic beverages found in the house that he could distribute a bottle every day for 2-3 persons. In the first half of January, they threw back a number of Soviet attacks. On 15 January 1945, he was wounded by shell shrapnel and was admitted to hospital, but after a week, and with his wounds still not healed properly, he returned to his unit. He acquired an oversized large boot with laces for his bandaged leg. Boosfeld did not mention what happened to his unit between 23 January and 10 February.

He continued his account on 11 February 1945, when, in the afternoon, he was ordered to report to the division's headquarters in the Tunnel (Budai Váralagút). When he arrived there, he found that everybody was eating, bathing and shaving. The division commander of the 8th SS Cavalry Division, → *Joachim Rumohr* assigned him to be at his side and gave him a handful of caffeine tablets and two aspirins for his pain. He joined the first wave of the breakout, which, in his words, "drowned in full-scale chaos. After those who were in the first lines fell, the masses at the back pushed more and more people forward, who were also killed. This all happened before we could cross the Margit Boulevard."[102] Near the Boulevard, at the very bottom of Várfok Street, a Soviet anti-tank shell hit the walls directly above his head, and his orderly, who was standing next to him, was wounded in the face. According to his memory, he was so shaken by the shock that he was hardly able to bandage his wounded comrade. At last, around midnight, they were able to leave the inner areas of Buda on the Margit Street – Ganz factory – Marczibányi Square route and were heading along the Vadaskert in the hills around Buda. Their movement was easier in this area because, beyond Marczibányi Square, they only met unprepared, heavily drinking Soviet troops who did not care about repelling enemy units. In the hills around Buda, he found *SS-Sturmbannführer* Friedrich Schippmann, commander of the 8th *SS-Pionier-Bataillon*[103] and *Erster Generalstabsoffizier* of the division, *Major i.G →Sven von Mitzlaff*, together with a few regiment commanders. On the morning of 12 February 1945, the group had grown to include 1,000–1,500 persons, but from his original unit, Boosfeld only had his orderly by his side. The majority of the group consisted of soldiers from his division, although several Wehrmacht soldiers and a few Hungarian *honvéd* soldiers also joined them. They hid in the Remete Hill (Remete-hegy) area for some time, then proceeded to go through the woods. They were a kilometre away from the main line of resistance when they had to wade through a stream. For some exhausted soldiers, this proved an impossible task, even though at specific locations, the stream was not more than five metres wide. Boosfeld lost his orderly here as well. He reached friendly lines in the late morning of 14 February 1945 at Somodorpuszta. He recalled that, beyond the Soviet main line of resistance, they had to climb a hill until they reached the first German positions. From his group, only 10 to 20 people remained at his side, and he only met *Major i.G.* von Mitzlaff later.

After he managed to escape, he slept for 36 straight hours. After that, he was transported by bus to Győr, where those who had escaped the breakout attempt were being collected in a school sports hall. From here, he was brought to Bratislava; he was transported from here by aircraft to the *Führerbunker* in Berlin, together with *→Hermann Maringgele*. Here, Adolf Hitler personally decorated both of them on 20 February 1945 with the *Ritterkreuz des Eisernen Kreuzes*. At the same time, Boosfeld received the *Nahkampfspange Gold* (Close Combat Clasp in Gold) because his days spent in close combat, including the breakout attempt, amounted to 57. He was also promoted to *SS-Hauptsturmführer*. According to his statement, he was the youngest in this rank. The award documents were signed by Hitler only on the following day, therefore the date of his award is stated as 21 February 1945.[104]

According to his recollections, he had to wait an extremely long time in the *Führerbunker* before he had the chance to meet Hitler. Hermann Fegelein was present. Their conversation lasted around 15 minutes. Hitler seemed to be a mentally exhausted, worn-out person, and he was shaking. His spotless speech and suggestive power at the same time was impressive. He asked Boosfeld about the breakout, the urban usage of *Panzerfausts* and the morale of the Hungarian Germans. Boosfeld replied of the latter that their morale began to decline as soon as the Red Army had occupied their homes. After the audience, Fegelein noted that "it was unnecessary to burden the Führer with such negative comments".[105]

Joachim Boosfeld around 1956

He spent the last period of the war in various hospitals; there is no information relating to his imprisonment. He could only return to work in May 1946. Between 1946 and 1947, he spent three semesters studying pharmaceutics at Hamburg University, and between 1950 and 1955, he studied at Bonn University's faculty of law. Between September 1947 and December 1949, he was an official at the *Pressedienst München* (Munich Press Service) under a false name – in reality, he was an agent of the *Organisation Gehlen*, a West German intelligence agency named after Reinhard Gehlen.[106] After this, he was a salesperson for a pharmaceutical company for two years, and for a short time he also worked as a real estate agent. In 1956, the *Bundeswehr* took him over, and he wrote in his personal files the following fields of interest: "politics, international law, Eastern Europe, history, music, intelligence (intelligence and counterintelligence courses)". Initially, he was assigned to the 11th Panzergrenadier Division in Oldenburg, and in 1970, he was promoted as the commander of the 1st Panzergrenadier Brigade. In 1972, he received a staff position at the *Oberkommando Bundeswehr*. He was the only former Waffen-SS officer to reach the rank of staff colonel in the *Bundeswehr*. He retired in 1981 and died on 19 June 2015.[107]

DECORATIONS	RANKS
• *Eisernes Kreuz II. Klasse* 1 January 1942	• *Stabsfeldwebel* 1 September 1941
• *Eisernes Kreuz I. Klasse* 30 March 1942	• *SS-Untersturmführer* 1 December 1941
• *Deutsches Kreuz in Gold* 30 December 1944	• *SS-Obersturmführer* 9 November 1943
• *Allgemeines Sturmabzeichen*	• *SS-Hauptsturmführer* 20 February 1945
• *Nahkampfspange Gold* 21 February 1945	• *SS-Hauptmann* (*Bundeswehr*) 1956
• *Ritterkreuz des Eisernen Kreuzes* 21 February 1945	

1944[108]

2012

BUCK, FRIEDRICH

Friedrich Buck was born on 30 January 1922 in Friedensthal in Bessarabia (today Mirnopillya, Ukraine) into a landowning family of medium means. With a large number of relatives (twenty persons), he resettled in the Third Reich in 1940. The *Rasse und Siedlungshauptamt* (*RuSHA*, Race and Settlement Main Office) provided a very disappointing evaluation of the family: many had been labelled with the least reliable "*Volksliste 4.*" label (this meant that the related persons had been marked as "renegade" and were thus excluded from military service). Although Buck's father had received a better evaluation and was sent for political training as well, he was, however, according to a subsequent assessment, of reserved personality and weak mental abilities and was deemed completely incompetent.

After this, it is something of a miracle that Buck's request to join the Waffen-SS in 1941 was granted (at this time, the recruitment requirements were still rigorous). At first, he was assigned to the SS Panzergrenadier Regiment *Der Führer* as a machine-gun operator. During the spring of 1942, he took part in the combat operations around Rzhev, and in the summer, after he was promoted to *SS-Sturmmann*, he asked for reassignment to the *SS-Kavallerie*. From then on, he served in the 1st SS Cavalry Regiment and, after the reassignment of unit numbers, in the 15th SS Cavalry Regiment. From the end of 1942, his unit suffered catastrophic losses at Medvedevo, but due to the perseverance of its soldiers, they were able to hold their positions. During these combat activities, Buck received, besides having been promoted to *SS-Unterscharführer*, the *Eisernes Kreuz II. Klasse* and the *Allgemeines Sturmabzeichen* (General Assault Badge). During the battle of Kharkov and the ensuing retreat, he became well-known for his dauntless

Friedrich Buck in the 1990s

and spirited conduct. He managed to reconnoitre and destroy Soviet forward artillery observer positions a number of times, as well as artillery and mortar positions. During these combat actions, he was decorated with the *Eisernes Kreuz I. Klasse* and the *Verwundetenabzeichen in Gold* (Wound Badge in Gold) for having been wounded five times. Buck also destroyed several tanks in close combat with hand grenade clusters and anti-tank mines.

Only a few details are known of his activities during the siege of Budapest. Buck, who had been promoted to *SS-Oberscharführer*, took command of the 5th (mortar) *Schwadron* of the 15th SS Cavalry Regiment upon orders from his superior, Oswald Krauss, due to the serious lack of officers. During this period, he organised a number of counteroffensives and repulsed several Soviet assaults. There is only one piece of data regarding his location during the siege, which is not verifiable by sources; however, according to this, he was mainly active around Bécsi Street, that is, in District III.[109] On 27 January 1945, he received the *Ritterkreuz des Eisernen Kreuzes* and the *Nahkampfspange Gold* via telegram. This combination of decorations was only awarded to 98 persons during the whole period of the Second World War. Based on his statement, he was also decorated with the Hungarian Gold Medal of Bravery.[110] According to his statement to *Der Spiegel* in 1976, →*Karl Pfeffer-Wildenbruch* handed over to him his own *Ritterkreuz des Eisernen Kreuzes.*[111] On the day of the breakout attempt, he was severely wounded by an artillery shell and, having remained in the city, was captured. This was the seventh wound he sustained. Due to his health, he was released from internment as early as the end of 1945. From then onwards, Buck worked with Bosch as a foundry technician.

In 1976 the *Ordensgemeinschaft der Ritterkreuzträger* (AKCR, Association of Knight's Cross Recipients) contacted Buck and later, in a ceremony in a *Bundeswehr* building in Bavarian Sonthofen, and to the accompaniment of the music of the *Präsentiermarsch*, two former SS officers, Johannes Göhler[112] and Gustav Lombard,[113] ceremoniously presented Buck with the *Ritterkreuz des Eisernen Kreuzes* (modified so as not to display the swastika) and a similarly changed

Nahkampfspange Gold. This has to be considered a unique gesture as, in cases where decorations were lost in the maelstrom of war, it was never a tradition to award them again. According to Buck's statement, given in his characteristic accent, this made him very happy (*"Die habbe mer a riesige Freid gmacht"*). It needs to be noted too that this was the first occasion upon which veteran *SS-Kavallerie* soldiers had gathered together; the police had banned a similar event in 1956. The ceremony sparked national outrage because colonel Herbert Mitzscherlich, an officer of the *Bundeswehr*, appeared at the event in uniform. He also presented a speech after the SS veterans' addresses and placed a memorial wreath together with the members of the *Hilfsgemeinschaft auf Gegenseitigkeit der Angehörigen der ehemaligen Waffen-SS* (*HIAG*, Mutual Aid Association of Former Waffen-SS Members). The media queried in whose name and upon whose command Göhler and Lombard felt entitled to award decorations of the Third Reich to anybody – however, it was never mentioned that Buck had actually already received these decorations earlier. As there was interest in the public domain, altered photographs were published in which Buck, in SS uniform, can be seen with the *Ritterkreuz des Eisernen Kreuzes* on display – of course, without a word from the media that these images were nothing more than forgery.

Friedrich Buck, who did not pay much attention to such issues afterwards, lived his last years in a care home and died on 25 September 2015.

DECORATIONS	RANKS
• *Eisernes Kreuz II. Klasse* • *Eisernes Kreuz I. Klasse* 7 October 1944 • *Allgemeines Sturmabzeichen* • *Nahkampfspange Gold* 27 January 1945 • *Verwundetenabzeichen in Gold* • *Ritterkreuz des Eisernen Kreuzes* 27 January 1945 • Hungarian Gold Medal of Bravery	• *SS-Unterscharführer* 1944 • *SS-Oberscharführer* January 1945

1942–1944[114]

BUNGE, HELLMUT

Hellmut Bunge was born on 1 June 1920 in Wanzleben in Prussia. His original unit was the 66th Infantry Regiment (*mot.*, later *Panzergrenadier*) of the 13th Panzer Division. He started his military service with this unit on 5 November 1937. In the Polish campaign he served as an anti-tank gun pointer, then from 10 September 1939, gun commander in the 14th (heavy weapons) Company of the regiment. He took part in the French campaign as well and was deployed in operations on the Eastern front. On 30 August 1941, he was reassigned to the *Infanterie-Ersatz-Bataillon 66* (the replacement unit for the 66th Regiment) stationed in Burg bei Magdeburg. His superiors had already taken notice of him; in his promotion recommendation, he was described as follows:

> He is of medium height and has a powerful appearance. He is a good sportsman and can endure the greatest physical hardships. He is an open, reputable person. He has a mature personality with a healthy sense of consciousness. He is energetic and a good national socialist. In combat with the enemy, he never failed as a section leader and a company commander.[115]

Between 16 September 1941 and 14 February 1942, he attended an officer candidate's course, and until 31 March 1942, he served as a training officer at the *Ersatz* unit. Thereafter he was reassigned to the regiment and served on the Western Front as platoon commander. From 5 October 1942 he was battalion adjutant at the 66/II Battalion. From 1 February 1943 he served as *Zugführer* of *Pionierzug* of the 66/8th Company; from 13 July 1943, he became the com-

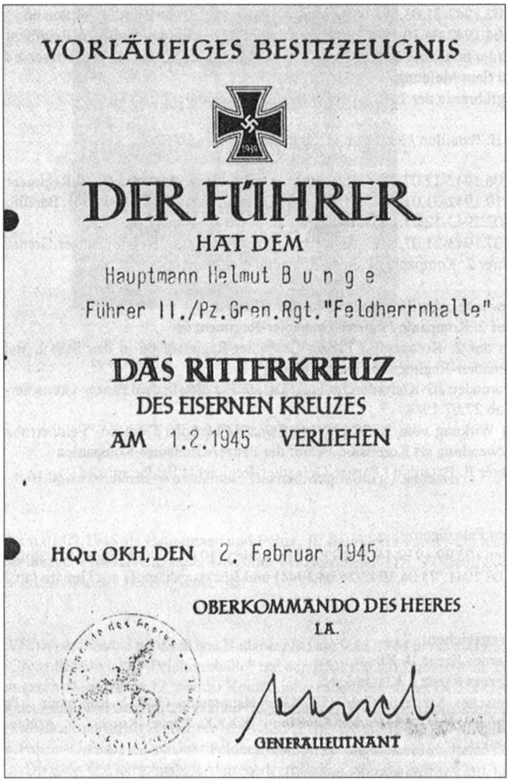

VORLÄUFIGES BESITZZEUGNIS

DER FÜHRER

HAT DEM

Hauptmann Helmut B u n g e

Führer II./Pz.Gren.Rgt."Feldherrnhalle"

DAS RITTERKREUZ

DES EISERNEN KREUZES

AM 1.2.1945 VERLIEHEN

HQu OKH, DEN 2. Februar 1945

OBERKOMMANDO DES HEERES

I.A.

GENERALLEUTNANT

Bunge's provisory document on awarding *Ritterkreuz des Eisernen Kreuzes*, which was handed over to one of his relatives

mander of the 2nd Company. His assessment from this time is very similar to that from earlier:

> …a calm man. He is a beloved comrade and has spotless political views. He has proven himself well in combat with the enemy. He is a good trainer and educator.

His only fault was that "he is not fresh enough".[116] However, it is probable that this was just an ill-willed remark from the person actually writing the assessment. On 25 August, he was lightly wounded in his left arm by an artillery shell; on 26 April 1944, he was severely wounded when his jaw was shot through. He was awarded the *Deutsches Kreuz in Gold* on 14 July 1944 – most probably honouring his combat actions in Bessarabia, where he had been wounded a few months previously. Most probably, these circumstances were connected to his promotion to *Hauptmann* at a very young age. After his recovery, he was transferred on 28 August 1944 to Panzergrenadier Division *Feldherrnhalle* as company commander.

Between November 1944 and February 1945, he was the commander of the 2nd Battalion of the Panzergrenadier Regiment *Feldherrnhalle.*

From his assignment, it is clear that his decoration must have been earned by showing personal bravery. From this period, only one account (connected to one of his section leaders) mentions him; in this, he is remembered as an understanding, cordial superior officer.[117] His unit was deployed in November for a short time on the Csepel Island at Lakihegy, then on the Valkó–Gödöllő line. From 6 December, it was in combat around Vác, then Dunakeszi–Fót, and then from 28 December around Rákospalota. From the first half of January 1945, his unit was located in the area of Újpest and District XIII. After relocating to the Buda side of the city, his unit was deployed initially in the southern areas of Buda. However, information on the battalion's activities from that point on is impossible to recover.

However, there is a radio telegram from 29 January 1945 that survived and in which →*Pfeffer-Wildenbruch* requested the decoration of Bunge. In the radio telegram, the following can be read:

> ...his battalion consisted of alarm troops and had no combat experience whatsoever; however, despite the initial critical situations, he managed to lead his unit to considerable victories solely based on personal example. Following the enemy achieving a considerable incursion and concentrating their forces, Bunge, upon a personal decision, attacked the enemy in the flank. With his personal deployment, he prevented the enemy from breaking through, which could have been extremely dangerous for the division.[118]

Bunge took part in the breakout attempt. He and his unit made it to the hills surrounding Buda via the Vérmező and the Kissvábhegy. On 14 February 1945, presumably in the area of Tök–Perbál, he was captured by the Soviets; he was released and returned home on 31 December 1949. Interestingly enough, when filing for prisoner of war benefits afterwards, he provided his place of service as such: "company commander, 66th Panzergrenadier Regiment, 13th Panzer Division". Most probably, he deemed his brief episode in Panzer Division *Feldherrnhalle* uncomfortable due to the unit's connections to SA. Afterwards, he worked in the postal service. He was not fond of remembering or talking about the war. When in 1990, a German historian sought to talk to him, Bunge only wrote that the *Wirtschaftswunder* ("economic miracle") that followed the war was much more important than the war itself and that he only hoped that the results of it would remain for the subsequent generations to enjoy.

> We want to forget the old days of war, all the more so because history is written by the victors. I ask you, therefore, not to make copies of my old pictures. I hope that you will have a more beautiful youth than I had. [119]

Hellmut Bunge died on 4 December 2006 in Herford.

DECORATIONS	RANKS
• *Eisernes Kreuz II. Klasse* 21 June 1940 • *Eisernes Kreuz I. Klasse* 14 February 1942 • *Panzerkampfabzeichen in Bronze* 14 February 1942 • *Nahkampfspange Bronze* 28 June 1943 • *Verwundetenabzeichen in Schwarz* 15 September 1943 • *Deutsches Kreuz in Gold* 14 July 1944 • *Ritterkreuz des Eisernen Kreuzes* 1 February 1945	• *Gefreiter* 11 October 1938 • *Unteroffizier* 19 October 1939 • *Feldwebel* 2 January 1942 • *Leutnant* 1 February 1942 • *Oberleutnant* 1 February 1943 • *Hauptmann* 20 May 1944

1941

CHARPENTIER, HANS-GEORG VON

Hans-Georg von Charpentier was born on 2 July 1902 in Strasbourg, which at that time belonged to Germany. In 1920, when the area was reattached to France, he relocated to the Saarland area of Germany. He had acquired agrarian qualifications and later worked as an independent horse-riding trainer.

With the newly awarded *Ritterkreuz des Eisernen Kreuzes* in December of 1942, in non-standard winter cap

For half a year in 1919, he served as a volunteer in a cavalry regiment and, from 1920 to 1930, held various leadership positions of lower rank leading positions in the right-wing paramilitary organisation *Wehrwolf.* In 1933 he joined the *NSDAP,* and in 1935 joined the SS. He also left the church. In December 1939, he applied for admission into the *SS-Verfügungstruppe* (*SS-VT*), the predecessor of the Waffen-SS. He served in the *Kavallerie* from the beginning. Until August 1941, he served as a *Zugführer* and from then on, until 15 December, as *Regimentsadjutant* at the 1st SS Cavalry Regiment before being appointed squadron commander. On 1 December 1943, he became commander of the 1st SS Cavalry Regiment. As *Regimentsadjutant,* he must have known about the mass murders committed by his unit because the organisation of the necessary logistical background was probably within his area of competence. From the end of October 1941, his unit was active on the frontline. On 17 March 1942, he was lightly wounded and also suffered a concussion at Toropino in Soviet territory.

He received the *Ritterkreuz des Eisernen Kreuzes* for his combat activities around Medvedevo in November-December 1942. His unit (3rd *Schwadron* of the 1st SS Cavalry Regiment) was nearly completely encircled, but Charpentier initiated counterattacks and, at his own discretion, also occupied a hill. During these combat actions, his *Schwadron* lost all but twenty of its personnel; at the same time, five hundred dead Soviet soldiers and five knocked-out Soviet tanks were counted lying in front of the *Schwadron* positions. From 1 December 1943 until his death, he was the commander of 18th SS Cavalry Regiment.

The assessment compiled by →*Joachim Rumohr* in June 1941 described him as follows:

> He is a determined and level-headed person. He is reserved and understanding. There are no known unique deficiencies, defects or manias. Mentally, he is active and bright. Physically, he has good abilities. He is an excellent rider. His service performance and knowledge are good. During his service, von Charpentier shows diligence and goodwill. He always strives

> to eliminate the deficiencies in his military expertise and knowledge and to educate himself further. His conduct towards his superiors is spotlessly perfect. He is respected by his comrades and by his subordinates as well.[120]

Rumohr supplemented the above with the following note on 10 November 1944: "The deficiencies of his military knowledge and performance are compensated by his well-considered practical measures and orders. Capable of commanding a regiment."[121]

There are almost no data available about his activities in Budapest. After Christmas of 1944, his command post was most probably in the southern part of Buda. During the breakout attempt, at an unknown location and unknown time (but in all probability still within the city bounds and before 13 February), he suffered lethal wounds. This is indicated by a document dated 20 February 1945, where he is listed among the registered dead.[122] Eyewitness accounts stored by the *WASt* also support the above facts.[123] On the other hand, the earlier commander of the division, *SS-Gruppenführer* Bruno Streckenbach,[124] wrote the following to one of his former comrades on 22 May 1960:

> Around July 1959, I spoke to Ernst Imhoff[125] in Wuppertal, who had also been a squadron commander. He told me that Charpentier was still alive and doing what he had done before the war: he had a riding school in Westphalia.[126]

DECORATIONS	RANKS
• *Eisernes Kreuz II. Klasse* 16 August 1941 • *Eisernes Kreuz I. Klasse* 21 January 1942 • *Allgemeines Sturmabzeichen* • *Verwundetenabzeichen in Schwarz* • *Ritterkreuz des Eisernen Kreuzes* 29 December 1942 • *Ehrenwinkel der alten Kämpfer* • *Julleuchter*	• *SS-Untersturmführer (der Reserve)* 29 October 1940 • *SS-Obersturmführer (der Reserve)* 15 July 1941 • *SS-Hauptsturmführer (der Reserve)* 16 March 1942 • *SS-Sturmbannführer (der Reserve)* 11 October 1944

1941–1942

DALLMANN, WERNER

Werner Dallmann was born on 7 April 1922 in Wangerin in Pomerania (today Węgorzyno, Poland). After attending elementary school, he was privately tutored for five years, then graduated from a merchant school. He joined the SS in 1940 and the *NSDAP* in 1941. In 1943, he left the Evangelical Church. From April 1940 to September 1942, he served in non-commissioned positions in the occupied territories of Poland. Based on his decorations – probably also during his short deployment to the frontline – he took part in frontline and partisan-hunting activities. After that, he was assigned to the SS Cavalry Division. He served on the frontline again; however, there are no known details of this service period of his, apart from the fact that he was wounded. In the second half of 1943, he attended the *SS-Junkerschule* in Braunschweig, afterwards working as a trainer there. On 1 June 1944, he was reassigned to the 22nd SS Cavalry Division, where he served as a platoon commander, then *Regimentsadjutant* at the 53rd Cavalry Regiment.

The combat actions during November 1944 caused considerable losses to his unit. Most probably, all three of his award recommendations were connected to the heavy combat he took part in. The first of these, for the *Deutsches Kreuz in Gold*, was handed in by →*Kurt Bartsch* on 11 December 1944; however, this was most probably deemed as underestimated and was changed to the *Ehrenblattspange des Deutschen Heeres*. The recommendation was signed by Himmler's liaison officer serving at the *OKH* on 28 December, and the decision was made on 5 February 1945.

According to the recommendation, he received the decoration for the following military actions:

On 3 November 1944, south of Pestszentimre, the Regiment established contact with the enemy; the connection with the neighbouring units was severed. The enemy infiltrated the gaps and threatened the Regiment with encirclement. Under the command of Dallmann, at the second attempt, an assault team was able to occupy Hill 129 on the left flank of the Regiment after heavy fighting, and they kept the hill in the face of constantly renewed attacks of the enemy until the connection with the Regiment was restored. With this, the gap was closed, the threat was lifted, and the Regiment was able to hold their acquired positions. On 4 November 1944, in the same location, Dallmann, with a reconnaissance patrol, restored connection with the right-wing neighbour, closed the created gap and brought the attack of the Regiment forward to the location 500 metres in front of the tank ditch southeast of Budapest. With this, he prevented an enemy attack that was in progress, which was completely eliminated by the subsequent assault of the Regiment. On 6 November 1944, in the area of Gyálpuszta, the attack of the Regiment was halted by enemy tanks and heavy counterattacks. It did not even seem possible that the occupied positions could be held. The assault group of Dallmann, which was sent to the location, could progress as far as the southern outskirts of Gyálpuszta, then flanked the enemy, and this forced the enemy attack to be aborted. With this action, Dallmann largely contributed to keeping the positions. On 8 November 1944, at Gyálliget, Dallmann was deployed with the Regiment's reserves to clear an incursion. They advanced until the southern edge of the village and caused the battalion-size enemy unit to flee in panic. On 9 November 1944 [without location], at the positions held by the 4th *Schwadron,* a deep incursion threatened to split the regiment in half. With the reserves of the regiment, Dallmann sealed the incursion, then initiated a counterattack and reoccupied the original frontline. On 19 November 1944 [without location], the enemy pushed an incursion on the left flank into the positions of the subordinated 9th [Hungarian] Police Company. The enemy had drawn continuous reinforcements to the incursion area and occupied Hill 119. There was a probability that the enemy would eliminate the whole position starting from the left side. Dallmann initiated a counteroffensive, drawing strength from the weak regimental reserves, pushed the enemy off Hill 119 and held the position against all subsequent enemy attacks. Thus, the reclaim of the earlier positions became possible, and the enemy threat was eliminated.[127]

It is not clear what Dallmann did to deserve the *Ritterkreuz des Eisernen Kreuzes*. Regarding this, in his personal file, only a telegram from the commander of the division, →*August Zehender* can be found, which states the following:

> I request the award of the *Ritterkreuz des Eisernen Kreuzes* to *SS-Untersturmführer* Dallmann in honour of his exceptional military conduct during the defence of Budapest. He is brave in all circumstances. He has repulsed with several counterattacks enemy attacks of superior numbers. He advanced beyond the requested point. He eliminated enemy assembly points. Today [30 December 1944], he was wounded.[128]

As the 53rd Cavalry Regiment was in combat around that time in the Pestszentimre–Pestszentlőrinc area, it is most probable that Dallmann performed the quoted actions around here. Dallmann continued to fight despite his injuries until he was wounded again. On his casualty files, it is stated, without citing the sources, that "he died from injuries, sustained in combat, in a hospital in the middle of January".[129] Gyula Steinert, who was a surgeon in the so-called Hospital in the Rock (*Sziklakórház*), remembered Dallmann's last hours as follows:

> Soon, a very young, barely twenty-year-old German officer is brought in by his comrades with abdominal wounds. We immediately took him to the operating room, and we operated on him. During the laparotomy [opening up his abdomen], it was revealed that the bullet pierced the bladder and the rectum and, after causing considerable internal damage, left the body near the sacrum. His bladder was sealed, and with a drainage tube, we closed the wound. However, the wound proved to be fatal due to the peritonitis that developed soon after. Two of his comrades were beside him all night, and I woke up several times to check on his state. He always ordered a charge and launched a counterattack in his feverish delirium. Poor Werner Dallmann – I still remember his name – became a victim of this horrible and aimless war. In the morning, we interred him on Bástya Boulevard [today: Tóth Árpád walk] in an unmarked grave.[130]

According to the patient admission log of the casualty clearing station of the Hospital in the Rock, Werner Dallmann was admitted on 15 January 1945 with bladder wounds and peritonitis. At 0100 hours on 19 January 1945, he was registered as dead. He was interred on 23 January 1945 in the grave dug opposite No. 7 Lovas Street. His remains were exhumed probably between 1945 and 1947. If this happened, then his unidentified remains are now resting in the

German Military Cemetery near Budaörs. At the same time, in the photographic database of missing personnel at the German Red Cross, Dallmann is registered as seen for the last time in Cegléd (in the internment camp there). Unfortunately, it is not known from whom this piece of information is derived, but it is certainly incorrect.

DECORATIONS	RANKS
• *Eisernes Kreuz II. Klasse* 28 September 1942 • *Eisernes Kreuz I. Klasse* 1 December 1942 • *Allgemeines Sturmabzeichen* 1 January 1943 • *Verwundetenabzeichen in Schwarz* 13 May 1943 • *Ritterkreuz des Eisernen Kreuzes* 17 January 1945 • *Ehrenblattspange des Deutschen Heeres* 17 January 1945 • *Deutsches Kreuz in Gold* 6 February 1945	• *SS-Unterscharführer* 20 April 1942 • *SS-Oberscharführer* 11 March 1943 • *SS-Untersturmführer* 1 March 1944

1944

DÖRNER, HELMUT

Helmut Dörner was born on 26 June 1909 in Mönchengladbach. He joined the police forces in 1927 and, from 26 November 1939, continued his service in the *SS-VT* in the rank of *SS-Hauptsturmführer*. He was assigned to the *Stab* of *Polizei-Panzer-Abwehr-Abteilung* of the *SS-Polizei-Division*. Until November 1944, he served in various positions in this division. In 1937, he left the Evangelical Church and joined the *NSDAP*. In 1940, he also joined the SS.

He took part in the French campaign and, from 1941, also in the campaign against the Soviet Union, during which he performed partisan-hunting duties. From September 1943, he served in Italy and, from the beginning of 1944, in Greece as the commander of *SS-Polizei-Regiment 8*. In Greece, the 4th SS Police Panzergrenadier Division and Dörner's regiment committed several atrocities against civilians. After the war, more than 200 persons stood trial for these deeds, but none of the cases ended with a conviction. Dörner's exact personal role in these mass murders is not known.

In August 1944, Dörner and his unit were only able to march northwards with considerable difficulties and thus escape from the encirclement, which was caused by Romania switching sides and the entry of Bulgaria into the war. From this date, his unit took part in combat activities around Temesvár–Szeged before being forced to retreat to the area between the Danube and Tisza rivers. According to the recommendation documents, the *Eichenlaub* awarded to Dörner at that time was for his activities in the battle of Debrecen, in which the 4th SS Panzergrenadier Division took an active part. According to the recommendation document, Dörner, in an armoured personnel carrier, broke through to an encircled battalion and organised its command and breakout from the encirclement so that the unit could take its equipment and wounded soldiers with it.

Helmut Dörner in the summer of 1944 in Greece. The photograph displays a camouflage coat fashioned from tent sheets.

Between 25 November and 6 December, he was reassigned to Budapest, but during this time, he retained his assignment as regiment commander – he signed award recommendations in this role. The reason for his reassignment is unclear: in theory, he would have had to attend a divisional commander course before this reassignment. In 1960 →*Pfeffer-Wildenbruch* wrote to Péter Gosztonyi that Dörner was initially assigned to Budapest to oversee the fortification works.[131] According to his personal files, on 2 December 1944, he was reassigned to the personal reserves of the *Reichsführer-SS*; however, in reality, he was assigned to the *IX. Waffen-Gebirgskorps,* where he could not receive staff positions due to his lack of qualifications. The data of his assignment are contradictory: according to some sources, he was sent to the *Haupt-SS-und-Polizeiführer* in Budapest, but according to other data, he was reassigned to the 22nd SS Cavalry Division. On 25 December 1944, a document states that Dörner commanded units of the 271st *Volks-Grenadier-Division* and some parts of the Kesseő group that had been forced back to Budapest. According to yet another document, Major General László Kesseő resented being subordinated to a person of lower rank and so left his unit. Because of this issue, the 6th Army initiated an investigation.[132] The next reference to Dörner can be dated to 9 January 1945, when he commanded a combat group on the Pest side, which most probably consisted of some of the smaller units of the 13th Panzer Division.[133] According to a German article published at the beginning of 1945 (taken up by various newspapers), he first commanded a regiment, then a division. Despite the propagandistic style of the writing,[134] it is worth citing the most important parts of the article which refers to Dörner:

> The man, who until now, oversaw only the smaller dimensions of regimental or divisional positions, soon knew the whole area of Great Budapest better than anyone else. He was rarely found at his desk in his office in the Castle. Instead, he travelled everywhere in his Skoda-Kübelwagen in the foregrounds of the outer city premises on the rain-sodden hills. The commander, who was hardened by many campaigns and battlefields, selected with steady hands the line widely embracing the sea of the houses from which the Soviet assault should be bounced back. Dörner has walked almost every metre of the defence line, which needs to be marked out there. Suppose we can set aside the internal political conflicts of Hungarian history during which the Castle was encircled several times; we can safely assume that since the Turkish wars in the 16th century, the city has not been besieged in earnest until now. Thus, Dörner could not find any defence lines upon which he could have built his own defences. He received the task from the acting commander of Budapest to create the deeply sectioned position system that was drawn in pencil on a map. Everybody who knows this 35-year-old Mönchengladbach warrior knows that he executed this task with full energy and commitment and with due swiftness and that he disregarded everything else that was unnecessary to be considered in that situation.[135]

The article contains a number of mistakes and inaccuracies. The most important of these is that the fortification plans for Budapest had already been prepared by the Hungarian high command in the summer of 1944 upon the basis of plans from the First World War, and during October 1944, the realisation of these plans had already started, even before Dörner's reassignment to Budapest. Also, it was impossible to conduct large-scale fortification works on the Pest side after December 1944 because the frontlines were already on the move by then. The author of the article probably only had the information that Pfeffer-Wildenbruch mentioned and then created a popularising article that had little in common with reality.

That is, the actual role of Dörner was certainly not in connection with the fortification works from the beginning of 1945 onwards. All evidence points to the fact that the command of the 13th Panzer Division was entrusted with the combat command of the entire Pest side of the city – this is all the more likely as the command of the 22nd SS Cavalry Division positioned here had very few qualified staff officers. Furthermore, the units of the Panzergrenadier Division *Feldherrnhalle* completely lacked command staff as they were stranded outside of the encirclement. This situation could have resulted in Dörner taking over the roles and duties of →*Schmidhuber*, who in turn was made superior to Dörner as the *Kampfkommandant* of the Pest side. This decision, according to the notes of the *Ordonnanz* officer of the 13th Panzer Division was probably not exempt from resentment on both sides, as Dörner behaved as Schmidhuber's superior. What is more, he forced Schmidhuber, who suffered from night blindness (nyctalopia), to return to the Pest side in the middle of the night in January 1945 when Schmidhuber relocated his combat post from Pest to Buda.[136] Dörner's own command post was in the Metropol Hotel on Rákóczi Street until 10 January 1945, when it was relocated to the City Hall of Budapest.

Today, it is not possible to conclude whether it is Dörner's or somebody else's handwriting that can be seen on the side of the report of the *IX. Waffen-Gebirgskorps* issued 10 January 1945. In one of the sentences of the report ("Despite the hardest of burdens and superhuman accomplishments, the morale of the units is high.") the word "high" was crossed over with blue, and somebody noted in hand: "Have you been out there?"[137]

From 18 January 1945, *Kampfgruppe Dörner* meant, in reality, the German reserves enclosed in the pocket from which units had to be handed over constantly to seal the gaps opening in the defence positions. For about a week, there was still hope that the largely combat-ready *Kampfgruppe* would be given permission to attempt an escape. On 26 January, Dörner, whose combat post around that time was at 23/a Budaörsi Street, could establish contact with the relieving forces that were able to advance as far as the Váli-víz stream during *Operation Konrad III*, but he was not granted permission to advance.[138] From this point, there is no evidence of Dörner taking part in the combat actions – it was not possible to execute any commands in that situation, as defence and resistance had disintegrated into separate combat actions of smaller groups. On 1 February 1945, he received the *Schwertern* (Swords) for the *Ritterkreuz des Eisernen Kreuzes* (Knight's Cross of the Iron Cross) besides the *Eichenlaub* (Oak Leaves). The reason for this decoration is unknown, and it can only be assumed that this was a form of "dismissal payment" for the commander who had already been forsaken. Dörner took part in the breakout attempt with the *Stab* of the *IX. Waffen-Gebirgskorps* in the Devil's Ditch. During this time, he was wounded somewhere around Bolyai Akadémia (Bolyai Academy). Staff Captain Ferenc X. Kovács met him after he was taken prisoner:

> I was taken to a villa on Béla király Street[139] [for interrogation]. There in the garden, I saw Dörner sitting under a tree, arm bandaged, and the cloth already soaking with blood (I knew him well because he had visited us at the division command several times); he looked very exhausted and worn

> and in a bad state of mind. Going past him, I was able to stop for a bit. We greeted each other, and he said: "Herr Hauptmann, sie (or diese) werden uns alle totschiessen." ["Captain, these will kill us all."] This still rings in my ear to this day. It might very well be that his assumptions were realised. I saw at the same place, on the road near the villa, I am not sure whether it was due to the rushing traffic or was deliberate, but there were rows of dead bodies in German uniform, crushed by Soviet tracked vehicles – ironed, if I may use this frivolous expression – and I had a strong sense of deliberation, as if they wanted to take revenge on them even in their death, and to humiliate and dehumanise them.[140]

This is the last data that can be uncovered about Dörner. The circumstances of his death are unknown; his remains are yet to be found.

DECORATIONS	RANKS
• *Eisernes Kreuz II. Klasse* 16 June 1940 • *Eisernes Kreuz I. Klasse* 19 June 1940 • *Infanterie-Sturmabzeichen in Silber* 2 October 1941 • *Deutsches Kreuz in Gold* 24 December 1941 • *Ritterkreuz des Eisernen Kreuzes* 15 May 1942 • *Nahkampfspange Silber* 24 September 1943 • *Eichenlaub* for the *Ritterkreuz des Eisernen Kreuzes* 16 November 1944 • *Schwertern* for the *Eichenlaub* 1 February 1945 • *SS-Ehrenring*	• *Unteroffizier (Polizei)* 6 October 1927 • *Feldwebel* (*Polizei*) 1932 • *Feldwebel der Reserve (Reichsheer)* 1934 • *Leutnant der Polizei* 20 April 1937 • *Oberleutnant der Polizei* 30 January 1938 • *Hauptmann der Polizei* 1 September 1939 • *SS-Hauptsturmführer* 1 January 1940 • *SS-Sturmbannführer* 1 April 1942 • *SS-Obersturmbannführer* 20 April 1943 • *SS-Standartenführer* 20 April 1944 • *SS-Oberführer* 15 January 1945

1944

DREXLER, WALTER

Walter Drexler was born on 25 September 1916 in Ulm. At 16, he joined the then-voluntary *Hitlerjugend,* and a year later, he joined the *NSDAP* and the SS. Because of his party activity, he was entitled to wear the *Alte Kämpfer* (Old Warrior) badge. In 1935, he left the Evangelical Church.

After graduating in 1934, he was assigned to the ranks of the *SS-Standarte "Deutschland"*, and between 1938 and 1939, he served for a year in the *SS-Totenkopfstandarte 2 Brandenburg* in Brandenburg (this unit contributed to the operation of the concentration camps). After this period, he was reassigned to the *Nachschubtruppen* (supply troops) of the *SS-Division "Reich" (mot.)*. He took part in the French campaign. By the summer of 1942, he was already the company commander of the 4th *(schwere) Kompanie* of the *Aufklärung-Abteilung* of the division. Between January and March 1943, he also took part in the Battle of Kharkov and the subsequent armoured battle at Kursk. On 1 November 1943, after being wounded twice, he was reassigned to the *Ersatz* (reserve) units.

This was when his quite embarrassing correspondence with the *Rasse- und Siedlungshauptamt der SS* (Race and Settlement Main Office, *RuSHA*, it belonged to Reich Security Main Office, *RSHA*) started. This organisation was authorised to settle marriage issues as well. This was because Heinrich Himmler was adamant that members of the SS married only with special permission, and the bureaucratic proceedings for such marriages had been assigned to this organisation. Drexler handed in his marriage request in 1940, which was accepted then. However, in the second half of 1943, somebody notified the *RuSHA* that Drexler's wife – who was working as a telephone operator at the *SS-Führungshauptamt* – "has a criminal record", though this fact was not stated in the marriage request documents. A lengthy correspondence commenced in which Drexler first expressed his surprise before requesting further details of the allegation. The officer of the *RuSHA* personally provided him details in Berlin: his wife had been convicted once for theft and twice for fraud in the first half of the 1930s – much earlier than she had actually met Drexler. Anyone who thought that this was the end of the story as far as the *RuSHA* was concerned would have been wrong. On 26 January 1944, the officer of the *RuSHA*, who held the rank of *SS-Hauptsturmführer* (that is, the same rank as Drexler's), sent a letter to him. Due to the very specific style of the letter, it is worth quoting a few lines from it:

> The sentences had been time-barred even before the marriage request was handed in in 1940. Therefore, it is only necessary to mention them cursorily. Your wife can call herself before all authorities, except the courts, as one without a criminal record. Therefore, you yourself have not handed in false data to the *RuSHA*. However, you must take it upon yourself to inform the *RuSHA* as soon as possible of what action you feel is necessary in light of your spouse's failure to disclose her convictions. The *RuSHA* is expecting your response no later than 15 March 1944.[141]

Although this case had no further details in Drexler's personal files, the officer could hardly have permitted to himself not to respond to this request. It is not clear what the *RuSHA* office might have expected in this case, having itself declared that it was the personal issue of a married couple. However, it is certain that such cases affected the promotions and careers of those involved. Himmler – and many of his direct subordinates – were maniacally pedant about watching the personal lives of their subordinates. The *RuSHA* even went as far as sending SS officers who were assessed in a negative manner into forced sick leave. For example, on 13 November 1939, Kurt von Gottberg was warned by the *RuSHA* that, "You have to report sick immediately due to severe heart problems and you will need to be sick [*sic!*]". Theodor Eicke, the commander of SS Panzer Division *Totenkopf*, had listed in his daily dispatches the names of SS officers who were punished for contracting venereal diseases and were sent to hospital.[142]

It is interesting that after the war, it was circulated that Drexler's wife was of Jewish origin. In the memoirs of Drexler's last company commander, preserved by Hans-Otto Wachter, he mentions that "the wife, who was regularly travelling with him in a trailer everywhere on the frontline from command post to command post, was a Jew, but few ever knew this. She was the one nursing my younger brother after he was wounded up until his death."[143]

However, there is no evidence of the Jewish origin of Drexler's wife in the marriage documents. It is hardly plausible that it would have been actually Drexler's wife who could have cheated the *Rasse- und Siedlungshauptamt der SS.*

Drexler spent the first half of 1944 at the *Das Reich* Division in France. However, he was reassigned to Hungary in the days after the Normandy landing of the Allies and was appointed commander of the *SS-Aufklärungs-Abteilung 8* of the 8th SS Cavalry Division. The unit was stationed then in Dunapentele (today: Dunaújváros).

On 12 December 1944, he was awarded the *Ritterkreuz des Eisernen Kreuzes* for the following military deed:

> [Between 4 and 7 November 1944] the *Aufklärungs-Abteilung* was assigned to clear the enemy incursion at Vecsés. In heavy and devastating urban combat (Drexler has lost 60 of his soldiers), he still managed to prevent the enemy from advancing further. However, he was not able to push the enemy back. The defence actions in the village during the night were unlikely to be successful due to our weak strength and the large superior numbers of the enemy. Drexler, on the other hand, realised the importance of defending this position, which affected the entirety of the defensive belt. Therefore, he continued attacking forward at his own discretion and reached the tank ditch. As he could not establish contact with his own troops to the left and right, he established hedgehog positions. Despite the lack of ammunition and the huge losses (110 soldiers, mainly enemy attacks from the rear), he held the position for three days before the enemy was completely annihilated with the help of a relieving manoeuvre. It was due to Drexler's command abilities that this considerable success could be achieved, which was incredibly important in the defence of Budapest.[144]

Drexler's unit was relocated to the Buda side around Christmas 1944 and took part in the assault attempt carried out by the armoured forces in Budapest towards Budaörs. After this, for a short period of time, his unit was positioned in the foregrounds of Kelenföld Railway Station and the vicinity of the Károly Király Barracks (today Maria Theresa Barracks), and then they had been in defence on the Buda side of the pocket, on the Margaret Island. It was Drexler's unit, too, that met the Soviet negotiators who appeared on the Buda side. Most of their vehicles were still in deployable condition at the end of January, and they also had the necessary fuel.[145] At the breakout attempt, they were tasked with covering the attack between Margaret Bridge and Mechwart Square in cooperation with the *Panzer-Aufklärungs-Abteilung "Feldherrnhalle"*. The remnants of the unit broke through next to the Bem Mozi (Bem Movie Theather) on 12 February 1945. They had been engaged in heavy combat at Vérhalom Square. From this point on, it is not possible to follow Drexler's fate: the sole fact that is officially known is that he was shot in the head in Kispest at 1100 hours on 13 February 1945.[146] Unfortunately, the sources do not provide any details on the cause or circumstances of this action; the most probable scenario is that a Soviet guard killed him after he was captured – however, even in this case, it is strange how he could have been appeared in Kispest as, due to the lack of bridges, the German captives were all driven towards the south, in the direction of Baja on the Buda side of the city. *SS-Hauptscharführer* Hans Bayer is the only person from Drexler's unit who made it relatively far: he was captured on 20 February 1945 in the Pilis Mountains after being turned in by a Hungarian civilian – however, he too had seen his commander for the last time in the city. Rudolf Köller, the former adjutant of Drexler, mentioned two further versions in a letter to Wolfgang Vopersal, the historian of the *HIAG* (Mutual Aid Association of Former Waffen-SS Members). The letter was written in 1984. Köller, in his letter, asked Vopersal what the source of the data was that stated that Drexler died in Stuttgart on 12 April 1962. At the same time, he mentioned that others had seen Drexler in an internment camp near Moscow. Based on our present knowledge, we are not able to resolve these discrepancies.

DECORATIONS	RANKS
• *Kriegverdienstkreuz II. Klasse mit Schwertern* 18 August 1941 • *Eisernes Kreuz II. Klasse* 24 February 1942 • *Eisernes Kreuz I. Klasse* 1 April 1942 • *Panzerkampfabzeichen in Bronze* 20 April 1942 • *Nahkampfspange Bronze* 25 January 1944 • *Ritterkreuz des Eisernen Kreuzes* 11 December 1944	• *SS-Untersturmführer* 11 September 1938 • *SS-Obersturmführer* 20 April 1940 • *SS-Hauptsturmführer* 20 April 1942 • *SS-Sturmbannführer* 21 October 1944

1940

EKESPARRE, ARTHUR CARL JOHANN VON

Arthur Carl Johann von Ekesparre was born on 8 January 1913 into a Baltic Swedish-German family on the Enneküss farmstead on Moon Island near Oesel (today Saaremaa) in Livonia, which at that time belonged to Russia (today this area belongs to Latvia and Estonia). On 1 April 1933, he joined, as a volunteer, the 8th Infantry Regiment (Prussian), which was then considered to be an elite unit. He was promoted to *Leutnant* on 20 April 1935. His subsequent promotions to *Hauptmann*, *Major* and *Oberstleutnant* had been approved all out of turn.

At the beginning of the Second World War, he was the commander of the *Maschinengewehr-Kompanie* of the regiment; in October 1940, he was assigned as regimental adjutant. His qualifications and assessments were all excellent and, most probably, this is why at the end of the year, he was reassigned to the 3rd Artillery Regiment (*motorisiert*) as a preliminary stage of the staff course (*Kriegsakademie*); for a month he also acted as the commander of the 29/II Battalion. This short period was enough for Ekesparre to receive the *Deutsches Kreuz in Gold*, awarded to him on 28 February 1942. Between February and August 1942, he attended the staff officers' course and was assigned temporarily to the *Wehrmachtführungsstab.*[147] From 15 January 1943 he was *Zweiter Generalstabsoffizier (1b)* of the 2nd Panzer Division, and in April he received a permanent position as a staff member. After that he served in staff positions in *Heeresgruppe B* stationed in France. He was reassigned as 1st *Generalstabsoffizier (Ia)* of the 13th Panzer Division on 30 October 1944.

He was awarded the *Ritterkreuz des Eisernen Kreuzes* on 15 January 1945. The recommendation documents did not survive, but it can be safely assumed that this decoration was connected to the combat actions of the 13th Panzer Division during November and December. At the beginning of October, the unit had successfully slowed down the offensive directed against the Hungarian capital, and between 7–14 December, it was also able to inflict considerable losses on the Soviet armoured forces in the area of Fót–Vác. Afterwards, they held the front-line section Fót–Rákospalota in the Budapest pocket. Before the encirclement was complete, the armoured units of the 13th Panzer Division, Panzer Division *Feldherrnhalle* and the Hummels of the latter were combined into *Panzergruppe "Feldherrnhalle"* and withdrawn from the frontline to the southern outskirts of Buda (among others, to Törökbálint) as there had been Soviet armoured units identified there. *Panzergruppe "Feldherrnhalle"* temporarily repulsed the enemy north of Budaörs.

In connection with the encirclement of Budapest and Ekesparre, the 4th adjutant of the 13th Panzer Division, *Oberleutnant* Ernst Schweitzer noted the following on the Christmas of 1944:

> Apart from my baptism by fire, I have never felt such a tremendous, terrible shock as this evening when the encirclement became an unchangeable, unmovable fact. I could also notice this in my comrades around me; hardly anybody ate anything. Instead, they escaped into chain smoking while turning over thoughts in their heads about how to escape the lingering doom over our heads. Luckily, the constant occupation required due to the reports and orders brought a sort of diversity and distraction. At 2300 hours, the *Ia* [*Oberstleutnant im Generalstab* Ekesparre] asks us to join him in his room for Christmas. We drink from his liqueur collection and take this man as an example of endurance and stature.[148]

In a physical and mental sense, Ekesparre could not spare himself from the extreme burden that prevailed during the siege. Around 10 January, a heated debate with →*Wilhelm Schöning* about whether the 66th Panzergrenadier Regiment should reoccupy the Lóversenytér turned into a shouting match. Schweitzer's memoirs remember these days as follows:

> ...the loss of his home in Pomerania did not escape him, and because of this, he completely turned inwards. He cannot sleep anymore; thus, he spends the nights reading and working and grabs every single opportunity to reach the positions of the unit commanders. I have shared these times with him and haven't missed a chance to gather information in the city. On the other hand, however, this made it possible for us to entrust the turning of our fate to the enemy action.[149]

Arthur Ekesparre took part in the breakout attempt with his adjutant, *Oberleutnant* Schweitzer. Around midnight, they left Margit Boulevard and advanced through the hills around Buda and towards the north-northwest. Their group soon grew to include several hundred people. They made camp in front of Solymár, and then, at dawn on 13 February, they took up quarters in the houses next to the Ürge Mill (Ürge-malom). At around 1100 hours, they woke to find Soviet units encircling them. According to the memoirs of Schweitzer, at that time, Ekesparre had already given up on his life: "he already told me that morning that he did not feel himself having enough strength to continue this exhausting march."[150] He stood up in the doorway of one of the houses, thus providing an excellent shooting target, and started to shoot at the Soviet soldiers.[151] We will never know precisely what happened at that house; we are only aware of the result of the events. Regarding the same moments, the following statement of Mátyás Boledovics was taken down for the record on 14 February, a day later:

> Yesterday, on 13 February 1945, at dawn, it was still dark outside when a Hungarian soldier demanded that we open the door, saying there were German and Hungarian soldiers there. A Hungarian colonel[152] announced that we were his captives and we were not permitted to go out or speak to anybody. We had to give up the buildings to them. Hungarian and German soldiers poured into the premises. They made boiled potatoes and we gave them all our stockpiled food. They were drying their clothes, and in the meantime, they were eating voraciously, especially the Hungarians, because the Germans still had some scraps of food left with them. Guards were standing outside, and they noticed around noon that there were Soviet troops advancing from Pilisvörösvár. The Hungarian colonel ordered not to shoot. However, a German general was nervous and fired at the five-member reconnaissance patrol; upon this, they went into cover, and then large numbers of Soviet soldiers attacked us. Heavy shooting began. The Hungarian colonel gave orders to show the white cloth they had found and ordered everyone out of the buildings. We took cover in the pantry. The colonel lastly told us that we were not at fault for anything and that we should tell everybody about this, and then he also went out. We stayed inside until the heavy shooting ended, and then Soviet soldiers came in. They also ordered us not to leave the house. Around evening time, other Soviets came, and they also interrogated us about every detail of the events and ourselves. They permitted us to be outside and to start cleaning up the house. Today, we established that sixteen Hungarian and German soldiers lay dead around our house. Approximately the same number of dead were to be found in the countryside near Pilisborosjenő, very close to us. There was one Soviet dead as well, who was taken away by

> his comrades. The Hungarian colonel was dead too, who was called, as far as I could make out, Vörösvári [Veresváry]. The wife or fiancé of one of the officers was also among the fallen. We have requested an immediate burial because we fear that with the coming of warmer weather, the dead bodies will quickly start to decompose and contaminate our water.[153]

Non-commissioned officer György Kárász, a military police officer of the *Budapest Őrzászlóalj* (Guard Battalion "Budapest"), described the events very similarly to the former description, especially noting the order from Veresváry about the surrender. However, he supplemented the latter with the fact that Veresváry, right after the surrender, "had suddenly drawn a pistol and shot one of the Soviet officers, upon which the Soviets murdered everyone. He also sustained several gunshot wounds, and it was pure luck that he survived this ordeal".[154]

The different interpretations of the event of death deserve attention. The massacre of the group was, in all probability, connected to the Hungarians and Germans putting up resistance to the arriving Soviets. As often happens in such circumstances, especially when the attacking party suffered losses, no mercy was offered to the captives. At the same time, it is also true that the number of dead soldiers found on the premises is much less than the number initially quartered in the buildings – this implies that some of them might have been able to escape (for example, Schweitzer) or some others were nevertheless taken prisoner. It is unclear who initiated the pointless fighting, and it may be considered a result of a series of coincidences.

DECORATIONS	RANKS
• *Eisernes Kreuz II. Klasse*	• Senior ensign 17 December 1934
• *Eisernes Kreuz I. Klasse* 4 July 1940	• *Leutnant* 20 April 1935
• *Verwundetenabzeichen in Schwarz* 30 August 1941	• *Oberleutnant* 31 May 1938
• *Nahkampfspange Bronze* 4 November 1941	• *Hauptmann* 18 March 1941
• *Deutsches Kreuz in Gold* 28 February 1942	• *Major* 1 January 1943
• *Ritterkreuz des Eisernen Kreuzes* 15 January 1945	• *Oberstleutnant* 1 October 1944

1942

ERDMANN, OTTO

Otto Erdmann was born on 10 October 1913 in East Prussia in Bromberg-Schwedenhöhe (now known as the Szwederovo district on the outskirts of Bydgoszcz in Poland). In 1932, he joined the *Reichsheer* as a volunteer, serving as a junior non-commissioned officer and a non-commissioned officer in the 25th Infantry Regiment and the 92nd Infantry Regiment. He took part in the Polish campaign, the French campaign and the Soviet campaign. On 15 April 1942, he was reassigned to the 120th Infantry Regiment (*mot.*) of Danzig. His assessment, compiled on 1 March 1944, describes him as follows:

> He has a mature, well-balanced personality. He is responsible and flexible. He is a professed national socialist who constantly cultivates himself. He has proven himself in battle against the enemy. He is a good trainer in the officer's course. Mentally, he is diligent and hard-working.[155]

In July 1944, he was reassigned to the 2nd Company of the newly formed 2110th Panzergrenadier Battalion *Feldherrnhalle*. In September, this unit was incorporated into the 66th Panzergrenadier Regiment of the 13th Panzer Division.

On 24 October 1944, Erdmann's unit, with the *Aufklärungs-Abteilung* and some armour of the division, launched an assault on the enemy positions south of Polgár, near Szihalom, attacked an entire artillery battalion equipped with 12.2 cm artillery pieces, and under the cover provided by the tanks, the Panzergrenadier*s* eliminated the Soviet defence. Erdmann personally distinguished himself during these combat actions, destroying altogether 21 artillery pieces (four were self-propelled) and 37 anti-tank guns. He put into use a captured artillery piece himself, and with this, he eliminated a still-resisting Soviet battery. As there was no possibility of transporting the captured equipment, Erdmann's soldiers were busy in the evening with destroying the weapons. Erdmann's superior officer, *Major* →*Georg-Wilhelm Schöning*, the commander of the 66th Panzergrenadier Regiment recommended him for the *Ritterkreuz des Eisernen Kreuzes,* which Erdmann duly received on 9 December 1944 in the presence of *Oberst* Dr Franz Bäke and *SA-Standartenführer* Bartel at the *Führerhauptquartier*. He was promoted to *Oberleutnant* due to the same combat action but had already received the promotion on 25 October.[156]

Erdmann remained within the encirclement.[157] His activities during the siege are unknown. Following the breakout attempt, he was registered as missing in action.

DECORATIONS	RANKS
• *Ritterkreuz des Eisernen Kreuzes* 9 December 1944	• *Fähnrich* 1 December 1942 • *Leutnant* 15 December 1942 • *Oberleutnant* 15 November 1944

1944

FEHRENSEN, WILHELM DR.

Wilhelm Fehrensen was born in Hannover on 12 December 1898. From January 1917, he served in the First World War as a common soldier, then as a non-commissioned officer. While serving in the Hannover 74th Infantry Regiment, he fought on the Russian Front and the Western Front. Thereafter, he graduated from medical university. On 15 September 1923, he joined the SA, where he served in high political ranks. From 1924, he was also a member of the *Stahlhelm* ("Steel helmet", organisation of frontline veterans). On 1 August 1936, he joined the SS and left the church. Within the SS, he immediately received the position of *Führer beim Sanitätsabteilung im SS Verfügungstruppen.* Between 1938 and 1939, he was assigned to the *SS-Totenkopfverbände*, which operated the concentration camps. Between March and April 1942, he worked as the leading medical officer in the Dachau concentration camp. In his position, it is obvious that he had knowledge about the fake medical experiments ongoing in Dachau. However, the nature and extent of his involvement is not clear. On 15 April 1942, he was assigned to the 6th *SS-Gebirgs-Division "Nord"* as *Kommandeur der Sanitätsdienst,* and from here, he was assigned to Budapest on 21 August 1944 as *Korpsarzt und Kommandeur der Feldlazarett* of the *IX. Waffen-Gebirgskorps*. On 17 September 1942, Heinrich Himmler sentenced him to disciplinary punishment. According to the warrant delivered to him:

> ...Between 1–2 June 1942 in the Zoppot [today: Sopot, Poland] Casino Hotel [you] as senior SS officer did not act against your comrades and did nothing to prevent the ensuing conflict. With this, you allowed the prestige of the SS to be degraded in the eyes of the general public. As an aggravating circumstance, you and your comrades had been heavily intoxicated.[158]

Unfortunately, the details of this case are not known; however, elsewhere in Fehrensen's personal files, it is noted that on that occasion, he was completely "drunk".

On 26 January 1945 he was awarded the *Deutsches Kreuz in Gold.* The recommendation issued five days earlier was sent by the *IX. Waffen-Gebirgskorps* via telegram:

> Fehrensen was personally active everywhere in the pocket despite the extremely difficult circumstances and the constant heavy artillery and mortar fire. It was due to him that the evacuation necessitated by the abandonment of the Pest side could be performed swiftly, which included the relocation of 4,000 wounded comrades.[159]

Initially, it was recommended that he receive *Deutsches Kreuz in Silber*. Still, during the process, this was changed, most probably because, in this way, the prestige of the award given to him could be even greater. *SS-Obersturmbannführer* Alfred Kment, SS liaison officer in the *Heerespersonalamt of the OKH*, notified the *IX. Waffen-Gebirgskorps* via *Heeresgruppe Süd* on the day of the award in a telegram.

In order to understand the duties and tasks assigned to Fehrensen, it is worth describing the German casualty attendance system in detail. In each section (consisting of approximately 30 soldiers), a *Sanitätssoldat* was present; furthermore, in each *Kompaniestab* (which again meant at least a section-strength), there was a person assigned with medical qualification as well as a *Sanitätssoldat*. Per each battalion, there was an *Assistenzartzt*, two *Hilfsärtzte* and a few *Sanitätssoldaten* comprising the crew of the field dressing station (*Truppenverbandsplatz, TVPL*). This was usually stationed next to the *Bataillonsstab* and served to take care of the wounded temporarily. From the field dressing stations, the wounded were taken to the main or division dressing station (*Hauptverbandsplatz, HVPL*). In theory, each division consisted of two ambulance companies (*Sanitäts-Kompanien*); each operated an *HVPL*, a dental surgery and a field pharmacy. This was supplemented by 30 to 35 red cross transport vehicles in each division. The officer responsible for medical assistance in each division was the *Divisionsartzt (Ivb)* in the *Divisionsstab*. The corps, including the *IX. Waffen-Gebirgskorps* did not have independent medical units but only organised and coordinated the medical units assigned to the different divisions. Occasionally, army medical units or other independent medical units were subordinated to it. In the case of Budapest, this was the *SS-Feld-Lazarett 500* in Szabolcs Street, but it was evacuated before the encirclement. At the same time, when the encirclement became permanent, this situation meant that the majority of the medical units and crew were stranded in Budapest and subordinated to Fehrensen together with the Hungarian medical units. By the end of the siege, a quarter (!) of the German defenders were qualified as wounded even though until 10 January, it was still possible to airlift some of the wounded soldiers out of the encirclement.

On the Buda side, following the encirclement, at least six to eight *HVPLs* were operating. The largest one was created in the cellars and basement of the Krisztina Boulevard wing of the Buda Castle (this is now used as the storage facility of the National Széchenyi Library). Apart from this, there were German wounded treated in the building of the Ministry of Finance on Szentháromság Square, in the National Archives on the Bécsi kapu Square; in the Old Hospital of St. John on Széna Square, in the so-called *Sziklakórház* and in the *Honvéd* Hospital No. 11 (today it is the University of Physical Education). Apart from the above-listed locations, there were at least one or two dozen smaller-scale medical stations towards the end of the siege because the *Honvéd* Hospital No.

11 was occupied by the Soviet troops at the beginning of February, and the Old Hospital of St. John at this point was in the frontline and therefore had to be evacuated.

There are practically no details available about Fehrensen's real activities. It is unlikely that he would have served as the caring angel of the hospitals in the besieged city, as none of the related memoirs[160] mention his name at all. He treated the issue of the wounded soldiers in an extremely inflexible manner. In the case of the Hospital in the Rock, for example, Fehrensen demanded that it had to be considered a combat area. On 24 January 1945, he suggested to the diplomat Friedrich Born, the Swiss national appointed by the International Committee of the Red Cross as its delegate in Budapest and who was responsible for the hospital, that he and his patients should leave and go over to the Soviet side. Fehrensen, at no point, showed a willingness to establish contact with the Soviets regarding this issue or being ready to help with the transport of the wounded.[161] It was also Fehrensen who ordered the *HVPL* of the 8th SS Cavalry Division to be relocated to the building of the National Archives. Lieutenant General Iván Hindy, commander of the Hungarian I Army Corps, could only order some personnel to save the most precious manuscripts. With the apparent lack of space, however, this was hardly possible. The German wounded soldiers were laid on medieval manuscripts, and thus, the precious archival sources were destroyed by blood and other bodily fluids or were irrecoverably damaged by other means.[162]

To make it possible to assess the role and responsibility of Fehrensen, it is worth considering the memoirs of Dr. Werner Hübner,[163] the field doctor of Panzer Division *Feldherrnhalle*. Hübner was himself wounded by a shell fragment to the abdomen when he arrived on the night of 9 February 1945 at the central military hospital in the Castle:

> It was a terrible sight; people were lying everywhere. There were no doctors or medical staff anywhere. All the patients in the large building were being treated only by Dr. Huml,[164] the doctor of the artillery regiment of the *FHH* [*Feldherrnhalle*] and one of our youngest assistant physicians. All of the medical officers started their own moral retreat following the example of their commanding general. When I asked *Unterartzt* Dr. Osten[165] who was on duty and where I could report, he told me he had not seen anybody on duty for days. As I was interested in the organisation of this place, I, at last, found the gentleman in command[166] during my observation walk, for whom my approach was extremely uncomfortable as he had not yet managed to clear his desk, which was full of champagne glasses and the remnants of the hearty meal he had taken. It would be better not to mention

the name of the leading medical officer as this cannot exactly be considered the most glorious part of the last days of combat medicine.

While we and the wounded in our care in the cellars could not eat well, here in the Castle, they were literally swimming in an abundance of provisions. The stores were full to the brim with heavenly delights about which we knew absolutely nothing. The poor wounded were only given soup brewed from horsemeat, while the gentlemen in the lower cellars did not lack a thing.

On the morning of 11 February 1945, rumours began to spread that the encircled troops were going to try to break out that evening. The full complement of medical personnel mingled with the wounded at once, which was extremely odd. The three of us who were working as doctors were ordered to present ourselves to the leading medical officer [Fehrensen] at 1800 hours. There, I met the surprisingly large medical staff residing in the Castle.

The leading medical officer sharply gave orders that at 1900 hours in the evening we were to gather with assault equipment at the Oroszlános Gate, from which the breakout attempt would be initiated. The doctors and 50 medical personnel chosen to remain with the wounded had already been appointed and made aware of their duties. All others were to follow his orders. The wounded would be handed over to the International Red Cross the next day.

In the meantime, the personnel of the dressing station were made aware of the plan by the *Stabsfeldwebel* of the central dressing station. When I arrived back at the bunker, there was an unbelievably deep silence there. The personnel of the dressing station were nowhere to be found. The appointed 50 medical personnel were also nowhere to be found. [...] In the large tunnel, where the signal vehicles of the corps were standing, it was apparent that there was a realisation that escape was impossible. A drunk doctor had grabbed command himself and tried to escape with the remaining personnel through a side tunnel, which ran from the Danube towards Budakeszi. The group started off with loud hollering – I did not see any of them again.

Now madness reigned in the Castle. The weeks of deprivation in the encirclement drove everyone almost crazy. The destitution, the misery and our grave concerns about the future led to actions for which individual persons could not be blamed [...] The wounded, in the meantime, realised that their caretakers had vanished and were pushed into an indescribable panic. In every corner of the underground hospital, gunshots were heard. No one wanted to be taken prisoner wounded.

> I managed to swiftly gather a few lightly wounded officers, a non-commissioned accounting officer and eight soldiers who could be deployed to the most important locations. The loudspeaker was still working, and thus, we were able to announce to the wounded that we were going to take care of them and from this moment on, we took all responsibility. Despite this, however, the suicides by gunshot continued.[167]

The medical personnel, however, did not only need to battle the surge of suicides. A three-member medical unit established a dressing station on the grounds of Buda Castle. Mrs József Szarka, who lived through the siege as a member of the personnel of the Castellanship (*Várkapitányság*), remembered the first moments after the looting began:

> [the Soviet soldier] at last forced me to look at the German soldiers he shot down. Next to the Mátyás-well lay, dead, the three doctors who had tirelessly worked to save the wounded; I recognised them instantly.[168]

Fehrensen took part in the breakout attempt at an unknown date and via an unknown route; he was last seen on 13 February 1945 in the woodland area near Buda, where he was leading a larger group of SS soldiers.[169] It is assumed that the remains of an *SS-Oberführer* that was uncovered in the 1990s near the Devil's Ditch (Ördögárok) can be identified as him.

DECORATIONS	RANKS
• *Eisernes Kreuz II. Klasse* 1914 • Bar to denote subsequent awards of the *Eisernes Kreuz II. Klasse* • *Verwundetenabzeichen in Schwarz* • *Eisernes Kreuz I. Klasse* 1939 • *Deutsches Kreuz in Gold* 26 January 1945 • *Julleuchter* • *Ehrendegen RFSS* • *SS-Ehrenring*	• *SS-Hauptsturmführer* 1 August 1936 • *SS-Sturmbannführer* 20 April 1938 • *SS-Obersturmbannführer* 1 October 1940 • *SS-Standartenführer* 1 September 1941 • *SS-Oberführer* 21 June 1944

1943

1943

GESCHKE, HANS-ULRICH

Hans-Ulrich Geschke was born on 16 May 1907 in Frankfurt an der Oder. He graduated from university with a degree in law and, in 1931, received an academic doctorate. In 1932, he joined the *NSDAP* and, a year later, the SA. He joined the *Sicherheitspolizei* even before the Nazi party came to power; his first workplace was in Dortmund. Between 1935 and 1938, he commanded the *Gestapo* office in Kiel. After a short service in Saarbrücken, he was sent to Prague, where he became the commander of the *Gestapo* unit there, which was considered extremely large with its strength of 800 members. His subordinated personnel described Geschke as ambitious and rigid; at the same time, he was described as someone who did not tolerate any "unnecessary" [sic!] excess – for example, in 1940, he prevented the burning of synagogues planned by the SA. At the same time, however, his name was closely connected to the most serious mass murder committed against the Czech people, which was ordered by Karl-Hermann Frank, *Höheren SS- und Polizeiführer* (Higher *SS* and Police Leader) of the Protectorate of Bohemia and Moravia. After the assassination of Reinhard Heydrich (leader of the *Protektorat Böhmen und Mähren* and the *Reichssicherheitshauptamt*) on 27 May 1942, Geschke coordinated the investigation and the hunt for the undercover agents, who had arrived at the end of the previous year from England by parachute. The investigation concluded with the discovery and annihilation of those responsible for the assassination. (They had been hiding in the crypt of a church in Prague, and after their hiding place had been uncovered by the *Gestapo*, they either fell in combat or committed suicide.) Geschke prepared the report on the Lidice massacre on 24 June 1942 – on that day, the adult population of the village named Ležáky were also exterminated, although neither village had any connections to the perpetrators of the assassination – the *Gestapo* simply assumed that the assassins had been aided in these villages. Altogether, 309 victims died in the retaliation surge. The mass murder itself was carried out by the German *Sicherheitspolizei* and the *Ordnungspolizei* with logistical help from the Czech police force (the Hungarian equivalent of the *Ordnungspolizei* was the gendarmerie and municipal police – *csendőrség* and *rendőrség* – without state security investigation unit). The person principally responsible for the retaliative actions was *SS- und Polizeiführer der Protektorat Böhmen und Mähren* Horst Böhme; Geschke took part in the organisation of the mass murders as Böhme's direct subordinate. The retaliation was carried out even though the majority of the Czech population was not hostile to the German invaders: tens of thousands of Czech people had come to pay their respects at Heydrich's funeral. The names of the villages of Lidice and Ležáky were deleted from land registers, and the extermination order was extended to include those who were friends or relatives of the inhabitants of Lidice. The retribution lasted for months and altogether claimed 3,188 lives (of these, 466 persons were executed because somebody in their circle of friends approved of the assassination of Heydrich).[170]

It is worth mentioning here that the Allies carried out only two successful assassination attempts against Nazi leaders: the *Generalkommissar for Weissruthenien*,[171] Wilhelm Kube, and Reinhard Heydrich. Both were important for the same reason – they helped secure the collaboration of the occupied territories. They were not "too savage" in the sense that such an approach might have proven counterproductive. From this viewpoint, these assassinations can be seen as intelligence "active measures" with the goal of increasing the terror inflicted by the Nazis on local populations, however hard it might have been for them in the short term because it was thought that this would shorten the war.

Operation Anthropoid, the codename for the assassination of Heydrich, was an idea instigated by Edvard Beneš, head of the emigrant Czech government in London, who was extremely troubled by the feeble way the Czech civilians resisted their fascist occupiers. He hoped that, as a consequence of the assassination, the mass murders by the Nazis would positively encourage Czech resistance and also increase the prestige of Czech emigrants.[172] His plan paid off. Largely as a consequence of the Lidice massacre on 5 August 1942, the British government changed its position and no longer considered itself bound to the Munich Agreement and, on 29 September 1942, Ján Masaryk, the minister of foreign affairs of the government-in-exile, issued a proclamation, previously approved by the Allies, that declared the Munich Agreement (and the First Vienna Award) null and void with retrospective effect. In this context, the Allies did not pay attention to the Slovak–Hungarian relationship at all and even generously ignored the fact that Slovakia happened to be an ally of Nazi Germany during the period in question (which indicated the complete weightlessness of Slovak political emigration). All this had fatal consequences from the Hungarian point of view: less than three years later, the annexed territories were returned to Czechoslovakia, and part of the Hungarian population was expelled from their homes.

Geschke was aware of the extermination of the Jewish population from the very beginning. This is proven by the fact that the first information and data about these actions were handed over to the Allies by an agent who was in contact with Geschke's driver. Geschke was also the prosecutor in the trial of Czech General Alois Eliás. From April 1939, Eliás was the prime minister and minister of internal affairs of the *Protektorat Böhmen und Mähren*, but he maintained contact with the government-in-exile in London. He was arrested on 27 September 1941 and accused of high treason, found guilty and sentenced to death. However, the sentence was carried out only after the death of Heydrich.[173]

In September 1942, Geschke became the Inspector of the Security Police and the Security Services in Posen, and on 17 December 1942, he was reassigned in the same position to Dresden. At his previous workplace, despite the shortage of time, he was introduced to the anti-Polish relocation programs organised with the help of the *RuSHA* and, in connection with this, the mass murders mainly aimed at Jews. Besides these actions, he might have run a separate concentration camp in Posen Fort VII, where executions were ongoing.

At the beginning of March 1944, Geschke and a few of his colleagues were reassigned to the Mauthausen concentration camp. Here, they had been told that they were to take part in the occupation of Hungary. Geschke officially became *Befehlshaber der Sicherheitspolizei und des SD* (*BdS,* Commander of the *Sicherheitspolizei* and *SD*) in Hungary on 17 April 1944. His direct superior was General of the Waffen-SS and the Police Forces Otto Winkelmann, who was the *Höheren SS- und Polizeiführer* in Hungary, and, in principle, even Adolf Eichmann was supposed to be his subordinate. However, Eichmann received orders directly from Berlin in Jewish-related issues and was not subordinated to Geschke in such cases. After the occupation, his first action was to arrest two hundred persons who, according to the Budapest telephone register book, held a doctorate and had at the same time "Jewish" sounding names. On 19 March 1944, he reported to Berlin that he had arrested 2,000 high-ranking Jews – it is highly probable that he had simply multiplied the number by ten.

Geschke's powers were just as clear as the relationship of the German occupation to the Hungarian statehood – that is, not at all. In principle, Geschke could only have acted against non-Hungarian citizens. However, it is true that this area initially required constant attention and effort on his part. The networks of Polish resistance in Hungary, the French and Italian communities turning away from the Vichy government and Mussolini, respectively, and suspected British–American or Soviet spies were uncovered by the *BdS* in almost every case with the help of the Hungarian political police. On the other hand, Geschke had also arrested many prominent persons of the Hungarian political scene. On 4 April 1944, he reported that he had already arrested 3,459 persons, the majority of whom were Hungarian citizens. Those who had been arrested were usually transported to either Germany or Auschwitz. Among these people were a number of members of parliament and the upper house as well. In certain cases, however, the Hungarian government managed to secure the release of certain individuals: for example, Geschke was forced to hand over Endre Bajcsy-Zsilinszky and Staff Colonel Gyula Kádár to the Hungarian authorities after a few weeks. However, in cases where those arrested had already been sent to the concentration camp at Auschwitz, there was no turning back; by then, such persons had witnessed the selection procedure, and thus, they became "bearers of secrets". For example, the Hungarian government tried to intervene in vain in the case of Grácia Kerényi[174] (the daughter of a famous professor of classical philology, Károly Kerényi), who was arrested on political grounds. Geschke, however, failed in a few cases relating to persons of importance: he did not manage to arrest the former prime minister István Bethlen, and prime minister Miklós Kállay also temporarily evaded him by escaping to the Turkish Embassy in Budapest. It is worth mentioning too that those arrested were robbed and, in many cases, cruelly tortured (Staff Colonel Gyula Kádár was robbed of his signet and wedding rings and was told: "down with these Jewish things").[175] We have no evidence of Geschke stepping up against the excesses committed by his subordinates.

Geschke lived in the villa at 9 Hermann Ottó Street, and his deputy and adjutant occupied the neighbouring villa at No. 7. Interestingly, the details of his activities during his time in Budapest are almost unknown. Soon after his arrival (before 26 March), Heinrich Himmler and Ernst Kaltenbrunner also visited Budapest. It was then definitively decided that the German occupation would basically consist of "consultation" since the majority of the reigning Hungarian political elite was more than willing to meet every demand of the German authorities. This was probably the reason that Geschke was not overloaded with other issues apart from the counterintelligence tasks mentioned above, and most probably, this is why we have so few sources describing his activities in Budapest. All of this is also supported by accounts given by other German officers. For them, including Eichmann, the time they spent in Hungary was, after the hasty work of the first few weeks, more like a carefree luxury vacation than work.[176]

The *Gestapo* already had a network of spies and collaborators in the city, whose numbers were close to a hundred – and many of them possessed high social status.[177] These included György Brunswik, the harbinger (logistics commander) of Miklós Horthy and many of the high-ranking officers of the gendarmerie forces together with Chief Rabbi Ferenc Hevesi.[178] Geschke, in principle, acted at a national level; for the issues related to Budapest, Alfred Trenker, then his successor, →*Reiner Gottstein,* were in command. His work was perfectly prepared by the Budapest network of the *Gestapo*: Geschke's unit arrived in Budapest with an already compiled list of arrests. His unit was, however, small: of the eight commands (*Kommando der Sicherheitspolizei, KdS*) under his rule, the largest was the one in Budapest, but nevertheless, it had only 33 personnel.[179]

However, the cooperation between the *Gestapo* and the Hungarian police forces was not always smooth. For example, Geschke filed a complaint against the leader of the *Magyar Állambiztonsági Rendészet* (Hungarian State Security Organization), Péter Hain (most probably because the latter had not coordinated his robbing sprees with the Germans). At last, Hain was deposed. The conflict between the Hungarian Ministry of Defence, trying to regain its sovereignty, and the *Gestapo* was a more serious case. On 5 June 1944, the chief of Department 21 of the Ministry of Defence, Staff Colonel Loránd Utassy, agreed with Geschke that in the future, the *Gestapo* could only arrest foreign nationals in Hungary via the Ministry of Defence. The Hungarian authorities used this as an opportunity to quietly release those arrested earlier. Consequently, after a time, in cases which aroused Geschke's suspicions, he did not keep to this agreement. However, he handed over Hanna Szenes[180] to the Hungarian authorities after she was captured as a British officer landing by parachute on Hungarian territory. From June 1944, Horthy demanded with increasing force the removal of the *Gestapo* from Hungary. These demands were unsuccessful, but the Hungarian State Security began to tap Geschke's phone lines, and the Hungarian gendarmerie was able to prevent the actions of the *BdS* in September 1944 when they wanted to clear the German prison in Gyorskocsi Street.[181]

The central office in Berlin became suspicious that in Hungary, there were no signs of any armed resistance or sabotage actions in preparation. "Kaltenbrunner called from Berlin and ordered us to check thoroughly because it was considered impossible not to have a resistance movement somewhere" – remembered Alfred Trenker. During the summer of 1944 Ernst Kaltenbrunner therefore ordered Geschke to uncover the underground movement by organising fake resistance. However, the Hungarian authorities assured them that such an action was completely unnecessary and the idea was dropped.[182]

In connection with Geschke's methods, it is worth mentioning that he even reported Trenker during the summer of 1944. According to the accusations, Trenker – despite repeated prohibition warnings by Geschke – was establishing contact with a social circle of persons, the leading figure of which was a millionaire called Németh:

> Trenker took part in numerous large-scale luxurious parties with this circle of people, the circumstances of which were incompatible with the gravity of the historical situation or his position as the leading officer of the security police.[183]

Unfortunately, the details of this case are not known; what we do know, however, is that from 21 July 1944, Trenker took part in the investigation of the assassination attempt against Hitler. The wording of the report is interesting not only because it is a testament to Geschke's narrow-mindedness but also because it speaks about the everyday lives of the members of the German security authorities in Budapest. Considering the fact that Geschke and his direct colleagues were living in lavishly furnished villas robbed from rich Jewish civilians, and there was a subordinate of Eichmann who specifically demanded Watteau paintings for his living quarters, it is particularly strange that they had accused Trenker of enjoying luxuries.

When the Romanians joined the Allies and declared war on Germany (23 August 1944), Geschke's situation changed completely. After the calm of the previous weeks, during which nothing worthy of notice happened, suddenly hurried actions were taken to prevent Hungary from attempting to conclude an armistice with the Allies. At the same time, Geschke ordered Eichmann, who found himself without a job, to relocate to the Oradea–Timișoara (Arad–Temesvár in Hungarian) area where he, as an experienced transport and logistics officer, had to organise the evacuation of the German population there. This action turned out to be a complete failure: the majority of German residents had no idea what awaited them and did not want to leave their homes where they had been living for centuries.[184] The abduction of Lieutenant General Szilárd Bakay and Miklós Horthy Jr. was, in part, Geschke's plan as well. Bakay, as the commander of the Hungarian I Corps of Budapest, was the most important person responsible for the military aspects of the armistice attempt and Geschke was aware of all these details due to his undercover informers. According to the report of Otto Winkelmann issued on 25 October 1944, on 6 October 1944, the first day of the Soviet offensive unfolding in the Trans-Tisza area, he himself gave orders to Geschke to initiate the action and demanded its execution within 24 hours.[185]

However, carrying out the abduction was not a smooth operation. In the evening of 8 October, Bakay and his adjutant, Captain Tibor Versényi, were abducted from the streets in front of the Hungária Szálló in a faked traffic jam. Still, the abduction of the young Horthy failed on the first attempt. At last, on the morning of 15 October, the young Horthy was also abducted from the Eskü (today Március 15.) Square with the help of two undercover agents who disguised themselves as leaders of the Tito-headed Yugoslavian resistance movement. Most probably, Geschke received the *Eisernes Kreuz II. Klasse* for this action. The reports fail to mention that the action did not go at all according to the plan and that its awkward execution played a major part in that.[186] Winkelmann's report also mentions that the abduction of the young Horthy was at first impeded by "stupid problems" and that the son of the Regent should have been able to realise that he was being ensnared on Eskü Square on 15 October – this was an indirect admission that there had been serious professional mistakes during the execution of the plan and that it only escaped discovery because the young Horthy was completely unsuspecting.[187] This is because the original plan was to arrest the young Horthy "in flagranti", right in the middle of a discussion with the resistance members. *SS-Sturmbannführer* Otto Skorzeny, however, did not wait long enough and was in combat with the Hungarian bodyguards before the arrest could be made. Furthermore, Geschke should have arrested Major General Károly Lázár, commander of the Guards, and Lieutenant General Kálmán Hardy, commander of the *Magyar Királyi Folyamerők* (Royal Hungarian River Patrol) as well, but he was unable to carry out these actions – Hardy was only arrested at midnight on 15 October by his own officers, and Károly Lázár only ceased fire in the morning of 16 October upon direct orders from the Regent.

Sometime before 24 December 1944, Geschke fled Budapest before the encirclement was complete. What is certain is that on 16 January 1945, as the head of the Security Police in Hungary, he was writing a letter of condolence from Balf to Éva Pataschits. Ferenc Pataschits was born in 1909 in the village of Dárda-Jenőfalva (today Darda-Podravlje, Croatia) and was forcibly drafted due to his assumed German origins, according to the German–Hungarian agreement, into the Waffen-SS. Most probably due to his age and limited physical capabilities, he was not assigned to a frontline unit but to the security police operating in Hungary (if he indeed had volunteered to join the SS, then it would be extremely strange that he only did this in 1944 when he could have joined much earlier). Pataschits, as a common soldier of an alarm unit of half a battalion strength within the SD (established in November 1944), died in combat on November 6. His remains were interred on 15 November at Kispest with military honours. On 23 November 1944, Geschke personally wrote a letter to the widow, Éva

Pataschits, but this letter was lost. The widow, who did not know anything about the events, wrote a letter on 18 December directly to Geschke to receive information. Geschke replied on 16 January.[188] At the same time Geschke reported to Berlin that he had been awarded the Order of the Holy Crown of Hungary. The last piece of information in connection with him is dated 4 April 1945: István Szappanos – the cousin of László Endre, former State Secretary for the Interior and commissioner for the evacuation of the Arrow Cross government – wrote in his diary that he met Geschke on 4 April 1945. (Interestingly, the diary does not comment on Geschke's person. However, given that "Colonel Geschke" was supposed to greet Endre's relatives, István Szappanos must have been aware of Geschke's identity).[189]

All these pieces of information are essential because, after 1945, several countries wanted to discover his whereabouts and hold him responsible for his actions. Geschke, however, was registered as an officially missing person as early as his stay in Budapest, and according to some publications, he died in the capital. The court in Frankfurt officially declared him dead in 1959. At the same time, however, as we have seen earlier, he was still alive in 1945, so rather than dying in Budapest, it is much more probable that he had switched identities and escaped to a country he deemed safe for himself.

DECORATIONS	RANKS
• *Eisernes Kreuz II. Klasse* 16 October 1944 • *Kriegverdienstkreuz II Klasse mit Schwertern* • *Kriegverdienstkreuz I Klasse mit Schwertern* • *Ehrenwinkel der alten Kämpfer* • *Ehrendegen RFSS* • Commander's Cross of the Order of the Holy Crown of Hungary with stars, war decorations and swords 20 December 1944	• *SS-Untersturmführer* 12 March 1935 • *SS-Obersturmführer* 13 September 1936 • *SS-Hauptsturmführer* 1937 • *SS-Sturmbannführer* 10 October 1938 • *SS-Obersturmbannführer* 9 November 1940 • *Oberst der Polizei* 26 March 1943 • *SS-Standartenführer* 9 October 1944

Around 1938

GOTTSTEIN, REINER

Reiner Gottstein was born on 10 August 1910 in Reichenberg in the Sudetenland (today Liberec, Czech Republic), which belonged to the Austro–Hungarian Monarchy at that time. His father worked there as a doctor. After the formation of Czechoslovakia, his family moved to Berlin. Gottstein graduated from university with a degree in law; he joined the SS in 1933 and was granted German citizenship in the same year. From 1934 onwards, he worked as a legal consultant for the *SS-Oberabschnitt Ost*; he joined the *NSDAP* in 1937. After graduation, in 1938, he applied to join the SD and, in the same year, also left the church. From the beginning, he was assigned to the Berlin centre of the *RSHA*. By 1941, he became the leader of the IID1st sub-department (radio, photography and film affairs) within the II department (organisation and administration). At the same time, he was active in other areas. He was, for example, a member of the working group led by Walter Rauff,[190] which was busy with the development of the "gas car" to be used for the mass extermination of the Jewish people.[191] In 1943, he was appointed as the deputy head of the *Gestapo* office in Düsseldorf. His first and last deployment outside Germany was in Hungary in March 1944. Initially, he led the SD office in Kassa (Košice) and then in Miskolc and, in this capacity, played an active role in coordinating the deportation of Jews. He worked with the Hungarian police to investigate the backgrounds of people deemed politically suspicious. It is not proven, although it is highly probable, that he took part in the elimination of the prison riot at Sátoraljaújhely that broke out on 22 March 1944, after which the pursuit of the escaped convicts continued until the first week of April (all captured escapees were executed). From 22 July 1944, he became the head of the *KdS* in Budapest after his predecessor, *SS-Obersturmbannführer* Alfred Trenker, was reassigned to Berlin.

We have only sporadic data on his activities until the takeover by the Arrow Cross – part of which is contained in→*Geschke*'s biography. Gottstein obviously played a significant role in the prevention of the armistice attempt as well. At the same time, there are no available sources regarding his actions around this time, as neither Otto Skorzeny nor others mentioned him directly. However, it is a fact that he received the *Eisernes Kreuz I. Klasse* and *II. Klasse* simultaneously for "capturing the son of the Regent and for occupying Buda Castle".[192]

After the Arrow Cross Party takeover, Gottstein had more opportunities and much greater freedom to act. From then on, he took part in investigations, in cooperation with the freshly created *Nemzeti Számonkérő Szervezet* (NSzSz, National Accountability Organization)[193] and with the state security group of Péter Hain, aimed mostly at deserted soldiers, hiding Jews and resistance members. There were large numbers of deserted German soldiers, many of whom were forcibly drafted Hungarian Germans and Alsatian French serving in the Waffen-SS. After the encirclement, Gottstein's most important task was probably the investigation of the Auxiliary Forces unit XIV/2. (*kisegítő karhatalmi század, KISKA*) in the Zugló area of Budapest and the action against the communist resistance group named Red Brigade. The action against the "Dallam" group is also worth mentioning – this was the only resistance group in Budapest led by an American officer, 1st Lieutenant Pál Kovács. The interrogations had been conducted partly by members of the *KdS* together with the Hungarian political police forces, and physical torture was often used to extract confessions. Survivors' accounts attest to being subjected even to torture with electrical current as well.[194] The Gottstein's command post was in Buda Castle after 16 January 1945, next to the *Számonkérő Különítmény* (Accountability Detachment), which also was forced to retreat there. Another office was situated at 30 Országház Street in the Castle District, in the contemporary Ministry of Internal Affairs building.[195]

It needs to be mentioned here that the purview of the *KdS* was, in theory, strictly separated from the task of the Hungarian gendarmerie and the "accountability forces". In the case of Hungarian nationals, the latter organisation had competence, while foreign nationals belonged to the scope of the *KdS*. Both organisations exchanged captives if it was decided that the person in question belonged to the authority of the other organisation. Cooperation became even closer during the siege due to the language barrier: the officers of the *KdS* did not speak Hungarian.

In theory, the investigation into the detonation on 22 November 1944 in the Metropol Hotel (58 Rákóczi Street) also belonged to the competence of Gottstein.

According to the academic literature, this action, which was executed by the "Szír Group", caused the death of 19 Waffen-SS officers.[196] However, all this is not supported in any way by the available sources. So far, not a single SS officer has been identified of those who would have lost their lives here because of the detonation, and it is also quite suspicious that no German documentary evidence of the event has been found. There were no dead Waffen-SS officers listed on the weekly officers' casualty report provided by *Heeresgruppe Süd*. All the evidence indicates that one of the surviving members of the partisan group, Gábor Csillik, who was "an employee of the Ministry of Internal Affairs" after 1945, greatly exaggerated the significance of his group's activities.

Gottstein was involved in discovering the hiding place of the Várnai group on the Ferenc-hegy (Ferenc Hill). Zseni Várnai and Zoltán Bokody wrote in connection with this at the beginning of 1945 the following:

> Our comrade János Kovács I. was captured by the *Gestapo* when he went into the cave for explosives. The said person, under torture, confessed and exposed our whole organisation. Our cave at the Ferenc-hegy was encircled by about 200 German and Arrow Cross bandits equipped with machine guns and flamethrowers who blocked the exits, and the approximately 16 persons who were inside were ordered to surrender. When this did not happen, the bandits put out of action everybody in the cave, inflicting death and injuries.[197]

Reality is much less romantic here, as well. There is evidence that only one person died during this action, and those arrested were given over by the Germans to the Hungarian authorities.[198]

In the days of the encirclement of Budapest, parts of the SD, including Eichmann and his group, and Gottstein's direct superior officer, →*Hans-Ulrich Geschke*, escaped. Consequently, Gottstein became the first and foremost authority regarding police- and politics-related matters in the capital. He was the one maintaining contact with the Hungarian police and the Arrow Cross Party organisations. In his confession dated 18 March 1951, Pál Szalai – who was a liaison officer of the Arrow Cross Party with the Hungarian police and later cooperated with Raoul Wallenberg in saving Jewish people – stated that on 31 December 1944 *General der Polizei* →*Konrad Hitschler* summoned Gyula Sédey, Chief Commissioner of Budapest Police, to appear before him in the presence of Gottstein:

> I myself do not speak German, but I could see that Gottstein was raving mad and shouting, and Hitschler was threatening Sédey and me. When we

> went away, I asked Sédey what they wanted, and he replied that they were not satisfied with the police and would hold us responsible if we continued to be lenient, especially regarding the Jewish question. Gottstein stated that Himmler demanded that not a single Jew should escape alive from the Budapest encirclement.[199]

Gottstein's most important and most horrific action would have been the extermination of the ghetto in District VII. All that is known about the details of this is that the Arrow Cross and SS men who gathered at the Royal Hotel on Grand Boulevard wanted to commit some kind of mass murder in the ghetto before it surrendered. In the heightened and panic-driven atmosphere reigning during the siege, some horrible rumours were circulating; one of these was the story about the undermining of the ghetto. It was obvious that there was no longer a realistic possibility of exterminating the whole population in the ghetto. However, there was still a chance to burn down some buildings and commit acts of mass murder locally. Given the terrible overcrowding in the ghetto, a few thousand people could have easily been killed. There was a demand for the murder itself both in the radical circles of the Arrow Cross and the SS. On the Arrow Cross Party side, clearing out all Jews from Budapest was a political program from the beginning, and among Gottstein's colleagues, there were many who, in previous periods of the war, had been active in killing and deporting Jews on the Eastern Front as part of either the death squads or various police units. What is more, there was also a large number of people who had experience in handling such matters: the I Battalion of the *SS-Polizei-Regiment 1* that was stuck in Budapest in the encirclement was comprised of personnel from Hamburg who had deported Jews from the Netherlands to Auschwitz before being deployed to organise similar actions in Poland and had recently escorted Hungarian Jew transports from Kassa (Košice) to Auschwitz. Pál Szalai mentioned earlier, and police officer Béla Kubissy,[200] commander of the police forces on the Pest side, later confessed at the people's tribunal, concordantly but independently of each other, that on the German side, the person responsible for the organisation of the pogrom against the ghetto was Reiner Gottstein and one of his subordinates, a certain *SS-Hauptsturmführer* Mumi (elsewhere: Mummi).[201] See further details of this case in the biography of →*Schmidhuber*.

Gottstein's excesses were noted even at the command of the Hungarian I Army Corps. At the beginning of February 1945, Lieutenant General Iván Hindy, in response to a question raised by the chief of staff of the Hungarian Defence Forces regarding Hungarian troops switching sides, stated that "sometimes the SS detains civilians and Hungarian soldiers without any reasonable suspicion and keeps them in horrendous circumstances, and these people owe their release solely to the intervention of the I Corps."[202] Unfortunately, we do not know exactly what cases Hindy was referring to here. However, it is a known fact that the Waffen-SS had committed a number of murders in the city. The most well-known such action involving non-Jews was the shooting of World Cup silver medallist kayaker Kamill Balatoni and four of his companions, carried out by an unidentified SS formation (most probably Gottstein's unit). Unfortunately, the details are unknown, and the only available source is a magazine article from 1945:

> 1945. While everyone in Pest was already happy with life, Buda was still burdened with death. Everybody was scared and silent in the cellar of the house under 16 Margit Boulevard. The cellar walls were trembling as if caught in an earthquake. There were sportsmen and sportswomen among the crowd hiding there, waiting to see what would happen. Kamill Balatoni, thirty-time Hungarian kayak champion, Miklós Kövér and Károly Nagymajtényi international kayakers, and János Wesszely, a talented kayak building master from Újpest.
>
> At once, everything seemed to stop, just like when a terrible storm abates. They were listening to the silence for a long time. Suddenly, footsteps were approaching on the other side of the door. Then the iron door opened. Soviet advance guards were standing in the doorway. Kamill Balatoni and his friends sprung up with unimaginable happiness. They were hugging the Soviet soldiers happily. Somebody from among the friends of Balatoni shouted: "If any German SS steps in here, we will kill him right here!" However, the Soviet advance guards were there only overnight, as they were given orders to retreat temporarily. Soon after that, SS soldiers came rushing into the cellar. Those hiding in the cellar watched in horror as one of the women hiding there greeted the Germans overly happily and spoke to them in a confident manner...
>
> For two or three days, sheer terror again descended into the cellar. One morning, Kamill Balatoni and three of his friends and an unknown young man from Kecskemét [...] were dragged away by the Germans.
>
> The shooting and the mortal agony of the five young Hungarian lives were not heard down there in the cellar...[203]

The article is especially interesting because this is the second source attesting to the fact that Soviet troops had temporarily held the building blocks north of Fekete Sas Street – in the related literature and contemporary official war diaries, it is stated consistently that the frontline in the last period of the siege was fixed at the line of the Margit Boulevard. According to the plaque in memory of the executed civilians, the arrest and execution took place on 7 February 1945, which means that the Soviets must have reached the building between 2 and 5 February 1945. From the fact that the arrest of Balatoni and his friends did not happen directly after the arrival of the German troops, we can conclude that this was again organised by either the special unit of Gottstein or another designated *SS-Polizei* unit. However, we cannot entirely exclude the possibility that the perpetrators were among those residing in the Arrow Cross party headquarters in nearby Kapás Street.[204]

Gottstein received the *Deutsches Kreuz in Gold* on 22 January 1945. It has not been possible to find the recommendation for this award. However, it is clear that it could only have been made in connection with his investigative tasks. In the same period, Ernst Kaltenbrunner, "in view of his untiring work in the deployments and the given combat mission in Budapest", recommended that he be promoted to *SS-Obersturmbannführer*.[205] This recommendation also shows that Gottstein had no formal military qualifications (the Czechoslovak army had not recruited him, probably because he was considered untrustworthy).

Gottstein's last decoration was the *Ritterkreuz des Eisernen Kreuzes*, awarded to him on 6 February 1945. This is more than unusual if we consider that this decoration was third in rank of Third Reich's decorations and was awarded for "military prowess and bravery" because, in this case, it was awarded to an intelligence agent who did not have any formal military education and had never taken part in any military deployment. Ernst Kaltenbrunner states in his recommendation:

> [Gottstein] made it possible to arrest and take out many saboteurs and deserters and eliminated the traitors among the Hungarian troops. *SS-Obersturmbannführer* Gottstein distinguished himself in defending the city with his personal presence and unflinchingly brave behaviour, and it was thanks to him that the Wehrmacht troops and Hungarian army forces deployed here were able to maintain their striking capabilities.[206]

Gottstein's unit carried out an increasing number of mass murders, even in the very last period of the siege. Of the members of the "Dallam" group, 15 people were executed on 15 January 1945 and on 5 and 6 February 1945, two, respectively; 26 persons were killed on 11 February 1945.[207] The exact number of the executed victims is unfortunately not known. The executions were carried out partly in the yard of the Ministry of Internal Affairs (30 Országház Street) and partly on the terrace of the winter garden of the Buda Castle. We also possess evidence that deserted Alsatian SS soldiers had been executed at that time by Gottstein's unit. The executions were partially legitimised with court martial sentences, and in order to be able to do this, a special court was set up during the siege, which was headed by a German and had two German and two Hungarian members.[208] After the siege, the castle guards counted 342 naked bodies in the Buda Castle at locations where the *Gestapo* and the *Nemzeti Számonkérő Szervezet* (National Accountability Organization) were active[209] – although it has to be mentioned that there is a possibility that at least some of these persons died of causes not connected to the above-mentioned organisations.

Gottstein was assigned to a 30-strong SD group attached to the *IX. Waffen-Gebirgskorps* in the breakout attempt. There are two accounts reporting his death. According to Kurt Wegener,[210] "on 13 February 1945, 20 km northwest of Budapest, he fell near Tök. Cause of death: submachine gun shots". The account of Helmut Liedtke[211] states, somewhat differently, and without mentioning the location, that "Gottstein was gravely wounded and was demanding that he should be shot dead. According to an account of a third person, an *SS-Hauptsturmführer* carried out his wish."[212]

DECORATIONS	RANKS
• *Eisernes Kreuz II. Klasse* 17 October 1944 • *Eisernes Kreuz I. Klasse* 17 October 1944 • *Deutsches Kreuz in Gold* 22 January 1945 • *Ritterkreuz des Eisernen Kreuzes* 6 February 1945	• *SS-Untersturmführer* 20 April 1938 • *SS-Hauptsturmführer* 30 January 1939 • *SS-Sturmbannführer/Polizeirat* (police officer) 1 October 1940 • *SS-Obersturmbannführer/Regierungsrat* 30 January 1945

1941–1944

HAMEL, HEINZ

Heinz Hamel was born on 27 November 1914 in Kröftel in Hessen. He first served in the 4th Company of the 528th Infantry Regiment. He was lightly wounded on 31 August 1941 and seriously wounded on 15 January 1942. After his recovery, he was reassigned to the Panzergrenadier Division *Feldherrnhalle*, where he served in the 5th Company. His officer's document file is unavailable, so his military career can only be partially reconstructed. He received the *Ritterkreuz des Eisernen Kreuzes* on 14 February 1945 as the assigned reserve *Oberleutnant* of the 5th Company of the Panzergrenadier Regiment *Feldherrnhalle*. The fact of the award itself is highly questionable because there is only one unfilled form to prove it.[213] He went missing during the breakout attempt. Certain witnesses heard that he was shot dead on Gellért Hill (Gellért-hegy). He was officially declared dead on 3 October 1961. There is no further data available regarding his promotions and other decorations.

DECORATIONS	RANKS
• *Eisernes Kreuz II. Klasse* • *Eisernes Kreuz I. Klasse* • *Ritterkreuz des Eisernen Kreuzes* 14 February 1945	• Dates of promotions are unknown.

HEUER, ALFRED

Alfred Heuer was born on 23 December 1920 in Altstadt in the Sudetenland (today, the town is called Staré Město pod Landštejnem, Czech Republic). His father was a laboratory worker. He joined the SS in 1939 and began his military service in the Waffen-SS on 24 October 1939 in the 3rd *Artillerie-Ersatz-Abteilung*. His first frontline service commenced in July 1941, when he was a radio section leader at the *II. Artillerie-Abteilung* of the SS Artillery Regiment *Das Reich*. He attended an officers' course between November 1941 and April 1942 (*SS-Junkerschule*). Later, he was reassigned to the artillery regiment of the SS Cavalry Division. He served as an officer assigned to the batteries, *Nachrichten-Zugführer* and *Abteilungsadjutant*. On 31 January 1944, he was awarded the *Deutsches Kreuz in Gold*. The recommendation mentions the reason for the award of the combat actions he had undertaken between 28 March 1943 and 17 October 1943. In the summer of 1944, he was reassigned to the 22nd SS Cavalry Division, where he served as adjutant at the *Stab* of the artillery regiment. His activities during the siege of Budapest are unknown, and it is also not known why he was recommended to receive the *Ritterkreuz des Eisernen Kreuzes*. It is even stranger that no contemporary documents could serve as proof for the recommendation and the award. However, two sources provide convincing evidence that the award was indeed granted to Heuer.

The first source is the confession of Walter Rosler,[214] made under oath, according to which, on 30 January 1945, he received his decoration together with Heuer at the command post of the 22nd SS Cavalry Division in the building of the Ministry of Commerce at 1-3 Lánchíd Street. Rosler received the *Eisernes Kreuz I. Klasse*, Heuer and →*Bartsch* both received the *Ritterkreuz des Eisernen Kreuzes* and → *Zehender* received the *Eichenlaub*. Unfortunately, Rosler did not mention the name of the officer officiating at the ceremony nor how the original decorations reached Budapest; he also did not mention whether an original *Eichenlaub* was awarded in the case of Zehender or a locally improvised copy, as happened with →*Wilhelm Schöning* (see details of this case in the Schöning biography).

The second source is the account of *Hauptmann* Franz Stockmann, the leading medical officer of the *I. Abteilung* of *Heeres-Artillerie-Brigade 959*. Stockmann encountered Heuer during the breakout attempt in the hills around Buda:

> The orders of the officers are unassured and hardly convincing enough. I am desperate. Ever since we moved out of the city, I have not eaten anything apart from half a loaf of bread and a few shards of chocolate. We can quench our thirst with snow.

A young SS officer who was part of the reconnaissance party voiced his opinion, which was the opposite of that of the *Oberleutnant.* He wanted to look for a shorter route to reach the German lines. I ask whether he could take me and Leutnant P[affrath] with him. He looks at us and, at last, agrees. His name is *Obersturmführer (Waffen-SS)* H[euer], *Ritterkreuz des Eisernen Kreuzes* holder and the adjutant of the artillery regiment of the 22nd *SS-Artillerie-Division.* He also takes with him a few SS non-commissioned officers he knew personally, so altogether, there are six of us soldiers in the group. [...]

In secret, I very much look up to H[euer]. He is bent over the map, his decoration, the *Ritterkreuz* is glimmering in the light of the petrol lamp, as he plans our further route. This is the first time I am standing face to face with him in a room, and I can talk with him undisturbed. Until now, we had been only out in the open, in combat next to each other against the snow and the enemy units, charging and escaping, constantly keeping all our senses and physical and mental strength on the edge.

So this is the brave young man who engaged the vastly superior enemy in infantry combat just two hours before and who boldly led us to this place. He does not want to wait for the larger units of our group; he rushes us to move on. [...]

A machine gun is howling in our trench, attacking from the left. The bullets lodge into the trench very close to me, almost right next to my head. We are shooting back. We can easily keep the infantry away, but then, to our horror, the tank returns and locates itself approximately 80 metres from our trench. Its barrel is pointed at us, and the first shot immediately comes towards us right away! It claws into the trench wall very close to my head while we crouch down in the muddy trench as much as we can. During the next few shots, we realise that from the movement of the barrel, we can deduce which trench section will be targeted next time, and we warn each other by shouting. Next to me, an SS officer is vomiting heavily from the stress while he tears off the insignia from his coat. I am bandaging a Hungarian comrade who is seriously wounded in the upper arm. Without achieving too much, after a while, the tank whizzes away towards the village.

It is silent now. We can renew our strength. Perhaps we could really hold out in this trench until darkness sets in. Only sporadic infantry fire. But then, all of a sudden, the tank's engine starts to roar behind us, and the monster is pushing itself up to the high ground approximately 20 metres away. First, we can only see the barrel, and then the whole vehicle slowly approaches our trench. Somebody shouts: "We're done now, it will pound us into the ground." Approximately eight metres from me, the tank rolls over the trench directly next to H[euer]. H[euer] throws a hand grenade bundle, which blows up without any effect under it. It would have been an easy job for the vehicle to drive on the edge of the ditch and, this way, chase us out from the trench right into the range of the infantry carbines or crush us in the trench. In the meantime, more tanks and assault guns appear from the village and position themselves right in front of us. With this, our situation becomes hopeless; any further resistance would mean suicide.

We notify each other by shouting, and we put our weapons on the edge of the trench. It is with a heavy heart that I part with my father's old World War I war pistol, which he gave me in 1943 with so much trust, on my last holiday. Then, with our hands raised, we climb out of the ditch and head for the Russians. Behind us, H[euer] is shouting: "A German officer never surrenders!" – and he blows himself up with hand grenades.[215]

DECORATIONS	RANKS
• *Eisernes Kreuz II. Klasse* 18 October 1941 (according to other sources, 26 November 1941) • *Eisernes Kreuz I. Klasse* 28 September 1942 • *Allgemeines Sturmabzeichen* 30 December 1942 • *Nahkampfspange Bronze* 1944 • *Deutsches Kreuz in Gold* 31 January 1944 • *Ritterkreuz des Eisernen Kreuzes* 30 January 1944 (?)	• *SS-Untersturmführer* 21 June 1942 • *SS-Obersturmführer* 30 January 1944

Around 1943

HITSCHLER, KONRAD

Konrad Hitschler was born on 21 December 1896 in Zweibrücken as the third child of the engineer Ludwig Hitschler. After graduating from high school, he was instantly enlisted, and after two months of training, he went to the Western Front with the Bavarian 22nd, then with the 23rd Infantry Regiments. His last First World War assignment was that of a company commander. After the end of the war, he was the adjutant of the commander of the non-commissioned officer school in Fürstenfeldbruck. He was also a member of the extreme right-wing Epp paramilitary unit.

In January 1920, he left the military and joined the Bavarian police. In May 1925, he was reassigned to the gendarmerie; until 1933, he served as one of the gendarmerie commanders in Pfalz. After the *NSDAP* rose to power, he joined the party in May (his membership number was 3,268,486). In April 1933, he was reassigned to the gendarmerie department of the Bavarian Ministry of Internal Affairs and became chief of the department in 1937. At the outbreak of the Second World War, he became the commander of *Feldgendarmerie-Abteilung (mot.) 682* and participated in the Polish campaign with this unit. On 20 April 1941, he was admitted into the SS; thereafter, he was assigned to the *SS-Personalhauptamt*. Between October 1941 and May 1943, he served as an inspector of gendarmerie and, at the same time, was the commander of the police training regiment in Oranienburg. From May 1943 to September 1944, he worked with the *Ordnungspolizei* in Simferopol, where he later became commander of this unit. Subsequently, until September 1944, he became the commander of the *"Schwarzes Meer"* unit of the *Ordnungspolizei*, which had its headquarters at the same location (later, it relocated to Romania). He was also one of the organisers of the SS unit, which consisted of Russian and Turkish volunteers. After that he was reassigned to Hungary, where he became the commander of the *Ordnungspolizei* in the staff of Otto Winkelmann. The location of his command post in Budapest is not known.

There is a deep obscurity veiling the activities of the *Ordnungspolizei* in Hungary. What is known with certainty is that the *Ordnungspolizei* established an office in each and every gendarmerie district (apart from Kolozsvár/Cluj). There were eight such offices, and they took an active part in the deportation of the Jewish population by guarding trains from the Hungarian borders until they arrived in Auschwitz (the gathering of Jewish people into ghettoes and loading them onto trains was organised and carried out by the Hungarian authorities). The offices most probably had a strength of no more than a hundred personnel. Apart from this, Hitschler in Budapest had an *SS-Wachbataillon* and a company of *Ordnungspolizei* at his disposal.[216] According to a report made in the summer of 1944, *Polizei-Nachrichten-Kompanie 304*, a specially assigned police regiment staff (with the III Battalion of *SS-Polizei-Regiment 21* and half of a *Polizei-Wachbataillon*) and a field police unit were stationed in Budapest. In addition, the 12/II *SS-Polizei-Bataillon* was stationed in Miskolc and the 20/II *SS-Polizei-Bataillon* was stationed in Barcs.[217] However, these units did not take part, or only in a very limited scope, in the anti-Jewish actions.[218] The summarised strength of the units subordinated to the *Höherer SS und Polizeiführer* (Higher SS and Police Leader, *HSSPF*) – including civilian workers, the SS military hospital, the water guards, and other units – was 2,097 in Budapest.[219]

According to a statement by Péter Gosztonyi – although this lacks proper sources – Hitschler commanded a police combat group during the siege. There is no evidence of this in any contemporary document. In contrast, it is thought-provoking that Hitschler was left out of the "shower of decorations", a fact which rather suggests that he did not command a combat force. The latter assumption is supported by the log of the Castellanship on 17 January 1945, which records Hitschler's visit and his measures concerning the Castellanship at a date and time when, according to Gosztonyi, Hitschler must have been preoccupied with saving the ghetto on the Pest side.[220] Hitschler, together with *Oberst der Polizei* Korff, set up his office at the Castle Command and, after its destruction, on 17 January, relocated to shelter No. 7–9.[221] At the beginning of February 1945, Hitschler became gravely ill with pneumonia (?), and as he was rendered practically immobile, he did not take part in the breakout attempt. According to the memories of a Hungarian nurse, she saw him in the early hours of 14 February:

> He was a short man. Tubes were going under the blanket attached to his body. I do not remember whether there were any fluids seeping through these tubes. He was lying there with his eyes closed, but he was alive.
>
> At once, Russians came in and were looking for weapons, if there was anyone who had not handed his weapons in yet. It seemed that they were content with everybody saying, "There are no weapons with anyone". They did not harm anybody, although a young Russian soldier, almost a child, started to shoot rounds into the ceiling next to the bed of the general. I was also standing very close and thinking he would shoot the general, but he did not do it. After the shooting, he went out of the room. I am unsure how much time elapsed after this incident, but suddenly, I noticed that the general had torn the tubes out of himself.[222]

A Russian biography of Marshal Timoshenko describes most probably the same event, although in a somewhat different manner:

> Two days after the end of combat activities, Timoshenko and Vorozheykin (?) went to the western side of Buda to inspect the Castle. It turned out that the many levels of the cellars were full of wounded German soldiers and officers.
>
> "The wounded must be taken care of immediately", ordered Semyon Konstantinovich. Then, they entered the room of the former military commander of the city (commandant). Well-fed, freshly-shaven fascists were on the beds. A few of them had generals' coats thrown over their blankets, and the double lightning insignia of the SS was clearly visible.
>
> When the marshals arrived, one of the generals tried to shoot himself in the head, but Vorozheykin's adjutant, Captain P. Pavlenko, snatched the gun from his hands. "So he must have done a lot to decide to do this", someone remarked. "We'll look into it. Everyone will be rewarded according to their merits", said Semyon Konstantinovich. "Let's go to the staff of the 2nd Ukrainian Front."[223]

Werner Jester, a wounded soldier in the *Feldherrnhalle* artillery regiment, met him just after the fire in the field hospital in the Castle: he, and a number of his fellow officers, survived the fire in a room of the castle bunker, which was closed by an iron door. These unfortunate people had to use their urine to cool the heated iron door.[224] According to one account, Hitschler, after that, gave his own *Kriegverdienstkreuz* to his saviour, Staff Doctor Werner Hübner (already mentioned in the →*Fehrensen* biography).[225] Hitschler died on 20 February 1945 in the Honvéd Hospital No. 11 in Budapest.[226]

DECORATIONS	RANKS
• *Eisernes Kreuz II. Klasse* 1914 • *Eisernes Kreuz I. Klasse* 1914 • Bar to denote subsequent awards of the *Eisernes Kreuz II. Klasse* 1939 • *Kriegverdienstkreuz II. Klasse mit Schwertern* • *Kriegverdienstkreuz I. Klasse mit Schwertern* • *Tapferkeits und Verdienstauszeichnung für Ostvölker (Ostvolkmedaille) Silber, II. Klasse* • *Julleuchter* • *SS-Ehrenring*	• *Leutnant* 11 October 1915 • *Oberleutnant der Polizei* 1 June 1923 • *Hauptmann der Polizei* 1 May 1925 • *Major der Polizei* 1 December 1935 • *Oberstleutnant der Polizei* 9 November 1937 • *Oberst der Polizei* 21 September 1941 • *Generalmajor der Polizei* 20 April 1944 • *Generalleutnant der Polizei* 30 January 1945

JANSA, ERNST

Ernst (Arnost) Jansa was born on 18 October 1899 in Prague in a Czech-German family; his father was a military officer. He graduated from a German high school and, in March 1917, joined the Austro–Hungarian *Feldartillerie-Regiment 19* for a one-year volunteer service. From October 1917, he was reassigned to the Alpine frontline in Italy, where he took part in the 12th Battle of Isonzo and then in the combat around Monte Grappa. During the latter, he received the *Grosse Silberne Tapferkeitsmedaille* (Silver Medal for Bravery, *Silberne Tapferkeitsmedaille I. Klasse*) – a high-status decoration considering his rank (cadet *Feldwebel*).

It is characteristic of his adventurous spirit that he reconnoitred enemy positions with aircraft a number of times as an artillery observer officer. In March 1918, he became the commander of an independent artillery battery escorting infantry. After the armistice, he attended university in Prague for a year.

From 1919 to 1938, he served in the Czechoslovakian army, his last rank being that of a captain – most probably, he was not promoted to higher ranks because of his ethnicity. On 28 October 1938, he was discharged, like other officers of the Czechoslovakian army of German and Hungarian ethnicity. After a period of probation spent in the *Reichsarbeitsdienst* (Reich Labour Service, a paramilitary organisation, *RAD*), he was taken over by the *Luftwaffe*; he Germanised his name to Ernst during this period. From the beginning, he was assigned to the anti-aircraft artillery. Until the end of 1939, he served at an airfield in Köthen and, after that, took part in organising and establishing several artillery units. His first major involvement in the war was commanding the 1st Battery of the 61st *Flak-Abteilung* from October 1942 on the French coast of the La Manche. He participated in the Balkans campaign with his unit, during which he received the *Eisernes Kreuz II. Klasse* and *I. Klasse* for destroying bunkers and tanks. In the operation against the Soviet Union, he was already the commander of this *Abteilung*, and his unit was active on the southern section of the frontline. A Wehrmacht report of 8 August 1941 mentioned him and his unit. After that, he took part in the combat operations as commander of the II *Abteilung* of *Flak-Regiment 24 (mot.)* until Stalingrad. Fortunately for him, he was wounded in the Caucasus during the combat actions at the Terek River and, therefore, was not trapped in the encirclement. After he recovered, his next assignment was to establish an anti-aircraft training school for ground combat (*Flak-Erdkampfschule der Luftwaffe*); however, during the autumn, he was deployed again at the front together with the training school personnel. On 25 October 1943, he took over the command of *Flak-Regiment 12* near Kirovograd and remained with this unit for the entire length of the war. After the armistice in Romania in August 1944, he was able to cover the retreat of the German units with his guns in the area of Râmnicu Sărat and Buzău. This action was essentially important as only those fragments of units saved this way were available to combat the 2nd Ukrainian Front and contain their advance for an entire month. His name was commended again in the Wehrmacht reports, and he was awarded the *Ritterkreuz des Eisernen Kreuzes*.

Only the *Stab* of his regiment was caught in the encirclement in Budapest and the 40/I, 42/I, 147., 241/II and 632nd (heavy) artillery *Abteilungen* were subordinated to it. The guns of these units were scattered at various locations in the city. It must be added that the entire Hungarian anti-aircraft artillery was also subordinated to Jansa and that these units had a considerably larger force than the Germans. Unfortunately, the text of the recommendation for the award of Jansa's *Eichenlaub* is not known. Still, he most probably received this decoration on 1 February 1945 in recognition of the enemy aircraft shot down during the encirclement. His decoration was the 726th of this award to be given.

On 12 January 1945, Jansa notified *Heeresgruppe Süd* that, in his opinion, the breakout attempt planned by the *IX. Waffen-Gebirgskorps* was unsound:

> The military success thereof is highly questionable [...], [furthermore] the change in the mood of the Hungarians sympathetic to us and the greatest loss of prestige is inevitable. The whole of the decent part of the Hungarian population, which has so far endured the sufferings with honour, would turn [on us] with contempt and hatred. At the same time, so far, it has done everything in our interests together with the Hungarian army. The lack of knowledge of the situation hinders the decision here. My suggestion: the deployment of larger parachute units in the Budaörs area and south of it in order to establish an airfield, as well as to clear the road leading to us. The consultation with the boss leads to similar results, but their passing on is questionable.[227]

Jansa seems to have thought at the time that Budapest was the best place to win the Second World War, as it did not even occur to him that the city would be militarily untenable in the long term.

He participated in the breakout attempt in the tunnel of the Devil's Ditch. In the Focșani prison camp, Ferenc X. Kovács witnessed that Jansa pretended to be a "Czechoslovak" national. On 15 December 1949, he returned home from internment but chose to live in West Germany. Jansa then found employment in business. From 1962, he also worked for an unknown period as a military adviser to the parliamentary fraction of the German Social Democratic Party (SPD).[228] He died in Puchheim on 25 September 1974.[229]

DECORATIONS	RANKS
• *Karl-Truppenkreuz* • *Tapferkeitsmedaille Bronze* • *Grosse Silberne Tapferkeitsmedaille* February 1918 • *Kriegverdienstkreuz II. Klasse mit Schwertern* • *Kriegverdienstkreuz I. Klasse mit Schwertern* • *Nahkampfspange Silber* • *Eisernes Kreuz II. Klasse* 9 April 1941 • *Eisernes Kreuz I. Klasse* 14 May 1941 • *Deutsches Kreuz in Gold* 25 February 1942	• *Fähnrich der Reserve* 1 March 1918 • *Leutnant* 1 October 1918 • *Hauptmann (Luftwaffe)* 1 May 1939 • *Major (Luftwaffe)* 14 May 1941 • *Oberstleutnant (Luftwaffe)* 1943 • *Oberst (Luftwaffe)* 1 January 1945

DECORATIONS	
• *Erdkampfabzeichen der Luftwaffe* 15 August 1942 • *Ritterkreuz des Eisernen Kreuzes* 31 October 1944 • *Eichenlaub* to the *Ritterkreuz des Eisernen Kreuzes* 1 February 1945 • Order of Military Merit IV grade with swords (Bulgaria) • Commander's Cross of the Order of Merit of the Kingdom of Hungary on war ribbon with swords 15 January 1945	

1944

KLETT, ALBERT

Albert Klett was born on 24 February 1916 in Romania, in Cobadin (Dobruja) in a landowner-farmer family. The family settled in the region at the end of the 19th century; they grew sugarbeet on 38 hectares. After elementary school, Klett attended the German high school in Nagyszeben (Hermannstadt, Sibiu in

Transylvania) while also taking an active role in the youth organisation of the German population. His last assignment was as a deputy *Gaujugendführer* (regional youth leader). In 1937, in Potsdam, he completed a training course for *Hitlerjugend* leaders and also completed a sports training course. From November 1938, he served with the cavalry in the Romanian army for two years and was discharged with the rank of lieutenant. In December 1940, Klett's family was repatriated to Germany as part of the *"Heim ins Reich"* program organised in the wake of the Hitler–Stalin pact. In 1942, his father, August Klett, became the head of a 400-hectare estate near Kutno named Dobrelin, in the territory known then as *Warthegau*. Albert joined the *SS-Kavallerie* almost immediately after his family had moved back home to Germany on 12 January 1941. For the Eastern campaign of 1941, he was assigned to the 5th Company of the 1st SS Cavalry Regiment. In May 1942, he was transferred to the *SS-Junkerschule* in Bad Tölz. Interestingly, he did not leave the church – this was a rarity among SS officers.

He received the *Ritterkreuz des Eisernen Kreuzes* in the autumn of 1944. At that time, he was the commander of the 6th Squadron of the 15th SS Cavalry Regiment. The exact date of the award is very difficult to determine. The actual action for which he received the decoration happened at the end of September, and the date of recommendation was 10 November 1944. The registry entry of the recommendation is dated 25 November at the relevant department of the *Heer,* but there is also a handwritten note that states 10 October 1944 as the date of decoration. In September 1944, Klett and his unit were in defence at one of the points of essential importance of the Maros defence line at Hill 463. Between 16–26 September, this section was subjected to seven company-strength, fifteen battalion-strength and four regiment-strength assaults. By 26 September, the strength of the companies in defence here dwindled to one-third of their original strength. Klett realised that, with an insufficient number of men, he had no chance of holding his position any longer and, therefore, decided to go ahead with a counterattack. Exploiting the situation, he attacked the flanks of the Soviet troops. With this move, he caused great confusion among the Soviet attackers, and when these began to flee in panic, they swept away the second Soviet attack wave behind them. With this swift action, Klett captured 13 machine guns, one flamethrower and a large amount of ammunition and counted 200 Soviet dead in front of the German positions.[230]

His unit took part in the defence of the Attila Line between Pestszentlőrinc and Üllő; in December 1944, he was in position near Pécel. From here, on the second day of Christmas, they were relocated to the Óbuda Brick Factory on the other side of the Danube, and on 27 December, they had their first active contact with Soviet troops. After that, they were in defence in the line of the

Goldberger Textile Factory in Óbuda for a more extended period. However, by February 1945, the remnants of the unit had been pushed back to the Southern Railway Station. On 9 February, they received orders to destroy their heavy equipment and fall back to the Castle.[231] Klett kept his unit together even then, and everybody received warm food a few hours before the breakout attempt – their first such meal in days, which for many would also be their last.

According to the account of Fritz Szigetter,[232] Klett was liked by everybody in his unit:

> Albert remained calm and [after the breakout] issued a few orders. He was the reference point on which we could rely. After breaching the last Soviet main line of defence, where Albert too was among the fallen, those who broke out were immediately picked up by those in the first German lines.[233]

According to Eduard Reimer, a squadron member, after the first wave, they left the Castle at eight in the evening and came under terrible artillery fire at Széna Square, which caused panic among them, and most of the unit dispersed. This was the last time Reimer saw his commander; he was taken prisoner the next morning. Konrad Augustin[234] saw him before he was wounded when, on February 14, 1945, in front of Szomor-Gyermely, Klett was fatally shot in the head. At the same time, in an article in an American revisionist magazine, it was stated without sources that he had been shot in the head in January 1946 in a Soviet internment camp.[235]

DECORATIONS	RANKS
• *Eisernes Kreuz II. Klasse* 25 October 1942 • *Eisernes Kreuz I. Klasse* 1 December 1942 • *Nahkampfspange Bronze* 14 October 1943 • *Ritterkreuz des Eisernen Kreuzes* 16 October 1944	• *SS-Untersturmführer* October 1942 • *SS-Obersturmführer* 30 January 1944 • *SS-Hauptsturmführer* 1944

1943

KORTH, SIEGFRIED

Siegfried Korth was born on 5 February 1922 in Grunewald. On 30 September 1940, he joined the Waffen-SS, where he was assigned to the 2nd Cavalry Regiment. From November 1941 to April 1942, he attended the *SS-Junkerschule* (officers' training school) in Braunschweig, after which he received a one-month platoon commander's training. In June 1942, he was assigned to the new SS Cavalry Division, then stationed in Dębica, where he was assigned as an adjutant to the 1st SS Cavalry Regiment commanded by Gustav Lombard. He served here as a platoon leader from the beginning of 1943 until May, when he took over the command of the 3rd Squadron. On 1 September 1943, he was wounded lightly; on 17 September, however, he was seriously wounded (he was shot in the chest by a small arms weapon). Afterwards, he received the *Deutsches Kreuz in Gold.* After his recovery, he returned to the 18/3rd Squadron; during the siege of Budapest, he was commanding this unit. An undated personal assessment, which is most probably from 1944, describes him as

Korth, Charpentier, Gustav Lombard, Johannes Göhler and Anton Vandieken in the autumn of 1943 on the frontline

follows: “he excels in his extraordinary richness of thought. His performance is of a very high standard. […] He is a natural leader, and he is suitable for a staff course.”[236]

The 18th SS Cavalry Regiment was deployed on the southern Buda frontline from the end of 1944. On 9 February 1945 Korth received the *Ritterkreuz des Eisernen Kreuzes.* The recommendation for it is not available, but the combat action for which he received it was most probably related to the fighting in Buda during January 1945.

He took part in the breakout attempt, and he reached the first German lines between 16 and 18 February 1945, that is, one or two days after the majority of the escaped soldiers arrived.[237] After the war, he did not maintain contact with his former comrades or speak about his memories of the war. Peter von Blankenburg, who was a former soldier himself and who made friends with Korth in 1947 at the agricultural college in Göttingen, briefly noted: “I have never asked my friend Korth why he was awarded the *Ritterkreuz des Eisernen Kreuzes*”. Korth himself never talked about this topic.[238] He later worked in agriculture and died on 27 September 1996 in Wertach.

DECORATIONS	RANKS
• *Eisernes Kreuz II. Klasse* 28 September 1942 • *Eisernes Kreuz I. Klasse* 1 December 1942 • *Allgemeines Sturmabzeichen* • *Deutsches Kreuz in Gold* 23 September 1943 • *Ritterkreuz des Eisernen Kreuzes* 9 February 1945	• *SS-Untersturmführer* 21 June 1942 • *SS-Obersturmführer* 30 January 1944

1939–1942

KRAUSS, OSWALD

Oswald Krauss was born on 21 October 1914 in Hamburg. He joined the SS on 1 August 1934 and the *NSDAP* on 1 March 1935. Between 1934 and 1937, he served in the *Leibstandarte "Adolf Hitler"* regiment and then became a trainer at the *SS-Junkerschule* in Braunschweig. Thereafter, he was reassigned to the police forces. After the annexation of the Czech Republic, he was assigned to the 205th *Polizei-Bataillon* in Kladno.

Obtaining a marriage licence was quite a painful process for him. The complexity of the procedure is well illustrated by the fact that Krauss handed in no less than 117 original documents to the authorities. However, this was still deemed insufficient. Krauss' father committed suicide when aged 50, and one of his brothers also committed suicide at only 26 years of age. The *RuSHA*, therefore, suspected that there must have been an inherited mental illness in the family. Finally, citing that the suicide happened not due to psychological reasons but because of the misery caused by the world economic crisis, they consented to the marriage, but only with the stipulation that the fact would not be entered in the SS genealogy book (*Sippenbuch der SS*).

Due to his personal files being incomplete, it is not known precisely when he was reassigned to the *SS-Kavallerie*. However, this must have happened before 1943. During the siege of Budapest, he was the commander of the 15th SS Cavalry Regiment. This unit was in combat from 25 December 1944 in District II and in Óbuda.

The recommendation of his *Ritterkreuz des Eisernen Kreuzes* has not survived, but a few telegrams that were kept in his personal files can shed light on additional related details. The most detailed of these was sent by *Divisionskommandeur* →*Rumohr* on the day of the award:

> On 2 January 1945, after days of hectic fighting for the control of Hill 300 [Mátyás-hegy], on its own initiative, he launched a flanking attack with his remaining thirty men, taking the high ground permanently. 90 Soviet soldiers lay dead, and many infantry weapons and five anti-tank guns [were seized].[239]

This attack was indirectly confirmed on the Soviet side as well, in the war diary of the 180th Rifle Division, where the combat activities around Hill 300 are mentioned a number of times. The 180th Rifle Division reported that it had lost 69 men killed and 212 wounded on the 2nd and 3rd of January.[240]

Oswald Krauss as a police officer, in ceremonial uniform

Krauss' subsequent movements in the encircled pocket can no longer be established. The only reference to his person can be found in one of Konrad Augustin's letters:

> Thus during the breakout I saw a regiment commander, *Sturmbannführer* Krauss, lying exhausted on the roadside, together with his adjutant. This happened on the night of the 13th to the 14th.[241]

Some sources give the place of death as Esztergom and the time as March 9, 1945.[242] However, there is no basis for this. It is not even likely that Krauss would have made it further north than the Buda Hills. In a document issued in the *Führerbunker*, dated 19 February, he is mentioned among the "officers confirmed to be dead," which was only possible if somebody from the main breakout group provided an eyewitness account.[243] As a consequence, his death must have happened before 15 February 1945.

DECORATIONS	RANKS
• *Eisernes Kreuz II. Klasse* 5 November 1943 • *Eisernes Kreuz I. Klasse* 20 September 1944 • *Ritterkreuz des Eisernen Kreuzes* 27 January 1945	• *SS-Untersturmführer* 12 March 1938 • *SS-Obersturmführer* 10 September 1939 • *SS-Hauptsturmführer* 3 January 1942 • *SS-Sturmbannführer* 11 October 1944

KRÄMER, PAUL

Paul Krämer was born in Leipzig on 26 September 1897 into an old family of craftsmen, his father being a stonemason. Krämer volunteered for military service in 1915. He fought on the Western Front as a member of the 107th and, from 1917, the 245th Reserve Infantry Regiment. Unfortunately, little is known about his decorations and ranks. He fought in the ranks during the First World War and suffered gas poisoning. He spent a total of 11 months at the front and was demobilised as a sergeant and squad leader. After the war, he served in the Leipzig Volunteer Security Regiment for a time. Like the Hungarian "detachments" of the time, this unit was formed to oppose left-wing organisations.

After his demobilisation, Krämer went into business. At first, he worked as a bank clerk, but by the outbreak of the Second World War, he was already a managing director of the company that ran the Leipzig Fair.

Krämer actively embraced National Socialism. He joined the SA in the 1920s, where he attained officer rank. What is known about his activities in the SA is that he was the adjutant of the commander of Leipzig *SA-Standarte*, *SA-Standartenführer* Carl Strobel.[244] He joined the *NSDAP* sometime between 1930 and 1932 – his membership number was 1,137,223. By 1937, he reached the rank of *Oberleutnant der Reserve*. On 20 January 1933, he was wounded. In his SA files only the following is stated: "open wounds on his head, inflicted during an attack by communists."[245] On 30 June 1937, he was involved in a pub brawl in Leipzig, although, according to the documents dealing with the issue, he was sober at the time. About the incident itself, we have only the witness account of the victim, a medical non-commissioned officer, Hermann Pätznik. According to this, in the late night hours, Pätznik sat down with two of his lady acquaintances and one of his comrades at a table where Krämer, who was unknown to him, and a sales clerk were already drinking. The sales clerk invited everyone to a beer, and the small company started talking. During the conversation, Krämer, dressed in civilian clothes, told Pätznik, wearing a uniform, "You were still in your swaddling clothes when I was already fighting in the Somme battles." Pätznik responded by swearing, to which Krämer punched him in the face. Pätznik did not retaliate because, as he testified, "Krämer, who was much smaller than him [164 centimetres tall], would have collapsed from a punch". The quarrel then continued outside the pub, and only a policeman from the local police station could separate the group.

No further details of the case are known. The police officer in charge of the case noted that Krämer had admitted the beating, that he intended to file a complaint for the verbal abuse he had suffered, and that he definitely would have said the same thing 20 years earlier to any newly appointed lieutenant who had been naughty towards him.[246]

He was promoted to reserve lieutenant on 1 July 1937, mobilised at the end of August 1939, and soon afterwards appointed a reserve captain. He participated in the French campaign with the 14th Infantry Division. He was subsequently transferred to the 52nd Rifle Regiment. During the development of the army that began in 1940, the regiment was subordinated to the newly formed 18th Panzer Division. Krämer took part in the Soviet campaign of 1941 with this unit, and with his troops, he reached as far as the Tula area. His assignments cannot be traced, but it is certain that by the beginning of 1942, he was already commander of the 52/II Battalion. On August 21, 1942, he was awarded the German Golden Cross.

On 12 February 1943, in the area of Smirniye (30 km east of Maloarkhangelsk), he was seriously wounded (his left arm was broken by a shot, and he received a shot in the chest). He was eventually discharged from the military hospital in Leipzig on 18 February 1944. As the 18th Panzer Division was being reorganised, he was reassigned to the *Ersatz* (reserve cadre) of 13th Panzer Division. He received his new frontline assignment on 25 October 1944 when he became commander of the 93rd Panzergrenadier Regiment, which was in combat between the Danube and the Tisza Rivers.

Before the encirclement of Budapest, the II Battalion of Krämer's regiment was withdrawn from the city. However, the heavy weaponry was partially left in Budapest. On 9 January 1945, the battalion, which was heavily decimated while deployed in the area of the Városliget (City Park), was subordinated to the 66th Panzergrenadier Regiment, and Krämer's duties from then on were limited to administrative tasks. His promotion to *Oberstleutnant* must have happened around this time. He was also recommended for the *Ritterkreuz des Eisernen Kreuzes*, but the details of this are unknown. He took part in the breakout and, while leading a group of wounded soldiers near Solymár, he met another escaping group. His comrades last saw him on the morning of 14 February in the southern part of the Pilis Mountains, not far from Pomáz. From then on, his fate is no longer traceable. By July 1958, Paul Griemsch reported to the *WASt* that Krämer "allegedly shot himself after he was wounded".[247] His bequest was destroyed by his family members in the 2000s.

DECORATIONS	RANKS
• *Friedrich August Medaille in Silber* • *Eisernes Kreuz II. Klasse* • *Eisernes Kreuz I. Klasse* • Bar to denote subsequent awards of the *Eisernes Kreuz II. Klasse* • Bar to denote subsequent awards of the *Eisernes Kreuz I. Klasse* • *Verwundetenabzeichen in Silber* • *Deutsches Kreuz in Gold* 21 August 1942 • *Ritterkreuz des Eisernen Kreuzes* 7 February 1945	• *Leutnant der Reserve* 1 July 1937 • Further dates of promotions are unknown.

1944

KÜNDIGER, HERBERT

Herbert Kündiger was born in Leipzig on 3 August 1910. His father was a shoemaker. Kündiger joined the *Reichswehr* in 1929. He had only achieved the rank of *Gefreiter* (lance corporal) by 1933, and, given this slow start, his later progression through the ranks is more than unusual. In 1935, he married Berta Eckhardt. Kündiger was admitted into the officers' ranks on 1 May 1940. He was wounded in 1941 and again on 13 October 1943 when he was shot in his shoulder blade. In June 1943, he was promoted to the post of commander of the newly established 261/III *Grenadier-Bataillon*. Soon thereafter, the unit was deployed between Smolensk and Nevel. During the heavy defensive combat, Kündiger showed extraordinary bravery, for which he received the *Deutsches Kreuz in Gold* as well as the *Verwundetenabzeichen in Schwarz*.

After his recovery, at the end of 1943, he was appointed commander of the 978/I Battalion of the 271st Infantry Division. The unit was in the process of being established in the Netherlands. From February to June 1944, the unit was stationed near Montpellier, close to the shores of the Mediterranean Sea, as reserves to *Heeresgruppe D*; afterwards, the unit was relocated to Normandy to prevent the Allied landing and invasion. In August 1944, the 271st Infantry Division, together with other different units, was trapped in the Falaise Pocket. Here, Kündiger again distinguished himself with his brave conduct. His combat group was encircled by American troops. However, he sealed off an incursion with the *Bataillonsstab* and then broke out with his unit to fight their way back to the rear positions, which he held despite receiving orders to retreat from there. He brought three artillery pieces into his positions, which were thus considerably reinforced and, with his actions, saved invaluable time for the retreat of the majority of the division.[248]

His assessment dated 19 November 1943 reads as follows:

> He has considerable unit experience, and his performance as an officer is excellent. He is big, strong, very diligent, and reliable, and he is ready to be deployed at all times. He is a good organiser and treats his subordinated soldiers correctly; with his superiors, he is open and respectful of authority. He has an extraordinary sense of duty, and he has distinguished himself a number of times in combat against the enemy.[249]

The majority of his division was crushed after August 1944, and the division was re-established in the area of Nyitra (Nitra, today Slovakia) in the autumn of the same year – this time, as 271st *Volks-Grenadier-Division* with the same unit number. Kündiger became, at that time, the commander of the 978th Grenadier Regiment. The *Heerespersonalamt* (Army Personnel Office) received his recommendation for the *Ritterkreuz* on 12 November 1944 to credit his conduct during the combat activities in France in August 1944. At last, the decoration was awarded to him on 9 December 1944. From November 1944, Kündiger was deployed again within the 271st *Volks-Grenadier-Division.* It was first assigned to guard the Danube, and then, from December onwards, they were in defence in the Margit line. After 24 December the 978th Grenadier Regiment and part of the artillery of the division were confined to Budapest after heavy fighting with the enemy in the area of Bicske and Budafok. Kündiger took over command of these artillery units. He had to use his best improvisational abilities during these days because contact with the divisional command had been severed, and the Soviet onslaught constantly created unforeseen situations that were extremely difficult to deal with. It was almost a miracle that an unbroken front line could be maintained on the southern outskirts of Buda.

After that, Kündiger's group was in combat on the Pest side of the city for a while. An order by *Kampfgruppe →Dörner* dated 9 January 1945 mentions that they were in defence to the right of the 66th Panzergrenadier Regiment and that the 318th *Landesschützen-Bataillon* was also subordinated to him.[250] Kündiger's combat post was on Kerepesi Street before 10 January 1945 and was relocated to the *Városháza* (City Hall) around 14 January. From 20 January, he relocated his command post to Buda, Holdvilág Street, and the *Sziklaközpont* (the Air Defense HQ in Budapest) on the Kis-Gellérthegy. Here, he has also distributed *Eisernes Kreuz* decorations to the subordinated Hungarian assault artillery personnel who had earned them during the combat actions at the end of December.[251]

The recommendation for the award of the *Eichenlaub* to Kündiger is unknown; there is only evidence that the decoration was awarded on 21 January

1945. It is, therefore, safe to assume that he received the decoration for his command actions during the heavy fighting at the end of December 1944. He was in position with his unit around the southern railroad embankment and withdrew from that location towards the Castle only on 8 February. What we do know about his movements around this time is that his command post was in the Gellért Hotel on 9 February.[252]

During the breakout, he was in command of a larger group. Heinrich Fothe[253] remembers his death the following way:

> On either 12 or 13 February, I and two of my comrades found Lieutenant Colonel Kündiger and his men. After we reached a clearing, Kündiger was severely wounded by gunshots fired by concealed Soviet guards. We took him to an isolated building, where, unfortunately, we had to leave him behind. He gave me the orders to command his battalion further. We must acknowledge the fact that he is dead. [...] After I returned home from my internment in 1953, I contacted Lieutenant Colonel Kündiger's family and related the fact that Kündiger collapsed in my arms with a gunshot wound. As there was no chance of getting medical attention here – which fact was acknowledged by Kündiger as well – he wanted me to give him back his pistol, which I had taken away. Thereafter, four soldiers took Kündiger to a house nearly 300 metres away. Before that, he gave me his maps and assigned me the task of leading his men towards Esztergom without any concerns for himself. As Kündiger had suffered extremely severe blood loss and his intestines were already spilling out where he had been hit, there can be no doubt that Lieutenant Colonel Kündiger was deceased.[254]

Interestingly, the news of Kündiger's suicide – although in a very limited way – had spread even before Fothe could return from his internment. A letter (dated 3 February 1950) written by Rudolf Haab, who served in Kündiger's unit, contained the following lines: "All we knew was that our commander, Lieutenant Colonel Kündiger, had killed himself because he could not reconcile this defeat with his political views."[255]

DECORATIONS	RANKS
• *Eisernes Kreuz II. Klasse* 26 June 1940 • *Eisernes Kreuz I. Klasse* 3 November 1941	• *Gefreiter* 1 July 1933 • *Unteroffizier* 1 April 1934 • *Feldwebel* 1 October 1936

DECORATIONS	RANKS
• *Infanterie-Sturmabzeichen* 20 August 1940 • *Deutsches Kreuz in Gold* 21 October 1943 • *Verwundetenabzeichen in Silber* 25 October 1943 • *Nahkampfspange Bronze* • *Ritterkreuz des Eisernen Kreuzes* 9 December 1944 • *Eichenlaub* to the *Ritterkreuz des Eisernen Kreuzes* 21 January 1945	• *Leutnant* 1 May 1940 • *Hauptmann* 1 October 1943 • *Major* 9 December 1944 • *Oberstleutnant* 21 January 1945

1942

1942

LIEBISCH, FRANZ

Franz Liebisch was born in the village of Georgswalde on 5 February 1921. He enlisted in the SS at a surprisingly young age, already on October 10 1938, and served in the *SS-Standarte "Deutschland"* until January 1942, after which he was transferred to the *SS-Kavallerie*.

In late 1942 and early 1943, he distinguished himself as a platoon commander of the 3rd Squadron of the 1st SS Cavalry Regiment in the fighting around

Medvedevo. After that, he was reassigned to the 4th Squadron of the regiment, where his superior was Johannes Göhler, who later became Hitler's adjutant. Liebisch was regarded as a modest, calm, reliable, extraordinarily diligent officer. On 3 August 1943, he was recommended for *Deutsches Kreuz in Gold*. However, it is uncertain whether he actually did receive the decoration. According to the recommendation, he breached a mine barrage near Mozhir, took a partisan camp in close combat and also acquired ammunition for heavy mortars.[256]

In 1943 he married Gertrud Klazek. His planned marriage provoked the resentment of the *RSSHA* because, as an SS officer, he had to ask permission for the intended church wedding. Liebisch first wrote a letter of apology, claiming that this was a mere formality and only necessary in view of his future wife's family. When he was told to submit his request to Himmler, detailing his reasons, he abandoned his plans for the church wedding.

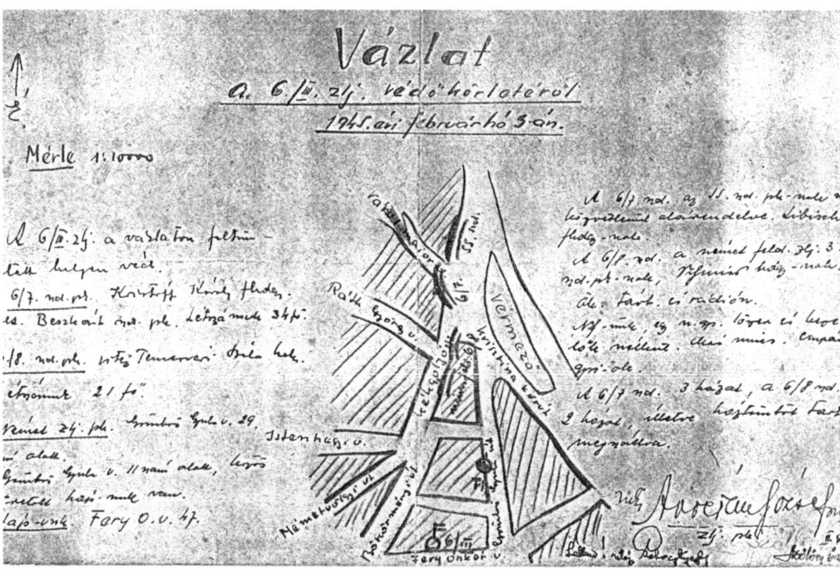

The sketch of Major József Adorján, drawn on 3 February 1945, on which he also mentions „Lieutenant" Liebisch in connection with the 6/7. Companies. During this period, the command post of the German superior battalion command was at 29 Gömbös Gyula Street (earlier and now Alkotás Street).

From the middle of 1944 until August 1944 he served in the personnel of the *Junkerschule* Tölz. During the siege of Budapest, he first served as the commander of 4th Squadron of the 16th SS Cavalry Regiment, however, from January 1945, he was in command of a theoretically battalion-strength unit.

The circumstances of his *Ritterkreuz* award are unknown. According to a surviving sketch, in the first days of February 1945, the Hungarian III Battalion of the 6th Regiment was also subordinated to him, and Liebisch was defending the Southern Railway Station and the northern part of the Vérmező. He also commanded one of the combat groups of the German 36th *Beobachtungs-Abteilung*.

During the breakout, he was wounded in the leg. His comrades took him with them for some time but had to leave him behind when they met a serious terrain obstacle. According to the account of →*Joachim Boosfeld* to the *WASt*:

> During a reconnaissance mission (approximately around 12 or 13 February), he was wounded in the leg due to a shell fragment hit. Thereafter, his comrades attempted to take him and other wounded comrades with them on makeshift stretchers. However, the groups were dispersed by the Soviet units hunting for them. The further fate of Liebisch is unknown.[257]

DECORATIONS	RANKS
• *Eisernes Kreuz II. Klasse* 2 August 1941 • *Eisernes Kreuz I. Klasse* 10 October 1942 • *Ritterkreuz des Eisernen Kreuzes* 9 February 1945	• *SS-Untersturmführer* November 1942 • *SS-Obersturmführer* January 1945

1942–1943

LINDENAU, DANIEL

Daniel Maximilian Otto Usdau Lindenau was born on 27 August 1914 in Danzig-Langfuhr (today, District Wrzeszcz of Gdańsk, Poland) into a military family; his father was a general. On 6 April 1934, he voluntarily joined the 1st (Königsberg) Infantry Regiment; in October, he was promoted to *Gefreiter*, and in December, he was promoted to *Unteroffizier*. From January 1935, he was assigned to the Dresden *Junkerschule*. On 20 April 1936, he was promoted to *Leutnant* and assigned to the 5th Company of the 1st Infantry Regiment. In January 1938, he was reassigned to 29th Infantry Regiment stationed in Crossen. However, in November, he served as the adjutant of the I Battalion of the 121st Border Infantry Regiment.

He received the *Eisernes Kreuz II. Klasse* during the Polish campaign and was promoted to commander of the 13th Company of the 121st Infantry Regiment in November 1939. During the campaign against the Soviet Union, he swiftly earned the *Eisernes Kreuz I. Klasse* as well. From August 1941, besides his duties as company commander, he also served as *Regimentsadjutant*. He was wounded performing these duties.

In the summer of 1942, he was reassigned to the 68th Infantry Division as the first adjutant. His staff training also commenced around this time. From November 1942, he served as the 2nd General Staff Officer in the supply group of the division HQ. From March to May 1943, he was reassigned to Berlin for staff training. Upon completion of staff training, he was admitted to the staff. From 10 August 1943, he served as the 2nd General Staff Officer of the 132nd Infantry Division. From 25 April 1944 he was reassigned to serve as the 1st General Staff Officer of the *Operationsabteilung* of the *bevollmächtigter General der Wehrmacht in Ungarn* (commissioned general of the Wehrmacht in Hungary who at that time was Hans von Greiffenberg). In this capacity, Lindenau was tasked with organising the unit establishments in Hungary, dealing with the current issues of the German occupying forces in Hungary and handling problems arising between the German and Hungarian organisations.

The date of his reassignment to the *IX. Waffen-Gebirgskorps* is not known. According to certain sources, this happened formally only on 30 December 1944. According to Lindenau's own account, however, he was already in the Chief of Staff position from 23 December 1944 when he arrived back in Budapest from Berlin via Vienna by an express train on which even a dinner was served.[258]

In the Waffen-SS, it was not uncommon to have staff officers reassigned from the Wehrmacht to higher-level formations because the Waffen-SS did not organise their staff training. At the beginning of 1945, we know of at least 23 such reassignments.[259] In Budapest, such mixing of officers and units was not uncommon even at lower levels of the units – this happened presumably because many officers who had previously lost their positions due to frontline events concentrated in the city. For example, several German rear commands (*Standortkommandantur, Korück 593, Kommandant des Rückwärtigen Heeresgebiets Süd*), the German military mission in Romania and a number of smaller units that had either lost their guns or their function previously were also in the city.

The reception of Lindenau among German and Hungarian officers was mixed, to say the least (in connection with this, see the →*Pfeffer-Wildenbruch* biography). It is not clear whether or not he was taken captive during the breakout attempt together with his superior. Péter Gosztonyi concludes that he left the Devil's Ditch (Ördögárok) in the area of today's Körszálló. However, Lindenau and his superior were interrogated together.

In connection with Lindenau, a telegram dated 1 February 1945, which he sent to the *Generalstabschef* of the 6th Army is worth mentioning. In this telegram, he "humbly reported" that he himself had been decorated with the *Ritterkreuz des Eisernen Kreuzes* and that Major →*Bodo Schaper* had received the *Deutsches Kreuz in Gold*. It is impossible to establish why he was convinced about these awards, but the telegram clearly states that he thought they had been awarded – unfortunately, the entire telegram correspondence of the *IX. Waffen-Gebirgskorps* and the 6th Army was lost; therefore, the contents of the telegrams exchanged directly before Lindenau's are also unavailable. It is highly probable that the *IX. Waffen-Gebirgskorps* communicated not only with the 6th Army but with *Heeresgruppe Süd* as well (in theory, their radio equipment would have enabled this). Therefore, if the former had been the only communication channel, it would have been unnecessary to report the award to the person previously awarded it. *Heeresgruppe Süd* initiated an investigation into the matter on 16 March 1945, and the request was forwarded to the *Oberkommando des Heeres* (*OKH*), which responded on 26 March by saying that "in the case of Major Lindenau, there has been no recommendation to award the *Ritterkreuz*. *Major* Bodo Schaper did receive the *Deutsches Kreuz in Gold* on 21 January 1945."[260]

Nevertheless, Lindenau, at the time of his captivity, stated that he had been awarded the *Ritterkreuz*. In 1959 (ten years after he returned from internment), he applied to join the Association of Knight's Cross Recipients, and his request was granted. He reasoned that *Generalmajor* Heinrich Gaedcke, *Generalstabschef* of the *Heeresgruppe Süd* had made the recommendation for the decoration. However, there is no trace of this recommendation apart from a 1959 transcript of a letter dated 15 March 1945 in which Gaedcke notified Lindenau's father that his son had been registered as a missing person and, at the same time, confirmed that Lindenau had been promoted to *Oberstleutnant* on 10 February 1945 and awarded the *Ritterkreuz*. Lindenau, in a letter to the Association of Knight's Cross Recipients, explained that he had been wearing the *Ritterkreuz* when captured and that the Soviets had taken it away from him. However, he failed to name any eyewitnesses to support this, although several officers from the *Korpsstab* of the *IX. Waffen-Gebirgskorps* were still alive at that time. Lindenau was so confident in his case that, even before the final decision of the Association, he purchased a miniature copy of the *Ritterkreuz*[261] (made without the swastika) for 2 marks and 50 pfennigs, which he wore on social events. He died on 29 August 1984 in Buxtehude.

DECORATIONS	RANKS
• *Eisernes Kreuz II. Klasse* 5 October 1939 • *Eisernes Kreuz I. Klasse* 13 July 1941 • Order of the Merit of the Kingdom of Hungary, Officer's Cross with war decorations and swords (based on his own account) • Romanian Order of the Crown, class IV with swords (based on his own account)	• *Leutnant* 20 April 1936 • *Oberleutnant* 1 January 1939 • *Hauptmann* 1 February 1942 • *Major* 20 January 1944 • *Oberstleutnant* 10 February 1945 (out of turn)

1943–1944

1943–1944

MAINKA, ERHARD

Erhard Mainka was born on 20 March 1913 in Reichenbach in Silesia (now Dzierżoniów, Poland). It is not known when he began his military career, but in all probability, he was first drafted in 1935. Until 1935, there was no general compulsory military service in Germany; therefore, those who belonged to the so-called "white years" (those who were 18 years of age between 1920–1935) did not do military service. In theory, from 1935 to 1939, weapons training was organised for these persons, but this lasted only a few months. In the case of Mainka, the first data available regarding his military service is that he was promoted to *Leutnant* on 1 January 1938 while a member of 8th Cavalry Regiment. On 10 October 1939, he was sent for cavalry training (*Kavallerie-Schule*). He took part in the Polish campaign with 28th *Aufklärungs-Abteilung* (reconnaissance battalion). On 10 January 1941, he was assigned as *Zugführer* in the 21st *Reiter-Regiment* of the 1st Cavalry Division. On 16 February 1942, he was reassigned to the 227th *Radfahr-Abteilung* (bicycle battalion) as a company commander. He was seriously wounded on the Eastern Front on 5 April 1942. From there, he was reassigned to the *Schwadron-Chef* position of the 336th *Radfahr-Schwadron* on 1 July 1942. His abilities and performance must have been recognised here, as soon after that, the *Oberkommando des Heeres (OKH)* reassigned him to the *Kriegsakademie*. On 1 June 1943, he was reassigned to the *Stab* of the 7th Panzer Division as an adjutant and then served in the same position in the *VII. Armeekorps*. On 1 August 1944, he was officially admitted to the *Stab*. From 1 September 1944, he served as the *Erster Generalstabsoffizier (Ia)* of the 22nd SS Cavalry Division.[262]

Almost nothing is known about his activities during the siege of Budapest, which can be related to the fact that the officers and personnel of the 22nd SS Cavalry Division had the most problems during the siege among the German units. Because of this, from the beginning of 1945, the units of the division were mostly deployed together with other units, and the Chief of Staff of the division had significantly fewer operational duties.

He sent his last message to his comrades outside the encirclement on the afternoon of 11 February 1945 by a still operational radio. The circumstances of his death are unknown.[263] According to the war log of the Soviet 109th Heavy Artillery Brigade, they found the body of an unidentified German *Generalmajor* in the area of the 12th Battery. This was most probably the body of Mainka: German staff officers wore two red stripes lengthwise on their trousers the same way as generals did; only the colour of their shoulder straps differed.[264]

DECORATIONS	RANKS
• *Eisernes Kreuz II. Klasse* • *Eisernes Kreuz I. Klasse* • *Anerkennungsurkunde des Oberbefehlshabers des Heeres für hervorragende Leistungen auf dem Schlachtfeld* 19 November 1942 • *Deutsches Kreuz in Gold* 30 January 1945 (?)	• *Leutnant* 1 January 1938 • Further dates of promotions are unknown.

1945

MARINGGELE, HERMANN

Hermann Maringgele was born on 29 November 1911 in the village of Tschars, in Südtirol, as the tenth child of an Alpine farmer family. After vocational training in tourism, he could only find work in the hotel industry with interruptions because he was called up for conscript service in the Italian army from 1932 to 1933 and was also sent to the Abyssinian theatre of operations between 1935 and 1937. Most probably, he became fed up with the Italian army and, therefore, in 1940, joined the Wehrmacht. As volunteers around that time were mostly directed to the Waffen-SS, Maringgele was also assigned to this organisation and first served in the 1st SS Cavalry Regiment. In the summer of 1941, he took part in the campaign against the Soviet Union and was seriously wounded on 22 September 1942. His role in the mass murders perpetrated by his unit is unclear. After that, he was reassigned to Warsaw to the *SS-Kavallerie-Ausbildung-und-Ersatz-Abteilung*. In 1943, he was reassigned to the 2nd *Schwadron* of the 15th SS Cavalry Regiment as platoon leader, a position he held until the end of the siege of Budapest. His rank at that time was *SS-Hauptscharführer*.

Before the siege of Budapest, Maringgele had already accumulated 35 close combat days. According to the recommendation for his decoration, after the encirclement of the Hungarian capital, he performed no less than 47 successful missions. During these missions, he eliminated a Soviet command post and a radio operator group, and destroyed a supply unit. With regard to his activities on the Buda side of the city, it is known that initially his command post was in the Pál-völgy Caves and the Restaurant Erdei Lak ("Forest Hut") at the foot of Remete-hegy (the building itself no longer exists, in its place today stands the *Erdei Lak Villapark* at 149 Szépvölgyi Street).

A few sections of the Hungarian University Assault Battalion were also subordinated to Hermann Maringgele.[265] On 28 January 1945, he was decorated with the *Deutsches Kreuz in Gold* via telegram.

During the breakout attempt, he reached the German lines with 60 persons via an unknown route. According to his award recommendation, he was the first to arrive amongst the units that attempted the breakout. He was ordered to Berlin together with →*Joachim Boosfeld*, where Hitler, by a spontaneous decision, awarded him the *Ritterkreuz des Eisernen Kreuzes* and the *Nahkampfspange in Gold* on 21 February 1945. The latter was awarded to him after 84 confirmed close combat days – by far the largest number of close combat days among the German soldiers. Moreover, he was promoted to *SS-Untersturmführer* for his brave conduct.[266] The text of the recommendation reads:

> During thirty-seven successful assault missions, some of which were conducted deep behind the enemy lines, he inflicted significant losses on the enemy and acquired valuable reconnaissance information. Because of his missions, conducted with bravery, and the success of which was based solely on his leadership abilities and personal example, he was able to stabilise the frontline in the section held by his regiment, and this contributed significantly to the fact that the frontline of the pocket on this section could be firmly held despite heavy enemy superiority. During the breakout attempt, Maringgele led a group of sixty persons, which he commanded with exemplary conduct behind the enemy lines and with which he reached, first among those in the encirclement, the German lines on 13 February 1945.[267]

Hitler signed the award documents the next day; however, the recommendation was only created on 24 February. Thereafter, he was reassigned to the *SS-Kavallerie-Ausbildung-und-Ersatz-Regiment* in Beneschau. At the end of the war, he was captured by American troops, and his decorations were taken from him.

After the war, Maringgele settled down in Germany. Most probably, he must have found it difficult to come to terms with the horrors of war: he almost never attended any comrade meetings and events, and he very rarely let anyone visit him. He died on 21 July 2000 in Solingen, Westphalia.

DECORATIONS	RANKS
• *Nahkampfspange Bronze* • *Nahkampfspange Silber* 1944 • *Nahkampfspange Gold* 21 February 1945 • *Eisernes Kreuz II. Klasse* 20 December 1941 • *Eisernes Kreuz I. Klasse* 22 June 1942 • *Deutsches Kreuz in Gold* 21 January 1945 • *Ritterkreuz des Eisernen Kreuzes* 21 February 1945	• *SS-Untersturmführer* 21 February 1945

1935

1943–1944

1965

MITZLAFF, SVEN VON

Sven von Mitzlaff was born on 16 May 1914 in Drosedow, Mecklenburg. His predecessors were committed to cavalry: his grandfather had been the commander of the famous horse training school in Hannover, and his father was a famous gentleman horseman and horse breeder. Sven learnt to ride when he was seven years old, and when he turned 19, he started his voluntary service in 1933 in the 4th *Reiter-Regiment*. As a gallop jockey, Mitzlaff won numerous awards and prizes despite his height of 185 centimetres. He had 153 individual victories. Considering that they had been achieved by 1939 when the Second World War abruptly ended his jockeying career, this is an exceptionally high figure.

From 1938, he served as *Schwadron-Chef* in 9th Cavalry Regiment, and from 10 November, was assigned as adjutant in the II *Abteilung* of the 9th Cavalry Regiment. However, he took part in the French campaign as squadron commander of the 6th *Schwadron* of the 2nd *Reiter-Regiment.*

On 28 June 1940, in consequence of a report signed as "Eugen Jost", a court martial procedure was begun against him. His unit was stationed near Paris at that time and was preparing to cross the Seine. Two weeks earlier, von Mitzlaff had been ordered to requisition horses. As he could not find appropriate horses in Paris, he visited the stalls of the nearby Maisons-Laffitte, which he knew from the newspapers because this was a location famous for French galloping sport. According to the report, von Mitzlaff, with a gallop calendar in his hand that included the best horses' data, gathered 30 thoroughbreds and called for them by their names. He then retrieved the requisition documents he himself had signed and tore them to pieces. At the same time, it was claimed that he had also taken a quantity of other equipment. It is characteristic of the stern discipline in the German army that the case immediately warranted a court martial procedure against von Mitzlaff. On 17 July 1940, the files reached the high command of the *Ersatzheer* (Replacement Army). The severity of the case was further increased by the fact that an order issued on 7 July 1940 by the leading veterinarian of the *OKH* specifically prohibited the requisition of thoroughbred horses. Von Mitzlaff's misconduct, therefore, seemed twice as serious.

Von Mitzlaff submitted his report on 24 August 1940. In this, he referred to the fact that he had been ordered on 24 June 1940 to carry out the requisition as many horses were missing in his unit. He denied the accusation that he would have taken the best sports horses (these horses were not even there anymore, a fact confirmed by the number of empty horse bays). At the same time, he confirmed that he had selected the horses with a French trainer but had not even considered the horses' names. As neither the owners of the horses nor the caretakers were available, he handed over two requisition documents for the two horses where he found at least one person who agreed to take these documents (the French trainer who helped him with the selection refused to take the requisition papers because, according to his statement, he did not know the owners). Furthermore, according to von Mitzlaff, he had never heard of a person called "Eugen Jost" and had taken only 17 and not 30 horses. His report was confirmed in every detail by his superior, and it was further added that the horses were currently at the 2/II *Abteilung*. The court martial trial began on 2 September 1940 at the 1st Cavalry Division. During the trial, it was proven that the *OKH* order regarding the prohibition of the requisition of thoroughbred horses had not been forwarded to the regiment. Von Mitzlaff only had four horses in his *Schwadron*, and their selection had not happened on the basis of their sports ability, and only the harnesses belonging to the horses had been requisitioned with them. Von Mitzlaff had indeed torn up two requisition documents two days later, but this happened because those horses had not been taken away. Von Mitzlaff was fully acquitted of the charges.

His assessment describes von Mitzlaff on 10 February 1941 as follows:

> He is of noble character, open, humble and very well-mannered. He is calm and acts with self-possession. He is a well-loved comrade and attentive superior. A skilful squadron commander, diligent and dutiful, energetic and purposeful. He is exceptionally committed and talented in horse matters. He is a superb gentleman rider. He distinguished himself in Poland, the Netherlands, and France as a brave officer and squadron commander.[268]

His later assessments were as enthusiastic about his person as this description. Interestingly, apart from his last assessment (dated 1 March 1944), where it is noted that he has an "excellent national socialist world view", there are no references whatsoever in any of his assessments to his views regarding National Socialism; however, his wide reading was mentioned several times. On the assessment dated 30 October 1941, his regiment commander added that "he is exceptionally brave and diligent, and a very good squadron commander, he is much more than he seems to be. Recommended to receive the *Deutsches Kreuz in Gold*".[269] (This latter decoration was not awarded to him this time.) From 15 December 1941, he became commander of the 5th (heavy) *Schwadron* of the 2nd *Reiter-Regiment*, however, served only for a short period in this position, as, due to his exceptional abilities, he was sent to attend a staff course (*Kriegsakademie*). As the first stage of staff training, from 1 March 1942, he was reassigned to the 7th Panzer Division, and from 16 June, he was further reassigned to the *VII. Armeekorps*. He attended a staff course in Berlin between 30 August and 7 November 1942. After that, he served as the *Zweite Generalstabsoffizier (Ib)* of the 132nd Infantry Division. From 1 August 1943, he was taken over to the *Stab* and served as the *Zweite Generalstabsoffizier (Ib)* of the *LXXXIX. Armeekorps* before being reassigned as the *Dritter Generalstabsoffizier (Ic)* (intelligence, counter-intelligence). He was wounded twice more at unknown dates. From 1 September 1944, he was reassigned as the *Chef des Generalstabes* of the 8th SS Cavalry Division.[270] His activities during the siege are unknown; according to his family, he was recommended to receive the *Ritterkreuz des Eisernen Kreuzes*. His command post was in the MOM factory until the beginning of February 1945.

During the breakout, he moved with the group of Ernő Billnitzer and →*Wilhelm Schöning* in the Buda hills; however, in the Zsámbék basin, he was with a much smaller group. He was twice wounded in the meantime: his chest and leg were shot through, most probably during the breakthrough of the last Soviet positions. With these wounds, he was still able to reach the first German lines, approximately 500 metres from there, in the early morning hours of February 14. According to his recollections, he would not have been able to make it that far had his comrades not helped him. As soon as his mother and one of his friends received the news that he had made it through, they set off from Mecklenburg without delay and, through a series of adventurous and considerably risky events, they eventually reached Baden bei Wien. It was a life-saving moment for Sven von Mitzlaff. His mother made herself in charge of tending to her wounded son and then transported him to his uncle's estate near Waging, Bavaria.

After recovering, Sven von Mitzlaff returned to equestrian sports as a trainer. He devoted his life to breeding thoroughbred horses and became very successful in the galloping sport. As a trainer, he had 1,764 confirmed victories (of these, seven were derby victories). His most successful student was a Hungarian emigré, Péter Alafi, who left Hungary in 1956; he had altogether 2,307 galop victories. Sven von Mitzlaff died on 3 December 1992 in Eitzendorf near Verden. According to the obituary of the German racing sport, he was "the true trademark of the German galloping sport; he had an unmistakable personality, he was well-known, well-loved, and respected by everyone, a true *Grandseigneur*".[271]

DECORATIONS	RANKS
• *Eisernes Kreuz II. Klasse* 6 October 1939 • *Eisernes Kreuz I. Klasse* 5 November 1940 • *Verwundetenabzeichen in Schwarz* 17 September 1941 • *Verwundetenabzeichen in Silber* • *Infanterie-Sturmabzeichen* 9 January 1942 • *Deutsches Kreuz in Gold* 27 January 1945	• Ensign 1 September 1934 • Senior ensign 1 December 1934 • *Leutnant* 1 April 1935 • *Oberleutnant* 1 August 1938 • *Rittmeister* 1 August 1941 • *Major (der Kavallerie)* 1 August 1943 • *Oberstleutnant* 20 February 1945

1944

MÖSSLACHER, ERHARD

Erhard Mösslacher was born on 16 June 1921 in Weißbriach in Karinthia. On 1 September 1939, he joined the ranks of the Waffen-SS. Initially, he served in the *Der Führer* Regiment. He took part in the French campaign, during which he was wounded on 3 May 1940. On 30 January 1942, he was reassigned to the *SS-Kavallerie*, and he was promoted officer around this time as well. He received the *Deutsches Kreuz in Gold* on 26 September 1943 – at that time, he was serving in the 6th Squadron of the 2nd SS Cavalry Regiment.

Mösslacher actively took part, with marked malevolence, in preparations for the deportation of the Hungarian Jewish population. This is all the more remarkable because among the officers of the 8th and 22nd SS cavalry divisions, he was the only one about whom such documents have survived. On 22 March 1944, that is, one day after his arrival to Hungary, Mösslacher was already preoccupied with terrorising the Jewish residents of the town of Paks. On that day, he appeared in the office of the head of local administration and handed in a decree that had eight points. According to that, Jews were subjected to curfew in the evening; Jews could not leave the town under any circumstances; they were prohibited from using any means of public transportation; their assets were to be taken into a complete inventory; their shops were to be marked with a yellow star; orthodox and reform Jews were to be listed by their religious leaders; the heads of the Jewish families were obligated to report to their religious leaders every day (!) at 1600 hours in person and, in the event this was missed, they had to pay "with their heads" and the religious leaders had to forward such data one hour later to Mösslacher. In case of any mistakes in the data or the escape of any Jews, Mösslacher threatened the community with the execution of "100 Jews".

He especially stressed that he would retaliate against black market activities above and beyond "the directions of the government".[272]

It must be noted here that Mösslacher had no authority to issue such regulations. Theoretically, not even Eichmann could issue such orders, as his capacity only allowed him to act in the field of "counselling". From the summer of 1944 to the end of the siege, Mösslacher was commander of the 6th Squadron of the 16th SS Cavalry Regiment. On 22 September 1944, he was wounded again at Ludas. He received his *Ritterkreuz* on 9 February 1945. The recommendation for this decoration is not known. However, it is almost certain that he received it for his combat activities in District XII of Budapest. In this period, his company was in combat in the Farkasréti Cemetery and Orbán Hill. Mösslacher took part in the breakout and, on 13–14 February, was in a group together with →*Albert Klett*, →*Friedrich Meier*, Fritz Szigetter and Konrad Augustin. The latter, in his letter about the death of Klett, refers to Mösslacher and writes that he was shot on 14 February 1945 at around 0500 hours, not too far from reaching no-man's-land.

His bequest, which did not contain documents created during the siege of Budapest, was sold by an American auction house for 12,500 dollars.[273]

DECORATIONS	RANKS
• *Eisernes Kreuz II. Klasse* 25 July 1940 • *Eisernes Kreuz I. Klasse* 25 February 1942 • *Deutsches Kreuz in Gold* 26 September 1943 • *Nahkampfspange Silber* 15 November 1943 • *Ritterkreuz des Eisernen Kreuzes* 9 February 1945 • *Osvolkmedaille Silber I. Klasse*	• *SS-Untersturmführer* 30 January 1942 • *SS-Obersturmführer* 23 April 1943 • *SS-Hauptsturmführer* 30 January 1945

1942

1943

MÜLLER, KURT

Kurt Müller was born on 20 August 1919 in Diedelkopf (Kusel). His father was a blacksmith. At the outbreak of the Second World War, he chose the career of a commissioned officer. He was assigned as a platoon leader to the 150th *Panzerjäger-Abteilung* on April 1, 1940. On 28 October 1940, he was reassigned to the 39th Panzer Regiment also as a platoon leader. On 15 July 1941, he was again reassigned, this time to the unit of *Panzer-Ersatz-Abteilung 33*, which was stationed in St. Pölten, where he was sent for officers' training. His assessment from 1942 describes him as follows:

> He is a straight, decent person. He is confident, firm and energetic in his appearance. He can convey the national socialist thought very well to others. As an officer commissioned to the company and the father of *Fähnrichs*, he demonstrates excellent knowledge and performance. He is an excellent trainer and teacher as well. Mentally active, physically sturdy and strong, however limited due to sustained wounds. He has conducted himself excellently in battle against the enemy. There are no weak traits in him. Summary of the assessment: well over average.[274]

On 5 May 1942, he was reassigned to the 129th *Panzer-Abteilung*; however, he has been reassigned again to the 33rd *Panzer-Ersatz-Abteilung* on 3 September 1942. This short period of time was enough for him to be awarded the *Deutsches Kreuz in Gold.*

On 13 September 1944 he was reassigned from 33rd *Panzer-Ersatz-Abteilung* stationed in St. Pölten to the 2110/3. *Panzer* Company. This unit had been used for the re-establishment of the 13th Panzer Division in Örkénytábor, Hungary. Here, Müller became commander of the 6th Company of the 4th Panzer Regiment. From the beginning of October 1944, he was deployed to combat activities. He took part in the armoured battle in the Debrecen area and the combat activities in the foregrounds of Budapest. On 13–14 November 1944, east of Nagykáta, according to the war log of the 66/I Battalion served as commander of one of the assault groups of the regiment.[275] Recommendation documents for decorations awarded to him did not survive, although his family remembered that he had received a decoration for knocking out tanks. His casualty files state that from November 1944, he was reassigned to the *IX. Waffen-Gebirgskorps* in an unknown position, however →*Wilhelm Schöning*, writing about him in his account of the war, states that on 30 December 1944, "he knocked out several Russian tanks from the shortest distance".[276] Schöning must have been two days wrong because the 3rd Tank Brigade of the 23rd Tank Corps reported the loss of nine of their tanks, which had been destroyed in the area of Rákospalota–Csömör on 28 December – the day on which the Soviets suffered their heaviest loss of tanks during the encirclement of the Hungarian capital. This evidence suggests that Kurt Müller's combat actions might have been in connection with these Soviet losses. On 29 December, the Soviet tank losses could not have been larger than four vehicles, and on the next day – while the Soviet troops breached the defence at Rákosszentmihály and occupied the majority of the area of the town – they lost only one tank. The 13th Panzer Division, under the personal control of *Oberstleutnant i.G.* →*Ekesparre*, launched two subsequent counterattacks during the afternoon: the first collapsed in the fire of Soviet anti-tank guns and mortars; the second was able to force its way into the western parts of Rákosszentmihály northeast of the circular railway but stalled in front of an anti-tank ditch. Due to the enemy's tanks and anti-tank guns, the 13th Panzer Division lost 4 or 5 tanks and 9 armoured fighting vehicles (although the unit's earlier losses had been insignificant). The last major tank combat during the encirclement of Budapest was fought on 31 December 1944: on that day, a Soviet assault breached the frontline of 66th Panzergrenadier Regiment, and only stopped west of the Kőbánya cemetery. It was here that the armoured units last participated in a counterattack in a larger group, which was unsuccessful. From then on, Müller was probably never deployed again in any large combat mission with his tank. According to a photograph of a Panther tank, on the barrel of which seven knock-out rings had been painted, it finished its duty on the Krisztina Boulevard near Vérmező. In all probability, this was Müller's vehicle.

Comrades who took part in the breakout attempt remembered seeing Müller outside Budapest on 20 February 1945. His fate is unknown. His family learned that Müller had been decorated with the *Ritterkreuz* on 21 March only from a radio broadcast.[277]

DECORATIONS	RANKS
• *Eisernes Kreuz II. Klasse* 9 July 1940 • *Eisernes Kreuz I. Klasse* 6 July 1942 • *Panzerkampfabzeichen* • *Deutsches Kreuz in Gold* 13 September 1942 • *Ritterkreuz des Eisernen Kreuzes* 7 February 1945	• *Leutnant* 1 April 1940 • *Oberleutnant* 1 April 1942

1944

1988

PHOENIX, HARRY

Harry Phoenix was born on 3 January 1913 in the small town of Zhagori (Schagarren in German, today Žagarė, Lithuania), which belonged to the Russian Empire at that time, into the Baltic German community. His father was an electrical engineer; therefore, the family belonged to the upper middle class. Phoenix was discharged from the Latvian army in 1934 as an artilleryman; after that, he graduated from the Riga Academy of Teacher Training. In 1939, he took part in a seminar at the Imperial Sports Academy in Berlin. After that, he voluntarily joined the Waffen-SS, where he was assigned to the artillery based on his earlier military training. During the French campaign, he received the *Eisernes Kreuz II. Klasse*, for his exceptional bravery, especially for knocking out French bunkers. In the summer of 1941, he was reassigned to the artillery regiment of the *SS-Division "Reich"* as *Geschützführer*. In this capacity, he was awarded the *Eisernes Kreuz I. Klasse* and *Infanterie-Sturmabzeichen*. From the beginning of 1942, he took part in the Eastern campaign as an officer and from June as commander of the 5th Battery. On one occasion, his battery found itself in the first line and managed to contain assaulting Soviet troops with handguns until reinforcements arrived. During the winter of 1942/1943, he served as a forward artillery observer and took part in several perilous missions on the frontline. Phoenix's reports saved infantry in the main line of defence a number of times because their precision enabled the artillery to provide them with support. At Medvedevo, the Soviets rushed through the "Phoenix radio unit" and cut it off from its own troops. However, the unit continued to direct the fire of their own artillery, which was stationed much farther back in safety. On another occasion, Phoenix held his command bunker for five hours with only eight of his men when the Soviets broke through the defences. In March 1943, he was freshly promoted to *SS-Obersturmführer* when he was wounded. At that time, he had already been decorated with the *Nahkampfspange in Bronze*, which seems quite unusual in the case of an artillery officer.

In August 1943, Phoenix was assigned to provide artillery cover for a sparsely occupied defence section. As expected, the enemy broke through, all the more so because the ammunition of the defensive artillery ran out. At that moment, Phoenix rallied his gun crews and launched an infantry counterattack, during which he was able to retake the initial positions. A few hours later, as an artillery observer, he found himself behind the Soviet lines with his two men. Somehow, they managed to make their way back to their own infantry lines, although Phoenix was wounded during the process. For these combat achievements, he received the *Deutsches Kreuz in Gold* and the *Vervundetenabzeichen in Silber* decorations on 16 January 1944.

On 19 March 1944, he took part in the occupation of Hungary with his division. His artillery regiment was stationed in the villages of Tolna and Baranya counties. Here, he became acquainted with his future wife, Erzsébet Rosenau, who was born in Vienna in 1922 but had Hungarian citizenship. She was a member of the *Volksbund* from 1939 and, at that time, led a boarding school for women in Hidas maintained by the *Volksbund*. Phoenix handed in his marriage request documents on 22 September 1944, and the wedding was held on 24 November 1944, after the siege of the capital started, and most probably in Budapest itself.

From autumn 1944, there is only sporadic data on Phoenix's combat activities. What seems to be certain is that he took part in the combat actions in Northern Transylvania and Hungary. After the middle of January 1945, having run out of ammunitions for his guns, he organised infantry assault groups from the gun crews. Phoenix's unit was deployed on the Buda side at various locations throughout the city. There are data confirming their presence on the southern railroad embankment, on the Kis-Sváb-hegy and at the Goldberger-factory in District III as well.

His unit, the 8th SS Artillery Regiment was assigned to the third wave of the breakout attempt. However, they never received orders to set off. At 0300 hours, on 12 February 1945, he decided to set off on his own initiative with his men (the remains of three batteries out of four). They headed for Rózsadomb from Szilágyi Erzsébet Boulevard, but their subsequent route is impossible to reconstruct. (Phoenix himself also tried to retrace the route they had taken at that time and returned to Budapest twice in the 1980s in an attempt to do so.) On 12 February, he successfully managed to escape the encirclement with approximately 300 men. He remembered the events as follows in his interview from 1988:

> At 0300 hours, at dawn, at our discretion, we set off as there were no orders of any kind from the Regiment, although they promised that they would notify us. The sky was slowly lightening, and we were going westwards on a really wide street out of the city; there were many dead bodies lying around there, so we turned towards the right. Perhaps we were going towards Rózsadomb. I wouldn't be able to tell exactly where we went. I visited Budapest twice later to find our route; I was walking up and down everywhere but couldn't find it. What is certain is that we set off from Mária Square.
>
> Our main route was crisscrossed with anti-tank ditches. I remember a column trying to get through them with *Schwimmwagens* and wounded comrades. It is certain that nobody made it through there. This was at dawn on 12 February.
>
> At the edge of a square, we noticed that it might be possible to get through there. I met von Hehn there, Rumohr's adjutant.[278] Hehn was an eyewitness to Rumohr being wounded, and he wanted to take him further with them, but Rumohr said, "You will have enough trouble without me," and then he shot himself in the head. Hehn was clearly shocked by these circumstances. He was not in a good shape either. I threw away my winter coat because it was too heavy, although I was quite a fit guy then. He, however, was carrying a large backpack with him. He said that his family

had nothing left and that he wanted to bring them a few small things. But I was thinking the last thing that you would need in such a situation was a large backpack like that.

We had seen that behind us, the Russian artillery was shelling the city in the snowstorm, but we were already past them at that time. We saw officers who took their wives with them; one of them had high heels, and she wanted to march in the mud in those. It could clearly be seen that this would not end well. We made direct contact with the enemy several times. Somewhere in the woods, we captured a Russian soldier who was mending telephone lines, and, as I knew a little Russian, I interrogated him. I was getting useful information from him because, westwards, the Russians were establishing a blocking line. Upon hearing this, I told my group we should spend the night in the woods. We slept upright. I found a large Hungarian coat in an abandoned house, which I used as a cover, and shared it with my friend Rasmussen from Schleswig-Holstein.[279] Unfortunately, those guarding the captured Russian soldier fell asleep, and this allowed him to escape. The next morning, when we continued our journey, we found that ahead, the enemy was waiting in front of us in trenches, but luckily, we also found a deserted cover. To the south of us, we saw a larger group of men, who also turned out to be Germans. A few Hungarians were with them, including a couple of Hungarian generals and the chief of staff of our division.[280] They asked me to lead the group forward. So suddenly, our group grew to include 2,000 men. We waited during the night, but then a Wehrmacht group came from the *Feldherrnhalle*, and they wanted to set off immediately. I warned them that the Russians were everywhere, but they did not heed my warning, and three or four hours later, they came back decimated. We also tried to break out. We went back towards the east, then northwards, and suddenly, no Russians were ahead of us. We aimed to outflank the Russians, and we succeeded. We only met small groups; these had around 30 men each, and from our 2,000-strong group, only those who had endured the forced march remained. Suddenly, we noticed Russian soldiers on a hillside a few hundred meters ahead of us. By then, we were already utterly exhausted. Luckily, I came to myself, and I had a soldier who served as a non-combatant auxiliary, being a Soviet national. I had captured him before, and I liked him so much that I did not let him be taken as a prisoner of war. He was very loyal and always was with us, so I knew he was in our column. I ran to him and said, “Rasilov, answer them in Russian if they ask something”. My knowledge of Russian would not have been enough for that.

This trick worked; we marched past each other, which was the most dangerous situation. Nobody had more than 10 bullets left, and defence would have been impossible. But we managed to get through this. There were a few other smaller-scale contacts with the Russians, but they were not a big deal.

And suddenly, we ran into the Soviet main line of defence. Here, a straight road led to the German main line of defence, a corduroy road. This seemed too dangerous for me, so I turned right. They were shooting at us from the left and the right, but we saw the tracer bullets, and we were able to dodge them every time. A few of our soldiers, though, chose the straight road, and they were captured. We were lucky; approximately forty of us made it through. I do not know who might have been behind us. When I got through, I gave my weapon to somebody, entered a dugout, sat down by the stove and immediately fell asleep. I woke up a few hours later when the stove began to warm up my frozen feet.[281]

His recommendation to receive the *Ritterkreuz* described him as follows:

...he was commanding the fight of the remnants of the artillery in Budapest. Thanks to his arduous activity, he was able to maintain fire support for the infantry elements even in the most challenging circumstances. In the battery positions, he let the enemy come as close as possible, and he held out to the end, repulsing a number of attacks from the enemy. Upon orders, he led a combat group of approximately 400 men during the breakout. Thanks to his exceptional combat direction, deep in the rear, it was possible to break through five enemy lines while being exposed to constant enemy attacks. With a last assault on the morning of 14 February 1945, he also managed to break through the Russian main line of defence.[282]

„My first school year 1965/66" – The photo of Harry Phoenix as form teacher

He was awarded on 21 February 1945, at the same time as →*Boosfeld* and →*Maringgele* received their decorations. Although a number of documents state that Phoenix also received the *Nahkampfspange in Gold*, Phoenix himself did not know about this, and he did not wear the decoration after the war either. However, based on the number of his close combat days, he most probably would have been eligible for that decoration.[283]

Due to frost injuries on both of his legs, he was transported to the hospital established in Semmering, Austria. After the war, he settled in West Germany, where he worked as a teacher. He died on 21 December 1999, and according to his will, his ashes were scattered into the sea.

DECORATIONS	RANKS
• *Eisernes Kreuz II. Klasse* 1 August 1940	• *SS-Untersturmführer* August 1941
• *Eisernes Kreuz I. Klasse* 2 October 1941	• *SS-Obersturmführer* 30 January 1943
• *Allgemeines Sturmabzeichen* 11 June 1941	• *SS-Hauptsturmführer* January 1945
• *Deutsches Kreuz in Gold* 16 January 1944	
• *Nahkampfspange in Silber* 1944	
• *Ritterkreuz des Eisernen Kreuzes* 21 February 1945	
• *Verwundetenabzeichen in Gold* February 1945	

1940–1943

RAEDER, KURT

Kurt Raeder was born on 7 January 1913 in Berlin-Friedenau. There is no data on the beginning of his military service; all that is known is that he was appointed reserve lieutenant in September 1940 and received the rank of first lieutenant in March 1942.

Between September 1940 and February 1942, he served as a platoon leader in the 4th Company of the 508/I Battalion of the 292nd Infantry Division.[284] He took part in the French and Soviet campaigns with this unit. On 10 August 1941 and again on 21 October 1943, he was wounded. He was reassigned to Panzergrenadier Division *Feldherrnhalle* reserves on 1 November 1943.

From the autumn of 1944, he served in the 60/I Battalion (according to other sources in 120/I) of the newly reestablished Panzergrenadier Regiment *Feldherrnhalle*. His service positions, deployments and combat actions in Hungary are completely unknown. As reserve first lieutenant, he received the *Ritterkreuz des Eisernen Kreuzes* on 21 January 1945. The recommendation documents for this decoration have not survived. On 13 February 1945, he was captured by the Soviets in Budapest. He was released on 31 December 1953. After the war, he returned to his earlier profession and also worked as a lay judge. The date of his death, as well as the dates of his promotions, are unknown.

DECORATIONS	RANKS
• *Eisernes Kreuz II. Klasse* • *Eisernes Kreuz I. Klasse* • *Ritterkreuz des Eisernen Kreuzes* 21 January 1945	• *Leutnant der Reserve* September 1940 • *Oberleutnant der Reserve* March 1942 • Further dates of promotions are unknown.

1943

REIßMANN, PAUL

Paul Reißmann was born on 17 January 1920 in Zwickau as the son of a waiter. After he finished elementary school, he trained to be a locksmith and then worked in this profession. From 1933, he was a member of the *Hitlerjugend* (membership was compulsory only from 1936 onwards). From August 1938 to 11 November 1939, Reißmann was also a member of the *Nationalsozialistische Kraftfahrkorps* (*NSKK,* National Socialist Motor Driver Corps). On 11 November 1939, he voluntarily joined the SS. Until 21 October 1940, he served as a *Kradschütze* before requesting reassignment to the *SS-Kavallerie* as an *SS-Sturmmann.* He and his unit were assigned securing tasks in Poland until the summer of 1941, and then, after the Soviet campaign, he served at the same rank in the eastern Polish territories. From August 1941, Reißmann's unit perpetrated a number of mass murders. However, his role in these crimes is not clearly defined.

As a consequence of the Soviet breakthrough, from 5 December 1941, the SS cavalry regiments were relocated to the frontline, where combat actions raged constantly until February 1942. During this period they lost 80 percent of their strength.

By the end of June 1942, at the Heidelager training field, the SS Cavalry Division had been established from the remnants of the SS Cavalry Brigade, which then received an entirely new regiment. Reißmann was reassigned to this new regiment. The unit was deployed in the Rzhev area during the autumn, and this was where Reißmann earned the *Eisernes Kreuz II. Klasse.*

In mid-February 1943, the unit was relocated to Bobrujsk, but a small detachment was deployed near Komarichi. It was here that Reißmann, as *Zugführer,* knocked out a Soviet tank. For that action, he received the *Sonderabzeichen für das Niederkämpfen von Panzerkampfwagen durch Einzelkämpfer* and the *Allgemeines Sturmabzeichen.*

In April 1943, the 3rd SS Cavalry Regiment was relocated back to the Heidelager training ground. After its refreshment and replenishment, the unit received unit number 17 (*SS-Kavallerie-Regiment 17*). Reißmann was reassigned to the 4th Squadron. The regiment spent half a year in the area of Warthegau. Their subsequent combat deployment commenced on 16 January 1944 in the area of Kovel, where a larger-scale Soviet breakthrough had to be sealed off. From the end of January, the regiment was engaged in heavy combat with the advancing Soviet troops at the River Striy. Kovel was a target of concentrated Soviet attacks due to its situation as an important railway hub, and by the end of March 1944, it was completely encircled. The German defenders broke out of the encirclement on 5 April 1944 with the help of a relief attack. By then, Reißmann had more than 30 close combat days in his records, earning him the *Nahkampfspange in Silber.* He also received the *Eisernes Kreuz I. Klasse* for these combat actions. The 17th SS Cavalry Regiment suffered heavy losses during these combat days, and Reißmann was wounded for the third time. Subsequently, the regiment was relocated to Hungary and incorporated into the 22nd SS Cavalry Division during its establishment. Reißmann was deployed in the Attila I Defence Line, in the foregrounds of Pestszentimre from 2 November 1944 with the 4th Squadron of the 17th SS Cavalry Regiment. After the Soviets breached the defensive positions, Reißmann's unit launched a counterattack that collapsed in the heavy Soviet artillery fire. During these combat actions, Reißmann knocked out a Soviet tank with a *Panzerfaust,* which blocked the road in a strategically important location; after that, Reißmann was able to reach an anti-tank ditch with his section. On the same day, the squadron commander was killed; therefore, Reißmann took over the command of the entire squadron. In the unclear, chaotic situation other units were also subordinated to him, together with an *Alarmkompanie* commanded by officers. He was able to hold positions for four days until, on 8 November, he was mortally wounded in the first trench during a Soviet assault.

Paul Reißmann around 1943

Two days later, his commander recommended Reißmann for the posthumous award of the *Ritterkreuz des Eisernen Kreuzes,* requesting that he be promoted retroactively to officer status. Reißmann received the award under an

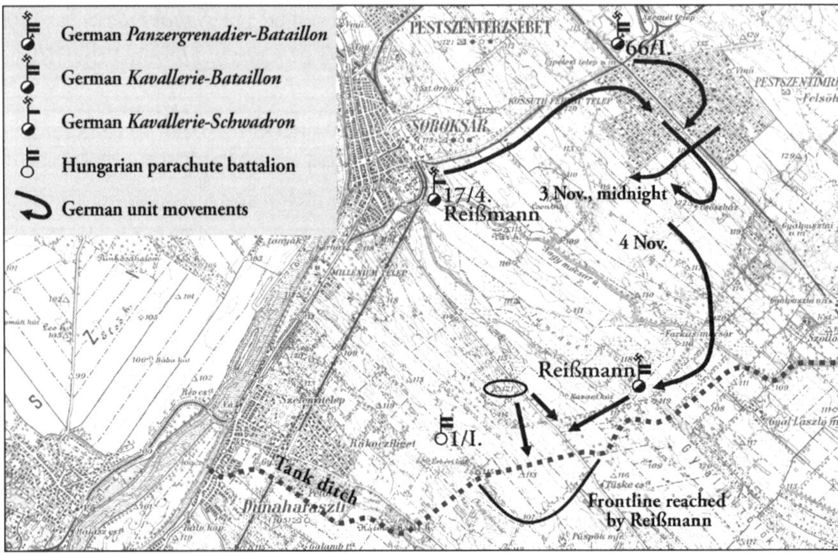

The draft of the combat actions of Reißmann on 3 to 8 November 1944

accelerated procedure four days after his death, and his promotion was also validated with retroactive effect as of 1 November 1944.[285]

DECORATIONS	RANKS
• *Eisernes Kreuz II. Klasse* 5 December 1942 • *Eisernes Kreuz I. Klasse* 4 March 1944 • *Sonderabzeichen für das Niederkämpfen von Panzerkampfwagen durch Einzelkämpfer* 14 March 1943 (second award 7 November 1944) • *Allgemeines Sturmabzeichen* 15 March 1943 • *Nahkampfspange Silber* 25 April 1944 • *Verwundetenabzeichen in Silber* 1 August 1944 • *Ritterkreuz des Eisernen Kreuzes* 12 November 1944	• *SS-Scharführer* 1 March 1943 • *SS-Oberscharführer* 19 November 1943 • *SS-Hauptscharführer* 1944 • *SS-Untersturmführer* 1 November 1944

1945

REMLINGER, HEINRICH

Heinrich Remlinger was born on 19 March 1882 in Poppenweiler near Ludwigsburg. He started his military service on 2 October 1902 in the *Ulanen-Regiment "König Karl" 19.* After his compulsory military service, he was promoted to non-commissioned officer. He served throughout the First World War in this *Regiment.* On 22 August 1914 he earned the *Eisernes Kreuz II. Klasse* for saving his wounded regiment commander and taking him out of the battlefield near Arlon, Belgium. In April 1916, he was promoted to officer candidate in recognition of the bravery with which he distinguished himself in the combat around the Somme in 1916. He also received the *Eisernes Kreuz I. Klasse* and the Military Merit Cross of Württemberg with Swords. On 1 August 1919, he was promoted to *Leutnant.* Until 1935, he served with the cavalry in various roles and, after that, served a year at the Neustettin Command (today Szczecinek, Poland). In 1936, he was reassigned to the reestablished Torgau military discipline centre (Fort Zinna), where he became the commander. According to an assessment as of 19 February 1941, he had a powerful militaristic personality, displayed a strong will and always strived to prevail. As per the assessment's description, he had been "the commander of the *Wehrmachtgefängnis des Deutschen Reichs* (military prison of the German Reich) in Torgau for a number of years now, enthusiastic and efficient, with a number of individual initiatives and strong organisational skills."[286] On 15 April, the following was appended to the above description: "he has earned unparalleled merits by organising military law enforcement in the Wehrmacht".[287] This note refers to the fact that from 1941 onwards, the *Strafbataillons* of the Wehrmacht were organised in the military prison in Torgau and incorporated into the orders of battle as units with unit numbers 500-. According to the accounts of eyewitnesses, the commander liked to "blabber", and it happened a number of times that he subjected the inmates to hour-long "tirades".

His promotion on 1 December 1942 to *Generalmajor* can be deemed extraordinary, as Remlinger had not completed any higher military or officer training – this is why he had not previously been considered for promotion, although, based on his age, he would have been eligible.

On 15 February 1943, he was assigned as the commander of *Feldkommandantur 541* in Paris; however, from 10 May 1943, he was reassigned to the Eastern Front, to the position of the head of *Feldkommandantur 186*, which was stationed in Opochka, at the rear area of the 18th Army in defence in the foregrounds of Leningrad. On 26 September 1943, he took over the command of *Standortkommandantur 241 Pleskau* (Pskov). In general, these command posts, which can be termed as "garrison commands", had no operational role. They ensured order throughout the rear areas; more precisely, their preliminary preoccupation was attending to administrative tasks and maintaining military discipline.

Little is known of Remlinger's activities during this period, even despite the fact that after the war, he was formally sentenced to death and was hanged for his activities here. The only available references are mentioned in his assessment dated 10 December 1943:

> He is exceptionally diligent, purposeful, precise and scrupulous, and has practical experience. He has an inclination towards pedantry. He is exact and unambiguous in giving orders, often theoretical and bureaucratic. He thinks strictly along national socialist notions and acts accordingly. During partisan deployments, he has executed smaller tasks that proved his good tactical sense and correct combat command abilities.[288]

He served in this position until March 1944. After that, he was reassigned as the *Kommandeur* of the *Kommandant des Rückwärtigen Armeegebiets 593* (*Korück 593*, in the rear area of the 6th Army). In this function, he also commanded the *Wehrmacht-Standort-Kommandantur-Budapest* (that is, the non-combatant units). As Budapest was packed with various rear area Wehrmacht and *Luftwaffe* units, Remlinger's position was anything but formal. On 7 December 1944, *Generalleutnant* Walther Krause took over the command of *Korück 593*, which was constantly being relocated westwards, and Remlinger was left to command the *Wehrmacht-Standort-Kommandantur-Budapest*.[289]

On 3 December 1944, the *Bevollmächtigten General der deutschen Wehrmacht in Ungarn*, Hans von Greiffenberg, provided an assessment of Remlinger for the last time:

> He has an energetic personality and a good sense of practicality. He set to work with great enthusiasm to deal with the difficult tasks of the freshly established *Wehrmacht-Standortkommandantur Gross-Budapest,* and he has achieved considerable success. He is aiming for higher achievements, and he can place himself in the correct spotlight. He is physically very fit, despite his age.[290]

There is almost no data available relating to his activities in Budapest. Nevertheless, from the SD phone book, it can be deduced that until the encirclement, his command post was in Hotel Wien at No. 16 József Körút and also in Hotel Astoria.[291] There are three major aspects based on which conclusions can be drawn about his personality and role.

The first such aspect is drawn from Remlinger's later trial. In December 1945, in Leningrad, in the Viborg Cultural Centre, the Soviets organised a grand-scale show trial. This was the third of eight show trials conducted in just six weeks between December 1945 and February 1946 – before this one, only two previous trials had been held in 1943.[292] The most important organizers of these trials were Viktor Semyonovich Abakumov, head of Soviet counter-intelligence, and Lavrentiy Beria, chief of *NKVD.* In the Leningrad process, eleven persons stood trial. Seven German officers received death sentences; they were accused of the mass murder of civilians and prisoners of war. Remlinger was sentenced to death for fourteen cruel partisan-hunting expeditions, setting hundreds of villages to fire, and murdering eight thousand "Soviet persons". The execution was conducted in public on 6 January 1946, one day after the death sentence was announced. Remlinger was executed in Leningrad on Kalinin Square, and according to earlier practices, the truck-hanging method was used.

Of the defendants at this trial, only one person managed to return home alive, and like those defendants who returned home later from similar show trials, he too described how brutally he was tortured during the interrogations.[293] In the case of Remlinger, however, it seems that torture was not practised, as based on his behaviour, he did not seem to be broken at all. Of course, it cannot be entirely excluded that, despite torture, their captors were not able to break him. Still, it is rather more probable, based on the records of the trials, that they did not exert extreme cruelty on Remlinger, who was considered the prime defendant. It is all the more probable, it seems, that it was easier to cast him in the role of the commander who denies everything. Nikita Petrov, who is researching the crimes committed in the Stalin era, noted in connection with the trial in Kharkov in 1943, that the aim of the state prosecutor, Andrei Vyshinsky, was to organise these show trials to portray the entirety of the German army as a criminal organisation. To achieve this, the ordinary enlisted soldiers and the generals were accused in the same trials – even if there was no connection between them.[294] In the case of Remlinger, they tried to prove that, during his command, the *Wehrmachtgefängnis des Deutschen Reichs* in Torgau was, in reality, a training ground for mass murderers. According to the prosecutor, German soldiers could be exempted from their court martial sentences if they set villages on fire and shot people down. For this, practical training was provided in Torgau, according to the state prosecutor.

Due to length limitations, a review of the complete Leningrad trial will be omitted from the present work. Nevertheless, it is worth noting that the trial itself was a peculiar mix of a show trial and prosecution of actual crimes. The use of the "amalgam process", named as such by Leon Trotsky, suggests this view as well; during such a procedure, various different cases and defendants who were not related in any respect to each other were deliberately mixed up to be able to discredit one with the other.[295] The core reality in these accusations is difficult to discern completely in retrospect. However, a few aspects may help in assessing the trial itself.

An essential feature of Soviet court proceedings, which was particularly prevalent in the case of show trials, was that judgments were handed down in a way that largely or completely followed the formal rules of procedure and gave the appearance of the rule of law. In the case of the trials against defendants who had committed war crimes, however, it is a widely known fact that in the Soviet Union during the years of the Second World War, unspeakably horrendous acts had indeed been perpetrated. Thus, even in a state governed by the rule of law, it would have been difficult to deal with the problem of "I was following orders", and a very extensive investigation would have been necessary to determine how much leeway and responsibility each accused had. Every German commander of an occupying force based on Soviet territory was implicated in at least one specific type of war crime, even if he was the most humane commander possible. These commanders could not dissociate themselves from the organised manhunt, called at the time "labour conscription", which in reality resulted in hundreds of thousands of people being forcibly transported to Germany as forced labourers. In the process, the occupying forces used a whole range of coercive measures, including the shooting of non-compliant people. At the same time, the methods used were extremely varied, depending on the location and the commander himself.

Most of the accusations aimed at Remlinger seem particularly absurd, as there was no large-scale partisan activity in the region in question, and the German assessment of Remlinger mentions smaller missions only. The exhaustive monograph on the Wehrmacht's occupation activities in the northern part of Russia does not even mention Remlinger's name, which is another indication that the "undertakings" mentioned were merely insignificant actions.[296]

During the trial, a few German witnesses were also called to testify against Remlinger; these witnesses were also defendants. Such witnesses would have, at best, been deemed biased against Remlinger in a correct, lawful trial, as they had previously been held at the Torgau prison. Furthermore, the majority of the defendants had not even been subordinated to Remlinger after Torgau. The Soviet witnesses who were called to testify spoke in general terms only. The prosecution also accused Remlinger of having taken part in the forced deportation of the civilians, to which Remlinger responded that these actions were within the responsibility of *Wirtschaftsgruppe Nord* and he had only executed the given orders. He denied ordering soldiers to shoot civilians and reasoned that the German witnesses had only "confessed" against him because they held personal grudges and had previously been his subordinates. He responded to the events listed by the court by denying they had happened at the time when he was a commander in Pskov. Remlinger corrected the court several times when it had, according to him, altered the text of the orders he issued. To the accusation centred around his political views, he responded that he had never been a member of any National Socialist organisations, including the *NSDAP*. However, he confirmed that he had been ordered by the division commander of the 285th *Sicherungs-Division* to set villages on fire and execute people but firmly denied having led even a single penal expedition. In connection with the burning of villages, he mentioned that during December, he received one to three reports of burnt-down villages daily. Under his own authority, he confessed to altogether two "partisan hunts" which were not associated with any deaths by the court. He stated proudly, and with exceptionally grotesque pedantry, that in Torgau "he raised persons who are of worth to the German society" [sic!] – with this, he most probably wished to reflect on the accusation that in Torgau mass murderers were trained under his command.

At a certain stage during the trial, the name of the location, Katyn, was also mentioned. Here, more than 22,000 Polish captives (primarily officers) had been murdered and buried in unmarked graves by *NKVD* units. Arno Diere,[297] a soldier serving in the 21st *Feld-Division* (*Luftwaffe*) confessed in connection with Remlinger that the "practical training sessions" of the Torgau prison were held in the Katyn forest. Pavel Luknitsky, who had been in combat in Budapest and was also present during the whole of Remlinger's trial, witnessed this confession as follows:

> Diere [confessed that he and] many others like him were taken to the forest during the night and dug huge graves. The dead bodies transported here on trucks were thrown into these graves by the SS soldiers – tens of thousands of Polish officers, Soviet people, Jewish people, and Diere took part in the burying of these large graves.
> "Can you approximately estimate how many bodies had been thrown into these graves?"
> "15,000-20,000 people," replies Diere calmly. And then he adds that he had seen a picture of one of the mass graves in a newspaper, and the inscription said: "The Russians did this..."[298]

We can entirely exclude the possibility that Katyn was mentioned as the individual idea of the prosecutor or one of the interrogation officers. As in other aspects of the trials, the decision regarding Katyn was made at the highest levels of authority. This is evident because lengthy coverages about the events of the Leningrad trial were published on the very next day in the Soviet-occupied zone of Germany, and these explicitly highlighted the case of Katyn, which had no connection to the sentence at all.[299] The purpose of mentioning Katyn during the trial must have been to connect the name of the city with the mass murders that Germans indeed committed; the intention was to discuss the details of this case in a separate trial. One year earlier, on 24 January 1944, the special Soviet committee tasked with "investigating" the case had already issued a statement about Katyn in which they blamed the mass murders, reputedly committed in the autumn of 1941, on the Nazis. The Soviet security service obviously knew that from December 1944, the Polish government in exile in London was also investigating the case, the documentation of which was published in English in February 1946, that is, a few weeks after the Leningrad trial. This publication had not yet explicitly named the perpetrators, but it made clear that the fate of the Polish officers had become untraceable in the Soviet Union. All evidence leads to the suspicion that the Soviet side utilised a specific pre-emptive tactic in connection with Katyn, which is why this issue was brought up in the Remlinger trial. At the same time, the Soviets were also granted their demand to have the Katyn massacre included as a German war crime in the Nuremberg trials commencing in November 1945 and at the same time as the opening of the Leningrad trials, Polish state prosecutor Roman Martini was charged with organising a show trial for the Katyn case – and of course, the defendants would be Germans. Martini, to his own demise, started having suspicions about the case very early on; it was, therefore, hardly a coincidence that on 28 March 1946, he was found dead in his own home in Krakow. After that, the idea of the Katyn show trial was abandoned.[300]

During the Leningrad trial, Remlinger responded in the following way to the prosecutor's questions:

> "How did you arrive in Budapest?"
> "Upon order from Berlin in April."
> "What kind of orders did you receive?"
> "The same as in Pskov."
> "Who did you shoot there?"
> "Nobody got shot."
> "Most probably the Jews."
> "Not a single Jew was shot. I have saved the lives of a large number of Jews, but you do not believe this."
> "Who shot them?"
> "Those who were always preoccupied with this: the SS, the *Gestapo*, and others. I do not have anything in common with these; when I had the chance, I saved the lives of Jews."
> "Where did you get captured?"
> "In Budapest, during the breakout attempt."
> "During the escape?"
> "We tried to break out from the castle that was under siege."
> "And you did not succeed in breaking out?"
> "We did not manage..."[301]

It is worth noting that Remlinger retained his composure and that even immediately before the death sentence was pronounced, he continued to refer to his humanitarian actions in Budapest. In reference to Remlinger's "last-words" statement, an eyewitness reported:

> He does not ask for clemency. If he is found guilty, he wants to die bravely because he would rather die that way than live longer in shame and dishonour. What he has heard, seen and, most importantly, read during his captivity about the Soviet Union makes him suppose that the Soviet Union is preoccupied with the truth. When it comes to confessions, however, one must be wary of people who are themselves guilty. You cannot rely on the confessions of people who are out for revenge. The special units had never been subordinated to him. He did not issue the orders presented by the court, including those ordering the killing of Soviet civilians. The trial has proven that what [the other defendants] are guilty of happened in Luga, far from the area that was under his jurisdiction. [Eyewitness]

> Sonnenfeld[302] lies, but he does not despise him for it; he only feels sorry for him. He is going to die for him. It is a shame, though, because he is a very skilled man, and with a different personality and character, he could be very useful for society. He had more than enough things to do in his own circle of authority. In connection with the events at Karamyshevo and Novoselye, he cannot say anything; he was given orders by his superiors, and the destruction happened because of a partisan attack. [...] He was not a fascist, contrary to what the prosecutor states. He was always open, and so he would confess to having been a follower of Hitler if he had been one. He led thousands of young men to the right path and is proud of this. And this has nothing to do with Hitler. The state prosecutor said that he was cruel. This is not true; he saved the lives of hundreds of Jews in Budapest. He did the same in Pskov but does not want to bring this up because otherwise, it would look like he was embellishing something. [...] In the event the court sentences him to death, he will die bravely. Perhaps this will help his wish that Germany and the Soviet Union could be reconciled with each other. That is, if his own nation were ever able to get up and heal, it could only do so with the help of the Soviet Union. If his death serves this purpose, then he will die happily.[303]

After 1945, in the people's courts in Budapest, nobody gave evidence that incriminated Remlinger despite the fact that all of the Arrow Cross Party members and prominent leading figures of the police and military authorities in Budapest were tried. It is also true, however, that Remlinger's name did not surface in a positive context either, even though a large number of eyewitness accounts are available in connection with the rescue of the Budapest ghetto in mid-January 1945. It is also worth mentioning that Remlinger left the Pest side on 10 January 1945, and when stationed on the Buda side, he would have been in no position to hear about the plans against the Budapest ghetto.

The only certain data regarding Remlinger's person can be extracted from the report Swiss diplomat Harald Feller submitted in 1946 about his experiences in Budapest. He is a very interesting person, as his direct superior was the Swiss Vice-Consul Carl Lutz, who was responsible for foreign interests and was one of the most important personalities in the history of the rescue of Jews in Budapest. Lutz was stuck on the Buda side of the city from 24 December 1944, therefore Feller had to arrange everything himself. Cases were abundant because the embassy's activities in saving the Jews were disturbing the Arrow Cross Party organisations more and more, in consequence of which the workers of the Swiss Embassy were subjected to severe atrocities. Furthermore, they were warned that if they did not abandon their Jew-saving activities, the Arrow Cross Party would no longer observe the extraterritorial rights of the Swiss legation ("the safe houses"). Feller mentioned in his report that on 2 January 1945, he initiated negotiations with *Generalmajor* Remlinger regarding the excess violence with which the Arrow Cross authorities operated. These negotiations took place in Hotel Astoria, where the *Wehrmacht-Standort-Kommandantur-Budapest* was stationed:

> [Remlinger and his adjutant, Major Fritz Schuster[304]] both immediately declared that, as representatives of the Wehrmacht, they would safeguard the extraterritorial rights of the Swiss Legation as long as they were able to do so and that, in this connection, they would do everything in their power if members of the Hungarian National Socialist terrorist organisation stormed the Swiss Legation – as they had warned us [beforehand] that they would do. When we asked how long this resistance could last, Remlinger, with a pessimistic gesture, pointed to the upper floors of the hotel and to the street, where everything was in flames. The artillery barrage that followed was a telling sign of the superiority of the attackers.[305]

Feller continued his report by saying that, based on the agreement reached with Remlinger, from then on, the German artillery unit stationed on Szabadság Square and the German *Sturmgeschütze* would ensure that the Arrow Cross Party did not bother the Swiss Legation. The neighbouring office in Vadász Street was probably also saved from further raids because of this agreement. It is worth further quoting Harald Feller's report in detail:

> The necessary arrangements [in the defence of the Swiss Embassy] were to be made by a German unit in charge of the artillery located on the square. Under the command of an *Oberfeldwebel*, these men were always ready to chase away the Arrow Cross Party men if they attempted to attack the Embassy. During the entirety of the duration of the siege, the actual *Reichswehr* units[306] always kept their distance from the SA and SS formations and the Hungarian Nazi units as well. [...] We have not asked for military guards to be dispatched because we already had a police guard, and we wanted to resort to military help only in the case of extraordinary emergency situations. From the very beginning, we were of the opinion that all military defence – which was also offered by the Hungarian side as well – had to be politely declined by us because the defence of the legation could be based solely upon extraterritorial rights and not on armed defence.

> The intervention of the German units was not necessary because we have made it clear and known everywhere that the above-mentioned German unit is in readiness. Therefore, the Arrow Cross militants did not dare come close to the legation. Apart from this, the circumstances in Szabadság Square worsened due to the increasing intensity of the combat actions, to the point that the armed gangs rather chose to hide in cellars, and this did not change after the departure of the German *Sturmgeschütze* after 14 January either.
>
> In this context, the German sergeant who prevented the SS units from blowing up the ammunition stored in the stock exchange building opposite the embassy by showing us how to defuse the explosives should be mentioned. The sergeant died in mid-January after being hit by a mortar shell.[307]

Three further events suggest that Remlinger might have had a role in preventing atrocities against the Jewish population in Budapest. On 16 October 1944, in a large-scale roundup, Arrow Cross Party militants had driven Jewish residents of District VI into the Tattersall (*Nemzeti Lovarda,* National Riding Hall). Some of those forced into the Tattersall had to march to the bank of the Danube in the evening, where the Arrow Cross Party was organising their execution. According to eyewitness accounts of survivors, this massacre was stopped by a German officer who had just arrived at the location on a motorcycle.[308] Considering that at the given date, Remlinger's *Wehrmacht-Standort-Kommandantur-Budapest* was the authority in charge and not →*Pfeffer-Wildenbruch,* the order must have come from him.

The second case is connected to the Jewish High School in Abonyi Street (today: Radnóti Miklós High School) where reserve Captain László Ocskay, under the guise of the 101/359. labour service company provided shelter for more than 2,000 people. The labour service company officially made clothes for the German army, but many women and children were also safely hidden in the building. At the end of November or the beginning of December 1944, the Arrow Cross Party units tried to eliminate the labour service company. Eyewitness and survivor Gábor Dénes was a small child during the events:

> One day (perhaps around noon), suddenly, all the adults came home, and we had to go to the inner yard for assembly. Armed Arrow Cross Party members were running everywhere, shouting orders.
>
> We were standing there for a very long time, and it was said that they would take us all, and they were waiting for the order. According to my memories, my mother was also afraid that they might just shoot us down then and there because she knew from the scarce news that in Budapest,

> there were mass executions everywhere. At some time – yet before the evening twilight, so around early afternoon – the Arrow Cross Party members suddenly vanished and German soldiers on trucks arrived in the yard. We were immediately sent back to the classrooms, to the "living rooms". From that date on, there was a German military guard constantly in the school, and they never harassed anybody and were guarding the Jews against the Arrow Cross militants. One afternoon, they just "disappeared", and the liberating soldiers arrived on the night of that day. (According to my mother's account, they were Romanian soldiers). My mother later mentioned many times that the German military commander had received a telephone call – asking for help – from the Jewish "commander" of the "local community".[309]

The event is known from various other sources as well.[310] During the roundup by the Arrow Cross Party militants, two labour service workers were able to sneak out of the building in Abonyi Street, and they warned Ocskay, who soon arrived with armed German soldiers and chased the Arrow Cross Party militants away. Unfortunately, we do not know exactly to whom Ocskay appealed in this case. It is certain, however, that the incident fell within the jurisdiction of the *Wehrmacht-Standort-Kommandantur-Budapest*, which was stationed at the time in Hotel Astoria and which Ocskay could easily reach. Considering that at that time, the City Command could only issue orders to the *Waffen-SS Wachbataillon* stationed in and around Hotel Royal and its surroundings on Grand Boulevard, it is logical to assume that they would have been the first to respond to the incident. At the same time, it is unlikely that Karl Pfeffer-Wildenbruch had anything to do with this event, partly because he was based in Buda all the time (around the date in question, in Werbőczy [Táncsics] Street) and partly because his position clearly implied that he was not responsible for the affairs of the rear areas.

The third case is related to the Danish legation. Its residency at 27 Kelenhegyi Street was stormed by Arrow Cross Party militants on 24 December 1944 and the following day. In both cases, they were looking for Wallenberg, who was not in the building. Instead, they took the cook, two Hungarian Jews she had hidden, and the embassy driver, who was soon released. It was the driver's intervention that likely led to the arrival of German soldiers who remained there until the end of the siege.[311]

In theory, during the breakout attempt, Remlinger was assigned, together with the commander of the *Wehrmachtstreifengruppe z.b.V. 26*, Eberhard von Oetinger,[312] to the 22nd SS Cavalry Division.[313] He was captured on an unknown date and in an unknown location. A contemporary account, however, provides details that give a clearer view of this case.

Dénes Kövendi[314] chose the exact day of the breakout attempt to visit his father and his sister, who were sheltered in the Baár-Madas High School. He set off from Kende Street in District XI. He knew nothing of the unfolding events and, taking a wide detour, he avoided the Castle District and the Southern Railway Station, took a route via the northeastern slopes of the Kis-Sváb-hegy and then crossed the Városmajor. On Hieronymi (today: Határőr) Street, three young men joined him:

> One of my companions was speaking a lot; he was telling stories about his war deeds: of course, they started wearing civilian clothes only very recently. We did not meet a living soul. However, as soon as we got to the avenue [*fasor*], on the opposite side, at least twenty dead soldiers were lying on the pavement. I think they were Hungarians and Germans as well. We did not check them out thoroughly, but we saw that on the ground floor of the building (it seemed to be a large shop, completely burnt out), even more dead soldiers were lying on the floor. It was a similarly gloomy scene, like in one of Bergman's films (perhaps in *Shame*), when the dead soldiers' bodies floated en masse on the surface of the sea. I still do not understand today how these soldiers ended up there, so many of them: we did not see other dead bodies in the vicinity, and obviously, nobody had either the time or the capacity to collect them in one place. Perhaps, during the breakout attempt, they were sheltering here to avoid heavy shelling, and later, they wanted to give themselves up, but instead of taking them captives, had they just been gunned down?
>
> I left my companions: they were going in another direction, and I had to go up Trombitás Street. I had heard in the autumn that a former classmate of mine lived there at number 2, so it was only natural that I should drop by and ask what was going on.
>
> As soon as I entered the building, I was genuinely frightened for the first (and last) time during the whole siege. In the stairwell from the front door of the building to the first floor were at least 10-15 people who appeared to be high-ranking German officers. Their uniforms were somewhat worn, but their gold stripes were shiny, and the red side stripes on the trousers of some of them were a striking contrast to the grey-clad corpses we had seen a few minutes earlier. I'll tell you, I was very frightened: we were programmed to think that we should be afraid of the Germans and that the Soviets would liberate us (albeit in a somewhat unpleasant way). Now, in my first shock, I felt that I had been taken prisoner by the Germans. I mumbled something to them about why I was there but did not dare men-

> tion my former classmate – I just wanted to get out of the gate as quickly as possible! I got the feeling that they were in no mood for world conquest, either. In fact, my appearance seemed to frighten them a little: they were probably thinking that if they were not going to escape capture, it should happen quickly. They asked me if I had seen any Russians. I told them no, not nearby. Can I go further up the street? – I asked, meaning, "Will you let me go free?" One of them said: *"Als Zivil können Sie gehen"* [As you are a civilian, you can go] – and I got out of there as fast as I could.[315]

Kövendi must have met Remlinger and his *Stab* because other high-ranking German officers could not have been there; →*Rumohr* and →*Zehender* were seriously wounded and had fallen, →*Dörner* was heading out with the Devil's Ditch (Ördögárok) group, and →*Hitschler* was lying in the hospital. Although staff officers could have also worn red side stripes on their trousers, only four such staff officers had been present in Budapest, and we have clear details on the movement and whereabouts of only two of them, →*Erhard Mainka*, and →*Bodo Schaper*.

Pavel Luknitsky, already mentioned above, in his memoirs published in 1968, recalls the last minutes of Remlinger's life as follows:

> Approximately five minutes before 1100 hours, the huge, three-tonne trucks arrived in the square via the wide gap. They turned and stopped right next to the gallows. On each gallows were five *NKVD* soldiers with battle helmets and drawn faces. I did not see the accused at once; they were covered by the sides of the trucks, lying down or half lying down. Suddenly, I could see their faces. […]
>
> Remlinger was sitting on the left, and Engel on the right on the fourth, last truck. This truck could not park properly for a while; it went into reverse and then forward again, but every time one of the wheels got stuck on one of the gallows' supporting beams, and it began to creak. The *NKVD* soldiers helped the driver, and in the end, he parked exactly where he was supposed to. Almost everything was right-angled. Remlinger was wearing his officer's cap, and over his jacket, and under his cloak, a fur sheepskin jacket, the same one he had been wearing when he was captured in Budapest. His trousers were held in place by a white rag belt, the knot of which was hanging on his stomach. Remlinger wore good boots; some of the defendants were wearing boots, and the others combat boots. […]
>
> Remlinger struck a general's pose, standing up straight and holding his head unusually high. In his posture, you could see the unnatural stress

but also his effort to be seen as someone who remained undaunted in all circumstances, and his face was always calm. [...] He was staring ahead of him, his eyes fixed on an obscure point somewhere; he clearly saw nothing; he just wanted to show that he was staring death right in the eye.

The silence was shattered by the sound of the truck's sides opening downwards. [...] The commandant waved his hand, and on all of the trucks, the fifth soldier put the ropes around their necks. [...] The trucks began to move at once, very slowly. [...] All accepted death in silence, without any gestures...[316]

DECORATIONS	RANKS
• *Eisernes Kreuz II. Klasse* 1914	• *Leutnant* 1 August 1919
• *Eisernes Kreuz I. Klasse* 1914	• *Oberleutnant* 1 January 1921
• bar to denote subsequent awards of the *Eisernes Kreuz II. Klasse* 25 September 1943	• *Hauptmann* 27 March 1927
• *Kriegverdienstkreuz II. Klasse* 1 June 1941	• *Major* 1 July 1933
• *Kriegverdienstkreuz I. Klasse* 1 December 1942	• *Oberstleutnant* 1 March 1936
• He had been awarded an unidentified decoration in Budapest.[317]	• *Oberst* 1 August 1938
	• *Generalmajor* 1 December 1942

January 1944

Autumn of 1944

RUMOHR, JOACHIM

Joachim Rumohr was born on 6 August 1910 in Hamburg. He joined the *NSDAP* in 1930 (his party membership number was 216,161), and in 1931, he joined the SS (His SS number was 7450). In 1935, he joined the Waffen-SS, where he was assigned to the 3rd Battalion of *SS-Standarte 2* (later *SS-Standarte "Germania"*). From May 1938, he was the company commander of the 12th Company of the *SS-Standarte "Germania"* stationed in Radolfzell, and with this unit, he took part in the Polish campaign in 1939 and the *Westfeldzug* in 1940. His company, however, had other missions: in November 1938, this unit burned or blew up and looted synagogues in Konstanz, Wandegg, Gailingen and Randegg, and abused captured Jews who were then transported to Dachau concentration camp. Rumohr's personal involvement, like that of the majority of the unit, is not documented, nor is there any record of him being ill during the period in question.[318] The least that we can state is that he must have seen the stolen goods gathered in the garrison's yard. He must have heard stories of the looting, beating and deportation of the local Jewish population (Radolfzell itself was declared "free of Jews" in 1936 because the local authorities managed to remove civilians considered to be Jewish or of Jewish origin by administrative means, and this fact was announced on posters at the entrances to the town). Moreover, it would be very unrealistic to assume that, as a company commander, he was not actively involved in these actions.

Rumohr was promoted to commander of the II *Abteilung* of the artillery regiment of the *SS-Division "Reich"* at the beginning of January 1941. He took part in the campaign against the Soviet Union from the beginning. On 1 June 1942, he was promoted to regimental commander of SS Artillery Regiment of the SS Cavalry Brigade. He received the *Ritterkreuz des Eisernen Kreuzes* for the winter combat actions at the Dnieper River in the autumn of 1943 and for the combat actions between Kremenchug and Kirovograd in the winter of 1943.

Most probably, he came into contact with Hungarian troops for the first time in the summer of 1943. At this time, he substituted the *Generalstabschef* of the SS Cavalry Division. In this capacity, he commanded the anti-partisan combat activities near Mozhir (among others, the so-called *Operation Seydlitz*), in which the Hungarian "Ordas" detachment also took part. These operations mostly failed, as on the one hand, the partisans escaped in time, and on the other hand, due to the unrest erupting in Volhynia, the troops making up the greater part of the unit's strength had to be relocated. The above-mentioned *Operation Seydlitz* was aimed at destroying the villages north of the Dnieper River. The balance sheet of the operation was as follows: 2,768 people "annihilated in combat", 2,338 persons "done for", 603 prisoners of war, 6,817 evacuated residents, 807 destroyed "gang hideouts" and 54 villages burnt down. Apart from this, the operation blew up four major ammunition stores and acquired 17 pieces of heavy weaponry, 14 machine guns, 43 light machine guns and 471 handheld weapons. According to a German report, they had also succeeded in routing the 50-strong command staff of the partisan group – however, a different report admitted that the operation had ultimately failed because the Saburov partisan units managed to break through the encirclement towards the west. It is a telling sign that the ratio of acquired weapons to the number of massacred partisans was 1:10. There is no surviving data regarding German–Hungarian casualties.[319] Although the partisans also suffered losses, these operations merely caused organisational problems for them because several storage locations and hideouts had been destroyed and a number of panicking partisans had deserted.[320]

Joachim Rumohr (second from the right) in the Soviet operational area in 1942

On July 1, 1944, Joachim Rumohr was appointed commander of the 8th SS Cavalry Division then stationed in Hungary for reorganisation. At that time, the division's command was in Baja. His unit in Northern Transylvania began fighting the Soviet troops advancing from Romania in early September 1944. His division

With one of his children in the summer of 1944, in Hungary

held the "Maros Line" for two weeks and played a key role in the operations. Rumohr knew the battlefield not only from his map table: he regularly visited the first positions in his *Schwimmwagen* (a small amphibious vehicle). He was a popular leader; his soldiers remembered him as an understanding and thoughtful commander. The *Wehrmachtbericht* issued on 9 October 1944 especially mentioned his name in connection with the combat activities in Transylvania, which was considered to be a rare and high honour.

During the siege of Budapest, the 8th SS Cavalry Division was in defence in the Attila Line between Vecsés and Pécel. On 24 December, Rumohr's units were the first to be alarmed and relocated to the Buda side of the city. The 8th SS Cavalry Division commanded the defensive operations on the Buda side, on the section between the Sas-hegy and the Kiscell Mansion in Óbuda, together with several subordinate Hungarian unit fragments. Rumohr's command post was first located in the Center in the Rock (*Sziklaközpont*) on the Kis-Gellérthegy, and was later relocated to the MOM factory.

According to the account of →*Helmut Friedrich,* the adjutant of 13th Panzer Artillery Regiment, on 26 January 1945, at the end of the briefing held by Pfeffer-Wildenbruch, when those present openly criticised Hitler's stubbornness, an SS general left in a huff, clattering his footsteps and shouting in a voice that could be heard by all: "It is now clear to me that our men must be burnt up in Budapest!"[321] Friedrich did not give a name, but it is almost certain that the commander in question was Rumohr!

At the end of 1944, with an unidentified Hungarian officer

Rumohr received the *Eichenlaub* on 1 February 1945. The decoration itself was actually delivered to the recipient: *SS-Unterscharführer* Bödecker, who was one of the soldiers of the *Nach-*

In the area of Vecsés, in November 1944 – in front of him, in a coat and with binoculars, stands Joachim Boosfeld

richten-Brückenkopf Budapest in Bratislava (Pozsony), mentioned in his memoirs, written in 1945, that he was tasked with forwarding the exact time and location of the air delivery of the *Eichenlaub*.[322]

There are multiple accounts of Rumohr's death. The majority of the accounts (from altogether six persons) are consistent in that they give the time and location of Rumohr's death as the evening of 11 February in Széna Square. According to this, Rumohr was wounded on the Széll Kálmán Square–Széna Square side of Várfok Street in the first hour of the breakout attempt. →*Joachim Boosfeld* saw him a few minutes after being wounded, as he was shouting orders, and a few minutes later still, he heard the news spreading that the *Divisionskommandeur* had fallen. Many eyewitnesses saw his dead body, together with the dead body of →*Zehender*. The most detailed account was provided by Johannes Theli, who said that Rumohr was "hit by a machine-gun round, which hit his lower body and thighs. As rescue was not possible, he shot himself".[323] However, two other accounts mention completely different circumstances. Endre Fazekas, a resident of Budapest, remembered as follows:

> [...] A prisoner of war was brought to the empty lot opposite us, the body of a fallen German general. They brought it to the street yard of our house at 33 Keleti Károly Street and covered it with a quilt. He was a middle-aged man, extremely well-groomed and dressed, who, according to the Russians, had failed to stop when warned and had therefore been shot. I only saw him lying on his back; there was no sign of a shot. At the end of one arm of his jacket was a ribbon with the inscription "Florian Geyer". The next day, however, his boots were no longer on his feet, and in the days that followed, he himself was taken away, so we did not bury him, an activity the Russians carried out with us in the area.[324]

Fazekas did not mention Rumohr by name, but Rumohr was the only one to wear the "Florian Geyer" armband in the rank of general. It is also possible, of course, that Fazekas confused the rank insignia and markings of staff officers and

November 1944, in the Attila I. defence line

generals. It is all the more possible because, as has been mentioned earlier, the shoulder straps were only slightly different; the red textile strip was also worn by officers belonging to the *Artillerie*, and staff officers could also wear two red side stripes (*Lampasse*) on their trousers. In the 8th SS Cavalry Division *Florian Geyer* only one staff officer was in service then, *Major i.G. →Erhard Mainka.*

There is yet another eyewitness account that is even more baffling. Kálmán Kohányi escaped from Hungary in 1956. On 11 February 1958, he sent a two-page letter in Hungarian to the Dortmund office of the German Red Cross. As this letter is a rare document, it is worth quoting a longer passage from it:

> [...] I report for registration that at the end of the Second World War, the commander of the German units defending Budapest and encircled in the Buda Castle area, SS General Joachim Rumohr, was captured by the Russians in the early morning hours of 12 February 1945 during an attempt to break out of the Castle after sustaining gunshot wounds to his head. The general, who was bleeding profusely, was laid on a ladder tied up by the Russians and taken to Budapest II district, 12 Bogár Street, where the commander of a Russian artillery division, a Staff Major [Major General?], the commander of the Russian artillery units providing artillery fire during the siege of the Castle had his headquarters. I myself was a resident of the above-mentioned building at 12 Bogár Street, and it was precisely because of the garrisoning of the Russian soldiers that all 21 residents of the five flats in the building were crammed into my flat. I saw SS General Joachim Rumohr, still alive, at 9.30 on the morning of 12 February 1945, from the first-floor window of the building, lying on a ladder in the courtyard, covered with his cloak, being laid out in the courtyard by the Russian soldiers who were carrying him. [sic!] I remember that the General's bullet wound in the left temple was oozing blood, and his complexion was very waxy

> yellow from the great loss of blood. He even noticed me peeping out from behind the window frame and looked up at me, but his eyes remained that way. His body was personally searched by the Russian Staff Major. His identity was established from the documents he had taken. His rank was visible anyway. At the request of the Russian Staff Major, the civilians of a nearby house dug separate graves for him and two other German soldiers of unknown identity. As I was then working for the Swedish Red Cross, he asked me to have a headstone made for the German General. He asked that the text of the headstone and the inscription on the cross be made according to the drawing on the side of our mailbox. He personally determined the direction of Berlin with a compass and ordered that the dead should be buried facing homeward, and I quote his words, "he deserves it; he died as a hero for his country". On the grave, the Russian Staff Major placed a German assault helmet. Unfortunately, I was unable to fulfil my promise of erecting a wooden cross on the grave, which was forbidden by the newly organised red armband police, which had been informed about it. The three graves were located on the then-empty plot opposite the building at 12 Bogár Street, Budapest II (Rózsadomb). I personally laid flowers on the graves every year on 12 February and 1 November at night. Otherwise, at all times of the year, the neighbouring residents used to lay flowers of condolence on the graves at night. This was going on until the night of 24 July 1949, when the Hungarian *ÁVÓ* [political police] dragged me away at night from my apartment at 12 Bogár Street mentioned above. Since then, I know nothing of the fate of the graves.[325]

The letter quoted above immediately raises several questions. Firstly, the writer of the letter used to run a Jewish children's home at 29 Bogár Street and also rescued people from the Óbuda Brickworks and Szent István Park on several occasions.[326] His brother was caught as a deserter and sentenced to death.[327] Kohányi served as an ensign in the First World War and spent a long time as a Russian prisoner of war – so in 1945, he was actually able to talk to Soviet officers. What is particularly interesting is that, as a rescuer of Jews, he did not find it at all controversial to look after the grave of an SS general. His gesture is quite understandable in view of the fact that the Jewish children's homes were not under threat from SS soldiers. In fact, it was SS soldiers who moved the sheltered children from 29 Bogár Street to the Légrády villa near the Baar-Madas Grammar School when the front line reached the former site. The Lutheran pastor and rescuer Gábor Sztehlo, who lived in the villa, was at first startled when SS soldiers banged on his door:

When I opened the door, I almost burst into laughter when I saw the little thing with characteristic Semitic traits around the neck of the German soldier, warming his cold hands on the soldier's neck. The well-built lad took the little creature off his shoulders with a serious look on his face and handed it to me with great care. By this time, I was crying rather than laughing. What God does to preserve these children! After the boys had arrived, I went to the commander of the German frontline section to thank him for his help.[328] He received me kindly and dismissed my thanks by saying that it was only natural... None of us had said anything about who these children were, but I immediately felt (and he told me once later) that he knew very well who they were and what kind of work we were doing.[329]

However, it is more difficult to explain how and why Rumohr was moved from Széna Square to Bogár Street. Kohányi would have had no reason to write untruths in 1958, and his report is quite detailed, so there is reason to believe that his story is true. The only possible explanation for the story is that Rumohr committed an unsuccessful suicide on the night of 11 February, and when the Soviets discovered the high-ranking officer the next morning, he was immediately taken to a higher headquarters. In the chaos of the outbreak, Rumohr's subordinates may not have realised that their commander was still alive. Zehender, who was lying in the same place as him, or at least not far from him, was probably not taken away because he was already dead.

The empty plot on Bogár Street was completely built up in the 1970s. Kohányi's letter may also have reached the Rumohr family, as a group of middle-aged and elderly German tourists were passing by at the time, looking for the body. In 1977, a report in the newspaper *Der Freiwillige* also seems to confirm Kohányi's version. In 1978, former SS soldier Georg Weiner visited Hungary and met his Hungarian comrades. Shortly afterwards, he received a letter from one of them:

[...] After the breakout attempt, as a resident of Buda, I simply went home and dressed in civilian clothes. Shortly afterwards, on 14 or 15 February, I noticed several Waffen-SS prisoners of war in uniform, accompanied by Russian soldiers, near my apartment on the Rózsadomb. There was also a Russian captain or major with this group. The POWs were carrying a wounded man. The man had attempted suicide but was still alive. Judging by his uniform, he was a senior SS officer. The group stopped in front of a house, and at that moment, the wounded man passed away. The German was then buried in the empty plot next to the house, a process

> in which civilians, including myself, had to assist. After the funeral, the Russian officer said that this dead German soldier had been extremely brave. As soon as normal administration is restored in Budapest, this grave should be reported immediately so that he can be buried with military honours later. The Russian officer, immediately after his death, put the German's personal papers in a tin box and placed it in his blouse pocket. During the search of the body at the funeral, a small pocket photo album fell out of another pocket. I kept this album for years, but what a misfortune. I lost it when I moved in the 1950s. Only one photo remained, showing a lady, presumably in Venice.[330]

The death of Rumohr is also registered in the war log of the Soviet 109th Heavy Howitzer Artillery Brigade, although in a slightly different manner:

> At dawn on 12 February 1945, at the [infantry] position of the 7th Battery on Kis Rókus Street, artilleryman Kuzmichev noticed that a group of German soldiers led by a general was trying to cross the street. Red soldier Kuzmichev fired a volley of submachine gun fire at the enemy group, who immediately fell to the ground and returned fire with rifles and submachine guns. Several soldiers from the 7th Battalion rushed to the aid of red soldier Kuzmichev, and a sustained firefight ensued. The fighting destroyed most of the German group, and a few prisoners were taken. At dawn, it was discovered that one of the bodies belonged to Major General Rumohr of the SS Cavalry Division.[331]

According to the war log, Lieutenant Colonel Gyula Takátsy[332] and Major Rudolf Schindler[333] were taken captives at the same location. Not far from there, at the perimeters of the 12th Battery, the dead body of another supposed *Generalmajor* was found (in reality, this was the dead body of the already mentioned *Major i. G.* Erhard Mainka).[334] According to the unit history of the 109th Heavy Howitzer Artillery Brigade, written after the war, the positions of the 7th Battery were near the junction of the Kis Rókus Street–Keleti Károly Street, and Rumohr was hiding behind a soda car standing out in the street when he was hit by the submachine gun round.[335]

The interesting moral lesson of this story is that eight sources report Rumohr dying in three different ways. His suicide, death and "murder". can only possibly be reconciled if we suppose that Rumohr, as a Rasputin-like figure, first tried to take his own life but failed, and then along with others (or maybe alone) tried to take part in the breakout attempt during which a Soviet soldier wounded him, in consequence of which he finally died on Bogár Street. The truth will, in all probability, never be fully uncovered. It is also not known where Rumohr's body finally ended up or even if the body was exhumed. If the latter is the case, then his remains lie in a plot reserved for unknown soldiers.

DECORATIONS	RANKS
• *Eisernes Kreuz II. Klasse* 14 November 1939 • *Eisernes Kreuz I. Klasse* 28 August 1941 • *Deutsches Kreuz in Gold* 23 February 1943 • *Ritterkreuz des Eisernen Kreuzes* 16 January 1944 • *Eichenlaub* to the *Ritterkreuz des Eisernen Kreuzes* 1 February 1945 • During the siege of Budapest, he was awarded an unidentified Hungarian decoration. • *SS-Ehrenring* • *Ehrendegen RFSS*	• *SS-Untersturmführer* 4 November 1933 • *SS-Obersturmführer* 2 November 1935 • *SS-Hauptsturmführer* 9 November 1938 • *SS-Sturmbannführer* 21 June 1941 • *SS-Obersturmbannführer* 1 November 1942 • *SS-Standartenführer* 20 April 1944 • *SS-Oberführer* 9 November 1944 • *SS-Brigadeführer* 15 January 1945

1940

SCHAARSCHMIDT, HERBERT

Herbert Schaarschmidt was born on 10 January 1920 in Werdau, Saxony. His father had a junk shop. He attended only elementary school. In his military documents, he stated that his qualification was "worker" and his occupation was "cleaner". He started his military service on 15 October 1940 at the *Flak-Ersatz-Abteilung 12* in Berlin-Lankwitz. At the beginning of 1940, he was reassigned to 8th *Flak-Regiment,* which was tasked with the defence of the Leuna Works near Merseburg, a factory that manufactured synthetic fuel. Soon after that, Schaarschmidt was reassigned to the I *Abteilung* of the newly established 42nd *Flak-Regiment* in Berlin-Lankwitz.

Schaarschmidt had been trained to handle the *Flakvierling 38* (1938-type 2 cm four-barrelled automatic cannon). This artillery piece was handled by an eight-member crew. Besides the *Geschützführer* (gun commander), the crew members were marked *Kanoniere* (K1 to K7). The gun-pointer (K1), seated on a gun control seat, adjusted the elevation and lateral direction with two crank handles, i.e. he moved the gun barrels. Meanwhile, he aimed an electric periscope at the aircraft to be fired on and operated the firing pedal with his right foot. This crew member handled the most important tasks: the faster the enemy plane was, the faster he had to move the cranks to keep the target locked in his sights. He was assisted in this by the range finder (K2), who stood behind him and continuously adjusted the range data on a small board. The data was shouted out to him by the person making measurements with the electric device (K5).

The ammunition handlers (K6 and K7) fed the ammunition, and the loading was done by a separate person (K3). This shows that the crew of such a gun had to work very closely together if it was to be successful. Schaarschmidt's first job was to operate the electric measuring device (K5), for which he completed a two-month course in the autumn of 1941 and a one-month course in the spring of 1942. His unit remained essentially in the German Reich until 1944, carrying out anti-aircraft duties. All that is known of his service is that Schaarschmidt had accumulated 39 live combat days before he was appointed *Gefreiter* on 29 November 1944.

In the autumn of 1944, the unit was reorganised as the I *Abteilung* of *Flak-Regiment 40* and relocated to Hungary. The unit fought in Budapest under the 15th *Flak-Division* until December. Schaarschmidt took part in these battles from the outset as a gun-pointer (K1) with the rank of corporal. He was awarded the Knight's Cross of the Iron Cross on 9 February 1945. The award itself is something of an anomaly, as during the entire Second World War, only five German soldiers were awarded this decoration for destroying enemy aircraft with artillery. In comparison, almost 200 soldiers from the *Heer*, the *Luftwaffe*, the *Kriegsmarine* and the *Flak* units of the SS were awarded the decoration for successfully attacking ground targets.

Due to a lack of sources, the combat action cannot be precisely dated. According to a newspaper article of 31 January 1945, Schaarschmidt shot down six Soviet ground attack aircraft with his automatic cannon under heavy enemy fire in ten days but also took part in ground fighting. Over the next ten days, he destroyed two more aircraft. All this was achieved with very low ammunition consumption: the four-barrelled automatic cannon used no more than 268 pieces of ammunition. Willi Carl, a soldier serving in the *Hundestaffel*, *SS-Sanitäts-Abteilung 8* of the 8th SS Cavalry Division was most probably writing about Schaarschmidt in his account as follows:

> An anti-aircraft gun is stationed between the [Mátyás] church and our building. The gun-pointer is a young, spirited lad who received the Knight's Cross today. He shoots down four or five planes a day.
>
> At exactly ten o'clock, the Russian planes come and drop their bombs on us, and he shoots at them without restraint, fulfilling his daily quota. He took particular pleasure in destroying a Soviet propaganda car in a single burst. From here we have a great view of the whole of Pest and, most importantly, a great view of the streets leading to the Danube opposite. When the Russians tried again to position the car with the loudspeakers and subject us to their propaganda slogans for all evening, he targeted the car so precisely that the whole thing fell to pieces on the first burst, and there was nothing left of the loudspeakers. It was a real pleasure at last.[336]

The further fate of Schaarschmidt is completely unknown. Considering that he received the *Eisernes Kreuz II. Klasse* on 19 December 1944, and the *Eisernes Kreuz I. Klasse* on 23 January 1945; it is probable that both decorations were awarded for the already mentioned twenty-day period of combat action. This is all the more probable because, in his case, the processing time of the award must have been longer: the recommendation for his award must have been sent to Berlin by the end of December – unless this was a case of an extraordinary recommendation, expedited by a telegram sent by →*Pfeffer-Wildenbruch* himself.

Schaarschmidt was obviously trapped in the encirclement; however, we do not know what happened to him after the end of combat actions. The vast majority of his unit did not survive the siege: 43 persons were registered as missing in action from his unit alone – however, he was not among them. Unfortunately, no summary list of the names of the enlisted men who took part in the breakout attempt and escaped successfully has ever been compiled. Therefore, whether he managed to get out of the capital is unknown. At the same time, there are no hospital treatments recorded on Schaarschmidt's personal files after 1943, and as his place of residence was not in West Germany but in the Eastern occupation zone of Germany, he was not eligible to apply for compensation for any period he might have spent in prisoner of war camps either; in other words, there is no information available to indicate whether he was a prisoner of war or not. The only available data in connection with him is the secondary copy of his paybook, which was found near Salzburg in the spring of 1945 and taken to the *Sudetendeutsche Bildungswerk* organisation, from which, in 1998, the document was transferred to the *WASt.*

The copy of the paybook was not kept by the owner but theoretically by the personnel department of his unit. Therefore, Schaarschmidt's paybook was empty after the autumn of 1944. With some degree of probability, it can be assumed that the headquarters offices of the unit had left Budapest in the autumn or a few weeks before the beginning of the siege, and as Schaarschmidt must have been registered as missing at the end of the siege, his paybook records were not updated at the headquarters. After 1945, Schaarschmidt had no connections with his past or the war – the authorities in East Germany would not have left too many possibilities for this. He lived to see the reunification of Germany and died in his hometown on 13 March 1993.

DECORATIONS	RANKS
• *Eisernes Kreuz II. Klasse* 19 December 1944 • *Eisernes Kreuz I. Klasse* 23 January 1945 • *Ritterkreuz des Eisernen Kreuzes* 9 February 1945	• *Gefreiter* 29 November 1944

1934

1938–1942

SCHACK, HANS VON

Hans von Schack was born on 6 April 1913 in Gotha as a descendant of the Coburg branch of a well-known northern German noble family. He attended the officer's training course and started his military service in 17th Cavalry Regiment. He took part in the Polish campaign of 1939 with the cavalry regiment subordinated to the 7th Infantry Division. From 14 February 1940, he served as the commander of the 8th Squadron of the *Reiter-Regiment 2* until 15 April 1941, when he was wounded. On 22 November 1941, he was reassigned to the reconnaissance company of the 559th Infantry Regiment. Between March and May 1942, he was the commander of the I Battalion of the 559th Infantry Regiment. His assignments after that are not known. On 25 January 1943, he was lightly wounded by mortar shells in the area of Kelkolovo, south of Lake Ladoga. Although wounded, he did not leave his military service post; however, two days later, he was seriously wounded by mortar shells again on his right leg. He was treated in hospital for an entire year. According to his assessment files from March 1944, due to his medical condition, he was to be reassigned to the armoured troops as *Abteilungscommandeur* (battalion commander). However, this was not realised. From January to August 1944, he was assigned to the German contingent in Romania as a cavalry training commander.[337] He was lucky to be part of the cavalry training course, as the cavalry advisors of the German contingent in Romania were subordinated to the cavalry officer training school in Sibiu (Nagyszeben); after the Romanian armistice, the officers serving there, led by colonel Joachim Macholz, were able to reach the Hungarian–German troops in the northern parts of Transylvania.[338]

According to his prisoner-of-war compensation form submitted in 1955, he was promoted to commander of 16th SS Cavalry Regiment of the 8th SS Cavalry Division in September 1944. During this period, one of his close relatives was executed for taking part in the assassination attempt against Hitler. From December 1944, the combat-ready parts of the Hungarian 12th Reserve Division, which was reported to have 76 officers and 1,183 soldiers in three groups called battalions, were subordinated to his regiment.[339] The recommendation documents for his award of the *Ritterkreuz des Eisernen Kreuzes* have not survived; however, a short article might shed some light on the causes:

> Four times the Bolshevists broke into the long and disjointed line of the regiment with the strength of two companies. Major Hans von Schack launched a counterattack with only twenty men, cutting the enemy's rear communication lines and relieving two encircled companies. Although a handful of his men were attacked by the Bolshevists from the north, he managed to disperse the enemy completely.[340]

As the 16th SS Cavalry Regiment was in defence around this time between the Orbán Hill (Orbán-hegy) and the Rózsadomb; the events described above most probably happened in this area. The same events have been described in a similar manner in the telegram of →*Pfeffer-Wildenbruch* sent to the 6th Army:

> [The Regiment of Hans von Schack] has, since the cauldron battle, repulsed and cleared 93 assaults of company-strength units and eight assaults of battalion-strength units. On 14 January 1945, acting on his own initiative and without considering the possible risks, he took his 20 men. He relieved two encircled companies, cutting off the enemy's lines of communication and scattering the enemy troops. He rebuilt the main line of defence at the most critical section of the defences and destroyed the enemy in the rear.[341]

It is worth noting that there was an extremely short time between the recommendation and the actual award of the decoration. Although Pfeffer-Wildenbruch's telegram is undated, the earliest date he could have sent it was 15 January 1945; just twelve days later, Schack had already received the decoration – at least on paper.

Schack took part in the breakout attempt and was captured at an unknown location on 13 February 1945. During his internment in 1950, he was sentenced to 25 years of correctional labour and the sentence was not altered by his appeal either. He was released on 13 December 1955. The government in West Germany paid him 5,760 German marks in compensation for his years spent in captivity – at that time, this was the equivalent of approximately 13 months of income. He lost his two children on 22 February 1945 in a bombing raid. Hans von Schack died on 3 April 1978 in Germany.

In April 2004, the Thies Auction House sold his documents and decorations for 12,500 EUR.[342] The *Ritterkreuz des Eisernen Kreuzes* was probably handed over to his wife in the first half of 1945 (unless the auction house added it later to the compiled inheritance).

DECORATIONS	RANKS
• *Eisernes Kreuz II. Klasse* 5 January 1940	• Senior ensign 1934
• *Eisernes Kreuz I. Klasse* 22 May 1942	• *Leutnant* 1 April 1935
• *Verwundetenabzeichen in Schwarz*	• *Oberleutnant* 1 August 1938
• *Ritterkreuz des Eisernen Kreuzes* 27 January 1945	• *Major* 1 February 1943 (extraordinary promotion)

1943–1944

SCHAPER, BODO

Bodo Johann Wilhelm Ernst Schaper was born on 13 May 1915 in Hamburg. Not much is known about the early stages of his military service, but it is safe to assume that he intended to serve as a commissioned officer from an early age. On 1 September 1939, he was assigned as platoon commander in the 9th Battery of III *Abteilung* of the 20th Artillery Regiment; by 19 December, he was already the *Abteilungsadjutant*. From 7 January 1941, he served as *Adjutant* in the 20th Infantry Division *(mot.)*. From 16 August 1942, he was assigned to the 11th Company of the 76th Infantry Regiment *(mot.)*, and from 16 October, he was reassigned to the III Battalion of *Grenadier-Regiment (mot.) 76*; however, at the same time, he had also been assigned to staff training by the *OKH*. During the latter, he served in the *Stab* of the 226th Infantry Division and *Korück 559*. From 6 December 1943, he attended the *Kriegsakademie*, and on 1 August, he was assigned as a staff officer.

In his assessment dated 9 April 1942, his superiors described him as "of superior knowledge and being extremely clever". According to his assessment dated 20 January 1943, he was a "sincere, honest personality, an enthusiastic soldier, who asked out of pure enthusiasm to be reassigned from the artillery to the infantry." The *Kriegsakademie Hirschberg* described him as follows:

> Tall, slim, athletic appearance. Honest and sincere personality. A calm and well-balanced person. He is fresh and has a good sense of humour; he knows what he wants and how to achieve it. He is ardent in his national socialist attitude. He has the appropriate skills in tactics. He performs reliably in

> every field. [...] He is interested in chemistry, technology, and war economy. His weak side: sometimes he is far too headstrong.[343]

After completing his studies at the *Kriegsakademie*, following the end of February 1944, his service assignments were hard to track accurately. In his personal files, it is stated that, for a short period, he was assigned to work with the commander of the *Sicherheitspolizei* in Cluj (Kolozsvár). However, there is no evidence of such an assignment, nor is it logical that a staff officer would have been sent there. In the same documents, it is also noted that from August 1944, he was assigned to the 560th Mapping Group belonging to *Armeegruppe Fretter-Pico*. In other documents, however, it is stated that from 5 August 1944, he was assigned to the *XIII. SS-Armeekorps,* which was under organisation at that time and was subsequently deployed on the French border.[344] This latter version of events is the most credible of all. He was assigned as the *Generalstabsoffizier (Ia)* of the *IX. Waffen-Gebirgskorps* on an unknown date, but certainly before November 1944.

Only scarce details of his activities are available during the siege of Budapest. Ferenc Kovács X., head of the operations department of the Hungarian I Army Corps, remembered him as being an understanding and correct comrade who frequently visited the frontline troops (as opposed to his superiors). Only one account is available regarding his death, and it is based on hearsay; as per this account, Schaper was killed by a direct artillery hit while taking cover in a cellar entrance.

On 17 February 1972, the *Deutsche Handelsvertretung* (German Commercial Representation) in Budapest (there was no embassy or legation at that time) sent his identification card and one of his name cards to the responsible authorities in Berlin after Istvánné Kurali found them in her father's belongings after his death. According to the woman, Schaper died between 10 and 15 February 1945 at the corner of Alkotás Street and Márvány Street, and was buried there by his father. A few years later, the body was exhumed and transported to an unknown location.

DECORATIONS	RANKS
• *Eisernes Kreuz II. Klasse* 3 October 1939 • *Eisernes Kreuz I. Klasse* 10 July 1940 • *Deutsches Kreuz in Gold* 22 January 1945	• *Hauptmann* 1 July 1942 • *Major* 1 July 1944

Around 1939

1940–1944

SCHITTHELM, KARL

Karl Schitthelm was born on 10 October 1910 in Marthashausen (today: Morzewiec) near Bromberg (today: Bydgoszcz, Poland), which at that time belonged to the *Deutsches Kaiserreich*. He was drafted in 1940 and assigned to the 6th Company of the 66th Infantry Regiment, which was being set up near Vienna, where he served as a courier. He served in this position for the entirety of the war; at the beginning of 1945, he held the rank of *Obergefreiter*. There is no data available regarding his political views or activities, but it is known that he was a member of the *NSDAP*.

He was decorated with the *Ritterkreuz des Eisernen Kreuzes* on 7 February 1945. The background for the award was that on 8 January 1945, between Herminamező and Törökőr, Schitthelm was separated from his unit during the retreat, and he alone delayed the advancing Soviet units for hours by holding a house in a key position. He achieved this by picking up abandoned weapons and running from window to window, firing from different positions, giving the impression that a larger German force was guarding the house. For this Schitthelm was awarded the *Eisernes Kreuz I. Klasse* and *II. Klasse* on 15 January 1945, at the same time as being recommended for the *Ritterkreuz* of the Iron Cross. The latter was awarded to him on 7 February 1945. The news reached Schitthelm; however, it is not known whether or not the decoration was actually awarded to him. Schitthelm was wounded during the siege of Budapest on an unknown date, but he remained mobile. During the breakout attempt, he went missing; he was last seen on the evening of 11 February 1945.[345] The Hildesheim Court declared him officially dead on 19 January 1962.[346]

DECORATIONS	RANKS
• *Eisernes Kreuz II. Klasse* 15 January 1945 • *Eisernes Kreuz I. Klasse* 15 January 1945 • *Ritterkreuz des Eisernen Kreuzes* 7 February 1945	• Dates of promotions are unknown.

Before 1934

January 1944

Autumn of 1944

SCHMIDHUBER, GERHARD

Gerhard Schmidhuber was born on 9 April 1894 in Dresden as the oldest son of a factory owner. He joined the Royal Saxon Army as a one-year volunteer on 1 April 1914, where he served in the 177th (12th Royal Saxon) Infantry Regiment.[347] His regiment served on the Western Front for the entirety of the war. On 26 September 1914, he was wounded in the right shoulder by a gunshot. On 16 April 1916, he became the *Adjutant* of the III Battalion of the 177th (12th Royal Saxon) Infantry Regiment. He took part in the combat actions around the River Aisne and the battles on the Somme. On 12 December 1917, he was promoted to *Regimentsadjutant*; however, he also commanded the *Minenwerfer-Kompanie* (mortar company) for a short period. On 21 January 1920, he was discharged and, as a civilian, worked first as a merchant, later taking over his father's cardboard factory. Apart from this, between 1924 and 1929, he was active in the *Jungstahlhelm Wiking* (a comradeship organisation) as *Ortsgruppenführer* (local group leader). He took part in the training of three different groups as well. On 29 September 1920, he married Helene Baumfelder, who was a British citizen; they had two sons together.[348] In 1933, he was employed again as *L-Offizier (Landesschutzoffizier)* – due to the restrictions of the Treaty of Versailles formally as a civilian employee; however, according to his assessment dated around this time, he was "too mild in his conduct, therefore, as of now, he is to be assigned only in case of increased emergency".[349] His future military career could not be deduced from such an assessment.

He was reactivated on 15 June 1934 as *Hauptmann* and assigned to 10th Infantry Regiment. On 10 November 1938, he was reassigned to 103rd Infantry Regiment and, in the first year of the war, served as the commander of the II Battalion here. With his unit, he took part in the Polish and French campaigns; he served in the Balkans, and from June 1941 on, he took part in the Soviet campaign. On 15 June 1940, his battalion was reorganised as a battalion of *Schützen-Regiment 103*. On 18 November 1941, he was seriously wounded near Rostov (both of his jawbones were shattered, and he lost his left eye). After his recuperation, on 1 May 1942, he was placed into the *Führerreserve* and assigned as a student at the *Panzertruppenschule*. On 11 July 1943, he was assigned as the commander of the 304th Panzergrenadier Regiment. With this assignment, he found himself right in the middle of the Battle of Kursk. He received the *Ritterkreuz des Eisernen Kreuzes* for his combat leadership activities in September 1943. Around this time, his unit was involved in preventive battles in the areas of Kiev and Chernigov against the superior Soviet troops.

His superiors during the war had described him at various times, as follows. In 1941: "He is an exemplary officer, a brave and energetic battalion commander, perfectly capable for the role of regiment commander, training school trainer and educator." In 1942: "He has distinguished himself several times with his personal bravery; in the gravest of situations, he has always been in the midst of the battle and moved his unit forward with the example of his personal bravery ."[350] In 1943, at the *Panzerschule Wünsdorf*: "As a reactivated officer, he lacks the years of peacetime experience and training. He tries to resolve all conflicts and hardships with untiring, arduous humbleness. He is harder on himself than on others." In August 1943, *Oberst* Fronhöfer wrote: "Self-aware, confident, balanced personality. He is well versed in the command duties of the warrant officer course, which he conducts with confidence and purpose. Has proven himself in the face of the enemy. Suitable for regimental command." *Generalmajor* Tröger, in the same place, added: "He is an able training course commander who is also a good candidate for commanding the entire school." January 1944, 2nd Panzer Division: "An exemplary officer with very high standards and ideals. He is not a rude personality; he has proven himself to be a perfect combat group commander in critical situations; he has a good sense of tactics and commands armoured units with confidence. He is able to pass on the national socialist ideals to his subordinates. His strong side is the subtlety and firmness of his character, which is paired with the utmost sense of responsibility towards himself and his subordinates. He is above average."[351] *General der Panzertruppe* Hermann Balck also noted his ability to get along with people, adding that "the excellence with which he does this has proven crucial in critical situations."[352]

Apart from this single note among these assessments, no information is available on whether Schmidhuber had identified himself with the national socialist ideology. In order to attempt to understand his personality better, two personal accounts are worth mentioning. On 16 October 1944, German field police intercepted a group of 20-30 Hungarian deserters in the Tiszántúl, whom they wanted to execute. Miklós Nagy, one of the deserters, spoke German, and a young German *Oberleutnant* interrogated him and then led him to Schmidhuber. Schmidhuber was, based on his appearance as described by Nagy, "a typical Prussian gentleman" and only interested in whether the Hungarians had experienced any mistreatment at the hands of the German units, as he wanted to punish those who plunder. Ultimately, the deserters were not harmed in any way and were quietly released.[353] During the siege of Budapest, Schmidhuber was allegedly worried about having taken a Persian rug from the Royal Palace of Gödöllő, where the command post of the division was stationed for a time. He gave 100 *Pengő*s (*Pengő* was the Hungarian national currency) to Staff Captain Benyovszky so that he could help a poor man with this money, as his conscience was troubled about the rug.[354]

On 1 February 1944, he was again placed into the *Führerreserve* and completed the 9th course at the *Kriegsakademie Hirschberg*. During this time, he received the *Deutsches Kreuz in Gold*, the recommendation for which has not survived; however, it seems to be obvious that he must have been rewarded for his combat leadership and personal bravery in November–December 1943, as his unit was transferred to France in early January 1944.

In May 1944, Schmidhuber took over the command of the 7th Panzer Division as an acting commander.

The unit first was in defence in front of the Carpathian passes, and then, from July on, a part of the *Heeresgruppe Nord*. On 9 September 1944, he was appointed acting commander of the 13th Panzer Division, which was being reconstituted in the Örkénytábor area, and on 1 October, he became full commander. Most of the corps had been destroyed in Romania two weeks earlier, and its reconstitution was made possible by the absorption of units from the 109th Panzer Brigade.

On 6 October 1944, Schmidhuber's division, before the completion of its reestablishment, was deployed in response to the offensive of the 2nd Ukrainian Front. The 13th Panzer Division played a significant role in the mobile manoeuvres of the armoured battle near Debrecen. It would be misleading if we consider only the combat strength of the 13th Panzer Division and the number of combat-ready tanks at its disposal, as the unit drew its strength mainly from the heavy weapons transported on armoured personnel carriers (heavy mortars, three-barrel automatic cannons, guns). The 13th Panzer Division was deployed in defence in the area of Valkó in November, and in early December, it was relocated into the Attila I Defence Line in front of Isaszeg and Gödöllő; from here, the 13th Panzer Division retreated north of the Mogyoród–Pécel line in mid-December. From the end of November 1944, the 10th Hungarian Infantry Division and the 12th Hungarian Reserve Division were also subordinated to Schmidhuber (the latter, however, was again subordinated to the 8th SS Cavalry Division from 10 December onwards). At the same time, the main Soviet attack was also shifted to the Schmidhuber group. On 20 December 1944, a *Wehrmachtbericht,* without mentioning the Hungarian troops, specifically highlighted his name:

> In the fierce defensive battles in the Budapest area, two divisions of officers, NCOs and men, composed mainly of SA members, the *Feldherrnhalle* Panzergrenadier Division under Major General Pape and the 13th Panzer Division under Major General Schmidhuber, distinguished themselves with outstanding courage and vigorous attacks.[355]

However, this was not as ideal in reality as it might have seemed from the article. It is unknown who within the German military leadership came up with the idea of "giving" the SA a division in addition to the *Feldherrnhalle* Panzergrenadier Division, which was initially made up of a small number of SA members.[356] The idea itself may possibly be explained by the "organised chaos" prevalent within the system created by Hitler; in this environment, Hitler's subordinates received varying prerogatives and privileges. These subordinates included members and representatives of the SA, which as an organisation significantly decreased in number and strength after 1934.

At the same time, by 1944, SA membership within the *Feldherrnhalle* Panzergrenadier Division was a rarity, as the majority of the founders had been killed first at Stalingrad and then in the Minsk area in the summer of 1944. Nevertheless, all soldiers in the division wore the brown *"Feldherrnhalle"* armband with white Gothic letters on a brown background, commemorating the Munich Beer Putsch, as a sign of the unit's association with the SA. *Feldherrnhalle,* or Field

Marshalls' Hall is a memorial building in Munich in front of which a brief armed confrontation with the police forces ended Hitler's coup attempt on 9 November 1923.

In September 1944, in Örkénytábor, the 110th Panzer Brigade *Feldherrnhalle* was subordinated to the 13th Panzer Division: the unit was previously established from the reserves of Panzergrenadier Division *Feldherrnhalle*; therefore, the soldiers serving in it wore the *"Feldherrnhalle"* armband. The officers of the 13th Panzer Division were not consulted about whether they wanted to work with the SA or, more specifically, with a unit under the patronage of the SA. Of the 16 officers included in this work who served within the 13th Panzer Division, only four were members of the SA,[357] and SA membership was definitely not prevalent among the enlisted men. It is not surprising, therefore, that within the 13th Panzer Division, many were repulsed by the connection with the SA – including the commander of the division.

Some of the soldiers did not even put on the brown *"Feldherrnhalle"* armband, all the more so because they had neither the time nor the opportunity to do so during the retreat and while cauldron battles were raging.[358]

It is characteristic of Schmidhuber's approach that he sent a report to the *Generalkommando* of the *III. Panzerkorps* regarding the combat strength of the Hungarian troops on 3 December 1944. In this report, he writes with great concern and understanding about the Hungarian army's problems. He blamed the low level of morale among the soldiers partly on the critically underdeveloped human resource management within the Royal Hungarian Army ("the provisions and attendance matters within the Royal Hungarian Army are not maintained and taken care of according to Wehrmacht standards").[359] Schmidhuber also criticised the Hungarian government's propaganda work as very counter-productive because it sharply contradicted the reality, which was apparent to everyone.[360]

From the middle of December 1944, the units of the 10th Hungarian Infantry Division were withdrawn from their subordination to the division command and resubordinated, in smaller groups, to the 13th Panzer Division. From the first half of January 1945, the 13th Panzer Division was the major force on the Pest side, and basically, Schmidhuber was in command. However, after relocation to the Buda side, the division's command duties practically ceased. The units, originally intended to stay in reserve, were deployed one by one on the various sections of the frontline in Buda, which left the *Divisionsstab* with mostly administrative duties. The war logs of the 13th Panzer Division kept until 29 December 1944 were airlifted out of the cauldron (presently, these documents either reside at an unknown location or have been destroyed). The remaining sections of the war logs, kept during the siege, were lost during the breakout attempt. Schmid-

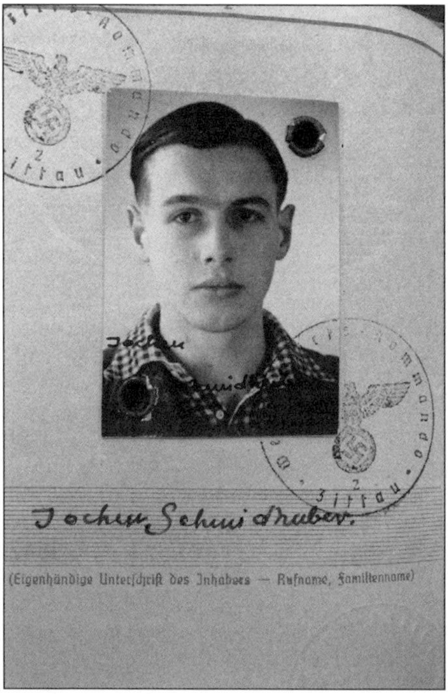

Service photographs of Schmidhuber's son, Jochen, who survived the war

huber learned of the death of his eldest son during the siege.

During the siege of Budapest, Schmidhuber's relationship with →*Pfeffer-Wildenbruch* was not entirely smooth and conflict-free. This was already apparent in the first days of 1945 when Pfeffer-Wildenbruch expressed his dissatisfaction regarding the strength of the 13th Panzer Division – he deemed the number of non-combatants too high – therefore, as a kind of political officer, he appointed *SS-Standartenführer* →*Helmut Dörner* as Schmidhuber's superior. The conflict was renewed on 16 January 1945 when Schmidhuber relocated his command post from the *Városháza* (City Hall) to Buda, however, Pfeffer-Wildenbruch ordered him, via Dörner, to immediately return to the Pest side, which was not an easy task in complete darkness via the destroyed bridges for an officer suffering from night-blindness – and the order had no sense whatsoever. On 2 February 1945, Schmidhuber held lengthy discussions with Pfeffer-Wildenbruch about the breakout. However, the commander of *Festung Budapest* remained adamant, even at this point. It also needs to be noted that until 6 February, the front was located in the vicinity of Sashegy and Farkasréti Cemetery, close to the Buda Hills, and this would have provided a much more favourable starting point for the endeavour than Széll Kálmán Square a week later.

Schmidhuber's most important deed was preventing the Arrow Cross Party and SS pogrom planned against the Jewish ghetto in District VII. The sources on the case are scarce as after 1948, the *ÁVH* (Államvédelmi Hatóság, State Security Police) was not interested in clarifying facts and events; on the contrary, it intentionally made the events even more obscure. One of the key witnesses, Police Chief Gyula Sédey, who had been taken captive in Budapest, was only handed over to the ÁVH by the Soviet authorities in 1950. After that, Sédey was tried and sentenced to death in a show trial, and only after the intervention of Olympic fencing champion Ilona Elek[361] was the sentence changed to life imprisonment. During the trial, Sédey was not even questioned about the plans for the destruction of the ghetto and its rescue, and he himself did not mention the matter, if only because he was not the main character in the story. It was only in his appeal that he indicated that he had risked his life to sabotage the planned operations and had thus succeeded in saving the inhabitants of the ghetto – which was in fact true, since he had previously ordered a hundred policemen to be stationed at the gates of the ghetto to protect it.

However, in 1945, it suddenly became important for a number of people that the events should be recorded for posterity. One such person was Pál Szalai, who was a former police liaison for the Arrow Cross Party, and thus, it was essential for him to be able to justify his actions. Between 1945 and 1951, he regularly appeared before the police to make confessions. During these interrogations, the story was expanded and enriched with further details, suggesting that the police were not utilising the information correctly. That is, in the case of repeated questioning, all the details that had been revealed during these years could have been assessed at once. At the same time, there is no apparent reason to think that there was a contradiction in what he said. On 17 February 1945, Szalai confessed the following at the political department of Budapest Police Headquarters, which was at that time stationed at 60 Andrássy Street:

> Gottstein, the head of the political department of the SS police, cited Adolf Hitler, who allegedly said that not a single Jew must escape the encirclement around Budapest. Gottstein then launched an operation to exterminate all Jews in the ghetto, as well as those who were residing in the so-called "protected houses". [...] On the last day, the commander of the police force deployed in the ghetto reported to me that an action was underway by the Arrow Cross Party, together with a number of Germans and police, to completely exterminate the ghetto. I telephoned German General Schmidhuber to ask him if he knew that his men, under the direction of the [Arrow Cross] Party organisation in District VII, were going to completely murder the inhabitants of the ghetto. On the German side, the operation would have been led by a captain called Mumi, and on the Party side by Vilmos Lucska.[362] The German general was persuaded by better judgment. He sent for Dr Ernő Vajna, the Party delegate from the West, and Major Kubisi [correct: Kubissy]. On my protest, he called Vilmos Lucska to account and immediately arrested one of the German soldiers who wanted to take part in the action.[363]

In September 1948, during his screening procedure, he added that the planned pogrom was to begin on the evening of the 15th and that some 500 SS soldiers had gathered at the Royal Hotel[364] because of this. In the 1948 trial of Imre Nidosi, he added that he had learned of the pogrom plan from "Miksa Domonkos[365] and others" and that Vilmos Lucska had been the responsible official for carrying it out from the Arrow Cross Party's side.

He first contacted Ernő Vajna, the Arrow Cross Party commissar, who dismissed him, saying that he knew about the matter and had even been involved in its management together with Nidosi.[366] The investigation protocol of the process also revealed that 500 Germans, 300 members of the Arrow Cross and 200 policemen had taken part in the operation. In his testimony, Szalai mentioned twenty-seven members of the party's military organisation from District VII, who were to be joined by other such members from other districts. At the time, he said that the German general "reacted sharply to the planned evil deed and took the following action: he disarmed the German sergeant present and sent a patrol to find Captain Mumi [...]".[367]

In his own trial, Vilmos Lucska denied all charges against him but admitted that Schmidhuber had summoned Mumi's man and had him disarmed and that the German general had indeed ordered Mumi's arrest (Lucska's denial was consistent with his denial of earlier murders).[368] Imre Nidosi, on the other hand, admitted that he had talks on the destruction of the ghetto and even related that the plans were finalised by 10 January:

> The idea was to let loose a large number of Party members and German soldiers on the ghetto overnight to carry out the necessary work and, after the liquidation was complete, to set fire to the ghetto. [...] However, before the operation was carried out, Kurt Rettmann was summoned, as I recall, by the German Wehrmacht commander in Budapest and General Schmidhuber, whose command post was in the City Hall building, and they protested against the planned operation. As I recall, Dr Vajna said something to the effect that Schmidhuber had threatened to impose military measures if we continued with our plans. At the same time, Vajna also said that Schmidhuber had probably called off the operation because of Wallenberg's intervention and said something to the effect that if Wallenberg had been caught, he would have been finished off. As I recall, about two days after this incident, we relocated to Buda, to the Foreign Ministry building where Erik Csiky had his headquarters, so the operation was not carried out.[369]

Police officer Ferenc Perjési, Pál Szalai's police liaison, confessed the following about this matter:

> A few days after I moved into the ghetto, I learned that members of the Arrow Cross Party, together with German soldiers, were planning to wipe out the entire ghetto in one big ambush. The meeting place for the participants was the Royal Hotel, which was widely known to be the place where the most trustworthy people of Nidosi gathered; therefore Nidosi must have known about this plan, and it is not entirely impossible that the whole plan was formulated on his direct orders. Of the action, or the possibility of it, I immediately informed Szalai, who took the necessary precautions and, in turn, informed the German General Schmidhuber, who, in the circumstances unknown to me, called off the whole action.[370]

The same was confessed by Police Captain Béla Kubissy (commander of the police forces in Pest), already mentioned in connection with →*Gottstein* on 6 March 1945, with the difference that he that he credited himself with saving the ghetto:

> I will also say that on 15 January, when the German SS forces wanted to massacre the ghetto (where there were supposedly 70,000 people) because of the alleged killing of eight German soldiers, I prevented this by going with Sédey to see the German General Schmidhuber and managed to prevent the armoured attack on the ghetto.[371]

In the context of the sometimes confusing testimonies, it should be noted that the people involved could not have known what the others would say or even whether General Schmidhuber was still alive or not. In any case, under the given political circumstances, it was inappropriate to praise the actions of a German general. It is obvious that the death of the eight German soldiers was a fiction invented by the perpetrators to justify their own murderous intentions.

It seems that a contemporary chronicler of that time was more interested in what really happened in the Pest ghetto in 1945 than the court. Jenő Lévai, in his book *The True History of the Miraculous Escape of the Pest Ghetto* (*A pesti gettó csodálatos megmenekülésének hiteles története*), based on what was said before the People's Court and on personal conversations, adds that Pál Szalai's initial impression was that Schmidhuber "kept himself at a distance from the German political generals who were there. Through a German *Oberleutnant* named Fritz, who was his interpreter, I immediately asked him to meet me". Schmidhuber then summoned Ernő Vajna and Kubissy, "whom he forced to prevent the evil deed as a result of my personal protest".[372] Another point in Szalai's favour is that he did not make himself the mastermind of the affair, but Wallenberg's colleague at the embassy, Károly Szabó. Szabó had already referred to this in his testimony to the People's Court in 1948:

> Around 10 January 1945, when Wallenberg was no longer in Pest or had gone to the Soviet troops to ask for help for his protégés, Pál Szalai came to me with the news that he had learned of a planned attack on the ghetto to be carried out by Arrow Cross men of District VII based in the Royal Hotel and German soldiers. [...] Szalai was confused and turned to me for help. I, as Wallenberg's representative, advised him to contact the commander of the German forces remaining in Pest and authorised him to protest on Wallenberg's behalf against the annihilation of the ghetto.[373]

This was, in turn, verified by the son of Károly Szabó as well, whose father later told the story this way:

> When Szalai asked my father for advice about the ghetto, my father immediately thought of the next room [next to the Arrow Cross liaison desk in the City Hall]. He suggested to Szalai that Schmidhuber was the "obvious" choice as he was the closest and that he should refer to Wallenberg as an authority (Wallenberg was not consulted); this would certainly help. Szalai did not speak German and talked to Schmidhuber through an interpreter. My father did not participate in this meeting; he only gave the idea.[374]

The fact that German and Hungarian soldiers had taken over the guarding of the entrances to the ghetto in the final days was confirmed by Lajos Kósa, a soldier of the I Battalion of the 6th Regiment. Kósa's unit was assigned to the 66/II Battalion of the 13th Panzer Division at that time. The company's strength at that time was 80-90 men, and the unit practically avoided any activity. Kósa recalls that around 15 January, they received orders in an envelope to occupy the ghetto area reinforced by a German platoon. The order was to remain there until the Arrow Cross evacuated Pest.[375]

There is also evidence that Schmidhuber had been approached earlier, most probably on 10 January, regarding the issue of the ghetto. This is not surprising since it had been part of the public discourse since January 1945 that the Arrow Cross was planning mass murder against the inhabitants of the ghetto, and these rumours were duly substantiated by the massacres that regularly took place. Per Anger, the second secretary of the Swedish legation and Wallenberg's assistant, recalled:

> The Arrow Cross Party members [...], driven by their fanatical hatred of the Jews, wanted to carry out a last-minute mass murder in the ghetto. When Wallenberg was informed of this, he demanded that the German commander, General Schmidhuber, prevent the massacre. Otherwise, he said, he would have Schmidhuber executed on the gallows as soon as the Russians arrived. Frightened by Wallenberg's words, Schmidhuber stopped the planned operation against the ghetto. In doing so, Wallenberg helped save another 70,000 lives.[376]

Per Anger (who, incidentally, mistakenly linked Schmidhuber to the SS, which is not a conclusive error given the chaotic circumstances) did not say whether he was present at the negotiation itself. It is also clear, however, that Schmidhuber did not fear prosecution because he had already reconciled to his fate as a soldier. His decision was motivated by moral considerations. Per Anger's account, which puts the date of the visit at 10 January,[377] is corroborated by Tamás Veres, Wallenberg's photographer, who told the Swedish diplomat Per Anger in 1979, János Dési in 1994 and the Washington Holocaust Memorial Museum in 2002 that Wallenberg had a meeting with a German officer around 10 January who gave him a paper stating that German soldiers were not allowed to enter the ghetto because it was under protection.[378] Veres presumably remembered the dates well, as his parents were shot by Arrow Cross members two days later. According to an interview with János Dési, this happened as follows:

Photo of Arrow Cross Party member Vilmos Lucska after 1945

> The secretary of the Swedish Embassy also managed to obtain a written promise from the German general that he would not allow the massacre to take place. Wallenberg asked Veres to make as many

> copies of the paper as possible. By this time, they were living in a cellar because the city was under siege. Wallenberg had Veres brought back to his parents' home, which had a small darkroom. Veres made contact copies of the document in the darkroom by candlelight as there was no electricity. He worked all night and managed to produce a good number of copies, albeit in a slightly stone-age way. Wallenberg came to pick him up the next day and thanked him but did not ask how he had managed without electricity or light. According to Veres, he didn't care about the details, especially as he didn't have the time for that – the important thing was to get the job done.[379]

On the German side, there is only one source that can be indirectly linked to the rescue of the Jews. This is not surprising, given that 99 percent of the documents produced during the siege were destroyed. Ernst Schweitzer, 4th adjutant of the 13th Panzer Division wrote the following about the identity check of a young SS soldier:

> He answered that he was cleaning up the ghetto. He proudly reported that he and his accomplices were executing thousands of people a day in the cellars of the Jewish quarter. I immediately took the young SS man, who was a "captured German" [i.e. of East European ethnic German origin] to the general, who arrested him and reported him to the Corps. He is taken away by an adjutant officer of the Corps. No one knows what will happen to him.[380]

An interesting fact about the anti-Jewish atrocities is that there is some evidence that the presence of the German military in itself had a moderating effect on the members of the Arrow Cross. Survivors of an execution on 20 December 1944 reported during the trial of Arrow Cross members based at the Royal Hotel that they had only escaped because the Arrow Cross men had stopped killing when the German soldiers appeared.[381]

In assessing Schmidhuber's role, it should be noted that with the exception of László Karsai,[382] even those historians who express doubts about the case admit that there was a plan to exterminate the ghetto and that Schmidhuber played a role in preventing its implementation. According to some views, however, it was Himmler,[383] not Schmidhuber, who made the final decision in this case. However, this hypothesis is not supported by any data; moreover, at the time in question, there was no longer any direct radio contact between Budapest and the *RSHA* – the only remaining channel was via *Heeresgruppe Süd*. In a matter of such importance, it would have taken longer for an answer to arrive from Berlin, and according to eyewitnesses, Schmidhuber made an immediate decision.

According to Karsai, however, there was no existing plan by the Arrow Cross Party to destroy the ghetto – the eyewitnesses simply made up their claims about the plan to destroy the ghetto and the story of its rescue in order to save themselves. However, this explanation is not sufficient and is inconsistent in many respects. On the one hand, it does not take into account that the eyewitness testimonies were recorded in such a way that many of the people in question were unable to speak to each other, making it impossible for them to agree on their false story. On the other hand, if these "false" statements were only aimed at saving themselves, there would have been no need to involve a high-ranking German officer. In theory, the usual line of communication did not even lead to Schmidhuber but to the head of the Wehrmacht Headquarters in Budapest, →*Heinrich Remlinger.*

It is also wrong to claim that the members of the Arrow Cross Party made their confessions about Schmidhuber under torture. Certainly, torture was involved in the case of these arrested persons. Still, it must be pointed out that even under these circumstances, they did not confess to all the mass murders they had committed – which leads to the conclusion that their confessions were not determined entirely by their torture. It should also be borne in mind that the investigators were not interested in extracting confessions that would only speak of a "plan", especially one that would effectively rehabilitate a high-ranking German officer. Karsai's argument that there was no plan to attack the Jewish ghetto is even stranger when we consider that all the witnesses in the People's Court trials confessed to this issue in unison, including Miksa Domonkos, one of the leaders of the ghetto. The events in Budapest under the rule of the Arrow Cross Party leave no doubt that there was an intention at the level of the party leadership to exterminate the Jews – and this was admitted by former Arrow Cross Party members who were agents of the State Security authorities in the 1960s.

Schmidhuber was awarded the *Eichenlaub* for his *Ritterkreuz des Eisernen Kreuzes* on 21 January 1945 for his leadership performance. The recommendation for this decoration has not survived. Observing the previous events, it might be assumed that Schmidhuber was awarded this distinction because of the previous combat performance of his division. Soon after that, he received another decoration. A letter from Győző Benyovszky, written during the siege, describes the events:

> [On 24 January 1945] together with my superior[384] and with the chief of staff of the other, 12,th Division[385] we walked to the German division com-

IM NAMEN D
VERLEI
DI
Hauptma
Stab/kgl.ung
EISERN
2. KL
Div.Gef.St.,

The Eisernes Kreuz-document of Győző Benyovszky, rolled up

> mander who was stationed in the caves of the Kis-Gellért-hegy,[386] who, together with members of his staff of officers, we recommended for the Hungarian decoration,[387] which was awarded yesterday in a ceremony.[388]

Schmidhuber started off with the second wave of the breakout attempt. He left his command post located in the vicinity of the Tunnel (*Budai Váralagút*) at 2030 hours, together with his staff. With the streets full of wrecked vehicles and advancing soldiers, he did not reach Széna Square until 2130.[389] His chances were very limited from the start, as his night blindness, as mentioned earlier, meant that he could see almost nothing in the dark. Running from Csalogány Street across Széna Square, he was fatally shot. *Hauptmann →Helmut Friedrich*, who started off immediately after him, recalled the events as follows:

> I was running through Széna Square with huge leaps, jumping over the tram rail, when I saw a familiar-looking cap among the bodies of my fallen comrades. It had a gold rim – the cap of the division commander.[390]

The news of his death was most probably reported by several officers who made it through to the German lines because, as early as 18 February, there was an entry in his personal files that he had fallen on 11 February 1945.

DECORATIONS	RANKS
• *Eisernes Kreuz II. Klasse* 9 May 1915	• *Reserve Leutnant* 8 September 1915
• *Albrechts-Orden Ritterkreuz II. Klasse mit Schwertern* 16 April 1916	• *Hauptmann* 15 July 1934
• *Eisernes Kreuz I. Klasse* 17 December 1917	• *Major* 1935
• *Verwundetenabzeichen in Schwarz* 3 September 1918	• *Oberstleutnant* 1 July 1941
• Bar to denote subsequent awards of the *Eisernes Kreuz II. Klasse* 29 September 1939	• *Oberst* 1 April 1942 (out of turn)
• Bar to denote subsequent awards of the *Eisernes Kreuz I. Klasse* 24 June 1940	• *Generalmajor* 1 October 1944
• *Anerkennungsurkunde des Oberbefehlshabers des Heeres für hervorragende Leistungen auf dem Schlachtfeld* 10 October 1941	
• *Panzerabzeichen*	
• *Deutsches Kreuz in Gold* 28 February 1942	
• *Verwundetenabzeichen in Silber* 7 April 1942	
• *Ritterkreuz des Eisernen Kreuzes* 18 October 1943	
• *Nahkampfspange Bronze* 2 November 1943	
• *Eichenlaub* for the *Ritterkreuz des Eisernen Kreuzes* 21 January 1945	

1944

1945

1987

SCHÖNING, GEORG-WILHELM

Georg-Wilhelm Schöning was born on 8 June 1908 in Gumbinnen, East Prussia (today: Gusev, Kaliningrad Oblast, Russia). He acquired a legal qualification without a pre-degree certificate. The wide scars on both sides of his face are probably the result of the fencing practices that were fashionable at the time and even compulsory in the various comradeship associations. He served in the 23rd Infantry Regiment, and after completing a series of reserve training courses, he was promoted to reserve lieutenant in 1937. In 1939, during the mobilisation, he was first assigned to the same unit; however, in November, he was reassigned to the 10th (heavy weapons) Company of the 244th Infantry Regiment.[391] He served with this unit in the French campaign. In the summer of 1940, he was reassigned to the 120th Infantry Regiment, where he was the commander of the heavy weapons company. He took part in the campaign in Yugoslavia and the occupation of the Greek island of Kythira. From 22 June 1941, he also served in the offensive against the Soviet Union. In this campaign, he received his first decorations. As early as 14 February 1942, he was awarded the *Deutsches Kreuz in Gold*, meaning that in less than half a year, he had managed to accomplish more than six major military achievements. In May 1942, during the capture of Kerch on the Crimean Peninsula, he especially distinguished himself as commander of a combat group and adjutant. He was then promoted to commander of the III Battalion of the 120th Infantry Regiment, which was a very strange position considering his status as a reserve officer. He was seriously wounded for the first time (on the ankle) on 8 August 1942 at Kalach. For his military achievements (the destruction of a Soviet bridgehead), he was soon awarded the *Ehrenblattspange des Deutschen Heeres*. A year later, he was awarded the highest

Romanian military order, the Third Class of the *Ordinul Militar de Război "Mihai Viteazul"* (Order of Michael the Brave), for the same deed. A total of just 386 of these decorations were awarded, and only 72 of them were to non-Romanian nationals.[392]

It was because he was wounded that he was not trapped in the encirclement of Stalingrad, as he was reassigned to an *Ersatz* unit after he returned to service. His assessment from 13 October 1942 describes him as follows:

> He is an exceptional personality. Much dynamism. He stands his ground perfectly in battle with the enemy. He demonstrates excellent military performance and skills. He is very caring. He is definitely a frontline soldier type. However, given his abilities, he is also capable of other positions and tasks, such as higher-level adjutant positions, liaison officer positions in higher-level command staff, instructor in military schools, etc.[393]

A few months later, a similarly positive assessment was compiled about him:

> He is very lively and full of temperament, attentive, energetic, very harsh against himself, and open without moderation. He is an ardent national socialist. He has proven himself to be an exceptionally good instructor of officers in the battalion and has good education skills. He has an excellent general education. He has a wide range of interests. His mind and thoughts are clear. Physically, he is fully capable of service.
> He is a definite leader type with captivating dynamism. He openly stands his ground and keeps to his opinion even before his superiors, and sometimes, he does not stop at being rude. He is not a pleasant subordinate. He is above average.[394]

Schöning was promoted to *Major* on 1 October 1943 and was assigned as battalion commander to the 1st Regiment of the Panzergrenadier Division *Feldherrnhalle*. His unit was deployed in the Vitebsk–Narva area to reinforce the 246th Infantry Division. During these combat actions, he launched a counterassault, advanced one and a half kilometres and managed to keep the frontline intact for 14 days against a superior enemy strength. For this deed, he was decorated with the *Ritterkreuz des Eisernen Kreuzes* on 7 February 1944. The photographs clearly show that on the day of the award, he was wearing an *Eisernes Kreuz II. Klasse* because his original decoration was not available. On 8 February 1944, he took over the command of the entire regiment, and soon after that, he was wounded again. Thanks to this, he was able to avoid the second destruction of the Panzergren-

In October 1944, during the armoured Battle of Debrecen, on the commander's armoured car after he had suffered a head wound

adier Division *Feldherrnhalle* in the summer of 1944. After he returned to service on 26 July 1944, he was assigned to Danzig as commander of the newly established 110th *Panzer Brigade*. This unit was among the best-equipped, most modern armoured units of the period. It was equipped with Panther tanks and *Drilling* triple automatic cannons mounted on armoured fighting vehicles (*Sd. Kfz. 251/21*). The establishment process of the unit had not been completed when, in August 1944, the 110th Panzer Brigade was relocated to Hungary to Örkénytábor. The majority of the equipment and supplies arrived here. Schöning's unit was subordinated to the 13th Panzer Division on 7 October 1944, where he was assigned as commander of the 66th Panzergrenadier Regiment. On 20 and 23 August 1944, in Örkény, the musicians of the 66th Panzergrenadier Regiment of the 13th Panzer Division even gave promenade concerts, and on 28 August 1944, Schöning's unit was watching the performance of the Burgtheater Vienna at Lajosmizse, not even suspecting that they would be deployed within weeks.

On 25 August *SA-Brigadeführer* Erwin Kübler, commander of the *SA-Standarte "Feldherrnhalle"* bestowed the name and cuff titles inscribed *"Feldherrnhalle"* on the *gepanzerte Panzergrenadier-Bataillon 2110/Panzer-Abteilung 2110* of the 110th Panzer Brigade during a ceremony held at Örkénytábor. During September of the same year, Schöning's unit was training for the march to Budapest to counter a possible armistice attempt; these military exercises were codenamed "Land". On 1 October, all soldiers serving in the 110th Panzer Brigade *Feldherrnhalle* received the *Felderrnhalle* cuff titles.

On 3 October 1944, Schöning's unit was alarmed and then subordinated to the 13th Panzer Division on 7 October 1944, where he was assigned as commander of the 66th Panzergrenadier Regiment. The unit had its first contact with the enemy on 8 October, due to the events of a few days before, when the tank corps of the 2nd Ukrainian Front destroyed the defensive positions of the Hungarian 3rd Army. Schöning took part in the armoured battle around Debrecen and the retreat towards Budapest, as well as in the defence of the city. Before the encirclement, he was ordered to take over the command of a *Panzer-Brigade* on the

Western Front; however, this did not take place. Due to the extreme firepower and efficiency of his units, Schöning was always deployed on the most threatened sections of the frontline, and his subordinates were falling one by one. On 10 October 1944, his driver was killed in a grenade launcher direct hit next to him. On 14 October 1944, Schöning himself was wounded in the head by shrapnel but remained with his troops. On 3 November, he was already in the area of Maglód–Gyömrő with his *Panzergrenadier-Regiment* and launched counter-strikes against the Soviet troops breaching the defence lines. His command posts were constantly relocated: the regimental command was relocated to the Kőbánya Brick Factory on 31 December 1944, then to the Kispest Tram Depot on 2 January 1945; on 3 January 1945 to the Kispest Telephone Center; on 7 January 1945 to the wholesale bakery; on 9 January 1945 to the Tram Depot next to the Keleti Railway Station; on 10 January 1945 to the Metropol Hotel, and between 11–15 January 1945 to the cellars of the City Hall. In Buda, the regimental command post was first located next to the MOM factory on Ugocsa Street, and from the end of January 1945, in the Castle Tunnel.

Aurél Salamon, a reserve lieutenant in whose apartment at 45 Fery Oszkár Street (today: Kiss János altábornagy Street) in Buda, one of the supply units of the 66th Panzergrenadier Regiment was quartered, remembered Schöning as follows:

> Their commander, Major Schöning, who was of Saxon or Prussian descent, did not allow any harassment. He was an older officer, and according to the old norms, he treated the local residents in a humane way.[395]

On 21 January 1945, Schöning, together with →*Schmidhuber*, received the *Eichenlaub* to his *Ritterkreuz* via telegram. During the siege, one of his soldiers made him from an aluminium spoon a replacement; however, it seems that he never received the original later, as his legacy only contained the aluminium one.

It is thanks to Schöning that we know that at the end of January 1945, 11 other German officers were awarded various Hungarian decorations together with him. The award documentation suggests that the recommendations for these Hungarian decorations were made collectively, that is, per unit, and not individually. Together with Schöning, →*Herbert Kündiger*, as a combat group commander, received the Officer's Cross of the Order of Merit of the Kingdom of Hungary. Four officers from *Panzerjäger-Abteilung "Feldherrnhalle"*, and five officers from the 4th Panzer Regiment received the Knight's Cross of the Order of the Holy Crown of Hungary; *Major* Max Frigger, the engineer officer of the 4th Panzer Regiment received the Officer's Cross of the Order of the Holy Crown of Hungary.[396]

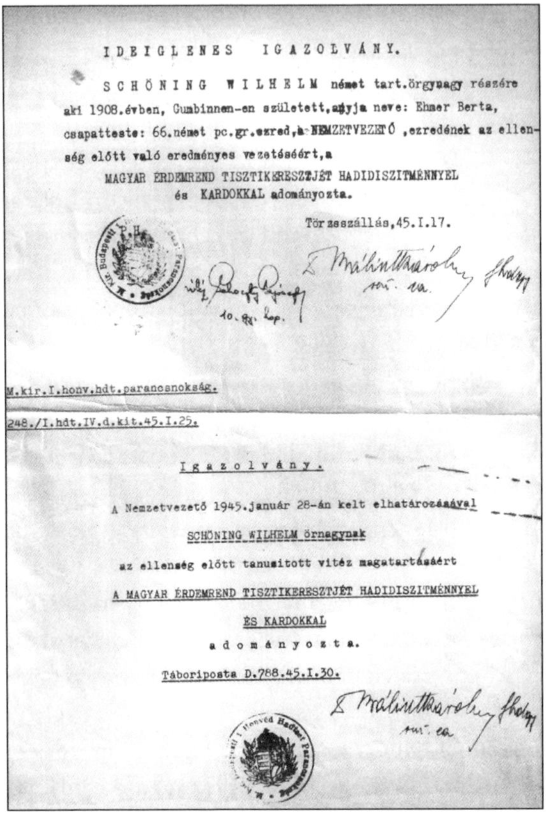

IDEIGLENES IGAZOLVÁNY.

SCHÖNING WILHELM német tart.örgynagy részére aki 1908.évben, Gumbinnen-en született, anyja neve: Ehmer Berta, csapatteste: 66.német pc.gr.ezred, a NEMZETVEZETŐ ,ezredének az ellenség előtt való eredményes vezetéséért, a

MAGYAR ÉRDEMREND TISZTIKERESZTJÉT HADIDISZITMÉNNYEL és KARDOKKAL adományozta.

Törzsszállás,45.I.17.

M.kir.I.honv.hdt.parancsnokság.

248./I.hdt.IV.d.kit.45.I.25.

Igazolvány.

A Nemzetvezető 1945.január 28-án kelt elhatározásával

SCHÖNING WILHELM őrnagynak

az ellenség előtt tanusitott vitéz magatartásáért

A MAGYAR ÉRDEMREND TISZTIKERESZTJÉT HADIDISZITMÉNNYEL

ÉS KARDOKKAL

adományozta.

Táboriposta D.788.45.I.30.

Georg-Wilhelm Schöning's Hungarian decoration document

Towards the end of the siege, Schöning was angered by the German war reports, which only mentioned the performance of the SS in connection with Budapest. Unable to persuade General Schmidhuber that the division should make a formal protest on this matter, Schöning sent the following message directly to the *OKH* on the Panzer Division's special radio channel, which was still in operation at the time and was used to report the names of fatal casualties on a daily basis:

> The honour of our soldiers demands that we declare, in connection with the radio reports heard here, that in addition to the Waffen-SS units, soldiers of two Wehrmacht divisions of all ranks are standing, fighting and falling west of Vérmező, as they have sworn to do. Lieutenant Colonel Wilhelm Schöning.[397]

Schöning took part in the breakout. His group was initially joined by the 4th Hussar Regiment, but he separated himself from them at Széna Square. His route took him through the Buda Hills, past János Hill, to the Szomor-Gyermely line. On the morning of 12 February, he took command of the main group of escapees. He was seriously wounded again in the no-man's-land between the two enemy lines. He remembered the breakout attempt in the 1960s as follows:

> After the regimental headquarters, together with the signal platoon, the company commanded by Stolley,[398] the maintenance units and a few

wounded soldiers who were still able to walk gathered at the eastern exit of the Tunnel, we managed to remain together as far as Mária Square, despite the indescribable chaos. However, the square was almost fully blocked, against orders, by the cars and panje horses of the 22nd SS Cavalry Division. When I tried to get out from behind the blocks of buildings into Széna Square, Stolley was shot in the leg, and I got a shell splinter into the back of thc head. After finding the rather clueless commanding headquarters of the 8th and 22nd Cavalry Divisions in a cellar north of the original breakout point, together with parts of the IX. SS Mountain Corps, to which Lieutenant Colonel Wolff had meanwhile joined, we went back the old way, crossing Széna Square, and there we set in motion the masses of soldiers in front of the square, in the square and behind the square and then led them up to Rózsadomb. Along the way, we fought off various command guards, sentries and small groups of Russians who opposed us. At dawn, we reached Hárs Hill in deep snow, took up a hedgehog position there, suffered casualties from Russian artillery, and could observe that the groups broken out to the northwest of us were being attacked by Russian ground attack aircraft and ground units. During the day, we were joined by another battle group under Wolff and a larger group of Waffen-SS soldiers under the command of the Chief Corps Medical Officer.[399] With the help of Stolley, who was holding his own despite his untreated wound, I took command of the whole group, assisted by Dr Seeger,[400] the Chief Divisional Medical Officer. In the ditch-lined woods north of Budakeszi, with small groups of 800-1000 men, we came up against a Russian blocking line the next morning, broke through it, and the following morning took up a hedgehog position on the heights east of the Zsámbék–Perbál line, while the Russians set up a blocking line around us. Between 8 and 9 p.m., we attacked this blocking position through a ravine I had reconnoitred, broke through with considerable losses, and by dawn were on the Russian front, which was moving westwards with artillery and headquarters. Meanwhile, the Waffen-SS group had left us. Unfortunately, I must add, because they were unlucky in their later westward movement. We turned northwest, and they were destroyed or captured by the Russian tanks and mechanised infantry that rolled past us. We broke through the Russian lines from the rear at 5 o'clock on the morning of the 14th and came under almost devastating fire from both sides so that, in fact, none of us was left intact. That was between 5 and 7 in the morning. I was badly wounded between the two lines and was carried to the German first line by Dr Seeger, who was also wounded there, and a staff sergeant. Stolley

> was wounded by the same bursting shell as me but also managed to reach our lines.[401]

A few days after reaching the German lines, Schöning described the final moments of the crossing to a war correspondent. As late as the 1960s, Schöning wrote that this part of the article, entitled "Comradeship is stronger than death", was completely true to reality (apart from the propaganda slogans not quoted here):

> Never in the four years of the Eastern Campaign had I seen such a barrage of fire as during the outbreak. We knew it was a matter of life and death because no one was thinking of surrendering. We ran down a mortar emplacement without taking cover and reached the edge of a forest, behind which we suspected German positions because of the rising light signals. I think most of the grenadiers in my unit were wounded. I saw, for example, a medic beside me with a bullet in his neck and a shattered right elbow, his pistol in his left hand. Just when we thought we had broken through the first line, we came under concentrated Bolshevist fire again in the no-man's land.
>
> I suddenly felt as if my legs had been torn off. Chief Medical Officer Seeger, who was charging at my side, tried to help. He leaned over me and was also badly wounded. As I had already fired all the bullets in my pistol, I ordered a lieutenant to shoot me, as I did not want to be taken prisoner. He shouted at me, "Only 2,000 metres to go, Lieutenant Colonel. You must succeed!" We crawled through the snow up a slope, the Chief Medical Officer at my side. Two of the wounded grenadiers in my group recognised me. The sergeant shouted to the lance corporal: "We can't leave our commander lying here. Come on, pick him up". Under heavy artillery fire, I was picked up and, with great difficulty, with my pierced legs, dragged two kilometres to the German positions. Seeger came along under his own steam.[402]

Schöning lived through the end of the war in a military hospital in Bad Elster, Saxony, first in American and then in Soviet captivity, from the latter of which he was released on 10 October 1945 because of his wounds. After that, he worked as a lay judge and was the legal adviser to the Employers' Association in Bochum. According to his family, he returned from the war a completely changed and embittered man – a fact that is reflected to some extent in his 1945 portrait. He was deeply troubled by the events and kept the clothes and objects he had worn at

"Official" photograph taken in the spring of 1944

the outbreak of war until his death. He kept up a lively correspondence with his comrades and took part in writing the history of his unit. His daughters did not really understand his attachment to the past, and the only family member with whom he could really talk about his experiences was the husband of one of his daughters, who had fled from Hungary to Germany in 1956.

The atmosphere that characterised these relationships is vividly illustrated in a letter written by his former subordinate Walter Oelsner on 16 April 1952:[403]

Dear Kamerad Schöning!

In your postcard, you mentioned those combat strongpoints on which our 110th Panzer Brigade rampaged seven years ago. I particularly remember our beautiful afternoon attack near Karcag and from there on to Nádudvar, but even more the afternoon attack in which you were slightly wounded. That firestorm was like true magic. The breakout of the neighbouring unit from Kaba and our fighting in the railway and road triangle, where we knocked out a couple of Soviet tanks at close range, still makes my blood boil. I could go on and on, but as a commander, you know better. We just have to keep remembering some of our good comrades who remained out there. [...] I'm particularly glad that you can now move without sticks. Because the fact that the Russians shot you in the legs during the escape is a really dirty move. One thing is for sure: the Russians hated our unit like the plague, and rightly so, because the 2 cm Drillings of our gunners spoke too direct a language to them. [...] A personal meeting would have been a thousand times better, and in that case, we would have had a decent drink, as is the old frontline custom. Best wishes to you and your family in the spirit of the old offensive hurrah:

Walter Oelsner

Schöning kept the clothes he was wearing during the breakout attempt and all his decorations in a suitcase until his death

Wilhelm Schöning died in Bochum on 2 November 1987 after a long illness.

DECORATIONS	RANKS
• *Eisernes Kreuz II. Klasse* 11 July 1940 • *Eisernes Kreuz I. Klasse* 12 August 1940 • *Deutsches Kreuz in Gold* 14 February 1942 • *Ehrenblattspange des Deutschen Heeres* 16 October 1942 • *Ritterkreuz des Eisernen Kreuzes* 7 February 1944 • *Eichenlaub* to the *Ritterkreuz des Eisernen Kreuzes* 21 January 1945 • *Ordinul Militar de Război "Mihai Viteazul"* third class 31 March 1943 • Officer's Cross of the Order of Merit of the Kingdom of Hungary with war decorations and swords 28 January 1945	• *Leutnant (der Reserve)* 1 October 1937 • *Oberleutnant (der Reserve)* June 1940 • *Hauptmann (der Reserve)* 1 March 1942 • *Major (der Reserve)* 1 October 1943 • *Oberstleutnant (der Reserve)* 1 December 1944 (with retrospective effect)

1944

SOLDNER, GUSTAV

Gustav Soldner was born on 18 September 1912 in Torgau as a son of a restaurant owner. After finishing high school, he was employed as a printing press worker. He joined the SA early on, where he reached the rank of *SA-Standartenführer* by 1941 (the rank equivalent to Colonel). He then served as *SA-Brigadeführer* Richard Schicke's adjutant; his last assignment was to organise the matters of the SA sports badges in the Elba–Magdeburg region, which suggests that, despite his high rank, he played a relatively minor role in the Nazi hierarchy.

After being awarded the *Eisernes Kreuz II. Klasse* and *I. Klasse,* he also received the *Deutsches Kreuz in Gold* on 29 October 1943 – by that time, he was commanding the 7th Company of the 66th Panzergrenadier Regiment. Soldner was recommended for the *Ritterkreuz des Eisernen Kreuzes* after the combat actions on 9–10 May 1944, when he and his unit (1st Company of the 66th Panzergrenadier Regiment) destroyed a Soviet bridgehead on the Dnester River even though his unit was surrounded. Temporarily, he took over command of the entire battalion, during which time 120 prisoners of war and 29 machine guns were captured. The decoration was awarded to him on 26 July 1944.

During the reorganisation of the 13th Panzer Division in the autumn of 1944, Soldner was reassigned as company commander to the 93rd Panzergrenadier Regiment. From 10 January, his unit, formerly under the 93rd Panzergrenadier Regiment of the 13th Panzer Division was incorporated into the I Battalion of the 66th Panzergrenadier Regiment of the 13th Panzer Division. Based on his *Feldpostnummer*, Soldner was assigned to the *Begleitskompanie* of the division in the last period of the siege. Of his activities in Budapest, there is only one letter available, written by his comrade, *Leutnant* Hans-Hermann Büllesbach,[404] to his widow:

Dear Frau Soldner!
As you have already learnt the fate of your husband from Sergeant Schulze, I do not want to miss the opportunity to write to you and express my deepest condolences. This is especially so because I had been together with your husband during the last times, and I came to know him quite well; therefore, I can understand your pain and grief completely, and I also hope, as you do, that we will be able to have a more favourable future ahead of us.

When your husband was wounded on 17 January by a shell fragment on his left leg, at first, he was slightly slumped. At that time, we were still hoping for the arrival of relief troops. Your husband was first accommodated at the divisional headquarters. However, I took him from there and transported him to the division's train, where we placed all our wounded comrades and were better off in terms of accommodation and supplies. We had plenty of time here to talk about many things that were troubling us. Your husband always had this admirable belief in victory. When the situation became hopeless, and we could no longer believe in relief, he was the most ardent supporter of the idea of the breakout attempt. From the beginning of February, he was able to walk a bit. He was often talking about you and his children and telling stories about the combat activities he was part of[405] and about his experiences during the war.

Before he was wounded, he was recommended by the regiment to receive the *Eichenlaub* for his brave conduct in the eastern part of the city. What came out of this, I do not know.

He was very hopeful when the order to start the breakout attempt arrived on 11 February. But in case he would not get out, he gave me and his orderly a letter for you. His orderly did not make it through. Furthermore, he gave me his *Nahkampfspange in Silber* as well, which I also received [according to the number of days I spent in close combat], and a portrait of himself as a keepsake, with the note, "What does not kill us, makes us stronger". Hereby, I send his *Nahkampfspange in Silber* as well as his letter to you.

During the breakout attempt, he was fighting ferociously at the spearhead and was partly the soul of our combat group. When it was not possible to advance, he moved forward and set everybody in motion. Finally, he became the leader of the whole group. Despite his wounds, he could walk fairly well.

When we set off around 0500 hours on 14 February to breach the last Soviet line, he was wounded by a shell fragment in front of me. I saw him jump into a ditch with staff intendant Pessel.[406] As I was hit on the thigh with an anti-tank gun fragment, I ran after them to the same cover. Your husband then said that he could not go further as he was wounded again. The staff intendant said the same. Close to the ditch, there was a Soviet bunker from which we heard talking. When I stood up, the Russians started to shoot at me from around 50 metres. Approximately 10-15 metres behind us, there were 5-6 more wounded German soldiers under a group of bushes. In the meantime, the attack advanced 300-400 metres. We had no soldiers left with us, so we could not take your husband with us either. We were too exhausted due to the lack of food and the hardships we went through. Upon my persuasion to try it once more, he said that he could not do it and said that I should try it alone. The days were hard, very hard, and we were grieving the loss of our beloved commander at that moment. Your husband said that he wanted to catch up with Captain Sauer,[407] and he wanted to be the same kind of commander he was. The soldiers who knew them both said that your husband was a second Captain Sauer.

Apart from me, only First Sergeant Toch made it out alive from the battalion. All other officers and enlisted men went missing.

I hope that I could say something in this letter that you wanted to know about your husband. In case you have further questions, please write to me at my address, as my new field post number has not yet been assigned.[408]

DECORATIONS	RANKS
• *Eisernes Kreuz II. Klasse* • *Eisernes Kreuz I. Klasse* • *Deutsches Kreuz in Gold* 29 October 1943 • *Ehrenblattspange des Deutschen Heeres* • *Ritterkreuz des Eisernen Kreuzes* 18 July 1944	• *Oberleutnant (der Reserve)* 27 February 1944 • Further dates of promotions are unknown.

1933–1935

1941

STIEGLER, JOHANN

Johann Stiegler was born on 3 November 1904 in the Saxony village of Mittelfrohna. He had already joined the SA before 1933, but this was not made official until after 1933. Among other positions, he also served as the driver of the SA commander in Chemnitz. There are only fragments of information available regarding his military career. He served as a volunteer even before the war, and he received tank destroyer training. At the beginning of the war, he was assigned to *Panzerabwehr-Abteilung 46* of the 44th Infantry Division and served in the Western campaign with this unit. In 1941, at an unknown date, he was promoted to *Feldwebel*. On 31 August 1941, he was awarded the *Eisernes Kreuz I. Klasse*. On 3 December 1942, in Stalingrad, he was lightly wounded and was again wounded on 24 December. This time, he was hit by grenade fragments, which caused wounds to his eyes (he temporarily lost his eyesight), buttocks, left forearm and chest – this proved a life-saver because he was airlifted out of the Stalingrad cauldron.

Thereafter, he remained in Germany for half a year before being assigned to the *Ersatz* unit of Panzergrenadier Division *Feldherrnhalle*, from which he was assigned to Hungary in September 1944. At that time, Stiegler served as a platoon commander in the 2nd Company of *Panzerjäger-Abteilung "Feldherrnhalle"*. The *Division* was in defence in the Attila Line and, between 6 and 12 December 1944, in the area of Dunakeszi–Vác–Galgamácsa, contained the advancing Soviet troops with defensive actions. The heavily worn units were to face the assault of the 5th Soviet Guards Tank Corps and the 25th Guards Rifle Corps at the beginning of December. On 7 December 1944, the units of Panzer Division *Feldherrnhalle* knocked out six Soviet tanks, on 8 December, they knocked out five; on 9 December, another five; on 11 December, they knocked out 20 and, three days later, on 14 December they knocked out four more.[409] A portion of these victories might be attributed to the *Sturmgeschütze* (of the 20 knocked-out tanks on 11 December, five were reported to have been knocked out by handheld weapons). Stiegler distinguished himself in the combat actions on 11 December when the *Panzerjäger* units of Panzer Division *Feldherrnhalle* were active. The importance of the combat actions on 11 December was related to the fact that units of the Soviet 25th Guards Rifle Division and 409th Rifle Division attacked that day with 60 tanks in the southwest direction between Csomád and Alsógöd. The Soviet units crossed the anti-tank ditch of the Attila I Defence Line and breached the frontline of the Panzer Division *Feldherrnhalle* on a four-kilometre wide and three-kilometre deep section. This incredibly dangerous situation was countered by Stiegler and less than six assault guns belonging to Panzer Division *Feldherrnhalle* (the unit possessed altogether eight StuG. III assault guns; however, on 15 December, only one of these was in combat-ready condition).[410]

There is one more combat deed connected to *Panzerjäger-Abteilung Feldherrnhalle 1*. On 27 December 1944, after 10 a.m. between Fót and Rákospalota, at benchmark point No. 132 and in the area of Sikátorpuszta (today, there are storage facilities of large grocery stores in the area), one of the battalions of Panzer Division *Feldherrnhalle* and three assault guns launched a counterattack against the 3rd Tank Brigade and 659th Rifle Regiment. This was helped by the wooded area northwest of benchmark point no. 132, where the Germans were able to cover themselves. Stiegel's assault guns destroyed three Soviet tanks and a number of Soviet infantry within 15 minutes. Thereafter, Stiegel's unit continued to push the attack towards the southwest and destroy two more tanks. At the end of the day, the Germans reoccupied Sikátorpuszta.

On 29 January 1945 →*Pfeffer-Wildenbruch* recommended Stiegler for this latter achievement for the *Ritterkreuz des Eisernen Kreuzes*. The recommendation describes Stiegler's actions as follows:

> [Stiegler as *Zugführer*,] on 27 December, was assigned the task to seal off the enemy breach with his four assault guns and to restore the previous main line of defence. He immediately started to position his assault guns and opened fire, and within 45 minutes, destroyed three T-34s and a number of infantry. Following these events, he went over to counterattack, knocked out two further tanks and destroyed enemy infantry. Stiegler did not consider his person but showed an extraordinary personal example and, by the energetic command of his assault guns, succeeded in preventing the dangerous breakthrough of the enemy. He had a decisive role in

VORLÄUFIGES BESITZZEUGNIS

DER FÜHRER
HAT DEM
Oberfeldw. Johann S t i e g l e r
Zugfhr. Pz.Jg.Abt."Feldherrnhalle"

DAS RITTERKREUZ
DES EISERNEN KREUZES
AM 1.2.45 VERLIEHEN

HQu OKH, DEN 2. Februar 1945

OBERKOMMANDO DES HEERES
IA.

GENERALLEUTNANT

The provisional documentation of Johann Stiegler's *Ritterkreuz des Eisernen Kreuzes*

keeping the integrity of the frontline and making it possible for the main line of defence to be restored.[411]

Apart from his deed, we hardly know anything about the fate of Stiegler – only a few of his letters written during the war survived. On 14 December 1944, he wrote that he purchased Christmas gifts for his two sons. On 18 December, he wrote about two of his assault guns being blown up and added that his full stash of cigarettes perished together with the assault guns. On that day, however, a new assault gun was allocated to him. In his last letter, dated 23 December 1944, he wrote that he had again been sent to the first lines with his assault gun.

After the war, his family heard stories of him swimming (!) over from Pest to Buda around the middle of January 1945, and he was admitted to hospital because of hypothermia. There is no data available on his later fate. The *Ritterkreuz des Eisernen Kreuzes* decoration was awarded in theory on 1 February 1945. However, the provisional documentation and the decoration itself were only presented to his wife at the end of February. Later, she wrote to the *WASt* that she had heard about the award on 25 February on the radio. The following day, a number of newspapers, in short articles, reported on Stiegler's decoration.[412]

DECORATIONS	RANKS
• *Eisernes Kreuz II. Klasse* • *Eisernes Kreuz I. Klasse* 31 August 1944 • *Ritterkreuz des Eisernen Kreuzes* 1 February 1945	• Dates of promotions are unknown.

1942–1944

ULRICH, EMIL

Emil Ulrich was born on 12 July 1921 in the village of Fürstenfeld in the region of Bessarabia (today: Cneazevca, Moldova). There are only scarce and intermittent data available that relate to his military service. What seems to be certain, however, is that he was already serving in the 120th Infantry Regiment *(mot.)* in 1942. He served throughout the war with this unit, which was one of the predecessor units of Panzergrenadier Regiment *Feldherrnhalle*. On 21 March 1944, he was lightly wounded in the left leg. On an unknown date, but certainly after 1943, he was promoted to the rank of *Zugführer*. On 2 September 1944, he was reassigned to the 5th Company of the Grenadier Regiment *Feldherrnhalle* of Panzergrenadier Division *Feldherrnhalle*.

He received the *Ritterkreuz des Eisernen Kreuzes* on 7 February 1945. The circumstances of the recommendation are unknown.

Ulrich was taken captive on 12 February 1945, and he only returned to Germany on 5 September 1949. His fate is unknown. In July 2019, a *Ritterkreuz des Eisernen Kreuzes* provisional award document was sold at an auction; the document had a facsimile signature of *Generalfeldmarschall* Erhard Milch and had been filled out for Emil Ulrich. However, the origin of this document is questionable.[413]

DECORATIONS	RANKS
• *Eisernes Kreuz II. Klasse* • *Eisernes Kreuz I. Klasse* • *Ritterkreuz des Eisernen Kreuzes* 7 February 1945	• Dates of promotions are unknown.

1943–1944

WEBER, RUDOLF

Rudolf Weber was born on 28 February 1917 in Vienna. There is very little information available about his military career. He served throughout the war as an enlisted soldier in the 4th Panzer Regiment of the 13th Panzer Division. What is known with certainty is that on 18 March 1940, he was serving in the 5th Company. On 25 August 1943, he was lightly wounded by an anti-tank gun projectile in the right eye. On 2 June 1944, he was lightly wounded again in a bombing raid.

He was awarded the *Ritterkreuz des Eisernen Kreuzes* on 14 February 1945. At that time, he was serving in the 9th Company of the 4th Panzer Regiment. The military achievement for which he received the decoration must have taken place in the second half of December 1944, but there is no information available regarding the details of this deed and its circumstances. It is known, however, that he held the rank of *Feldwebel* at that time, and his assignment connected him to tanks. At the end of the siege, most probably during the breakout attempt, Weber went missing.

DECORATIONS	RANKS
• *Eisernes Kreuz II. Klasse* 2 May 1943 • *Eisernes Kreuz I. Klasse* • *Ritterkreuz des Eisernen Kreuzes* 14 February 1945	• Dates of promotions are unknown.

1941–1942

WENDRINSKI, GUSTAV

Gustav Wendrinski was born on 23 January 1923 in Bratislava. He joined the SS at an unknown date but before 1942. He distinguished himself in the Kharkov armoured battle and earned the *Eisernes Kreuz I. Klasse*. In 1944, he was already serving as a platoon commander in *SS-Panzerjäger-Abteilung 8* of the 8th SS Cavalry Division.

According to his Slovakian biographer, Wendrinski was fluent in Russian and took part in destroying altogether 41 Soviet tanks. Of these, two were destroyed in the area of Vác–Acsa between 5 and 14 December, each with a *Panzerfaust*. He lost his way in the evening of 5 December 1944 with his tractor and was saved from being trampled down by the advancing Soviet tanks only by the cover of darkness. The recommendation for the award of the *Ritterkreuz des Eisernen Kreuzes* mentioned the same action as the reason for the award of the decoration:

> In unclear circumstances, without infantry cover, he assaulted a number of tanks, knocked out three of them, and then delayed the enemy infantry with a machine gun until his gun could relocate. Cut off from his unit, he dressed as a Hungarian civilian, destroyed two Soviet tanks with a Panzerfaust, and captured a tractor from the Soviets, which he managed to bring back to his own positions.[414]

He took part in the breakout attempt and, according to unconfirmed reports, he died in the area of Csobánka due to a shot in his heart. As his identification tag has not yet been uncovered to this day, the circumstances remain a matter of speculation.

What is certainly known of him is connected to the surviving war log of the 1st *Zug* of the 1st *Schwadron* of the *SS-Panzerjäger-Abteilung 8* (8th SS Cavalry Division). The war log was most probably kept by *SS-Oberscharführer* Gerhard König, who fell on 13 February 1945 during the breakout attempt along with a number of his comrades in the area of the Reiter Ditch (Reiter-árok) near the Malom-erdő at Pilisvörösvár. The war log begins on the day of 19 October 1944, and Wendrinski is mentioned twice. On the date of 20 November, the log reads: "*Oberscharführer* Wendrinski [and his comrades] remained at the baggage train". After the note dated 11 December 1944 ("reestablishment of the platoon and its subordination to the 6th Squadron of the 15th Cavalry Regiment"), the next day, the following is noted: "two guns lost, Wendrinski remains in the village with two men. Under cover of the night, he knocks out two pieces of enemy armour with *Panzerfaust* in close combat. Thereafter, *Oberscharführer* W. approaches the tractor. He succeeds..."[415] – from that point, the pages of the war log are missing; most probably, they were torn out and remained with König's dead body.

DECORATIONS	RANKS
• *Eisernes Kreuz II. Klasse* • *Eisernes Kreuz I. Klasse* • *Ritterkreuz des Eisernen Kreuzes*	• Dates of promotions are unknown.

1939–1942

1942

WOLFF, HELMUT

Helmut Wolff was born on 5 September 1911 in Sommerau in Eastern Prussia (today: Ząbrowo, Poland). His original occupation was a butcher; he joined the Wehrmacht on 1 May 1930 as a professional soldier. He was assigned to the 3rd Infantry Regiment. He married in 1936. At the mobilisation, he was reassigned to serve in the Infantry Regiment, with which he was in combat in the area of Graudenz (today: Grudziądz), Modlin and Warsaw as platoon commander. On 17 August 1940, he was further reassigned to the 156th Infantry Regiment. He served in this unit until 1944. Wolff was promoted to *Leutnant* on 1 April 1940. His assessment dated 1 February 1941 described him as follows:

> Slightly short, but with a good posture: good, soldierly appearance. He acts with a natural demeanour; he is energetic and determined. His out-of-service conduct is excellent as well. He is humble with his superiors and objective, righteous and caring towards his subordinates. He is a beloved person among his comrades, without pushing himself into the spotlight, with his calm and humble personality. He is a reserved and trustworthy person who does not open up by himself, only if he is contacted directly. Due to his natural military instincts, he has good skills and knowledge. His judgement is fair and clear, and he can be used especially well in unit service.[416]

With his unit, Wolff took part in the Yugoslav and Eastern campaigns. Until 19 October 1942, he was a company officer, as well as the commander of the 4th Company of the 156th Infantry Regiment; thereafter, he was assigned as

With his wife and his son in 1942

the commander of the 13th (heavy infantry gun) Company of *Grenadier-Regiment 156*. From 1943, he was the commander of the I Battalion of the 156th Grenadier Regiment until he was wounded on 3 February 1943. On 3 February 1943, he received the decoration of the *Deutsches Kreuz in Gold*. His promotion to higher ranks was swift: he was promoted to *Hauptmann* on 1 April 1942, to *Major* on 1 May 1943 and *Oberstleutnant* on 9 November 1944.

At an unknown date, but presumably during the autumn of 1944, at the re-establishment of the Panzer Division *Feldherrnhalle*, he was promoted to the commander of one of the battalions of the Panzergrenadier Division *Feldherrnhalle*. His assessment, dated 2 March 1943, describes him as follows:

> He is a fresh and energetic officer, dynamic and vigorous in combat. In critical situations, he makes decisions swiftly and takes responsibility for his actions. He personally throws himself into action. He is less skilled in tactical questions, and he commands his own battalion by personal example. He has a positive attitude, self-confidence, and firmness of character. His comrades respect him. His strength: he is dashing in combat. His weakness: he pushes himself into the spotlight a bit too often. He does not have a good grasp of the administrative operation.[417]

After completing the staff officer course, he received similar positive comments in his new assessment:

> He is mentally fresh and diligently learns about the tasks of leading a regiment. During his command, he successfully led an ambush employing radios, and during this, he displayed good tactical skills. He is a born leader.[418]

Helmut Wolff (right) with one of his comrades between 1942 and 1943

From the beginning of October 1944 he took part in the fighting of his division with his unit, and on 2 November 1944, he carried out a very successful counterattack near Gyón, 50 kilometers southeast of Budapest. He was presumably awarded the Knight's Cross of the Iron Cross, but was only awarded the *Ehrenblattspange des Deutschen Heeres*. On 2 November 1944, near Gyón, Wolff and his unit assaulted the advancing Soviet troops, and he was therefore recommended to receive the *Ritterkreuz des Eisernen Kreuzes*, but at that time, he only received the *Anerkennungsurkunde des Oberbefehlshabers des Heeres*. He took over the command of *Panzergrenadier-Regiment Feldherrnhalle 1* of Panzer Division *Feldherrnhalle* on 30 December 1944, after the former commander of the regiment, Erich-Friedrich Jung, was fatally shot in the head earlier, near Kőbánya, during a reconnaissance mission. He received his *Ritterkreuz des Eisernen Kreuzes* on 21 February 1945. The recommendation for this award did not survive. Therefore, we can only assume that he must have earned it with his distinguished conduct between December 1944 and January 1945. It is also possible, however, that his decoration was connected to three other SS officers who were also taking part in the breakout attempt. He dictated a separate report after the breakout attempt on his experiences of urban combat: from this report, it seems evident that he must have taken part in the command of his soldiers directly from the frontline.[419] His unit around this time was in combat in Újpest and thereafter in the districts of southern Buda.

On 11 February 1945, he broke out with his unit from the encirclement. In the hills around Buda, he belonged to →*Schöning's* group; he reached the German lines on 14 February with them in a terrible condition, seriously wounded (this was the seventh occasion on which he was wounded). His son saw him as late as the beginning of March 1945 in splints, with crutches and in plaster, with cannulas and drains protruding from his back due to the bullets still lodged in his body. Despite his serious condition, he took part in combat actions in April 1945 on Czech territory. He was taken captive on 9 May 1945 at Pilsen (Plzeň, Czech Republic). The American troops twice extradited him to the Red Army as he escaped the first time. He also escaped from Soviet internment, yet again in Czech territory. However, he was found by civilians in a ditch, half-dead from hunger, and was extradited to the Soviets again. In 1949, in a show trial, he was sentenced to 25 years of correctional labour. He was released on 4 October 1953.

He was also employed by the *Bundeswehr* from 1956 as *Oberst*, and first served in the *Münsterlager Panzerschule.* In 1958, he became a commander of the 32nd Panzergrenadier Brigade, and from 1961, he was the commander of the *Panzerschule* in Münster. Thereafter, until his retirement and at his own request, he was tasked with organizing the matters of the reservists in one of the military districts; after his retirement, he settled down in Schleswig-Holstein.[420]

DECORATIONS	RANKS
• *Eisernes Kreuz II. Klasse* 23 July 1941 • *Infanterie-Sturmabzeichen* 27 October 1941 • *Eisernes Kreuz I. Klasse* 3 November 1941 • *Deutsches Kreuz in Gold* 3 March 1943 • *Anerkennungsurkunde des Oberbefehlshabers des Heeres für hervorragende Leistungen auf dem Schlachtfeld* 7 January 1945 • *Ritterkreuz des Eisernen Kreuzes* 21 January 1945 • *Nahkampfspange Silber* 15 February 1945 • *Verwundetenabzeichen in Gold* 15 February 1945 (?) • Knight's Cross of the Order of Merit of the Kingdom of Hungary with war decorations and swords January 1945	• *Gefreiter* 1 May 1935 • *Unteroffizier*-candidate 14 March 1934 • *Unteroffizier* 1 April 1934 • *Feldwebel* 1 November 1935 • *Oberfeldwebel* 1 October 1936 • *Leutnant* 1 April 1940 • *Oberleutnant* 1 December 1940 • *Hauptmann* 1 April 1942 • *Major* 1 May 1943 • *Oberstleutnant* 9 November 1944 • *Oberst (Bundeswehr)* 1956

1935

1944

ZEHENDER, AUGUST

August Zehender was born on 28 April 1903 in Aalen; his father was a merchant. After completing elementary school, from 4 August 1920 until 3 August 1932, he served in the *Reichswehr.* He served in the 4th (machine gun) Company of the 3rd (Württemberg) Infantry Regiment stationed in Bad Cannstatt. His last rank in the *Reichswehr* was *Feldwebel.* After his discharge, he worked as a trainer at different sporting schools for three years. In October 1935, he had not yet been admitted into the *SS-Verfügungstruppe*; however, a month later, he was. In the related documentation, there is a reference that indicates the importance of SS membership for Zehender: "He has refused various positions offered to him in the *Luftwaffe* and the *Heer* in the hope that he can utilize his skills and knowledge in the ranks of the SS."[421]

He was promoted to *SS-Obersturmführer.* Presumably, around this time, he left the Evangelical Church. According to his assessment, dated 1935: "he is a fully trustworthy national socialist and as an educator, trainer and commander he is fully capable of membership of the *SS-Verfügungstruppe.*"[422] On 1 May 1937, he joined the *NSDAP.* Between 1935 and 1942, he served in the *SS-Standarte "Deutschland"* (later *SS-Regiment "Deutschland"*) as platoon, company and battalion commander. His assessment from 1937 describes him as follows:

> He is an exemplary trainer specializing in machine-gun handling. Regarding the overall racial assessment, he is of the Dinarian type; his character is spotless, and he is reputable, slightly too sensitive, and purposeful. His behaviour is always blameless.[423]

On 17 December 1937, *SS-Standartenführer* Felix Steiner, commander of the *SS-Standarte "Deutschland"* at that time, added the following note to Zehender's assessment:

> His skills have tactical boundaries. Within a battalion or a company, he reliably accomplishes his tasks. He is not yet capable of executing the tasks of a battalion commander. For this, he needs to make up for his tactical deficiencies and raise his general cultural level.[424]

The latter circumstance is only briefly and indirectly mentioned in later assessments: "Mentally he possesses moderate abilities, he is rather drawn to practical questions."

His first fiancée died on 29 February 1939 of tuberculosis. Besides this personal tragedy, he had other official problems as well: it turned out that the *Ru-SHA* prompted an investigation and uncovered that when Zehender handed in his marriage request documents, he submitted medical reports on his fiancée's health that did not take into account a previous operation that had left her infertile. However, for members of the SS, this was a sufficient reason not to allow the marriage. Finally, on 14 January 1942, he married his second fiancée, and the couple had a son.

Until the summer of 1942, Zehender served in *SS-Regiment "Deutschland"*, firstly as commander of a rifle battalion and then as the commander of the motorcycle battalion. He participated in the Polish, French and Soviet campaigns and was seriously wounded in June 1941. After his recovery, on 16 June 1942, he was reassigned to 2nd SS Cavalry Regiment, immediately becoming its commander.

Between 26 and 28 November 1941, south of Baturino, despite being ordered to retreat by the division command, he did not do so and persevered in keeping his position. This had a significant impact on later events, as keeping these positions proved to be of essential importance during the winter combat at Rzhev. However, the strength of the regiment dwindled to a mere 533 soldiers in just a few days. Zehender was recommended to receive the *Ritterkreuz des Eisernen Kreuzes*, which was awarded to him on 10 March 1943. On 4 July 1943, he took over the command of the recently established (by reorganization) 17th SS Cavalry Regiment.

On 1 May, he was appointed as acting division commander of the 22nd Cavalry Division.[425] He was most probably not assigned as its permanent commander due to his lack of training – Zehender had not completed a staff officer course and, therefore, was not eligible to command an entire division. It should

August Zehender (on the left) in the summer of 1943, somewhere around the Pripyat' swampland

be noted that although several sources refer to the unit as *"Maria Theresia"*, this was not an official designation. It is also unclear why the unit received a collar tab different from the other SS divisions: a cornflower. However, a number of possible explanations for this circulated among veterans of the division: before 1938, the cornflower had been the symbol of the Austrian national socialists; it was also Maria Theresa's favourite flower. According to a satirical paper (!), issued in 1944 and distributed only within the division, the cornflower was the symbol of "Heinrich Himmler tea" – this was an allusion to the peculiar eating habits of the *Reichsführer-SS* who was a vegetarian.[426] The establishment of the unit was made possible by the German–Hungarian agreement concluded on 14 April 1944, in accordance with which Hungary passed on to Germany those Hungarian citizens liable to military service who had identified themselves as of German ethnicity during the 1941 census, as well as those of whom it was possible to establish "the fact of being of German ethnicity". The drafting process was organized by the German drafting committees together with *Volksbund* activists and the Hungarian Royal Gendarmerie forces. Those who did not comply were given over by the Hungarian authorities to the Germans; also, there was no right of appeal against the decision made by the drafting committees. The Ministry of Defence was allowed to retain a maximum of 10.55 percent of those found eligible in case these persons were of essential importance in either the military industry or in any other field essential to the Hungarian Royal Army.

In the documents related to the establishment of the new division, it was initially called 22nd "Hungarian" or "Volunteer" SS Division, although both of these designations were quite loose and far from the truth. The decision that the new unit was to be set up as a cavalry unit only was made as late as the beginning of May 1944. The division was set up on the base of the 17th SS Cavalry Regiment, which earlier had suffered devastating losses at Kovel, and was reassigned from the 8th SS Cavalry Division. According to the original plans, the division would consist of three cavalry regiments: the 52nd (renamed from 1st SS Voluntary Cavalry Regiment); the 53rd (renamed from 2nd SS Voluntary Cavalry Regiment), and 54th (renamed from the 17th SS Cavalry Regiment), as well as further divisional units that were consistent with the organization of the 8th SS Cavalry Division. The serious lack of experienced officers was addressed by incorporating primarily Hungarian volunteers who had applied earlier, but there were also reassignments from the Wehrmacht and, furthermore, a significant number of Soviet volunteers – a group that accounted for almost 10 percent. The necessary number of horses were purchased entirely in Hungary. Due to this, Zehender worked in close cooperation with *SS-Obersturmbannführer* Kurt Becher, who officially headed the committee for purchasing horses in Hungary. It is a telling detail that Zehender also became friends with Adolf Eichmann, whom he accompanied on riding excursions.[427] The units of the division were located in the area of Kisbér and Győr, as well as in the villages of the Zsámbék basin.

Zehender even helped Eichmann receive a decoration. At the beginning of September, he let Eichmann take a truckload of artillery ammunition, a few guns and two platoons of soldiers, all originally belonging to Zehender's division. We can only assume that these units were part of *Kampfgruppe Ameiser*. After the war, the survivors of this unit were obviously not interested in having their actions related to Eichmann made public. In any case, in September 1944, Eichmann had these units assist with the evacuation of a military hospital in the area of Oradea–Timişoara (Arad–Temesvár). Their main task was to organize and evacuate those residents of the area who were of German ethnicity. However, this could only be partially accomplished. A few days before the breach of the frontline, Eichmann returned to Budapest, and for his achievements, Zehender awarded him the decoration of the *Eisernes Kreuz II. Klasse*.[428]

Zehender's last assessment was dated 6 September 1944:

> He is honest and has a trustworthy personality. His temperament is fresh and agile. His military skills are very good. Based on his service, he can be rated as excellent. He is diligent, intellectually of good capabilities, and a great comrade.[429]

In the spring of 1943, soon after his decoration

Zehender's division was deployed on 2–3 November 1944 in the Attila I Defence Line on the Dunaharaszti–Soroksár–Pestszentimre section. The division suffered significant losses in the first half of November 1944 – 13 officers fell, 35 officers were wounded, and two went missing. The complete losses amounted to 1,403 persons, and almost 80 percent were lost between 3 November and 8 November 1944. Looking exclusively at the numbers, this might not seem devastating, and the fact that much more than the prescript number of fresh soldiers had been allocated to the division covered these extreme losses (in the middle of December 1944, the division still had 2,168 enlisted soldiers more than its originally prescribed strength). However, if we take the number of officers into account, the losses provide a much worse picture. The division had a required strength of 400 officers, and considering the enlisted surplus, the unit would have needed at least 480 officers. However, only 233 officers were left by December, and half of the non-commissioned officers were missing. It was partly because of this situation and the low morale of the enlisted personnel, many of whom did not even speak German, that Zehender's division was the least steadfast unit during the siege of Budapest.

There is little information known about Zehender's actions and movements within Budapest. What is certain is that, during November 1944, the divisional command was located in the Gschwindt Liqueur Factory in District IX, at 9 Ipar Street; later, from 9 January 1945 until the end of the siege, they were relocated to the cellars of the building of the Ministry of Commerce at 1–3 Lánchíd Street. The building, most probably due to the proximity of the Chain Bridge and the Tunnel, was hit several times; after 1945, it was demolished, and nowadays, there is a park in its place, with the Zero Kilometre Stone.

After the abandonment of Pest, the 22nd Cavalry Division practically ceased to exist as an independent military unit. Its combat groups were deployed at various points in the city.

Zehender's task during the breakout attempt would have been to lead a group advancing in the main direction after the first wave broke through. There are a number of surviving accounts of his death. According to certain people, he was seriously wounded and then committed suicide. According to one account, he was wounded while he was sitting in a *Schwimmwagen* on Csalogány Street when a house in the bay of Széna Square (Széna tér) near him got a direct hit, and the falling debris covered his car. Fritz Landauer[430] remembered the events after the war in the account he provided to the *WASt*:

> When I arrived here at 2300 hours with my combat group, due to the incessant fire strikes the Soviets were showering on us, there were indescribable scenes in the gathered, large groups of people there. I tried to disengage my group from the chaos, and I wanted to receive orders from division commander Rumohr, as it was said that he was there as well, trying to make sure that the breakout went uninterrupted. When I forced myself through towards the anti-tank ditch on Széna Square, I was told that both Rumohr and Zehender were seriously wounded and had been taken to the nearby houses.
>
> I have only seen both of them dead. An SS officer present described the events as follows: Rumohr and Zehender, due to their serious wounds and due to their inability to take further part in the breakout attempt, committed suicide.[431]

The news of Zehender's death quickly spread among the soldiers. His body was most probably thrown into the anti-tank ditch on Széna Square and was exhumed from there during the course of 1945.

DECORATIONS	RANKS
• *Eisernes Kreuz II. Klasse* 13 September 1939 • *Eisernes Kreuz I. Klasse* 18 June 1940 • *Deutsches Kreuz in Gold* 16 October 1942 • *Ritterkreuz des Eisernen Kreuzes* 10 March 1943 • *Eichenlaub* to the *Ritterkreuz des Eisernen Kreuzes* 4 February 1945	• *SS-Obersturmführer* 9 November 1935 • *SS-Hauptsturmführer* 20 April 1937 • *SS-Sturmbannführer* 13 December 1940 • *SS-Obersturmbannführer* 19 November 1942 • *SS-Standartenführer* 20 April 1943 • *SS-Oberführer* 16 October 1944

2.

MILITARY PERSONNEL DECORATED WITH THE *DEUTSCHES KREUZ IN GOLD* DURING THE SIEGE OF BUDAPEST

1942–1944

BISCHOFF, HELMUT

Helmut Bischoff was born on 26 March 1920 in Inspringen near Pforzheim. He joined the SS on 1 November 1938 and was promoted to officer in 1943. He started his service in the *Aufklärungs-Abteilung* of *SS-Panzerdivision "Das Reich"* (or rather its predecessor). In 1943, he married Helene Honecker. The interesting aspect of this marriage is that a number of members of the Honecker family were active communists, and after 1971, Erich Honecker became the leader of East Germany. Bischoff was reassigned in July 1944 to the 8th SS Cavalry Division, where he was assigned as commander of the 1st *Schwadron* of the *Aufklärungs-Abteilung 8*. He was awarded the *Deutsches Kreuz in Gold* on 12 December 1944. He received the decoration as commander of the 1st *Schwadron* of the reconnaissance battalion for combat actions in Transylvania. After the Second Vienna Award, the village of Nagycserged (in Romanian: Cerghid) on the Romanian side of the Romanian–Hungarian border, together with the surrounding hills, was occupied by his unit on 5 September 1944. Although the Romanian counterattack retook the village and encircled his unit, Bischoff soon went into action again. On 11 September, an enemy armoured attack advanced as far as Oláhkocsárd (Cucerdea). Bischoff, by exploiting the terrain features and a large downpour, approached the village with his unit undetected and subsequently cleared it of the enemy in close combat. The recommendation for his decoration mentioned some of his other deeds:

> On 23 September 1944, the enemy crossed the river unnoticed in the Maros line and took Hill 429 with an assault. Bischoff launched a counterattack with his *Schwadron* and retook the positions. On 23–24 September

> 1944, the enemy occupied Marosorbó. Bischoff launched a night attack with his unit that had considerably reduced strength. They entered the village, resupplied themselves with weapons and ammunition, and then proceeded to defend the village against seven enemy counterattacks. He only gave up the village with the remainder of his *Schwadron* when the positions became impossible to hold due to the heavy firing of the enemy. On 25 September 1944, near Marosorbó, the remainder of Bischoff's unit, together with other soldiers from other units, stood opposite Hill 463 to aid the company in defence there. On 3 October 1944, Bischoff's unit faced an enemy force of the strength of two Romanian battalions during a counterattack. Despite their weakness, Bischoff immediately went into combat and made the enemy flee. However, due to the complete lack of heavy weapons support, the enemy consolidated their strength and started another attack. Bischoff, however, repulsed every enemy attempt.[432]

The last of the military actions mentioned in connection with his decoration took place on 20 October 1944 at an unknown location where he reoccupied a defensive section previously taken by the enemy.

There are no data regarding his movements and actions in Budapest. It is known that his *Aufklärungs-Abteilung* was in combat around the area of Vecsés in November 1944, in December at Maglód, and after Christmas on the Buda side of the city, in the area of Budaörs. On 29 December 1944, one of Bischoff's subordinates, *SS-Unterscharführer* Josef Bader, met Soviet military envoy Ilya Afanasievich Ostapenko and also escorted him on his way back for some distance.

Bischoff's further actions and movements cannot be reconstructed. Of his death, Fritz Landauer noted the following, based on hearsay:

Helmut Bischoff between 1942–1944

> On 14 February 1945, northwest of Budapest, at Torbágy, he was taken captive while seriously wounded (shot in the upper thigh).

> Allegedly, he died on 14 February at Torbágy. As he was not able to walk, the Soviets shot him dead.[433]

This latter assumption is strengthened by the fact that his dead body was recovered from Biatorbágy.

DECORATIONS	RANKS
• *Eisernes Kreuz II. Klasse* 5 August 1941 • *Eisernes Kreuz I. Klasse* 22 February 1942 • *Allgemeines Sturmabzeichen* 20 April 1942 • *Nahkampfspange Bronze* 14 January 1944 • *Deutsches Kreuz in Gold* 30 December 1944	• *SS-Untersturmführer* 10 March 1943 • *SS-Obersturmführer* 30 January 1945

1944

BÖGLMÜLLER, JOSEF

Josef Böglmüller was born on 21 July in Landsberg am Lech, in Bavaria. He was ranked *Oberleutnant* and commander of the 1st and 2nd Battery of the 271st artillery regiment. He received the *Deutsches Kreuz in Gold* on 28 January 1945. The recommendation has not survived. From the dates, we can assume that the combat actions for which he was recommended were related to the Soviet 23rd Rifle Corps' river crossing at Ercsi and the ensuing fighting. Böglmüller did not survive the siege of Budapest, although he was officially declared dead only in 2004. His remains were exhumed at that time from the Új köztemető in District X.

DECORATIONS	RANKS
• *Deutsches Kreuz in Gold* 28 January 1945	• Dates of promotions are unknown.

BOLLACK, HELMUT

Helmut Jakob Adolf Bollack was born on 27 August 1921 in Sinsheim. During the siege of Budapest, he was the commander of the *Stabsbatterie* of the I *Abteilung* of the 271st artillery regiment; however, he most probably also took over the command of the *Abteilung* itself during the encirclement. He fell on 24 January 1945 on the Buda side of the city. He was posthumously awarded the *Deutsches Kreuz in Gold* on 4 February 1945, so the recommendation for the award must have been handed in earlier.[434]

DECORATIONS	RANKS
• *Deutsches Kreuz in Gold* 4 February 1945	• Dates of promotions are unknown.

1943–1944

BRESINSKI, BRUNO

Bruno Bresinski was born on 23 March 1919 in Kartlow near Wismar. There is very scarce data about his military service before 1944; however, it is known that in 1943, he served in the 6th *Schwadron* of the 3rd SS Cavalry Regiment. He received the *Deutsches Kreuz in Gold* on 6 February 1945. The circumstances of the award are unknown; it is, however, known that at that time, he was ranked *SS-Hauptscharführer* and was a platoon commander in the 17th SS Cavalry Regiment. It is probable that he successfully reached the German lines, as there is no data relating to his capture. Bresinski died on 17 January 1998 in Germany.[435]

DECORATIONS	RANKS
• Hungarian Bronze Medal of Bravery 26 November 1944 • *Deutsches Kreuz in Gold* 6 February 1945	• Dates of promotions are unknown.

BUTTKEREIT, JOHANNES

Johannes Buttkereit was born on 3 November 1912 in the village of Russ bei Heydekrug (today: Rusnė, Lithuania) in East Prussia. Between 1934 and 1935, he served his compulsory military service in one of the artillery regiments of the Lithuanian army. His occupation was a forester. He joined the SS on 22 March

1939. The details of his military service are unknown. However, it is known that from the end of 1941, he served on the Soviet front with the artillery regiment of the SS Cavalry Division. In the summer of 1942, he attended the *SS-Junkerschule*. Thereafter, although still before the siege of Budapest, he was awarded the *Eisernes Kreuz I. Klasse* and *II. Klasse*. During the siege of Budapest, he was commander of the 6th Battery of the 8th SS Artillery Regiment. According to survivors' accounts, he led a combat group in District III (in the area of the Bécsi Street) and he was recommended for the *Ritterkreuz des Eisernen Kreuzes* as well. Buttkereit was awarded the *Deutsches Kreuz in Gold* on 27 January 1945. According to some of his surviving comrades, he was also awarded the Knight's Cross of the Iron Cross. He successfully took part in the breakout attempt. On 8 May 1945, near Salzburg, Buttkereit was taken captive by American troops. His family and comrades knew nothing of his fate, and wild theories began to circulate. On 15 October 1951, the *WASt* recorded a statement about him from a certain August Dambauer, according to which Buttkereit "shot himself in the head, together with the entire *Regimentsstab* during the night of 11 February 1945, in the area of Budaörs, as the planned breakout attempt was revealed and so failed".[436] Buttkereit died in Germany on 30 October 1975.

DECORATIONS	RANKS
• *Eisernes Kreuz II. Klasse* • *Eisernes Kreuz I. Klasse* • *Deutsches Kreuz in Gold* 27 January 1945	• Dates of promotions are unknown.

DRÜCKER, BERNHARD

Bernhard Drücker served in the rank of *Feldwebel* in the 3rd Company of the 93rd Panzergrenadier Regiment. He received the *Deutsches Kreuz in Gold* on 28 January 1945. There are no further data available regarding his person.

DECORATIONS	RANKS
• *Deutsches Kreuz in Gold* 28 January 1945	• Dates of promotions are unknown.

EICHEL, WILLI

Willi Eichel received the decoration *Deutsches Kreuz in Gold* on 23 February 1945 as an *Oberfeldwebel* serving in the 13th Panzer Artillery Regiment. There are no further data available regarding his person.

DECORATIONS	RANKS
• *Deutsches Kreuz in Gold* 23 February 1945	• Dates of promotions are unknown.

1938

FINDEIS, EUGEN

Eugen Findeis was born in Budapest on 7 September 1908; his father, Andreas Findeis, was a Hungarian citizen and served as a *Hauptmann* in the Austro–Hungarian Army. His mother, Vonicka Leopoldina, was born in Vienna.

His family returned to Austria after 1918, and Findeis attended high school there. On 4 August 1933, he joined the ranks of the *Österreichische Artillerie-Abteilung 1*; thereafter, he attended the *Theresianische Militärakademie* in Wiener Neustadt. The Wehrmacht took him over on 1 April 1938 and promoted him to *Leutnant*. He served in the war initially as the adjutant of the *Beobachtungs-Abteilung 28* and was then reassigned as the commander of the 2nd Battery of *Beobachtungs-Abteilung 33*. On 26 August 1941, he was seriously wounded by a shell hit. In the summer of 1942, he was assigned to work with the *General der Artillerie* at the *OKH* as an instructor. On 6 November 1943, he was assigned as commander of the *Beobachtungs-Abteilung 43*.

His assessment dated 25 March 1944 described him as follows:

> He has an excellent personality. He has a great sense of duty, responsibility and personal bravery. He has distinguished himself in battle against the enemy. He has excellent service records. He has in-depth knowledge of mathematics and physics. He is a first-class *Schallmeßmann* [sound measurement expert]. He reworked the training materials of the *Schallmeßbatterien*. He has a perfect national socialist attitude. He is also a good comrade and very considerate. He possesses extraordinary theoretical and practical skills in the field of sound measurement. He is especially experienced as an artillery observer who had the bad luck [sic!] of having served in the *OKH* because, due to this, he was only later assigned as battalion (*Abteilung*) commander. Therefore, he had disadvantages during promotions.[437]

Because of the above, his out-of-turn promotion to *Major* had already been considered; however, soon thereafter, Findeis was discharged from his commander position and was court-martialled. He was accused of having knowledge of many criminal deeds perpetrated by his subordinates and failing to report them. According to the charges against him, he did not report a soldier who lost a coat and an electric measuring device near Nikopol, *Oberleutnant* Brandt who placed a carbine in a car that was to be blown up, thereby causing losses to the army, and lastly, he did not report artilleryman Jaeger when he left a trailer to its fate during the retreat, upon which was a car, a motor vehicle and cables. On 19 September 1944, the court-martial cleared Findeis. It stated that the loss of the coat and the electric measuring device had not happened at all and that although the soldier carrying these items dropped unconscious from exhaustion during the retreat, one of his comrades took over the items and saved them. In connection with the carbine case, it was established that the weapon did not even belong to Findeis' unit but had been found; therefore, losing it was not considered a real loss. At last, in connection with the trailer, it was established that salvaging it would have been completely impossible during the retreat. With this, there were no obstacles in the way of promoting Findeis to *Major*.

At an unknown date, but still in 1944, Findeis became the commander of *Beobachtungs-Abteilung 43* and took part in the battle for Budapest with this unit. However, only parts of the unit might have become stuck in the cauldron, a supposition which is further strengthened by the fact that only three of its officers were regarded as missing in Budapest. There is no data regarding Findeis' movements and actions during the siege. Likewise, it is not known why he received the *Deutsches Kreuz in Gold*. The only contemporary document that mentions his name is the breakout attempt order, which assigned Findeis' unit to the group led by *Major →Ernst Kreipe*, commander of the I *Abteilung* of *Heeres-Artillerie-Brigade 959*.

DECORATIONS	RANKS
• *Eisernes Kreuz II. Klasse* 12 January 1941	• *Leutnant* 1 April 1938
• *Eisernes Kreuz I. Klasse* 5 September 1941	• *Hauptmann* 1 April 1942
• *Verwundetenabzeichen in Schwarz* 27 August 1941	• *Major* 1 August 1944
• *Deutsches Kreuz in Gold* 23 February 1945	

1943

FINGER, JOHANNES

Johannes Finger was born on 3 November 1923 in Bottendorf near Burgwald. There is no information about the first phase of his military service, except that he served in the artillery regiment of the *SS-Polizei-Division*. From here, he was reassigned, before the end of 1943, to the 8th SS Cavalry Division. On 29 December 1943, near Kucherovka, he was lightly wounded. He received the *Deutsches Kreuz in Gold* on 27 January 1945 as reserve *SS-Oberscharführer* and forward observer of the 8th Battery of the 8th SS Artillery Regiment. However, at the time of the award, he was already serving in an infantry combat group as a courier. He took part in the breakout attempt; around midnight on 11 February 1945, he successfully passed the frontline on Széll Kálmán Square. On the Rózsadomb he and his comrades were engaged in heavy combat, during which they had to occupy a number of houses in order to be able to advance. In the woodland, they were heading in the direction of Tök–Perbál when they reached the edge of the wooded area. His group contained approximately 2,000-3,000 men by then. Finger himself remembers the events as follows:

> As we did not have heavy weapons, we had to wait for the night to set in. I was in the middle of the group with the officers. I was just reporting the results of my reconnaissance mission, which confirmed the area southeast of our location as empty ground, when suddenly we heard Soviet shouts of "Hurrah! Hurrah" from the north. We heard the sound of combat, rifle and machine-gun fire, and the complete northern grouping was fleeing backwards in panic. A few of them even raised their hands; these were shot down by [their own officers]. However, the core of the men had not lost their minds. We created a continuous line and took cover, letting the enemy come closer. The enemy had superior numbers and was transporting machine guns on skis. Although they were advancing carefully, we were able to surprise them with directed fire, and after approximately five minutes, we were able to assault them while shouting "Hurrah!" They were leaving their wounded, the machine guns and dead comrades behind and were running for their lives. This was their last attempt to try to contain us in the woods. [...] We were starting off late; we assaulted the Soviet blocking line, a lot of snow, further combat, and complete exhaustion. The wounded were shooting themselves dead. I parted from the spearhead and from the large group. Around 0900-1000 hours on 14 February I reached the first Soviet lines, with approximately 150 soldiers from all units, all branches. We were lucky as it seemed there were Bulgarians or Romanians ahead of us. I was able to guess this from the clothing of a few of the dead bodies. I myself saw only 40-50 soldiers reaching the first German lines at 1100 hours on 13 February until a cavalry unit,[438] which did not make the slightest effort to help us, reached the Soviet main line of defence.[439]

After the war, Johannes Finger married a Swabian girl relocated from Tolna, whom he met in the summer of 1944 during his training. Starting from the 1980s, they frequently visited Hungary. Finger died on 27 April 2004 in Burgwald-Bottendorf.

DECORATIONS	RANKS
• *Deutsches Kreuz in Gold* 27 January 1945	• Dates of promotions are unknown.

1941–1944

FISCHER, ERNST

Ernst Fischer was born on 16 February 1912 in Dortmund. On 1 October 1933, he joined the ranks of the SA, and on 1 May 1937, he joined the *NSDAP*. Initially, he served in the ranks of the III Battalion of the 271st Infantry Regiment, then in the Panzergrenadier Division *Feldherrnhalle*. He was later promoted to non-commissioned officer. During the course of 1942, he was seriously wounded, and his left index finger was amputated. During the summer of 1944, he served in the headquarters company of the 110th Panzer Brigade *Feldherrnhalle*. He was awarded the *Deutsches Kreuz in Gold* on 16 January 1945 as a senior ensign; at that time, he was serving in the escort company of the 13th Panzer Division. Thereafter, he was promoted to *Leutnant*. During the siege of Budapest, he went missing.

DECORATIONS	RANKS
• *Eisernes Kreuz II. Klasse* • *Eisernes Kreuz I. Klasse* 13 September 1942 • *Nahkampfspange Bronze* • *Verwundetenabzeichen in Silber* 15 March 1944 • *Deutsches Kreuz in Gold* 16 January 1945	• Dates of promotions are unknown.

1943

FLÜGEL, WOLFGANG

Wolfgang Flügel was born on 3 July 1921 in Leipzig. His father, the intendant of the racecourse in Leipzig, had joined the National Socialist movement, which subsidized equestrian sports. His long commitment to the movement was honoured with a *Goldenes Parteiabzeichen*. Flügel left the church as early as 1 May 1934, that is, at 13 years of age – he was most probably influenced by his father (his mother committed suicide in 1932, which later caused problems for Flügel during his admittance process to the SS as, in theory, there was a no admittance policy in effect for anyone suffering from a hereditary illness or had suicides in their family).

Flügel's family history is anything but simple. His first wife, Brigitte von Hase, grew up in an anti-Nazi environment. Her uncle, Major General Paul von Hase, was an important figure in the anti-Hitler conspiracy as the *Stadtkommandant* (city commander) of Berlin in 1944. He was court-martialled by a Nazi court and later executed in Plötzensee in August 1944. Brigitte von Hase did not live to see this, however, as she died suddenly of a tragic illness in 1942. Flügel remarried during the war.

On 1 September 1939, he joined the *NSDAP*. While serving in the Reich Labour Service (*Reichsarbeitsdienst, RAD*), he took part in the Polish campaign as a member of a transport unit. After serving his time in the *Reichsarbeitsdienst*, on 1 October 1939, he was admitted to the *SS-Junkerschule* in Tölz. After completing officer's training, he was sent to the SS Riding School in München-Reim, which was led by Hermann Fegelein. Flügel was hoping that as a dressage rider, he would be able to compete in the Olympics planned for the year 1940, but this plan was shattered by the war.

Flügel was deployed to the Soviet frontline with the 1st SS Cavalry Regiment. His role in the mass murders perpetrated by this unit is unclear. On 30 January 1942, he was reassigned to the 3rd *Schwadron* of the 2nd SS Cavalry Regiment. On 7 March 1942, he was lightly wounded near Rzhev. From May 1942 to April 1943, he was assigned to the reserve units in Munich; during his stay there, he met his future second wife in a coffee house, and they married on 24 April 1944. After this, he attended a short officers' training course in Bromberg and was then assigned to the *SS-Kavallerie-Ersatz* in Warsaw. Subsequently, from 25 July 1943, he was assigned to the *SS-Flak-Ausbildungs und Ersatzregiment* in Munich.

In June 1944, he was assigned to Pécsvárad, where he, as platoon commander, took part in the reestablishment of the 4th *Schwadron* of the 15th SS Cavalry Regiment of the 8th SS Cavalry Division. From 26 July 1944, he was promoted to *Schwadron-Chef* and took part in the combat actions unfolding in Northern Transylvania. Between November and December 1944, his unit was in defence in the line of Pécel–Maglód in the positions of the Attila I Defence Line. On 4 November 1944, he was lightly wounded on the hand by a shell fragment. According to a letter he sent home at that time, he was hoping to receive an "extraordinary decoration" very soon. Two weeks later, however, he wrote:

> Unfortunately, my promotion to *SS-Hauptsturmführer* was not realized due to my young age. But later it will surely come true. Most probably there will even be more. I had to hand in a few dozen after-action reports to the Division.[440]

At the beginning of December, he was, for a short time, withdrawn from the frontline due to diphtheria. Afterwards, he returned to his unit, which was in defence on the Pécel–Maglód frontline and the next two weeks were relatively calm. However, on Christmas day, Flügel had to relocate to Buda. His unit was defending the frontline in front of the Pál-völgy Caves. Dénes Vass, a former soldier of the Ist University Assault battalion, remembered Flügel as follows:

Wolfgang Flügel in parade uniform, with his wife in 1943

> He was a strict soldier; he ordered a poor Swabian boy from Óbuda, who went home without permission, to be shot dead as a warning. The dead body lay there on the edge of Szépvölgyi Street. On his chest, there was a sign with a German and a Hungarian inscription. At one time, I brought a document to Flügel's command post, which was approximately a hundred metres away from 1st Lieutenant Babinszky's command post. It was awfully cold, and I was shivering in my thin coat; even my teeth were clattering. After I reported to Flügel, he was smiling as he asked: "Are you afraid, volunteer?" I tried to reply in excellent German that no, I was not afraid, I was just freezing. Flügel laughed and pulled out a bottle of *pálinka* from under his desk, filled a full water glass, and gave it to me: "Drink it!"[441]

There is almost no further information on Flügel's subsequent movement and actions. On 27 January 1945 he received the *Deutsches Kreuz in Gold* that he had been waiting for so much. Gyula Kokovay, who served with Dénes Vass, remembered that on the day of the breakout attempt, Flügel was keeping his positions in Ostrom Street.[442] It was also Kokovay who most probably last saw Flügel alive, on 12 February 1945, in the hills around Buda:

> The Germans walking in front of us stopped, so we also stopped, and as we did not know what was happening, I went forward with the captain to check. At the head of the column, the senior officer of the Germans, *SS-Obersturmführer* Flügel, was lying in the snow and was shouting that he had enough of this madness, everything was in vain, and that he wouldn't go a step further and so on. His men were just standing around him...[443]

From this moment on, we do not have a clear view of the unfolding events. The news, which was passed on to the family later and based on hearsay, reported Flügel's suicide in a railway tunnel with his own pistol. If this account is valid, the suicide must have happened at the Piliscsaba Railway Tunnel.

DECORATIONS	RANKS
• *Eisernes Kreuz II. Klasse* • *Eisernes Kreuz I. Klasse* • *Deutsches Kreuz in Gold* 27 January 1945	• *SS-Untersturmführer* 30 January 1942 • *SS-Obersturmführer* 9 November 1943

1939

Around1980

FRIEDRICH, HELMUT

Helmut Friedrich was born on 6 April 1914 in Frankfurt am Main. He was an Evangelical Church member and a youth group leader until 1934, and he even visited Hungary and Bácska (which then belonged to Yugoslavia) with a youth group. He attended teacher training college in Weilburg but, after graduating, worked as a teacher for only six months as he was drafted; he was only able to return to teaching in the autumn of 1945. He served only in the 13th Artillery Regiment.[444] He took part in the Polish and French campaigns and, in 1941, in the Soviet campaign, during which he served as commander of the 2nd Battery. He even reached the Caucasus. On 30 August 1943, he was wounded by a shell fragment on his face and hands. After recovering from this wound, he received a new assignment as the reserve *Hauptmann* and *Adjutant* of the commander of the artillery regiment. On 8 March 1945, he received the *Deutsches Kreuz in Gold.* An interesting aspect of the award of this decoration is that Friedrich was in the Soviet internment by then.

The recommendation for the decoration has not survived. Therefore, it can only be assumed that it was made partly in connection with Friedrich's actions around Budapest and partly in recognition of his unit's retreat from Romania and Bulgaria during August 1944. His last action was remarkably adventurous: on 29 August 1944, what was left of his unit started off from the Danube delta, and by swimming across the Danube and marching via Bulgaria and Belgrad, they reached their own lines (of the whole 13th Panzer Division, only 14 officers and 84 soldiers survived this way). It is characteristic of his modesty that he never spoke of his decoration to anyone, not even to his sons or the author of this work, nor did he mention it in his biography.

Helmut Friedrich with the author in 1995

At the end of August 1944, the 13th Panzer Division sent him to the *Führerhauptquartier Rastenburg* (the Führer's Headquarters, the *Wolffschanze*) to acquire information on the possibility of re-establishing the *Division*. According to Friedrich, this was possible because of the extremely valuable repair and maintenance units of the 13th Panzer Division managed to escape the encirclement and fought their way through the Carpathians. The firepower of *Panzer-Artillerie-Regiment 13* was considerably increased because some Hungarian artillery units were also subordinated to it. According to Friedrich's memories, during the combat actions around Gödöllő, they could carry out fire strikes against the Soviet troops with more than 71 artillery pieces. This situation ended abruptly when the capital city was encircled: as the regiment had very scarce supplies, only the most essential actions could be carried out.

Friedrich served during the entirety of the siege by the side of the regiment commander. He received his last letter from home in the cauldron on 27 December 1944 and managed to send out his last letter to his wife, in which he openly wrote about the grave situation, on 31 December. At that time, he still thought that, due to their shortage of ammunition, the siege would not last more than two weeks (it was characteristic of him that he never cared for any censorship, although he could easily have been court-martialled for disclosing this information). From 18 January, his unit was relocated to the tunnels of Gellért Hill. His last command post was in Fő Street, not far from the exit of the Tunnel. He took part in the breakout attempt, most probably starting off with his group towards Csalogány Street or Hattyú Street, with the first wave of the breakout. With his commander and *Generalmajor* →*Schmidhuber*, they arrived at the scene at 2000 hours in the evening. In the crowd, they were separated, but he was still an eyewitness to Schmidhuber's death. Around Fény Street, he was wounded in the leg, and soon thereafter, the fingers of his left hand were wounded. Nevertheless, he pressed forward via Városmajor, along the line of the cog-wheel railway, and then spent the day with his comrades not far from the Esze Tamás School at an abandoned building site, hiding in large concrete tubes. The following night was spent in a weekend house not far from the upper sections of the Diós-ditch

(Diós-árok). They spent the third and the fourth night east of Budakeszi in the attic of an abandoned house. He was taken captive there on 15 February 1945.

In the summer of 1945, Friedrich was released from the Cegléd internment camp due to his injuries. He returned to the eastern part of Germany as the leader of a larger group of wounded soldiers and, from there, moved to the western zone in 1947. The *WASt* still registered him as missing in action even years after the end of the war. On 24 April 1953, *Oberleutnant* Ernst Schweizer, *Adjutant* of the *Generalstabsoffizier (Ia)* of the 13th Panzer Division made a statement that he had last seen Friedrich at midnight on the day of the breakout attempt in Margit Street. Friedrich was an elementary school teacher between 1947 and 1979 in Sinntal-Weichersbach; he also played the organ in the local church and led the church choir as well. He had five children and ten grandchildren. After retiring, he worked on valuable local historical works and was one of the leading officials of the local evangelist church. He died in his home on 11 November 2006.

DECORATIONS	RANKS
• *Eisernes Kreuz II. Klasse* • *Eisernes Kreuz I. Klasse* • *Verwundetenabzeichen in Silber* • *Deutsches Kreuz in Gold* 23 February 1945	• Dates of promotions are unknown.

GEORGS, HEINZ

Heinz Georgs was born on 31 December 1920. He started his military service in the 13th Artillery Regiment of the 13th Infantry Division *(mot.)*; the 13th Panzer Division was formed by renaming the 13th Infantry Division *(mot.)* in the same year. It is not possible to date exactly his promotion to reserve *Leutnant*; however, it must have happened after 1942. At an unknown date, he was assigned to the 8th SS Cavalry Division, where he, despite being a Wehrmacht officer, took over the command of the 2nd Company of the *Panzerjäger-Abteilung* (the 2nd Company was equipped with *Jagdpanzer 38(t) Hetzers*). He was recommended for the decoration of *Deutsches Kreuz in Gold* on 6 January 1945. The reason for this is not known. Georgs took part in the breakout attempt and was among the few who managed to reach the German lines. (His name was typed as "Georgy" in the report about the successful breakout attempt, but this is a typo.)

DECORATIONS	RANKS
• *Eisernes Kreuz II. Klasse* • *Eisernes Kreuz I. Klasse* • *Deutsches Kreuz in Gold* 6 January 1945	• Dates of promotions are unknown.

1931

1932

GÖRCKE, WILHELM

Wilhelm Görcke was born on 7 September 1912 in Büsingen near Schaffhausen. In 1931, he joined the SS, and in 1936, he attended an *SS-Junkerschule* (officer training course); thereafter, he was reassigned to the *Leibstandarte-SS "Adolf Hitler"* where he served as platoon commander and subsequently battery commander. After a number of reassignments and a longer period of frontline service (he served on the Karelian frontline as well), he was assigned in June 1944 to the 8th SS Cavalry Division as commander of the 8th Artillery Regiment. After the establishment of 22nd SS Cavalry Division, he was assigned to take over the command of the 16th SS Artillery Regiment stationed in Italy at that time; however, this was not possible due to the encirclement of the Hungarian capital. During the siege of Budapest, Görcke most probably remained the regiment commander of the 8th SS-Artillery Regiment. His unit was in position in the area of Soroksár–Dunaharaszti between November and December 1944. However, it had lost almost all of its artillery pieces on the Pest side by the middle of January 1945.

Görcke's fate during the siege is not possible to trace. It is not known why he was awarded the *Deutsches Kreuz in Gold*. What seems to be true is that he took part in the breakout attempt, and after 16 February 1945 (!), he reached the German lines. He was the one who notified Joachim Gröppler's widow of the death of her husband on 15 February 1945. (Joachim Gröppler was the commander of the III *Abteilung* of the 8th SS Artillery Regiment).[445] Görcke, however, went missing shortly thereafter. His widow had to reopen the case so that Görcke could be legally pronounced dead in 1956, as it turned out that in 1952, he was mistaken for a non-commissioned officer who had the same name and was born at the same time.

DECORATIONS	RANKS
• *Verwundetenabzeichen in Schwarz*	• *SS-Standartenjunker* 9 November 1935
• *Eisernes Kreuz II. Klasse* 28 September 1939	• *SS-Untersturmführer* 20 April 1936
• *Eisernes Kreuz I. Klasse* 13 September 1941	• *SS-Obersturmführer* 12 September 1937
• *Deutsches Kreuz in Gold* 27 January 1945	• *SS-Hauptsturmführer* 30 January 1940
• *Ehrendegen RFSS*	• *SS-Sturmbannführer* 21 June 1943
• *SS-Ehrenring*	• *SS-Obersturmbannführer* 30 January 1945
• *Julleuchter*	
• *Finnischer Orden des Freiheitskreuzes (Vapaudenristin ritarikunta) 3. Klasse* 1 December 1941	

GREGER, FRIEDERICH

Friederich Greger was born on 22 December 1915 in Voxtrup near Osnabrück. He attended a commercial school. On 9 November 1933, he joined the SS. In

1935, he left the church and applied to join the Waffen-SS in the same year. His assignments are only known from 1941: at that time, he was serving as platoon commander in the *SS-Flak-Abteilung "Ost"*. His unit was subordinated to the SS Cavalry Division in September 1942. From 10 October 1943, he was the commander of the 3rd Battery.

During the combat actions around Budapest, he was wounded. In December 1944, he served at the *Abteilungsstab* of *SS-Flak-Abteilung 8* of the 8th SS Cavalry Division, then he was put in command of a *Kampfgruppe*. He was awarded the *Deutsches Kreuz in Gold* on 30 December 1944. According to his recommendation dated 5 November 1944, he received the decoration for two military deeds which had been accomplished between 28 August 1943 and 4 November 1944. Of these, only the latter was related to Budapest:

> Greger, with his personal involvement and determined behaviour, prevented the enemy from breaching the frontline when he swiftly assembled groupings and directed them to eliminate the danger. This helped to keep and reinforce the defence line.[446]

From January 1945, his fate is no longer traceable.

DECORATIONS	RANKS
• *Eisernes Kreuz II. Klasse* 8 February 1942 • *Eisernes Kreuz I. Klasse* 2 June 1942 • *Allgemeines Sturmabzeichen* 1 May 1942 • *Verwundetenabzeichen in Silber* 1 November 1943 • *Nahkampfspange Silber* 4 November 1943 • *Deutsches Kreuz in Gold* 30 December 1944	• *SS-Untersturmführer (der Reserve)* 1 September 1941 • *SS-Obersturmführer (der Reserve)* 30 January 1943 • *SS-Hauptsturmführer (der Reserve)* 20 April 1944

GROSSMANN, HEINZ

Heinz Grossmann was born on 1 August 1918. His personal files are not stored in the *Bundesarchiv*. Therefore, there is little information available regarding the details of his military service. Initially, he served in the 13th Artillery Regiment.[447] On 31 August 1941, he was wounded near Dnepropetrovsk. His last assignment, from January 1945, was as the commander of the II *Abteilung* of the 13th Panzer Artillery Regiment; prior to this, he held the rank of reserve *Oberleutnant* and was the commander of the 2nd Battery.

The decoration *Deutsches Kreuz in Gold* was awarded to him on 28 January 1945. On 13 February 1945, he was taken captive west of Budapest at an unknown location. He was released on 22 December 1948.

DECORATIONS	RANKS
• *Deutsches Kreuz in Gold* 28 January 1945	• Dates of promotions are unknown.

1944

1989

HABERSTROH, FRITZ

Fritz Haberstroh was born on 17 May 1921 in the village of Kamperbuch in the Moers district near Düsseldorf. His father was a miner. After attending elementary school, Haberstroh trained to be a carpenter; in 1933, he joined the *Hitlerjugend*.

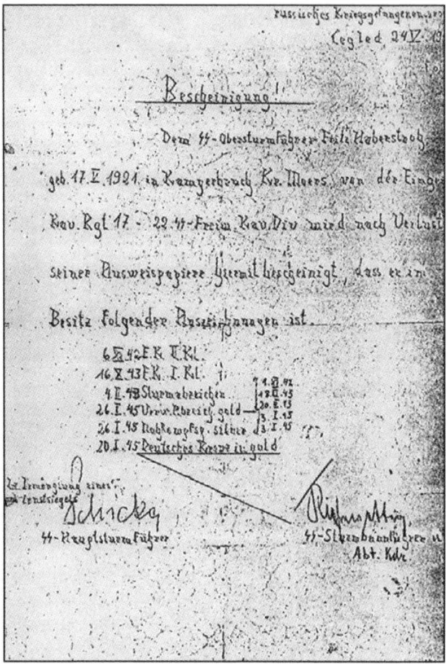
Cegléd, 24.V.

Bescheinigung!

Dem SS-Obersturmführer Fritz Haberstroh geb. 17.V.1921 in Kamperbruch Kr. Moers von der Kav. Rgt. 17 – 22. SS-Freiw. Kav. Div. wird nach Verlust seiner Ausweispapiere hiermit bescheinigt, dass er im Besitz folgender Auszeichnungen ist.

20.I.45 Deutsches Kreuz in Gold

SS-Hauptsturmführer

Abt. Kdr.

Decoration document of Haberstroh from the internment period

He was admitted to the SS on 1 January 1940, and at the same time, he also left the Evangelical Church. He was trained at the *SS-Nachrichten-Ausbildungs-Abteilung 2* in Unna; his first assignment was in the 3rd SS Panzergrenadier Regiment *"Deutschland"*, where he served in a radio section. He took part in the French and Soviet campaigns with this unit. He attended an officer training school between November 1941 and April 1942 (*SS-Junkerschule*). On 17 April 1942, he was assigned to the 17th SS Cavalry Regiment, where he served as an officer in the signal company. As the commander of an infantry alarm unit, he also took part in the combat actions around Kovel between March and April 1944.

In the summer of 1944, he was reassigned as platoon commander in the 2nd (radio) Company of the 22nd SS Voluntary Cavalry Division was established in Hungarian territory. On 5 January 1945, he was seriously wounded in Budapest – his left leg had to be amputated. He was decorated with the *Deutsches Kreuz in Gold* on 30 January 1945. The circumstances of the award are unknown. He did not take part in the breakout attempt due to his condition and was subsequently taken captive. His award of the above-mentioned decoration is especially interesting, as a special document regarding him survived. After being taken captive, Haberstroh lost his documents (most probably Soviet soldiers robbed him); however, his decorations must have been very important to him, therefore on 24 May 1945, in the Cegléd internment camp, together with his former commander *SS-Sturmbannführer* Hans Kiesewetter[448] and a witness, he filed for the following document to be created for him *"in Ermangelung eines Dienstsiegels"*, that is, "in the absence of official stamps". The reader should note that the following document is incorrect and incomplete in terms of the date of the awards:

> Certificate!
> We declare that Fritz Haberstroh, born on 17 May 1921 in Kamperbuch, Moers district, serving in the 17th SS Cavalry Regiment (22nd SS Volunteer Cavalry Division), lost his personal documents. Therefore, we attest that he is the owner of the decorations listed below.

Haberstroh, due to his medical condition, probably could have been released from internment before 1946. Until his death on 14 June 2002, he remained an active member of the SS comradeship organizations.

DECORATIONS	RANKS
• *Eisernes Kreuz II. Klasse* 6 December 1942 • *Eisernes Kreuz I. Klasse* 16 October 1943 • *Allgemeines Sturmabzeichen* 4 February 1943 • *Nahkampfspange Bronze* 22 April 1944 • *Nahkampfspange Silber* 26 January 1945 • *Verwundetenabzeichen in Gold* 26 January 1945 • *Deutsches Kreuz in Gold* 30 January 1945	• *SS-Untersturmführer* 21 June 1942 • *SS-Obersturmführer* 21 June 1944

HAHN, FRITZ

Fritz Hahn was born on 11 May 1914. Initially, he served in the enlisted soldiers' ranks and participated in the Polish, French and Soviet campaigns. He was wounded at least four times. He received the decoration *Deutsches Kreuz in Gold* on 28 January 1945 as *SS-Hauptscharführer* serving in the 11th *(Pionier) Kompanie* of the 93rd Panzergrenadier Regiment of the 13th Panzer Division. At an unknown location and unknown date, he was taken captive. There is no information available on the date of his release. However, he was certainly still alive in 1961.[449]

DECORATIONS	RANKS
• *Eisernes Kreuz II. Klasse* • *Eisernes Kreuz I. Klasse* • *Verwundetenabzeichen in Silber* • *Deutsches Kreuz in Gold* 28 January 1945	• Dates of promotions are unknown.

1939–1940

HASENBEIN, ERICH

Erich Hasenbein was born on 29 June 1916 in Königsberg (today: Kaliningrad, Kaliningrad Oblast, Russia). He joined the Wehrmacht in 1935, and in 1938, he was promoted to reserve *Leutnant.* During the entirety of the war, he served in the 66th Panzergrenadier Regiment of the 13th Panzer Division. The 66th Panzergrenadier Regiment was created in 1942 by renaming parts of the *Schützen-Regiment 66.* On 23 May 1941, he was appointed commander of the signal platoon of the regiment. On 1 January 1941, he was promoted to *Oberleutnant.* Then, on 1 January 1943, he was promoted to *Hauptmann* out of turn. The reason for this promotion was stated as follows:

> In the second and third battles of Kharkov in June 1942, as well as in the combat operations northwest of Kalach, he was able to lead his company to battle with his personal dynamism, and with adamant persistence, he was able to keep the defence positions with outstanding success. Despite the serious wounds he suffered before Kalach, he remained with the unit and, even before his complete recovery, took over his company with the usual dynamism when the temporary commander was also killed. On 20 September 1942, he was again wounded and had to be transferred to the main casualty clearing station of the Division. [450]

After the reorganization of the 66th Panzergrenadier Regiment in the summer of 1944, he became the commander of the II Battalion of the the 66th Panzergrenadier Regiment. He took part in the siege of Budapest with his unit and was always in the frontline. On 6 January 1945, a Soviet assault group almost captured him at his command post. After 16 January 1945, he was deployed on the Buda side with his units west and southwest of the Southern Railway Station. Around this time, these units were provided with artillery support by the assault guns of Tibor Rácz (and the 1st assault artillery Battalion). With German and Hungarian support, Hasenbein's battalion temporarily reoccupied the clothing storage of the Hungarian army on Daróczi Street. He was awarded the *Deutsches Kreuz in Gold* on 20 January 1945.[451] The circumstances of the recommendation are unknown.

While commanding a counterattack on 9 February 1945, he was wounded in the leg. Although →*Schöning* acquired a working *Schwimmwagen* for him, there are no data indicating whether or not Hasenbein was able to take part in the breakout attempt. What is known is that, around 12-14 February 1945, he was taken captive. He was certainly alive in 1965 because in that year he wrote a letter to the *Bundesarchiv* in connection with his service period.

DECORATIONS	RANKS
• *Eisernes Kreuz II. Klasse* 1 July 1940	• *Leutnant (der Reserve)* 1938
• *Eisernes Kreuz I. Klasse* 14 September 1941	• *Oberleutnant* 1 January 1941
• *Deutsches Kreuz in Gold* 16 January 1945	• *Hauptmann* 1 January 1943 (out of turn)

HASLEHNER, FERDINAND

Ferdinand Haslehner was born on 21 November 1921 in Linz. He joined the Waffen-SS on 1 April 1938. On 1 October 1942, he was appointed as a non-commissioned officer.

His first known unit of service was the 1st Company of the *SS-Flak-Abteilung* of the SS Cavalry Division (from 1943: 8th SS Cavalry Division) – he remained with this unit until the end of the siege of Budapest. On 10 September 1943, he was lightly wounded.

On 6 January 1945, he was awarded the *Deutsches Kreuz in Gold.* At that time, he served as *SS-Oberscharführer.* He was promoted to *SS-Untersturmführer* in January 1945. From that point on, his fate is unknown.[452]

DECORATIONS	RANKS
• *Deutsches Kreuz in Gold* 6 January 1945	• *SS-Oberscharführer* before 1945 • *SS-Untersturmführer* January 1945

1943

HEHN, VIKTOR VON

Viktor Richard Heinrich Adrian von Hehn was born on 4 February 1907 in Riga into an old Baltic noble family. He and his younger brother Jürgen came into contact with the National Socialist movement very early (Jürgen von Hehn was one of the leading figures in the cultural robbing of the eastern territories; besides this, he also played an active role in the appropriation of the Jewish libraries in Budapest). Viktor von Hehn joined the SA in 1936, the SS in 1940 and the *NSDAP* in 1941. Apart from this, he was also the deputy commander of the *Deutsche Volksgemeinschaft* in Latvia, which was founded on National Socialist principles. Despite this, von Hehn was not entirely suitable for the system, given his abilities and characteristics. It was most probably an inherited illness or medical condition that resulted in his assessment as follows: "In a hereditary, biological regard, supporting him is not acceptable. Moderate support given to him is not objectionable on racial grounds."[453]

From the summer of 1941, von Hehn was in service in the 6th *Einsatzkommando* of the *Einsatzgruppe C*. This unit perpetrated a large number of mass murders and other atrocities (by the end of the year, the *Einsatzgruppe* reported the extermination of 95,000 persons, two-thirds of which can be connected to the Babij Jar massacre near Kiev). There is no surviving information indicating the extent of von Hehn's involvement in these murders. From February 1942, he was assigned to attend the *SS-Junkerschule* and subsequently served in the Artillery Regiment of the 8th SS Cavalry Division. On 28 September 1942 he received the *Eisernes Kreuz II. Klasse*, then on 22 December 1942, the *Eisernes Kreuz I. Klasse.*

He participated in the combat actions in Hungary as the commander of the II *Abteilung* of the 8th Artillery Regiment of the 8th SS Cavalry Division and as the *Adjutant* of the *Divisionskommandeur*. He received the *Deutsches Kreuz in Gold* on 20 January 1945. The circumstances of the award are unknown.

Von Hehn took part in the breakout attempt. →*Harry Phoenix* met him in the evening hours of 11 February 1945 and was astounded that von Hehn was bringing with him a large backpack that was making him exhausted at the very beginning of the breakout action. Phoenix suggested that he should throw away everything that was unnecessary, but von Hehn, who was an eyewitness to →*Joachim Rumohr* being wounded earlier, responded that he really wanted to save the valuables he collected for his family, referring to the fact that they had lost everything in the Baltic area. It is not known what could have been in his backpack as he could not have legally acquired any valuables, and his reference to his family is equally strange because his wife and child were dead by that time. We only have two further accounts about his fate: Heinz Melchinger and Günther Scherzinger, both of whom took part in the breakout attempt, testified in 1953 that they had witnessed von Hehn committing suicide in a wine cellar 20 km from Budapest.

DECORATIONS	RANKS
• *Eisernes Kreuz II. Klasse* 28 September 1942 • *Eisernes Kreuz I. Klasse* 22 December 1942 • *Nahkampfspange Bronze* • *Allgemeines Sturmabzeichen* • *Deutsches Kreuz in Gold* 20 January 1945	• *SS-Untersturmführer (der Reserve)* 9 May 1942 • *SS-Obersturmführer (der Reserve)* 20 April 1943 • *SS-Hauptsturmführer (der Reserve)* 20 April 1944

1939–1944

HELLER, HANS

Hans Heller was born on 9 August 1915 in Geislingen. Of his military service, the only data available is that he was seriously wounded on 10 November 1942, on 11 February 1943, on 24 October 1943 and on 10 May 1944, and, furthermore, he was lightly wounded on 27 February 1943 and on 22 September 1944. According to *Gefreiter* Maikath's report dated 27 February 1945, Heller received the decorations *Deutsches Kreuz in Gold* and the *Verwundetenabzeichen in Gold* at the beginning of February 1945 (in reality, on 28 January 1945).[454] At that time, he served as a non-commissioned officer in the 3rd Company of the *Panzer-Aufklärungs-Abteilung 13*. He was last seen on 13 February 1945, south of Piliscsaba, in the wooded area. The authorities in Horb declared him officially dead on 31 July 1967.

DECORATIONS	RANKS
• *Verwundetenabzeichen in Gold* 28 January 1945 • *Deutsches Kreuz in Gold* 28 January 1945	• Dates of promotions are unknown.

HENNIG, HANS

Hans Henning, as *Oberfeldwebel* of the 5th Company of the *Heeres-Pionier-Brigade 127* received the decoration *Deutsches Kreuz in Gold* on 8 March 1945. There is no other information available regarding his person.

DECORATIONS	RANKS
• *Deutsches Kreuz in Gold* 8 March 1945	• Dates of promotions are unknown.

HERRMANN, KARL

Karl Herrmann was born on 6 August 1922. On 1 February 1945, he received the *Deutsches Kreuz in Gold* as the commander of the IV *Abteilung* of the 271st Artillery Regiment of the 271st *Volks-Grenadier-Division*. There is no further information available regarding his person.

DECORATIONS	RANKS
• *Deutsches Kreuz in Gold* 1 February 1945	• Dates of promotions are unknown.

HOLZ, EWALD

Ewald Holz, serving in the 93rd Panzergrenadier Regiment of the 13th Panzer Division received the *Deutsches Kreuz in Gold* decoration on 20 January 1945. No other information is available regarding his person.

DECORATIONS	RANKS
• *Deutsches Kreuz in Gold* 20 January 1945	• Dates of promotions are unknown.

1940–1944

KAMMERER, ERICH

Erich Kammerer was born on 11 January 1912 in Strasbourg. The details of his military service history are difficult to reconstruct due to missing parts in his personal files. He was wounded on 8 August 1941. From the autumn of 1944, he was known to be serving as the commander of *Beobachtungs-Abteilung 36* of the 36th Infantry Division and, therefore, must have served during the siege of Budapest.

On 20 January 1945, he was wounded in his right leg due to debris falling on him after an air raid. He received the decoration *Deutsches Kreuz in Gold* on 12 February 1945. There are two accounts of his death available. One of his comrades, Heinrich Schumacher, wrote an extremely detailed letter to the *WASt* on 3 July 1962, in which he describes the events as follows:

> After a discussion at one of our command posts, he started off with his driver named Klaus towards the Margit Bridge. I was watching him from the window as *Hauptmann* Erich Kammerer's vehicle got a direct hit and was burning with high flames. Half an hour later, *Leutnant* Gorni came to us and told us that Kammerer and his driver were dead. Gorni fell soon thereafter in the same area.[455]

At the same time, however, the survivors of the unit recorded a document on 5 March 1945 in Sopron which provides different data. In this document, five soldiers of the unit who successfully survived the breakout attempt gave an account of the fate of their 179 comrades. Non-commissioned officer Eckert stated about Kammerer:

> He was marching with us vigorously with the aid of a stick. Non-commissioned officer Kledtke and I were supporting the wounded Gefreiter Hermann. Therefore, we lost sight of our commander around 0300 hours at dawn on 14 February.[456]

It seems that this event must have happened northwest of Nagykovácsi, at the edge of the Zsámbék basin or already in the area of Perbál. The location of the remains of *Hauptmann* Kammerer is unknown to this day.

DECORATIONS	RANKS
• *Deutsches Kreuz in Gold* 12 February 1945	• Dates of promotions are unknown.

1944

KEITEL, KARL-HEINZ

Karl-Heinz Keitel was born on 2 January 1914 in Wolfenbüttel as the eldest son of Wilhelm Keitel, who later became *Generalfeldmarschall*. Like his father, he chose a military career. From 1934, he served in various cavalry units. In 1938, he married the daughter of *Generaloberst* Werner von Blomberg; it is interesting to note that Keitel's father had a very bad relationship with Blomberg. In June 1943, Keitel was reassigned to the *Schule für Schnelle Truppen Krampnitz*; thereafter, he served in *Kavallerie-Regiment Nord*, which was active in the Baltic area. During the summer of 1944, for a short period, he served

SS-Sturmbannführer Keitel in November 1944 in the Attila I. defence line, most probably with Major László Pokorny. The person in the middle is a German police officer from the *SS-Polizei-Regiment 1*

as the commander of the *Radfahr-Abteilung* of the 20th *Felddivision* of the *Luftwaffe* stationed in Northern Italy. On 5 August 1944 – most probably upon his own request – Keitel was transferred to the Waffen-SS, where he was appointed commander of the 17th SS Voluntary Cavalry Regiment of the 22nd SS Voluntary Cavalry Division on 20 October 1944.

He was recommended to receive the decoration *Deutsches Kreuz in Gold* on 14 December 1944 by division commander →*Zehender* based on the following military deeds:

> On 22 November 1944, the Soviets, after having crossed the Csepel Island, launched a surprise assault and broke into the positions of the Hungarian troops, repulsed the Hungarians from their securing positions, and reached Tököl and Szigetszentmiklós. The objective of the enemy was to advance in the direction of Csepel in order to be able to advance even further towards Budapest via the bridge there.[457]
>
> *SS-Sturmbannführer* Keitel, with two companies of the regiment and with subordinated Hungarian soldiers, immediately went into attack against the Russians, advancing into Szigetszentmiklós. During his daring attack, Keitel, leading the small combat group, fought his way from house

to house, street to street and reached the southern edge of Szigetszentmiklós, where he established positions on the railway embankment and stopped all of the assault attempts of the Russians. [...] On 23 November 1944, the Russians managed to breach the main line of defence, positioned on the railway embankment, and reach the regimental command stationed in the middle of the village. *SS-Sturmbannführer* Keitel retained a few of his men, and the Hungarians who were retreating launched a counteroffensive and, with his unrelenting counterattacks, repulsed the enemy back to their point of departure. After a short reorganization of the regimental reserves, Keitel went into the attack again and, in heavy woodland combat, reached the ravine one and a half kilometres south of Szigetszentmiklós.

On 24 November 1944, the Soviets, following heavy artillery preparation, renewed their attack along the railway embankment with approximately 800-1,000 soldiers and assaulted the 1st *Schwadron* of the 17th Cavalry Regiment in defence there. Thereafter, they advanced northwards, flooded the streets, then turned towards the west and tried to encircle the village of Szigetszentmiklós. *SS-Sturmbannführer* Keitel, with five couriers, resisted the enemy and, with dynamic combat command, appeared in different streets every time and shot at the enemy, throwing them in disorder. It was in this way that the recapture of the occupied parts became possible, the relief of the casualty clearing station and the swift establishment of a new line of defence, first at Hill 105, then at Hill 99 and east of it was achieved. It is to the personal merit of *SS-Sturmbannführer* Keitel that he led by personal example and flung himself into action and, with the best possible combat command, prevented the enemy from breaking through.

On 11 December 1944 at Dunaharaszti, supported from three sides by heavy weapons, the enemy created a salient in our main line of defence and occupied Hill 113 as well as the Millenium Settlement, which was a position of essential importance for the defence. This posed the threat of breaching the lines starting at Soroksár towards Budapest. Furthermore, the enemy also had the opportunity to target our positions from the newly occupied areas on the Csepel Island 10-12 metres downwards. With the help of a single platoon providing the reserve for the regiment, *SS-Sturmbannführer* Keitel launched a counterattack. He distinguished himself and, leading by personal example, Keitel pushed his soldiers further and further, fighting in heavy urban combat for every metre and every house. In a combat action lasting for hours, they retook the original positions. By deploying reserves and with artillery support, *SS-Sturmbannführer* Keitel continued his attack the next day. With daring and dynamic assaults, he reached Hill 112 and Hill 113 despite the heavy enemy fire. From this location, Keitel advanced further to the northern edge of Dunaharaszti, causing heavy losses to the enemy, who began to retreat and also acquire weapons.

This success was only due to Keitel *Sturmbannführer*, who, as usual, turned the situation to his advantage and cleared the area of the enemy intrusion.[458]

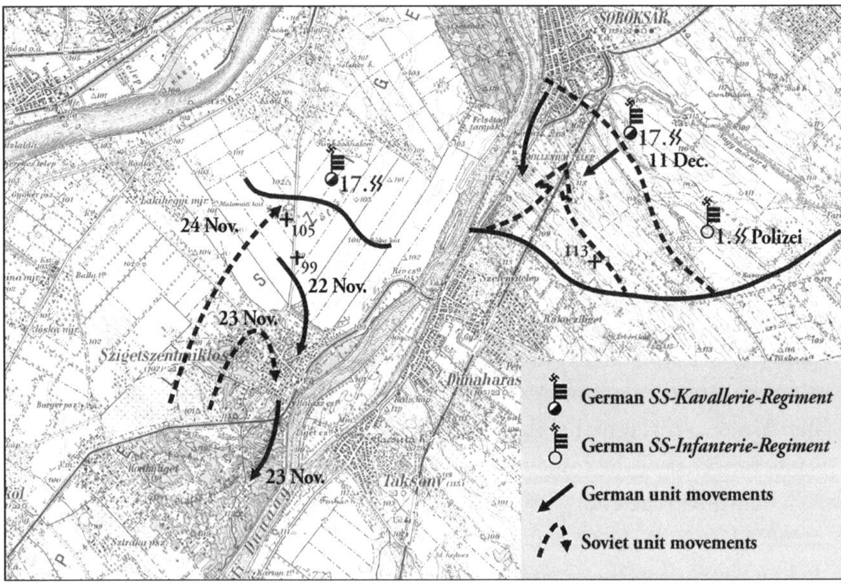

Karl-Heinz Keitel's reconstructed military advance in November-December 1944

On 12 December 1944, Keitel was seriously wounded, and this was the reason he did not remain in Budapest when the city was encircled. He received the *Deutsches Kreuz in Gold* on 6 February 1945 – it is necessary to note that for the combat actions around the Csepel Island →*Bruno Meiert* and →*Adolf Möller* received the same decoration (for a detailed description of these combat actions, see the biography of Adolf Möller). After having recovered, he commanded a combat group of the 37th SS Cavalry Division. On 9 May 1945, he was captured by American troops and released on 15 March 1946. In the 1960s, he handed over his father's inheritance to the *Bundesarchiv Freiburg* (*Abteilung Militärarchiv*). He was interviewed by the British historian David Irving. He died on 2 December 1968 in Köln.

DECORATIONS	RANKS
• *Eisernes Kreuz II. Klasse* • *Eisernes Kreuz I. Klasse* • *Nahkampfspange Bronze* 13 December 1944 • *Verwundetenabzeichen in Schwarz* 13 December 1944 • *Deutsches Kreuz in Gold* 6 February 1945 • *Deutsches Reichssportabzeichen*	• *Rittmeister* 1 July 1942 • *SS-Hauptsturmführer* 5 August 1944 • *SS-Sturmbannführer* 6 August 1944

KERKAU, OTTO

Otto Kerkau was born on 7 February 1911 in Plön, Holstein. He started his military service probably around 1939 in the 1st SS Cavalry Regiment. He was awarded the *Eisernes Kreuz II. Klasse* on 28 September 1942 and the *Eisernes Kreuz I. Klasse* on 20 February 1944. On 10 January 1942, he suffered a serious frost injury on his right hand.

He received the decoration *Deutsches Kreuz in Gold* on 27 January 1945. At that time, he was serving with *SS-Panzer-Aufklärungs-Abteilung 8* of the 8th SS Cavalry Division as reserve *Hauptscharführer*. The circumstances of the recommendation are unknown.

According to his comrade Peter Becher, Kerkau died in 1947 in a Soviet prisoner-of-war camp. This data was updated with some details by the Soviets: the place of death was specified as Prisoner-of-War Camp No. 146 in Georgia, and the date was specified as 5 February 1947.

DECORATIONS	RANKS
• *Eisernes Kreuz II. Klasse* 28 September 1942 • *Eisernes Kreuz I. Klasse* 20 February 1944 • *Deutsches Kreuz in Gold* 27 January 1945	• Dates of promotions are unknown.

KLAUSS, HANS-HEINRICH

Hans-Heinrich Klauss was born on 15 December 1919 in Wiedenborstel, Schleswig-Holstein. He trained to be a car mechanic. In January 1941, he joined the Waffen-SS and was assigned to SS Panzergrenadier Regiment *"Nordland"* of the SS Panzergrenadier Division *"Wiking"*. In April 1942, Klauss was reassigned to *SS-Flak-Abteilung "Ost"*, which was part of the SS Cavalry Brigade (which served as the base for creating the 8th SS Cavalry Division). He took part in the siege of Budapest as the commander of the 2nd (3.7 cm) Battery of the *SS-Flak-Artillerie-Abteilung 8*. With this calibre, it was possible to reach targets up to 6,500 meters away and engage air and ground targets as well. During the siege, until Christmas 1944, the *Flak-Artillerie-Abteilung* was mainly deployed against air targets; however, after that, it was deployed mainly in urban combat against ground targets. Klauss' unit was in combat during January 1945 in the northern parts of Buda.

He received *Deutsches Kreuz in Gold* on 27 January 1945. The recommendation has not survived. Klauss took part in the breakout attempt, and he successfully reached the German lines, most likely on February 14.

In April 1945, he was appointed as commander of *SS-Flak-Abteilung 32*. On 18 May 1945, he was captured by the Americans near Liezen in Styria. He was released on 5 January 1948.

DECORATIONS	RANKS
• *Deutsches Kreuz in Gold* 27 January 1945	• *SS-Untersturmführer* 30 January 1942 • *SS-Obersturmführer* 30 January 1944

1940–1944

KRAETZIG, LOTHAR

Lothar Kraetzig was born on 20 January 1910 in Frankfurt am Main. His civilian qualification was that of a salesman. There is only scarce information available relating to his military service. In November 1939, he was assigned to *Kolonne 58*. On 16 October 1943, he was reassigned to the *Kraftfahr-Ersatz-Abteilung 9*. Until November 1944, he served as reserve *Leutnant* in the 93rd Panzergrenadier Regiment of the 13th Panzer Division before being reassigned to *Panzer-Aufklärungs-Abteilung 13* of the same division, where he served as commander of a reconnaissance platoon. Later, he took over the command of the 1st Company (according to other sources, it was the 3rd Company). He received the decoration *Deutsches Kreuz in Gold* on 4 February 1945. On 11 February 1945, he took part in the breakout attempt but went missing shortly thereafter. His further fate is unknown.

DECORATIONS	RANKS
• *Deutsches Kreuz in Gold* 4 February 1945	• *Leutnant* 1 April 1944

KRÄMER, GABRIEL

Gabriel Krämer was born on 22 April 1914. His original profession was customs officer. There is very scarce information available on his military service; it is known, however, that on 25 February 1944, he was wounded. In August 1944, he was reassigned from the *Ersatz* units to the Panzergrenadier Division *Feldherrnhalle.* He received the decoration *Deutsches Kreuz in Gold* on 9 February 1945. At that time, he served in the rank of *Oberleutnant* and was the commander of the 9th Battery of the *Panzer-Artillerie-Regiment Feldherrnhalle*. He was captured by the Soviets on 20 (!) February 1945, in either Budapest or in the vicinity of the capital, and he was released from internment on 10 October 1952. As he did not provide the location at which he had been captured in his prisoner-of-war compensation request, it is not known how he managed to hide from the Soviet troops for eight days.

DECORATIONS	RANKS
• *Deutsches Kreuz in Gold* 9 February 1945	• Dates of promotions are unknown.

1940–1944

KREIPE, ERNST

Ernst Kreipe was born on 17 March 1913 in Celle. He chose a military career. The different steps of his military service are difficult to reconstruct because his personal files are incomplete. It is known that in the summer of 1941, he was a member of the German military contingent that was sent to Romania. His task was to facilitate the training of the Romanian army. According to one of his assessments, "due to his excessively open opinions on the Romanian circumstances, his work suffered hindrances on certain occasions". At the same time, as a recognition of his work, he was decorated with the Order of the Crown of Romania (Coroana României) IV Class with Swords.

In the summer of 1944, he took over the command of the I *Abteilung* of the *Heeres-Artillerie-Brigade 959* established in Romania. He served in the rank of *Major* at that time. After Romania's armistice, the unit was able to retreat beyond the Carpathian Mountains. From the end of 1944, *Heeres-Artillerie-Brigade 959* was stationed in Budapest. Kreipe's unit struggled with a lack of ammunition; therefore, from the beginning of 1945, they acted as an infantry combat group. He received the decoration *Deutsches Kreuz in Gold* on 10 February 1945. According to his comrade Fritz Gelsenkirchen, Kreipe was seriously wounded in the initial hours of the breakout attempt, and it was presumed that he would soon die. He is recorded as missing in action.[459]

DECORATIONS	RANKS
• *Deutsches Kreuz in Gold* 10 February 1945 • Order of the Crown of Romania (Coroana României) IV Class with Swords	• Dates of promotions are unknown.

KUNZ, JOSEF

Oberfeldwebel Josef Kunz received the decoration *Deutsches Kreuz in Gold* on 10 February 1945. He was serving at that time in the 2nd Company of the I Battalion of *Heeres-Pionier-Brigade 127*. There is no other information available regarding his person.

DECORATIONS	RANKS
• *Deutsches Kreuz in Gold* 10 February 1945	• Dates of promotions are unknown.

MAZUREK, FRANZ

Franz Mazurek was born on 23 November 1918. He received the decoration *Deutsches Kreuz in Gold* on 27 January 1945 as reserve *SS-Oberscharführer* while serving in 8th SS Artillery Regiment of the 8th SS Cavalry Division. There is no other information available regarding his person.

DECORATIONS	RANKS
• *Deutsches Kreuz in Gold* 27 January 1945	• Dates of promotions are unknown.

MEDLA, HENRY

As *Oberleutnant*, he served in the II Battalion of the 978th Grenadier Regiment of the 271st *Volks-Grenadier-Division.* He received the decoration *Deutsches Kreuz in Gold* on 4 February 1945. No other biographical data on his person is available.

DECORATIONS	RANKS
• *Deutsches Kreuz in Gold* 4 February 1945	• Dates of promotions are unknown.

MEHLES, GÜNTHER

Günther Mehles was born on 23 April in Altdöbern. In September 1941, he joined the 1st SS Cavalry Regiment of SS Cavalry Brigade. Until 13 October 1942, he served as adjutant of 2nd SS Cavalry Regiment and was promoted to officer at this time as well. From April 1944, he served as the *Adjutant* of the 16th SS Cavalry Regiment of the 8th SS Cavalry Division. In the second half of 1944, he was assigned as *Schwadron-Chef* of the 5. *Schwadron* of the 15th SS Cavalry Regiment (8th SS Cavalry Division),[460] and in November, he was promoted to *SS-Obersturmführer.* He received the decoration *Deutsches Kreuz in Gold* on 14 November 1944 – most probably for the combat actions he took part in while he was deployed in the Transylvanian region. He fell in January 1945 on the Buda frontline; a Soviet sharpshooter shot him dead close to his command post. His remains were recovered in the 1970s on the plot of the house at 84 Szépvölgyi Street.

DECORATIONS	RANKS
• *Eisernes Kreuz II. Klasse* 28 September 1942 • *Eisernes Kreuz I. Klasse* 12 April 1943 • *Nahkampfspange Bronze* 16 November 1943 • *Deutsches Kreuz in Gold* 14 November 1944	• *SS-Untersturmführer* 6 June 1942 • *SS-Obersturmführer* 11 November 1944

1942

MEIER, FRIEDRICH

Friedrich Meier was born on 28 May 1911 in Marchtrenk, Upper Austria. He was a professed National Socialist and joined the *NSDAP* on 1 October 1931 and the SS on 28 February 1932. During the battle for Budapest, he was ranked *SS-Hauptsturmführer* and was commander of the 1st Company of *SS-Panzer-jäger-Abteilung 8* of the 8th SS Cavalry Division. Meier was recommended for the decoration of *Deutsches Kreuz in Gold* on 26 November 1944, basically for his distinguished conduct during the combat actions of the division in Transylvania and Eastern Hungary (he was recommended to receive this decoration earlier as well; however, he did not receive it at that time). Meier's unit arrived in Budapest considerably late because it had been temporarily subordinated to the 76th Infantry Division. His last notable military deed, which was also recorded in the recommendation, was performed on 17 November 1944 in the area of Gyöngyös. He received the decoration on 20 January 1945. During the breakout attempt, he was, for a short time, together with the group, which also consisted →*Mitzaff*, →*Phoenix* and →*Klett*. On the morning of 14 February 1945, he fell in the area of Tök–Perbál. A comrade of Erich Gäfigam saw Meier's dead body on the roadside and recognized him.

DECORATIONS	RANKS
• *Eisernes Kreuz II. Klasse* 28 September 1942 • *Eisernes Kreuz I. Klasse* 25 August 1943 • *Allgemeines Sturmabzeichen* • *Kriegverdienstkreuz II. Klasse mit Schwertern* • *Deutsches Kreuz in Gold* 20 January 1945	• Dates of promotions are unknown.

MEIERT, BRUNO

Bruno Meiert was born on 4 March 1917 in Königsberg. He spent his military service between 1936 and 1938 in Gleiwitz (today: Gliwice, Poland). Thereafter, he joined the police force and became a member of the *Allgemeine SS* on 18 January 1939. From the autumn of 1940, he was the commander of the cavalry platoon of *Polizei-Bataillon 306*, and as such, he perpetrated a series of mass murders. His methods were so horrendous (he also shot down infants and the captured people were dragged to the mass graves at bayonet point) that *Oberleutnant der Polizei* Klaus Hornig, whose unit should have assisted Meier in perpetrating these crimes, openly refused to work with him and warned his own subordinates that, according to paragraph 47 of the *Militär-Strafgesetzbuch* (military law code), orders that clearly fall under the definition of a crime do not need to be carried out. In one actual case, they were ordered to execute 780 Soviet prisoners of war for whom no kind of trial had been initiated. Furthermore, Hornig called Meiert, whose clothes were dirty with the blood and spilt brains of his victims, an "SS prick" [*sic!*] in public and called his methods "GPU-methods" in reference to the earlier name of the Soviet state security organization. Hornig was arrested a few months later and sentenced to five years in a concentration camp – not because of the event mentioned above, but for listening to enemy radio stations. After the war, Meiert explained that he participated in the mass murders because he could not order his subordinates to do what he could not do himself.

On 20 April 1943, he was reassigned to the *SS-Kavallerie-Ersatz*, where he became the commander of the 5th *Schwadron* of the 15th SS Cavalry Regiment of the 8th SS Cavalry Division. In the summer of 1944, he was reassigned as first *Adjutant* in the 22nd SS Cavalry Division.

Meiert was recommended to receive the *Deutsches Kreuz in Gold* decoration in November 1944. The recommendation document stated the following:

> [On 22 November 1944] After the surprise advance of the Russians on the Csepel Island, *SS-Hauptsturmführer* Meiert was given the task of stopping the retreating *honvéd* soldiers and establishing a new defence line along the Tököl–Szigetszentmiklós railway line. By this time, the Soviets had breached the positions much deeper, were standing at benchmark point No. 102, and had occupied several large hangars. *SS-Oberführer* Zehender gave new orders in that area. With the support of a swiftly relocated company there, they were to launch a new attack. The situation was unknown, and Meiert knew nobody in that company.
>
> Regardless of advancing Soviet troops on the left and on the right, Meiert set off and, driving his men forward, repulsed the enemy behind the railway embankment; there, they established positions and kept them against all subsequent attacks. This made it possible to draw forward the neighbouring units as well. However, Meiert's most important deed was that it was possible to salvage important aircraft material stored in the large hangars by commanding the swift advance. On that day, it was possible for two Messerschmitts to take off from there.
>
> On 25-26 November 1944, *SS-Haupturmführer* Meiert was tasked with keeping the line from benchmark point No. 102 to Szigetszentmiklós on the Csepel Island. The enemy constantly assaulted the positions from the direction of Szigetszentmiklós and was repulsed in heavy, bloody fighting. Meiert was the heart of the defence. Again and again, he showed extraordinary courage and was a personal example to his men to keep fighting.
>
> The enemy managed to breach the positions of his right-hand neighbour, a Hussar company. The Soviets arrived in a large fruit orchard, which spanned as far as the direct rear of Meiert's unit. With a few couriers, Meiert stopped those retreating, and despite a fire assault from infantry units using mostly explosive shells, he launched a counterattack. In heavy combat, personally fighting in the first lines, he forced the Soviets to retreat step-by-step and managed to recapture the previous main line of defence.

This success was of essential importance because losing ground against the Soviets would have given them control over the Tököl–Csepel route, and they could have assaulted Csepel without any difficulties.

The *Adjutantur IIa* (responsible for personal issues of officers of the given unit) of Panzergrenadier Division *Feldherrnhalle* described Meiert's military deed on 28 November 1944 as follows:

> Meiert as an officer of the I *Alarmbataillon* of the 22nd SS Cavalry Division, between 24-26 November, with his personal bravery, helped tremendously in keeping back the Soviets who were advancing southwards from the north. With his battalion, the members of which were mostly insufficiently trained soldiers, he occupied the railway embankment at Szigetszentmiklós and, with this, made it possible to repulse the Soviet attack near the Hermina-major. During these combat actions, he displayed extraordinary stamina and endurance and evoked the immense trust of his soldiers. Attacking at Szigetszentmiklós, he dragged his whole battalion with him. Considering these combat actions the division is convinced that Meiert deserves to be recommended for the decoration *Deutsches Kreuz in Gold*.[461]

Fortunately for Meiert, he did not remain in the encirclement, most probably

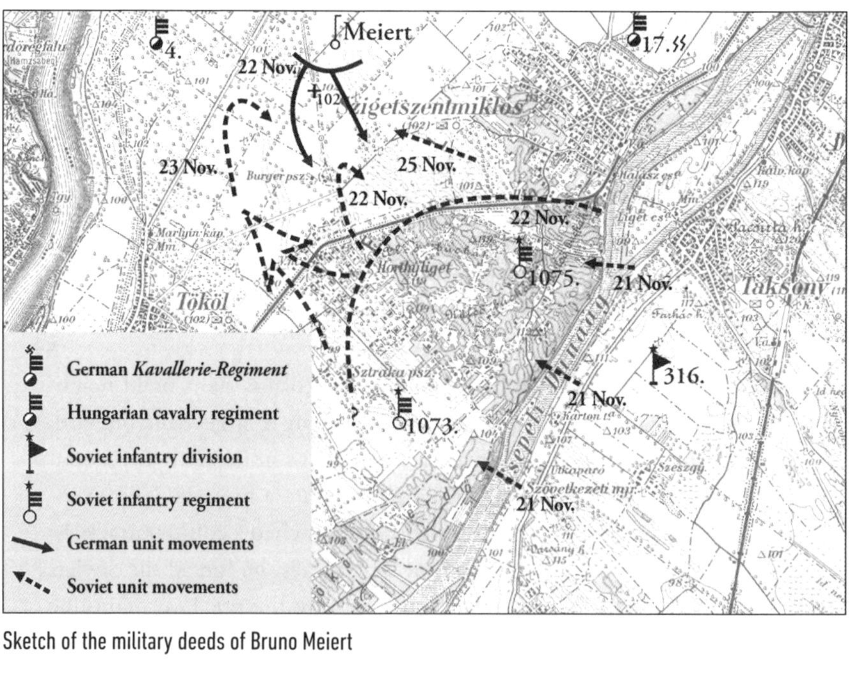

Sketch of the military deeds of Bruno Meiert

because he was lightly wounded. He received the decoration *Deutsches Kreuz in Gold* on 6 February 1945. Between 3 January and 15 February, he attended a battalion commander training course and then was assigned to the 37th SS Cavalry Division.

His fate is not traceable after the war. Until 1951, he hid in Germany, and from 1957, the police forces employed him again – however, after an investigation into his background, he was fired. Thereafter, he settled into business life. In his own words, after the start of the investigation, he had dedicated his life to making contact with former comrades – it seems his efforts were not in vain, as Meiert was acquitted. The trial itself spanned from 1961 until as late as 1973. The majority of the witnesses did not remember anything. And Meiert claimed that he only carried out orders.[462] He died in 2003.

DECORATIONS	RANKS
• *Deutsches Kreuz in Gold* 6 February 1945	• Dates of promotions are unknown.

MEISSNER, WALTER

Walter Meissner was born on 4 October 1920. During the siege of Budapest he was serving in the heavy weapons *Schwadron* of the 15th SS Cavalry Regiment of the 8th SS Cavalry Division as *SS-Hauptscharführer*. He received the decoration *Deutsches Kreuz in Gold* on 27 January 1945.

We only have one detail about his fate during the siege of Budapest: according to a transcript of an International Red Cross document dated 9 May 1967, he had fallen in the city.

DECORATIONS	RANKS
• *Deutsches Kreuz in Gold* 27 January 1945	• Dates of promotions are unknown.

METZIG, HEINZ

Heinz Metzig was born on 13 October 1924 in Friedeberg. He started his military service on 20 May 1942 in the *SS-Polizei-Division*. However, he was transferred from there to the *Kavallerie* at an unknown date. He was promoted to *SS-Untersturmführer* in March 1944. During the siege of Budapest, he served as an assigned officer of the 1st *Schwadron* of the 53rd SS Cavalry Regiment of the 22nd SS Cavalry Division. Near Pestszentimre, on 10 November 1944, he was seriously wounded (his throat was pierced by a shell fragment, and his left hand was bruised by a bullet). He received the *Eisernes Kreuz II. Klasse* on the same day; he also received the *Eisernes Kreuz I. Klasse* on 20 November 1944. He was awarded the Knight's Cross of the Order of the Holy Crown of Hungary with swords on 13 January 1945. He also received the decoration *Deutsches Kreuz in Gold* on 30 January 1945 – in all probability for the same reason, which indicates a rather peculiar awarding policy. In 1974, the Siegen authorities legally pronounced him dead.

DECORATIONS	RANKS
• *Eisernes Kreuz II. Klasse* 10 November 1944 • *Eisernes Kreuz I. Klasse* 20 November 1944 • *Deutsches Kreuz in Gold* 30 January 1945 • Knight's Cross of the Order of the Holy Crown of Hungary with swords 13 January 1945	• *SS-Untersturmführer* 1 March 1944

MEYER, CLAUS-DIETRICH

Claus-Dietrich Meyer was born on 28 June 1917. During the siege of Budapest, he received the decoration *Deutsches Kreuz in Gold* on 26 January 1945 as the commander of the I Battalion of *Heeres-Pionier-Brigade 127*. The circumstances of the award are unknown. Severely wounded at the end of the siege, he was captured on 12 February 1945, at one of the casualty clearing stations in the castle. Until May 1945, he was cared for in the military hospital established in Gömbös Gyula Street (formerly and latterly Alkotás Street) before being transferred to the Cegléd internment camp. He was transported to the Soviet Union from there. He was released on 13 August 1948.[463]

DECORATIONS	RANKS
• *Deutsches Kreuz in Gold* 26 January 1945	• Dates of promotions are unknown.

MITTELBERGER, OTTO-EUGEN DR.

Otto-Eugen Mittelberger was born on 16 March 1910 in Götzens, Tirol. He studied medicine. From 1929, he took part in the events and rallies of the *Deutsche Nationalsozialistische Arbeiterpartei* (*DNSAP,* the Austrian National Socialist party), of which he was a member. In 1931, he joined the *NSDAP*, and in 1934, he was imprisoned a number of times for his political activities. Soon after the *Anschluß*, he joined the *Allgemeine-SS* and the Waffen-SS (in the former, he reached the rank of *SS-Standartenführer*). Until 1941, he served as the commander of various SS hospitals. From 1 January 1941, he was assigned to serve in the *SS-Regiment "Der Führer"* for four months as the unit's medical officer. Thereafter, he was reassigned to Himmler's personal staff – the circumstances and details of this reassignment are unknown. Still, the least that can be said is that, in this position, he must have known everything about the organized genocide taking place in the Soviet Union. From October 1941 until March 1942, he was the commander of the *Sanitäts-Kompanie* of the SS Cavalry Brigade and was wounded once during this service. Thereafter, he was again assigned to the *Ersatz* units (*SS-Sanitäts-Ersatz-Abteilung*). Between 20 November 1942 and 3 June 1943, he was the commander of the Waffen-SS troops in the Netherlands. Then, until 1 March 1944, he served as the appointed commander of the *SS-Arzt-Akademie Graz*. Thereafter, he was assigned as medical officer of the 8th SS Cavalry Division. He was promoted on 30 January 1945 to *SS-Obersturmbannführer*. He was awarded the decoration *Deutsches Kreuz in Gold* on 9 February 1945. There is no information available regarding his activities around Budapest; he was legally registered as dead in 1947.[464]

DECORATIONS	RANKS
• *Deutsches Kreuz in Gold* 9 February 1945	• *SS-Obersturmbannführer* 30 January 1945

MÖLLER, ADOLF

Adolf Möller was born on 15 December 1918 in Bornhorst. In 1937, he left the church, and in the same year, he joined the *NSDAP*. He became a member of the Waffen-SS in 1940. He served with the *SS-Kavallerie* from the beginning. On 30 November 1942, and later, on 27 November 1944 near Soroksár, he was lightly wounded. He was recommended to receive the *Deutsches Kreuz in Gold* decoration on 5 December 1944. This recommendation was based on the Csepel combat situation, where Möller took part in the combat action as the commander of the *Stabs-Schwadron* of the 17th SS Voluntary Cavalry Regiment. The Soviet troops launched attacks to occupy Csepel Island on 2 November, 4 November, 7 November, 15 November, and 21 November 1944. However, these attacks were repulsed by the 1st Hussars Division which had to defend a 51-km long frontline.[465] On 22 November 1944, the Soviet 316th Rifle Division carried out a forced river crossing south of Taksony on the Ráckeve branch of the Danube and breached the frontline of the 1st Hussars Division in defence there.

The combat command during this period in the Budapest bridgehead was conducted by the *III. Panzerkorps*. Thereafter, significant troops were relocated to the Csepel Island to repulse the Soviet attack: two battalions and one *Artillerie-Abteilung* of Panzergrenadier Division *Feldherrnhalle*, the cadet-battalion of the Hungarian I Army Corps, and 13 Hetzers (most probably from the 22nd SS Cavalry Division). On 24 November, the Soviet troops occupied Tököl and Szigetszentmiklós, however, on the next day, the *Panzergrenadiers* of Panzergrenadier Division *Feldherrnhalle* reoccupied most of the area of Szigetszentmiklós for a short period.

Möller's decoration recommendation document describes the events as follows:

> On 22 November 1944, the Soviets launched a surprise assault and breached the defences on Csepel Island. *SS-Obersturmführer* Möller established contact with three persons in the shortest time possible via one of the branches of the Danube and personally led a reconnaissance patrol, which was essential for establishing a new blocking position. Because his signal soldiers were no longer available, he repaired the wires himself and kept the signal lines working, which was essentially important for further combat command.
>
> On 23 November, the Soviets breached Szigetszentmiklós on Csepel Island with large forces. *SS-Obersturmführer* Möller launched a counter-attack with twenty men and, with extraordinary courage and dynamism, repulsed the enemy, who outnumbered him ten to one. During the coun-

> teroffensive, he displayed truly exceptional courage and foresight. Due to his swift and decisive action the Soviet attack did not realize its aim to reach Budapest by advancing northwards on Csepel Island.
>
> On 24 November, the Soviets assaulted Szigetszentmiklós with a force approximately twenty times larger than ours. *SS-Obersturmführer* Möller distinguished himself even in this situation with his extraordinary calmness, and with a smaller group, he covered the retreat of weaker units, and with his perseverance, he made it possible to establish a new defence line. When the situation seemed almost desperate, Möller performed a counterattack with 4-5 couriers, confused the enemy troops, and made it possible for the regiment's casualty clearing station with the wounded to be evacuated, and also bought time for the irreplaceable vehicles to retreat. During these combat actions, Möller displayed extraordinary calmness and bravery and offered an exceptional personal example with his perseverance.[466]

It is not entirely impossible that the text of the recommendation contains the actual truth. However, there are also reasons to suspect that the person describing the events tended to shed a positive light on them. In retrospect, it is impossible to clearly discern how many soldiers were present at the locations during these events. However, it is known that until 25 November 1944, only the units of the 316th Rifle Division took part in the river crossing at Csepel Island, with an approximate strength of 6,000 soldiers; however, they were in combat on the whole island, from Szigetszentmiklós to Ráckeve. In the first five days of the operation, the 316th Rifle Division reported the loss of altogether 179 dead. Works studying the combat actions around Csepel Island only describe smaller-scale combat actions in the relevant period: Szigetszentmiklós was defended by approximately 200 German and Hungarian soldiers without any artillery support and performed only delaying actions.[467]

After he was lightly wounded on 27 November 1944, he was transported to *SS-Feldlazarett 500 (SS-Fela 500)* established in Budapest. He was most probably not evacuated from there as his family received no news of him after December 1944. In 1973, the Eutin authorities declared him legally dead.

DECORATIONS	RANKS
• *Deutsches Kreuz in Gold* 7 January 1945	• Dates of promotions are unknown.

1944

MÜNCHOW, LEOPOLD VON

Paul Georg Alexander Leopold von Münchow was born on 4 March 1884 in the village of Lippehne (today: Lipiany, Poland) into an ancient Pomeranian noble family. Münchow was very active during his youth: in 1897, when he was thirteen years old, he started to organize a youth movement called *Jungsturm.*[468] It was similar to the scout movement, but it preceded it by a couple of years (the scout movement did not begin in Germany until 1909). He took part in the leadership of the *Jungsturm* until 1914. By that time, the organization (which welcomed everybody regardless of class or religious differences) had spread throughout Germany.

He started his reserve officer service in the *Husaren-Regiment "Fürst Blücher von Wahlstatt" Nr. 5* and, as a visible sign thereof, until 1945 was permitted to wear the "*Totenkopf*" emblem of the Prussian cavalry next to the rosette and *Reichsadler* on his service-cap. In 1910, after completing legal studies, he went on to serve in his original regiment. In 1914, he was reassigned to the 2nd Life Hussars, "The Queen Victoria of Prussia" Regiment. The details of his First World War military service are unknown. However, his Bulgarian, Turkish and Austro–Hungarian service medals suggest that he must have held several different positions at various service locations. Von Münchow even received the decoration *Ehrenritter des Johanniterordens* (Knight of Honour of the Order of St. John).

What is certain is that von Münchow was discharged in 1920 as the general staff officer of the 36th Infantry Division and then became the imperial leader of the *Jungsturm*. During this period, the *Jungsturm* had organizations based outside of Germany, not only in Vienna and Prague but also in New York and São

Paulo as well. Von Münchow published the *Jungsturm's* songbook, in which 50 of the 555 songs were written by himself. Later, as a civilian, he became a *Kreisrat* (a position approximately equivalent to district counsellor).

After 1920, attempts were made in several provinces to ban the *Jungsturm* on the grounds that it was involved in party politics. However, the *Reichsgericht* (Imperial Court of Justice) dismissed these claims on each occasion on the basis that such accusations were groundless.

From 1932, the *Hitlerjugend* seemed to be increasingly concurrent with the *Jungsturm*, but with a membership of more than 25,000, the *Jungsturm* was still the largest youth organization in Germany. During the period of the Nazi takeover of power, the *Deutsche Pfadfinderverband* (German Scout Association) completely joined the *Jungsturm* – most probably to avoid being disbanded. However, the National Socialists were not prepared to tolerate the *Jungsturm*. In order to avoid being officially disbanded, on 13 October 1933, von Münchow disbanded the organization himself. Despite this, he was targeted by the *Gestapo*: he was arrested a number of times and prohibited from travelling outside of Germany.

He voluntarily applied to start his military service again in 1939. As a reserve officer, he was first assigned to the *Kommandant des rückwärtigen Armeegebiets 593*, which was responsible for the rear area of the 6th Army, then at an unknown date, he was promoted to the commander of *Korück 586*. He was most probably very active in this position as he received repetition clasps to his *Eisernes Kreuz I. Klasse* and *Eisernes Kreuz II. Klasse*, received during the First World War. He was also wounded on 30 March 1943, despite holding an office position far from the actual frontline. In the summer of 1944, he served as the *Personalstabsoffizier (IIa)* to the Commander of German Troops in Denmark (*Befehlshaber der deutschen Truppen in Dänemark*).

He was most probably assigned to Budapest in November 1944. His office was located in Buda Castle. It is characteristic of →*Pfeffer-Wildenbruch* that he tasked von Münchow, until the encirclement of the city, with providing news of the military situation to the Hungarian I Army Corps – expressing with this that he deemed the Hungarian Corps to be a territorial organization rather than a fellow army combat unit. On 19 December 1944, the high command of the 6th Army ordered von Münchow, who was assigned to the *IX. Waffen-Gebirgskorps* to immediately return to *Korück 593* (the rear area command for the 6th Army).[469] It is not known whether or not von Münchow complied with this order, but unlike him, the majority of those serving in *Korück 593* were not trapped in the encirclement of Budapest. Hardly any details about Münchow's movements and activities are known afterwards. It is known, however, that he received the decoration *Deutsches Kreuz in Gold* on 1 February 1945. In connection with this, the files recording decoration awards mark his place of service as "*Kampfkommandant Budapest*".[470] From this, we may conclude that he volunteered to command some kind of a combat group – it is unlikely that he would have received the decoration for his office work. According to a website primarily occupied with family tree research, "he died as the last defender of the Budapest airfield".[471] The assumption is that this is a reference to the Vérmező. However, there is no indication as to where this information came from. Von Münchow's personal files contain the only information as follows: "Missing in Budapest as of 15 February 1945." In 1977, the Langen authorities legally pronounced him dead.

DECORATIONS	RANKS
• *Braunschweigischer Kriegsverdienstkreuz* (War Merit Cross) *I. Klasse* • Bar to denote subsequent awards of the *Eisernes Kreuz II. Klasse* 1914 • Bar to denote subsequent awards of the *Eisernes Kreuz I. Klasse* 1914 • *Kriegverdienstkreuz I. und II. Klasse mit Schwertern* • *Verwundetenabzeichen in Silber* • *Deutsches Kreuz in Gold* 1 February 1945 • (Bulgarian) Order of Military Merit IV grade with swords • Gallipoli Star (Ottoman War Medal/ Harp Madalyasi/Eiserner Halbmond)	• Dates of promotions are unknown.

OTTO, HELMUT

Helmut Otto was born on 10 October 1906 in Oederan, in Saxony. During the siege of Budapest, he served as commander of the 2nd *Schwadron* of the 53rd SS Cavalry Regiment of the 8th SS Cavalry Division. He fell on 4 November 1944 near Pestszentimre. The details of his military actions are unknown; he received the decoration *Deutsches Kreuz in Gold* after this period. His rank at that time was *SS-Obersturmführer.*

He also received a Hungarian decoration, namely, the Knight's Cross of the Order of the Holy Crown of Hungary with swords.

DECORATIONS	RANKS
• *Deutsches Kreuz in Gold* November 1944 • Knight's Cross of the Order of the Holy Crown of Hungary with swords 13 January 1945	• Dates of promotions are unknown.

PAUL, REINHARD

SS-Oberscharführer Reinhard Paul received the decoration *Deutsches Kreuz in Gold* on 6 February 1945 while serving in the 6th *Schwadron* of the 17th SS Cavalry Regiment of the 8th SS Cavalry Division. There is no other information available regarding his person.

DECORATIONS	RANKS
• *Deutsches Kreuz in Gold* 6 February 1945	• Dates of promotions are unknown.

1940–1942

1962

PANCK, BERNHARD

Bernhard Panck was born on 27 February 1915 in Usedom; his father was a farmer. In 1937, he joined the Wehrmacht as a volunteer. He initially served in 5th Cavalry Regiment; in 1939, he was ordered to attend *Junkerschule*.

In the first period of the war, he served as a platoon commander in *Aufklärungs-Abteilung 175*, formed by 5th Cavalry Regiment. On 1 April 1940, he was promoted to *Leutnant*. During the Soviet campaign, he served in *Aufklärungs-Abteilung 12* of the 12th Infantry Division. In February 1942, he was severely wounded (shot in the knee). After his recovery, he was assigned to the German military contingent and sent to Romania. He was assigned to a cavalry officer training school in Bucharest and one in Sibiu (Nagyszeben, Hermannstadt). To his luck, the armistice of Romania found him in Sibiu, from where he and his comrades were able to make an orderly retreat to northern Transylvania. Here, he immediately took over the command of the 1st *Schwadron* of the 16th SS Cavalry Regiment (8th SS Cavalry Division). Within a short period, he was wounded three times, but he did not leave his unit. On 16 December 1944, he received a short leave due to having pressing family matters to attend to, but he was unable to return to his unit. He was sent back to his original unit, Reiter-Regiment 5, subordinated to the 4th Cavalry Brigade which was in combat near the Vértes Hills at that time. He was also assigned as the commander of the 1st *Schwadron*. In May 1945, he spent a few days in American captivity.

After 1945, he initially worked as a manager of a large estate. Five years later, he had to abandon this workplace due to conflicts with the estate's owner. He then worked in an iron foundry, a job that required hard physical labour, but after five years, he was promoted to the factory's mid-level management. At that time, he began to apply for service in the *Bundeswehr*. After a few rejections, his application was finally accepted, and he was admitted as *Hauptmann* in 1962.

The award of the *Deutsches Kreuz in Gold* for him is questionable as there are no traces in his personal files that he knew he had been awarded the *Deutsches Kreuz in Gold* on 14 February 1945. However, his name is on the list of those who have received the decoration.

DECORATIONS	RANKS
• *Eisernes Kreuz II. Klasse* 27 February 1940 • *Eisernes Kreuz I. Klasse* 3 September 1941 • *Verwundetenabzeichen in Schwarz* 18 March 1942 • *Nahkampfspange Bronze* October 1944 • *Verwundetenabzeichen in Silber* November 1944 • *Verwundetenabzeichen in Gold* 16 March 1945 • *Deutsches Kreuz in Gold* 14 February 1945	• *Leutnant* 1 April 1940 • *Oberleutnant* 1 April 1942 • *Hauptmann* 1 May 1945

1938–1941

PLÄNK, WILHELM

Wilhelm Plänk was born on 16 January 1911 in Redingen, Luxembourg. He joined the SS before 1939, and in July 1942, he was the commander of the 7th *(Radfahr) Schwadron* of the 1st SS Cavalry Regiment of SS Cavalry Division. In this position, it is certain that he had taken part in perpetrating the mass murders the unit committed.

During the siege of Budapest, from November 1944, he was the commander of 52nd SS Voluntary Cavalry Regiment of the 22nd SS Voluntary Cavalry Division. For reasons unknown, he remained outside the encirclement. He was awarded the *Deutsches Kreuz in Gold* on 21 January 1945 for his combat activities during September-December 1944. The recommendation for this decoration has not survived. He was captured by the Soviets on 12 May 1945 near Strakanitz (today: Strakonice, Czech Republic). He was released on 16 October 1955.

DECORATIONS	RANKS
• *Deutsches Kreuz in Gold* 21 January 1945	• Dates of promotions are unknown.

PLESCHINGER, KARL

Karl Pleschinger was born on 4 October in the village of Kalbe near Magdeburg. On 1 May 1932, he joined the *NSDAP*; however, after two months, he stopped paying his membership fees and, therefore, did not fulfil the probation time necessary for full-time membership. In November 1936, as an employee of the *Deutsche Arbeitsfront*, he misappropriated 39 *Reichsmarks*, and for what he had done, he was sentenced to one month in prison. In 1938, the *NSDAP* was also involved in his case for unknown reasons (at this time, Pleschinger most probably wanted to renew his previous membership). According to related documents, the police identified him as a communist party member and enemy of the state, and consequently, the *NSDAP* opened a special observation document in order to track his possible requests for membership. Contrary to all this, after 1939, at an unknown date, he joined the ranks of the Waffen-SS, and there is no information about whether his previous issues caused him any problems.

During the siege of Budapest, he served in the 6th *Schwadron* of the 18th SS Cavalry Regiment of the 8th SS Cavalry Division. He was awarded the decoration *Deutsches Kreuz in Gold* on 10 February 1945. The details of the recommendation are unknown. At this time, he was serving as *SS-Hauptscharführer*.

DECORATIONS	RANKS
• *Deutsches Kreuz in Gold* 10 February 1945	• Dates of promotions are unknown.

1943–1944

PRÄGER, WALTER

Walter Präger was born on 29 May 1920 in Berlin. He received the decoration *Deutsches Kreuz in Gold* on 28 January 1945 while serving as reserve *Leutnant* in the *Stabskompanie* of the 93rd Panzergrenadier Regiment of the 13th Panzer Division. In October 1944 →*Schöning* recommended Präger for the *Ritterkreuz des Eisernen Kreuzes,* but the recommendation was not approved. He was last seen on 13–14 February 1945, together with →*Paul Krämer*, north of Solymár.

DECORATIONS	RANKS
• *Deutsches Kreuz in Gold* 28 January 1945	• Dates of promotions are unknown.

1942–1944

REINHARD, KARL-WERNER

Karl-Werner Reinhard was born on 20 September 1919 in Berlin. In the absence of his personal files, it is known that he served in the I Battalion of the 4th Infantry Regiment during his military service. However, until 20 March 1941, he was recorded as serving in *Schützen-Regiment 7*. In the first half of 1943, he was reassigned to the 8th Company of *Panzer-Lehr-Regiment 130* of *Panzer-Lehr-Division*. At the end of August 1943, he was further reassigned, this time to the 2nd Company of Grenadier Regiment *Großdeutschland* in combat in the area of Bryansk. At the same time, he was assigned to train in a non-commissioned officer course. He was wounded on the following dates: 7 July 1941, 3 October 1941, 1 October 1943, 27 October 1943, and 12 January 1944. At the time of the siege of Budapest, he served in the 15th SS Cavalry Regiment of the 8th SS Cavalry Division as a Wehrmacht officer (although, according to his *Feldpostnummer*, he was registered at the *Divisionsstab*). Reinhard received the decoration *Deutsches Kreuz in Gold* on 27 January 1945; at that time, he was serving in the rank of *Hauptmann*. The circumstances of the latter recommendation are unknown. Reinhard went missing during the siege of Budapest.

DECORATIONS	RANKS
• *Deutsches Kreuz in Gold* 27 January 1945	• Dates of promotions are unknown.

RICHTER, HERBERT

Herbert Richter received the decoration *Deutsches Kreuz in Gold* on 28 January 1945 as reserve *Oberleutnant* serving in the II Battalion of the 978th Grenadier Regiment. Details regarding his person and the recommendation for the decoration are unknown.

DECORATIONS	RANKS
• *Deutsches Kreuz in Gold* 28 January 1945	• *Oberleutnant (der Reserve)*

RÖSCHMANN, ERNST

Ernst Röschmann was born on 24 July 1913 in Bremen. He joined the *NSDAP* and the SA in 1931. From 1935, he was a full-time member of the SA, and in 1938, he took part in the burning down of the synagogue in Bremen as *SA-Sturmbannführer*. In 1939, he started his military service; his first documented service unit was the 6th Company of the 401st Infantry Regiment. He took part in the combat around Budapest as reserve *Hauptmann,* serving in the I Battalion of the *Füsilier-Regiment* of the Panzer Division *Feldherrnhalle*. On 25 November 1944, he was seriously wounded (previously, he was wounded on two occasions). He received the decoration *Deutsches Kreuz in Gold* on 6 January 1945; the circumstances of the recommendation are unknown. It is not possible to determine whether he had been trapped in the city within the encirclement. After 1945, he worked as a salesperson. He died in 1967.

DECORATIONS	RANKS
• *Deutsches Kreuz in Gold* 6 January 1945	• Dates of promotions are unknown.

ROSENFELDER, FRITZ

Fritz Rosenfelder was born on 6 October 1908 in Pirmasens. He was originally a shoemaker and worked as an independent craftsman as one of the owners of the Theleld und Rosenfelder shoemaker factory. He joined the *NSDAP* in May 1933; he joined the *SS-Kavallerie* on 5 November 1939. In 1942, he served as *SS-Unterscharführer* in the 2nd Battery of the I *Abteilung* of the 8th SS Artillery Regiment. On 10 September 1943, he was wounded near Novosevsky (or Novgorod Seversky). On 21 June 1944, in consideration of his military capabilities, he was promoted to *SS-Untersturmführer* without having attended *Junkerschule*. According to the related documents,

> Rosenfelder has excellently distinguished himself in all of the missions in Russia, primarily as a forward artillery observer and observer officer, with his endeavouring spirit, sense of responsibility, caution and personal bravery that he retained throughout the most difficult situations.[472]

During the encirclement of Budapest, he fell on 28 December 1944 at Kelenföld. He received the decoration *Deutsches Kreuz in Gold* posthumously on 27 January 1945 as the appointed officer of *Stabsbatterie* of the I *Abteilung* of the 8th SS Artillerie-Regiment. The circumstances of the recommendation are unknown.

DECORATIONS	RANKS
• *Deutsches Kreuz in Gold* 27 January 1945	• *SS-Unterscharführer* • *SS-Untersturmführer* 21 June 1944

ROTHE, FRIEDRICH

Friedrich Rothe was born on 7 May 1920. During the war, he was wounded six times, twice seriously. From the end of 1944, he served as the commander of the 6th Company of the 93rd Panzergrenadier Regiment. In February 1944 and on 1 January 1945, he was promoted out of turn to *Oberleutnant* and subsequently to *Hauptmann*, which suggests that his military capabilities and deeds were deemed to be extraordinary. On 20 December 1944, his unit was retrieved from the frontline near Budapest and transported to the Garam River to support the Hungarian 2nd Armoured Division. Rothe was wounded for the last time on 24 February 1945 at Kéménd, where his left shinbone was pierced. He received the decoration *Deutsches Kreuz in Gold* on 22 March 1945, most probably partly for his military deeds in Budapest. At the end of the war, he was captured by American troops. He was released from the internment on 5 August 1945. He was still alive in 1967.

DECORATIONS	RANKS
• *Deutsches Kreuz in Gold* 22 March 1945	• *Oberleutnant* February 1944 (out of turn) • *Hauptmann* 1 January 1945 (out of turn)

1941–1944

RUTZKE, PAUL

Paul Rutzke was born on 31 January 1915. He served in the army from 1936; he was promoted to *Leutnant* on 1 October 1939. At that time, he was serving as signal platoon commander of the 184th Infantry Regiment of the 86th Infantry Division. He served in the Polish and French campaigns. On 16 June 1940 he was awarded the *Eisernes Kreuz II. Klasse*, and from 1 August 1941, he was the commander of the I *Abteilung* of *the* 184 the Infantry Regiment of the 86th Infantry Division. At that time, he was serving in subordination to the German

11th Army on the southern sections of the Soviet front in the area of Kherson. In 1943 or sometime later, he was reassigned from the 184th Infantry Regiment to Panzergrenadier Division *Feldherrnhalle*. In August 1943, he was a drill officer at an infantry officers' school. In the summer of 1943, he served with the *Feldersatz-Bataillon* of Panzergrenadier Division *Feldherrnhalle*, took part in combat actions in Romania during August and fought his way back from the encirclement. In November, he was reassigned to the I *Abteilung* of the Grenadier Regiment *Feldherrnhalle*. During the siege of Budapest, he served as one of the adjutants of Panzer Division *Feldherrnhalle*, and later, during the encirclement, he served as an appointed officer of *Panzergrenadier-Regiment Feldherrnhalle* of the Panzer Division *Feldherrnhalle*. It is not possible to trace what happened to him during the siege; according to a statement of an eyewitness, he was killed in February 1945. He was awarded the decoration *Deutsches Kreuz in Gold* on 23 February 1945. However, the circumstances of the award are unknown. The Mülheim-Ruhr district authorities legally registered him dead in 1964.

DECORATIONS	RANKS
• *Eisernes Kreuz II. Klasse* 16 June 1940 • *Eisernes Kreuz I. Klasse* 1 August 1941 • *Deutsches Kreuz in Gold* 23 February 1945	• *Leutnant* 1 October 1939

1935

1941

SANDER, FRIEDRICH

Friedrich Sander was born on 15 December 1908 in Goch near Kleve. He trained to be a mechanic. In 1927, he joined the *Reichsheer*, where he served until 1939 at the rank of *Feldwebel*. In 1935 he was married. In the Second World War, he initially served as a platoon commander in *Panzerjäger-Abteilung 178* of the 178th Infantry Division. On 10 October 1939, he was promoted to *Oberleutnant*; during the course of 1942, he was officially promoted to officer (he had already requested this in 1940 but was rejected at that time). He received the *Eisernes Kreuz II. Klasse* on 17 July 1941 and the *Eisernes Kreuz I. Klasse* on 15 August 1941.

Friedrich Sander in 1942

On 16 March 1943, he was appointed as commander of *Panzerjäger-Abteilung 87* of the 25th Panzer Division, and on 1 February 1944, he was promoted out of turn to *Major*. His assessment dated 1 March 1944 described him as follows:

> He is a calm, reserved personality. He is more than what he shows. Excellent national socialist behaviour. He is brave and always ready to be deployed. As *Panzerjäger-Abteilung* commander and as commander of alarm units, he distinguished himself in combat. He is also very calm in critical situations. A good organizer. Mentally fresh and lively. Physically strong and resilient.[473]

After a short period spent in *Panzerjägerschule Mielau* (today: Mława, Poland), he was reassigned on 8 September 1944 as commander of *Panzer-Abteilung Feldherrnhalle* of the Panzergrenadier Division *Feldherrnhalle*.

During the siege of Budapest, he acted in close cooperation with the Hungarian assault artillery troops. He received the decoration *Deutsches Kreuz in Gold* on 13 January 1945. However, the recommendation document has not survived. He took part in the breakout attempt; one of his soldiers stated that, on 13 or 14 February, he saw Sander for the last time when he was wounded near a brick factory (most probably the Solymár Brick Factory). At the same time, according to the summarized report of the Soviet 23rd Rifle Corps dated 16 February 1945, Sander was commanding a group of approximately 400 men when he attempted a breakout in the direction of Budakeszi-north–Julianna-major, Hill 554–Budajenő but was captured near Budajenő. No data are available on his subsequent fate.[474]

DECORATIONS	RANKS
• *Eisernes Kreuz II. Klasse* 17 July 1941 • *Eisernes Kreuz I. Klasse* 15 August 1941 • *Deutsches Kreuz in Gold* 13 January 1945 • Knight's Cross of the Order of the Merit of the Kingdom of Hungary with swords 28 January 1945	• *Oberleutnant (der Reserve)* 10 October 1938 • *Hauptmann* 1942 • *Major* 1 February 1944

SCHAFFNER, OTTOMAR

Ottomar Schaffner was born on 19 July 1914 in Köln. He started his military service in the ranks of the Waffen-SS. In November 1941, he was promoted to reserve *SS-Untersturmführer*. In January 1944, he was wounded near Kovel; at that time, he was the commander of one of the *Nachschub-Kolonne* of the 8th SS Cavalry Division. In the autumn of 1944, he assumed command of the 6th *Schwadron* of the 17th SS Cavalry Regiment of the 22nd SS Cavalry Division. According to his decoration recommendation, two of his military deeds are related to Budapest:

> On 3 November 1944, at the time of the Soviets breaking through south of Budapest, Schaffner quickly assembled his men and engaged the enemy and repulsed them beyond the anti-tank ditch. The attack was halted three times due to the heavy enemy fire and the counterattack of eight enemy tanks. It was Schaffner who, displaying extraordinary bravery, led his men, always encouraging them to advance, knocked out three tanks, repulsed the enemy and retook the anti-tank ditch.[475]

Schaffner fell on 7 November 1944 near Dunaharaszti. At the beginning of 1945, he was decorated with the Knight's Cross of the Order of Merit of the Kingdom of Hungary with swords. He also received the decoration *Deutsches Kreuz in Gold* posthumously on 6 January 1945.

DECORATIONS	RANKS
• *Deutsches Kreuz in Gold* 6 January 1945 • Knight's Cross of the Order of Merit of the Kingdom of Hungary with swords 1945	• *SS-Untersturmführer (der Reserve)* November 1941

1944

SCHMEDDING, ERNST

Ernst Schmedding was born on 17 December 1894 in Barop near Dortmund. He served in the First World War in unknown ranks and positions and then took part in the German–Polish conflict of 1919 as a member of the Silesian *Freikorps Oberland*. From 1920, he served in the police force. He was reassigned to the SS on 5 January 1942; at that time, he was *Oberstleutnant der Polizei* (in the security police). Interestingly, he never joined the *NSDAP*. On 27 July 1942, he was appointed commander of *Polizei-Panzerabwehr-Abteilung* of *SS-Polizei-Division*. On 1 September 1943, he was reassigned to the 13th *Waffen-Gebirgs-Division der SS "Handschar" (kroatische Nr. 1)*, where he was appointed commander of the artillery regiment.

→*Helmut Dörner*, who, like Schmedding, was promoted to *SS-Standartenführer* at the same time in April 1944, commented on Schmedding's promotion: "For me, it is painful that Himmler mentions me on the same page with Schmedding". This suggests that Schmedding might not have been very popular. His superior commanders were also not overly satisfied with Schmedding. His assessment, dated the summer of 1944, described him as follows:

> An open, sincere personality. Often helpless and avoids hardships. He has proven himself in battle. His service performance is acceptable under intensive supervision and direction. Mentally, he has medium capabilities. He has good physical abilities. A good comrade. He is capable of training and leading an officer staff if he is closely observed and is obliged to do so. In a tactical sense, he is below average. He does not have strong assets. Weakness: too little dynamism. Barely [the word crossed out] meets the requirements of being a regiment commander and only under close supervision.[476]

Ernst Schmedding with Heinrich Himmler (left) at the beginning of 1944 on the inspection of the 13th *Waffen-Gebirgs-Division der SS "Handschar" (kroatische Nr. 1)* on the Neuhammer training grounds

On 8 August 1944, he was reassigned to the *IX. Waffen-Gebirgskorps,* where he served as a commander of the artillery. His activities during the siege of Budapest are unknown. He received the decoration *Deutsches Kreuz in Gold* on 22 January 1945, most probably in a sort of automatic way that was due to his position. This assumption is strengthened by the fact that →*Gottstein* and →*Sobotta* received the same decoration on the same day, and the latter also performed office duties. Schmedding took part in the breakout attempt with →*Pfeffer-Wildenbruch's group*; he was captured on 12 February 1945.

On 12 December 1949, his trial lasted five minutes, and he was sentenced to 25 years of correctional-disciplinary camp labour. He was released on 18 October 1955. He died while on a vacation trip: on the night of 23 December 1963, he was one of the victims of the Laconia leisure ship catastrophe when the ship burst into flames and claimed 127 lives near Funchal, Madeira.

DECORATIONS	RANKS
• *Eisernes Kreuz II. Klasse* 1914 • *Eisernes Kreuz I. Klasse* 1914 • Bar to denote subsequent awards of the *Eisernes Kreuz II. Klasse* • Bar to denote subsequent awards of the *Eisernes Kreuz I. Klasse* • *Schlesicher Adler* (Silesian Eagle) *I. Klasse* • *Schlesicher Adler* (Silesian Eagle) *II. Klasse* • *Deutsches Kreuz in Gold* 22 January 1945	• *SS-Standartenführer* 20 April 1944

SCHONERT, WERNER

Werner Schonert was born on 1 September 1922 in Arnstadt, Thuringen. He served from 1940 until the end of the war in the 66th Panzergrenadier Regiment of the 13th Panzer Division. He was wounded twice in 1943; at that time, he was serving in the 11th Company of the 66th Panzergrenadier Regiment. On 2 March 1944, he was reassigned to the 8th *(schwere) Kompanie* of the 66th Panzergrenadier Regiment and, for a short period, served as *Bataillon-Adjutant.* He received the decoration *Deutsches Kreuz in Gold* on 9 February 1945. The details of the recommendation are unknown. According to the notes of his regiment commander, →*Georg-Wilhelm Schöning*, on 29 December 1944, Schonert, acting alone, destroyed a ditch section that had been previously abandoned by Hungarian troops and then subsequently occupied by the Soviets, meanwhile acquiring a number of machine guns and heavy machine guns. On 6 January 1945, he knocked out a tank with a *Panzerfaust.*[477] According to the register in connection with the award of the decoration, he was at that time the commander of the 2nd Company of the 66th Panzergrenadier Regiment. He took part in the breakout attempt and was captured on 14 February 1945, northwest of Buda. He was released from internment on 30 March 1949.

DECORATIONS	RANKS
• *Deutsches Kreuz in Gold* 9 February 1945	• Dates of promotions are unknown.

SCHRADER, ERWIN

Erwin Schrader was born on 16 July 1911 in Essehof near Braunschweig. His father was a farmer. After Schroder received his *Obersekundareife* (that is, after attending six years of secondary school), he worked in a bank office for two years. He joined the *NSDAP* on 1 November 1929. However, he left this organization on 10 January 1930 because he applied to join the ranks of the Wehrmacht, where he was assigned to serve in the 15th *(Preussischer) Reiter-Regiment* of the 3rd Cavalry Division. Earlier, Schrader was also a member of the *Hitlerjugend* and the SA. He was a professed National Socialist, which can clearly be seen from the fact that in 1937 while serving as a non-commissioned officer in the Wehrmacht, he requested permission to wear his *Reichsparteitag* badge of 1929 on his uniform. His request was denied based on the regulations in effect.

During the war, until February 1944, he served as a non-commissioned officer and platoon commander. After serving in *Aufklärungs-Abteilung 152* of the

52nd Infantry Division, in October 1943, was reassigned to the 1st Company of *Füsilier-Bataillon 9* of the 9th Infantry Division. His assessment from 26 March 1943 described him as follows:

> He is an especially reputable, straightforward person, independent colleague and skilled organizer. Mentally and physically, he has excellent capabilities. He possesses a healthy ambition, dynamism and readiness to act. He has proven himself excellently in battle against the enemy. He is an old member of the Party.[478]

In January 1944, he was promoted to *Leutnant.* On 7 November 1944, after the death of →*Ottomar Schaffner*, he took over command of the 6th *Schwadron* of the 17th SS Cavalry Regiment of the 22nd SS Cavalry Division. There is no information available on why and how he ended up in Budapest. He received the decoration *Deutsches Kreuz in Gold* on 10 February 1945; the circumstances of the recommendation are unknown. He went missing during the breakout attempt.

DECORATIONS	RANKS
• *Eisernes Kreuz II. Klasse* 15 November 1941 • *Eisernes Kreuz I. Klasse* 18 August 1943 • *Kriegsverdienstkreuzs II. Klasse* 7 September 1941 • *Verwundetenabzeichen in Schwarz* 15 November 1941 • *Nahkampfspange Bronze* 9 December 1943 • *Infanterie Sturmabzeichen* 13 December 1943 • *Deutsches Kreuz in Gold* 10 February 1945	• *Leutnant* 4 January 1944

1939

SOBOTTA, KARL-HEINZ

Karl-Heinz Sobotta was born on 29 December 1912 in Berlin-Schönefeld, into a middle-class family. He joined the SA and the *NSDAP* on 1 March 1933, and he left the Evangelical Church in 1937 (presumably, he joined the *Allgemeine SS* at this time). For half a year, he worked for the SA; thereafter, he completed his labour service, and then he was drafted. During his 14 months of military service, he served at *Pionier-Bataillon 4* and then *Pionier-Bataillon 8* and was discharged with the rank of *SS-Oberscharführer*. He joined the police forces on 1 July 1936, where he worked in the field of maintaining public order (his last service post was in Recklingshausen). During the establishment of the *Polizei-Division* in October 1939, he was assigned as commander of the 2nd Company of *Polizei-Pionier-Bataillon* of *Polizei-Division* at the rank of *SS-Hauptsturmführer*. During the French campaign, on 9 July 1940, he was lightly wounded on the upper right arm when he was hit by a shell fragment. In the Soviet Union, on 22 March 1942, he was again wounded by shell fragments on both of his hands (prior to this, in the first months of 1941, he completed a *Pionier-Offizier* training course). He was promoted to Waffen-SS officer on 1 April 1942. In January 1943, he was reassigned to *SS-Pionier-Bataillon 8* of SS Cavalry Division; he commanded the reorganization of the unit in Dresden and Cracow in April as well. On 19 March 1944, this unit was the first of the 8th SS Cavalry Division to cross the Croatian–Hungarian border: two groups assaulted the Drava bridges near Osijek (Eszék), and another crossed in small boats. (During this deployment, an SS soldier died, and a Hungarian 1st Lieutenant was seriously wounded). Later, *SS-Pionier-Bataillon 8*, positioned in the villages of Harta–Dunaegyháza–Dunaföldvár, was supplemented with a third company, and Sobotta was promoted to *SS-Sturmbannführer*. His assessment from

Karl-Heinz Sobotta around 1942–1944

this time was very positive, and his commander highlighted that "he is devoted to his service arm with extraordinary zeal and commitment".[479] At the end of August 1944, his battalion was first relocated to the area of Szeged–Dárda, then deployed as the river defence on the Maros River and subsequently in the combat actions around Torda. Sobotta commanded the unit until 30 November 1944, when he was assigned as assault engineer commander of the *IX. Waffen-Gebirgskorps.*

During the siege of Budapest, he was, among other things, responsible for organizing the demolition of the Danube bridges (on the other hand, it was the Soviets who tried to destroy the bridges at all costs before the detonations initiated by the Germans).[480] He received the decoration *Deutsches Kreuz in Gold* on 22 January 1945. However, the recommendation relating to this award has not survived. During the breakout attempt, Sobotta went with the *Divisionskommand* and was captured together with →*Pfeffer-Wildenbruch.* He described his later fate as follows in his reminisces, written in February 1954:

> On 12 February, I was captured. A female Soviet guard pointed at my badges and decorations and said, "Nix gut dieses", and took all of my possessions from me. The further stages of this bitter journey were the Hungarian and Romanian temporary camps until I arrived in Kiev in August 1945. Until the summer of 1946, the camp was more or less led according to international standard rules. After that, the famous "antifa campaign" started. The political warmongering knew no bounds, and the very effective measures of the Soviets

shut off everybody who was against the "antifa" campaign. Thus, I had been transported as a "hardly controllable person" to Penalty Camp No. 50 in Kiev, from which I was admitted to hospital as early as October 1946 with severe dystrophy and acute laryngitis. I had hardly survived the latter when I contracted dysentery. I was close to death, with my weight being only 44 kilos. I was really very close to completely giving in to the situation. Only the hope of seeing my wife and my children again gave me strength to persevere. So, I survived this crisis as well, and I gathered myself anew. Until 1949, as a staff officer, I did not have to go to work outside; I took part in the work of the prisoner-of-war authorities.

1949 again brought a turning point. The "red mill" started working again. It was evident to us for a long time now that, despite all of the promises made towards the West, the Soviets did not even think of releasing all of their prisoners of war by the end of the year. The hunt for war criminals had begun, most of the time, by bringing up ridiculous accusations. It was often the case that the cook was a war criminal because "with his work, he was increasing the combat potential of the Nazi Wehrmacht", or a priest because "he was praying for the victory of the Hitler army", etc. The success of the Soviet law meant for tens of thousands, as well as me, 25 years of correctional-educational labour camp, which was only a substitute for the death penalty, which had been abolished. Reason: my battalion was also fighting against partisans. Throughout the whole world, such rogue units taking part in armed combat are called bandits or insurgents and are dealt with accordingly, but in the Soviet Union, they were called peaceful Soviet people.

All of this happened on 11 November 1949, not long before the announced last date of release. I had spent half a year in Prison No. 1 in Riga. It especially needs to be mentioned that the prisons are considered to be by far the cleanest places in the Soviet Union. Thereafter, we were sent east together with serious convicted criminals (close supervision, floodlights, bloodhounds). At last, I was sent near Sverdlovsk [Yekaterinburg] beyond the Urals. From the day of the sentence, all prisoners of all ranks had to do hard physical labour. It is understandable how hard this was for those older persons if we consider that this hard labour primarily meant earthworks and building works. Many of them ended their labour and their imprisonment with heart attacks.

During these times, relatives and other helpful people tried to help from home. Many would have died due to the worsening food conditions if the packages sent from home had not been there. […] I can live again, and I can be happy again in the company of my wife, children, and friends, but thousands still wait for these moments. But how long?[481]

Sobotta was allowed to return home in October 1953. The authorities in Gelsenkirchen sent a private bus to the Friedland Transit Camp for him and five of his comrades. According to newspaper articles, his homecoming was turned into a sort of public celebration.

After a few months of recuperation, he returned to the police forces, working in public order; in 1959, he was reassigned to Dortmund. He was actively involved in the work of the *International Police Association* (*IPA*). He died on 14 July 1971.

DECORATIONS	RANKS
• *Deutsches Kreuz in Gold* 22 January 1945	• *SS-Sturmbannführer* March 1944

STAHLBERG, WERNER

Werner Stahlberg was born on 11 January 1919 in Kiel. His father was a telegraph engineer. Stahlberg joined the SS in 1935 and joined the *SS-Verefügungstruppe* on 30 April 1937, where he was assigned to serve with the *Nachrichten-Truppen.* He was promoted to *Offizier* in the summer of 1942.

Stahlberg's marriage relations were somewhat complicated. On 24 November 1943, he applied to have his marriage request processed in an expedited manner; his marriage to Miss Holz was planned for 6 December 1943. However, on 4 December, the *RuSHA* notified Stahlberg that further investigations were necessary because the family name "Edelsheim" found within his fiancée's family "sounds Jewish". Upon this, Stahlberg renounced his marriage request with the explanation that his fiancée was indeed partly of Jewish descent. On the same day, however, he handed in a new marriage request, this time naming a certain Miss Gertrud Graf. The planned marriage date was 4 January 1944. The *RuSHA* officers were furious:

> In my opinion, this relationship with Miss Graf could not have been too long; otherwise, how could he hand in a marriage request with another woman four weeks before that? We are not here to process marriage requests for every SS officer every four weeks. The gentlemen are requested to consider such requests carefully before they hand them in. Please note that Miss Holz's alleged Jewish background is certainly not proven by documents in our care.[482]

Stahlberg's military service and decorations can only be partially reconstructed. What is certain is that, from the summer of 1943, he served in the 8th SS Artillery Regiment of the SS Cavalry Division in the rank of *SS-Obersturmführer*. On 4 November 1943, he was awarded the *Eisernes Kreuz I. Klasse* decoration. In his personal files, there is a note that, on 27 January 1945, he was awarded the decoration *Deutsches Kreuz in Gold*. However, the recommendation is not available.

Stahlberg took part in the breakout attempt and succeeded in getting out of the city. However, his further fate is unknown.

DECORATIONS	RANKS
• *Eisernes Kreuz I. Klasse* 4 November 1943 • *Deutsches Kreuz in Gold* 27 January 1945	• *SS-Untersturmführer* 21 June 1942 • *SS-Obersturmführer* 9 November 1943

STEINBERGER, ERNST-MARTIN

Ernst-Martin Steinberger was born on 27 April 1921 in Saalfelden, Austria. Little information is available about his military service: on 26 May 1942, while serving in the SS Cavalry Division, he was wounded, which led to his hospitalization in Riga. On 30 December 1944, while serving in the 2nd Company of the *SS-Flak-Abteilung 8* of the 8th SS Cavalry Division, he received the *Deutsches Kreuz in Gold.*

According to Herbert Worring's statement, recorded on 10 July 1972, Steinberger fell on 6 February 1945 in Budapest.

DECORATIONS	RANKS
• *Deutsches Kreuz in Gold* 30 December 1944	• Dates of promotions are unknown.

TAPPEINER, JOSEF

SS-Oberscharführer Josef Tappeiner received the decoration *Deutsches Kreuz in Gold* on 10 February 1945 while serving in the 3rd *Schwadron* of the 18th SS

Cavalry Regiment of the 8th SS Cavalry Division. There is no other information available related to him. Tappeiner died on 24 November 2010.

DECORATIONS	RANKS
• *Deutsches Kreuz in Gold* 10 February 1945	• Dates of promotions are unknown.

TAUER, HERBERT

Reserve *Hauptmann* Herbert Tauer received the decoration *Deutsches Kreuz in Gold* while serving as commander of the 6th Company of the 66th Panzergrenadier Regiment of the 13th Panzer Division on 22 December 1944. There is no other information available relating to him. Tauer died on 29 August 2013.

DECORATIONS	RANKS
• *Deutsches Kreuz in Gold* 22 December 1944	• Dates of promotions are unknown.

THOMA, JOHANN

SS-Oberscharführer Johann Thoma received the decoration *Deutsches Kreuz in Gold* on 8 February 1945 while serving in the 16th SS Cavalry Regiment of the 8th SS Cavalry Division. There were no other data available relating to his person.

DECORATIONS	RANKS
• *Deutsches Kreuz in Gold* 8 February 1945	• Dates of promotions are unknown.

1961

WALLER, KARL

Karl Waller was born on 13 December in Wölchingen, Baden. He joined the SA when he was 13 years old, and a year later, he was also admitted to the *NSDAP*. From 1 August 1934, he served in the *Reichsheer*; at an unknown date (most probably around 1937–1938), he joined the Waffen-SS. This assumption is also strengthened by the fact that he left the Evangelical Church in 1938.

He took part in the Polish and French campaigns. Before 1942, he served in the *SS-Totenkopf-Infanterie-Regiment 2* of *SS-Division "Totenkopf"*, established mainly from former guard personnel of concentration camps, where he served as platoon commander. On 1 January 1942, he was reassigned to *SS-Schützen-Regiment "Thule"* of *SS-Division "Totenkopf"* and served in this unit until 1 August 1943. He was deployed in heavy combat actions in the Demyansk pocket as well. He was wounded twice (20 April 1942, shot in the thigh; 25 July 1943, shell fragment hit in the knee). Thereafter, he was reassigned to the *Ersatztruppen* of the *SS-Panzer-Aufklärungs-Abteilung 1* of the 1st SS Panzer Division. After attending a short training course and a reassignment to the *SS-Panzer-Aufklärungs-Abteilung 17* of the 17th SS Panzergrenadier Division, on 20 July 1944, was assigned as commander of *SS-Panzer-Aufklärungs-Abteilung 22* of the 22nd SS Cavalry Division.

He was married on 24 May 1942. He tried to get married earlier, but the process was halted by the *RuSHA* because one of his fiancée's parents had refused to identify the grandfather.

Very little is known about Waller's movements and actions in Hungary. Almost nobody survived from his unit. The establishment and equipping of *SS-Panzer-Aufklärungs-Abteilung 22* of the 22nd SS Cavalry Division had not yet been completed when the frontline reached the outskirts of Budapest. At that time, the unit was deployed near Soroksár and remained there until Christmas 1944. Thereafter the *SS-Panzer-Aufklärungs-Abteilung 22* of 22nd SS Cavalry Division retreated via Kőbánya towards the inner parts of the city. In the middle of January 1945, Waller's unit was already in combat on Margaret Island. His movements thereafter are not possible to retrace; it is only known that he was captured on the second day of the breakout attempt.

He was released from internment in 1955. However, according to available sources, his return home was dated 12 October 1956. The *Bundeswehr* took him over in 1958, and he became the commander of the 1st *Panzeraufklärungsbataillon.*

DECORATIONS	RANKS
• *Eisernes Kreuz II. Klasse* 1940 • *Eisernes Kreuz I. Klasse* 1941 • *Ostmedaille* • *Panzerkampfabzeichen Bronze* • *Infanterie-Sturmabzeichen* • *Verwundetenabzeichen in Silber* • *Deutsches Kreuz in Gold* 30 January 1945 • *Ärmelschild Demjansk* • Knight's Cross of the Order of the Holy Crown of Hungary with swords 13 January 1945	• *SS-Untersturmführer* 20 April 1939 • *SS-Obersturmführer* 20 April 1941 • *SS-Hauptsturmführer* 20 April 1942 • *SS-Sturmbannführer* 9 November 1944

1943–1944

WASSERSLEBEN, HERMANN-ERICH

Hermann-Erich Wassersleben was born on 7 March 1920 in the small town of Zahna in Saxony. On 16 January 1944, he was wounded in the left jaw. He was promoted to *Leutnant* on 1 July 1944. He came to the Hungarian theatre of war in November 1944 as company commander in the I Battalion of the 978th Grenadier Regiment of the 271st *Volks-Grenadier-Division*. His unit was first deployed in November 1944 in the area of Ercsi–Érd. After the encirclement of Budapest, the battalion was stranded in the capital, and at the end of December 1944, it was in combat in the area of the southern railway embankment. According to the reminisces of Péter Városy, a cadet of the Hungarian 1st assault artillery battalion, written in the 1980s, his unit provided fire support for Wassersleben's unit with their Zrínyi assault guns a number of times.

Leutnant Willy Eberz notified Wassersleben's widow on 14 February 1945 of the death of her husband. The letter is an interesting document due to its peculiar style, despite the fact that no exact details about the circumstances of Wassersleben's death can be derived from it. It can only be assumed that Eberz did not want to tell lies about this matter and, therefore, did not write anything reassuring (for example, that "he died immediately", which is a recurring feature in such letters):

> Dear Madam Wassersleben!
>
> Mine is the hard task to notify you of your husband's heroic death on 28 December 1944 in Budapest.

With the death of Lieutenant Wassersleben, the battalion lost an excellent soldier and an officer with exemplary bravery. He was a comrade who always thought about his men, cared for them, and was also a righteous superior officer. His principle was this: always do more than what you seem to be. He lived his life along this principle in front of the eyes of his soldiers, and he never demanded more of his men than he did of himself. His soldiers loved him and were always near him. Is there anything more a German officer could want?

In all hardships and difficult situations, he displayed a true man's heart and unbroken will to win. His life was a testimony to the Führer and the great ideals of Germany, and that is the way we execute our obligations out here. He was loved and respected among the officers: he was open and straightforward, and his adherence to his obligations will remain unforgettable.

The fate of soldiers made him face great tasks, and these were all completed by him in an exemplary manner. In difficult situations – when both the battalion commander and his adjutant were wounded – he took over command of the I Battalion of the 978th Grenadier Regiment.

For the combats in Budapest and around Budapest, the Führer awarded him on 26 January 1945 (according to the division's order) with the decoration of the German Cross in Gold as a visible sign of his behaviour and soldier's performance.

He loved you and your child with deep, concerned love, and we talked about our home and our families a number of times. He gave his life for his concern about his fatherland. His heroic death will help his child to build a better future.

Dear Madam Wassersleben! I can fully understand your pain in losing your husband, and it is also evident to me that no words can abate your pain; however, I would like to ask you something: please believe me when I say I want to share your pain and sorrow as a human being and as a comrade of your husband.

Beyond all grief, I ask you to be proud that your companion was such a straightforward, moral and brave German officer.

The confidence in the fact that he has fallen for our seriously threatened German nation, for our Führer and Great Germany, should serve as a consolation for you and your child.

In closing my letter, let me express my deepest personal condolences. I am at your service anytime you need advice or action in these difficult times.

With my silent condolences, I remain faithfully yours,

Willy Eberz, lieutenant and battalion adjutant

P.S. Unfortunately, I could not notify you earlier as I myself only returned to my unit yesterday after recuperating from my wounds.[483]

DECORATIONS	RANKS
• *Eisernes Kreuz II. Klasse* 17 October 1943 • *Eisernes Kreuz I. Klasse* 1 February 1944 • *Deutsches Kreuz in Gold* 26 January 1945	• *Leutnant* 1 July 1944

WEBER, WILLI

Willi Weber received the decoration *Deutsches Kreuz in Gold* on 10 February 1945; he was then serving in the rank of *SS-Oberscharführer* in the 3rd Company of *SS-Panzer-Aufklärungs-Abteilung 22* of the 22nd SS Cavalry Division. There were no other data available relating to his person.

DECORATIONS	RANKS
• *Deutsches Kreuz in Gold* 10 February 1945	• Dates of promotions are unknown.

WELTNER, ANDREAS

Andreas Weltner was born on 14 September 1907 in Rödelsee near Kitzingen. There is only scarce information available regarding his military service. He started his service on 28 August 1939 at the 2nd Company of *Panzer-Abwehr-Abteilung*

645. He received the decoration *Deutsches Kreuz in Gold* on 7 January 1945 as *Feldwebel* in the 2nd Company of *Panzerjäger-Abteilung Feldherrnhalle* of Panzer Division *Feldherrnhalle*. There is no other information available related to his person.

DECORATIONS	RANKS
• *Deutsches Kreuz in Gold* 7 January 1945	• Dates of promotions are unknown.

WERNISCH, OSKAR

Oskar Wernisch was born on 31 August 1917 in Rudelsdorf near Landskron. There is scarce information regarding his military service. He served as lieutenant in *Beobachtungs-Abteilung 43* during the siege of Budapest. He received the decoration *Deutsches Kreuz in Gold* on 29 January 1945. Wernisch went missing at the end of the siege.

DECORATIONS	RANKS
• *Deutsches Kreuz in Gold* 29 January 1945	• Dates of promotions are unknown.

WOLF, HEINZ

Heinz Wolf received the decoration *Deutsches Kreuz in Gold* as *SS-Unterscharführer* serving in the 2nd Company *SS-Panzerjäger-Abteilung 8* of SS Cavalry Division on 27 January 1945. There is no other information available relating to his person.

DECORATIONS	RANKS
• *Deutsches Kreuz in Gold* 27 January 1945	• Dates of promotions are unknown.

ZICK, HELMUT

Helmut Zick was born on 12 March 1920 in Hannover. He started his military service in the ranks of *Artillerie-Ersatz-Abteilung 13* in November 1939. On 8 April 1940, he was reassigned to the headquarters of the II *Abteilung* of the 13th Artillery Regiment of the 13th Infantry Division. In April 1942, he was reassigned to the 3rd Battery of the I *Abteilung*, however, soon afterwards, was reassigned to attend artillery officer's training until 27 September 1942. On 23 May 1943, he was reassigned to the 4th Battery of the II *Abteilung*. On 28 June 1943, he was further reassigned to *Artillerie-Ersatz-Abteilung 13*. His service unit during the siege of Budapest cannot be reconstructed. Presumably, he served in the rank of *Leutnant* as the *Abteilungsadjutant* of the II *Abteilung* of the 13th Artillery Regiment. *Oberleutnant* Ernst Scheizer last saw him on 13 February 1945 two kilometres from Solymár. Subsequently, he was registered as dead based on second-hand information. Later, it was coincidentally revealed that he was, in fact, alive, had been captured and had spent time in Soviet internment before returning home. This arose because, at the beginning of 1945, a bank deposit book with his name on it was found in Munich and in 1956, the authorities started a legal process regarding this book. During the legal proceedings, it was revealed that Zick was alive. He was decorated with the *Deutsches Kreuz in Gold* on 23 February 1945.

DECORATIONS	RANKS
• *Deutsches Kreuz in Gold* 23 February 1945	• Dates of promotions are unknown.

3.

PERSONNEL DECORATED WITH THE *EHRENBLATTSPANGE DES DEUTSCHEN HEERES* DURING THE SIEGE OF BUDAPEST

BÜCHNER, WILLY

Willy Büchner was born on 31 January 1915 in the village of Schweina in Thüringen. He started his military service in 1936 in the ranks of *Korps-Pionier-Bataillon 49*. In the same year, he was sentenced to pay a fine of 28 *Reichsmarks* for committing assault and battery. At the beginning of the war, he was already serving as a non-commissioned officer in *Pionier-Bataillon 152* of the 52nd Infantry Division, and continued to do so until 14 October 1943. His further career path cannot be retraced. On 14 June 1940 he received the *Eisernes Kreuz II. Klasse* and, on 17 July 1940, he received the *Eisernes Kreuz I. Klasse*. On 20 July 1942, he was awarded the *Verwundetenabzeichen in Schwarz*, and on 20 August, he was awarded the *Verwundetenabzeichen in Silber*. On 7 April 1942, he was awarded the *Allgemeines Sturmabzeichen*, and he also received the decoration *Deutsches Kreuz in Gold* on 5 September 1943.

He distinguished himself early on with his military capability, proven by the decorations listed above. On 30 November 1942, he was promoted to *Leutnant* without attending the officers' training course. On 1 May 1944, he was also promoted out of turn to *Oberleutnant*. His assessment described him as follows:

> He is a fresh, open and impulsive character with engaging dynamism. He is an extremely dedicated soldier. He is very self-conscious. He enforces his will. He is a definite leader type and very responsible. He is an ardent national socialist. He has distinguished himself in battle against the enemy. He is a dashing, dapper officer [...]; he needs to supplement his existing knowledge.[484]

He was awarded the *Ehrenblattspange des Deutschen Heeres* on 5 February 1945. The details and circumstances of the award have not survived, although it seems evident that this was in connection with the events that led to his death on 20 November 1944. At that time, he was the commander of the 2nd Company of *Pionier-Bataillon Feldherrnhalle* (most probably, he was reassigned here in the summer of 1944). Büchner was fatally wounded at an unknown location; in the period in question, the Panzergrenadier Division *Feldherrnhalle* was in combat at a number of locations from Maglód to Gyöngyös. Büchner's remains were interred in Lot 140 in the New Public Cemetery (Új köztemető).

DECORATIONS	RANKS
• *Eisernes Kreuz II. Klasse* 14 June 1940 • *Eisernes Kreuz I. Klasse* 17 July 1940 • *Verwundetenabzeichen in Schwarz* 20 July 1942 • *Verwundetenabzeichen in Silber* 20 August 1942 • *Allgemeines Sturmabzeichen* 7 April 1942 • *Deutsches Kreuz in Gold* 5 September 1943 • *Ehrenblattspange des Deutschen Heeres* 5 February 1945	• *Leutnant* 30 November 1942 • *Oberleutnant* 1 May 1944 (out of turn)

1944

KEMPNY, WALTER

Walter Kempny was born on 6 July 1917. He was wounded on 23 August 1941 on the right leg, and again, he was seriously wounded by shell fragments on 26 December 1943 on his right hand, right face, both of his legs and left shoulder. During this period, he served in the 10th Company of the Grenadier Regiment

Feldherrnhalle of Panzergrenadier Division *Feldherrnhalle*. After his recovery, he returned to the division in August 1944. At an unknown date, he received the *Eisernes Kreuz II. Klasse* and the *Eisernes Kreuz I. Klasse*.

The decoration *Ehrenblattspange des Deutschen Heeres* was awarded to him on 5 February 1945. At that time, Kempny served as *Oberfeldwebel* in the 1st Company of Panzergrenadier Regiment *Feldherrnhalle*. The details of the award are unknown. It can only be assumed that Kempny was originally recommended to receive the *Ritterkreuz des Eisernen Kreuzes* for a military deed sometime during December 1944. It is not certain that Kempny himself was notified of the award. He served in Budapest until the breakout attempt; after the war, he was registered as missing in action with this information.

DECORATIONS	RANKS
• *Ehrenblattspange des Deutschen Heeres* 5 February 1945	• Dates of promotions are unknown.

PICHLMAIER, MAX

Max Pichlmaier was born on 4 April 1920 in Dillingen. The details of his military service are unknown; what we know is that he started his military service in the 40th Panzergrenadier Regiment of the 17th Panzer Division, and from the autumn of 1944, he commanded the 1st Company of the 66th Panzergrenadier Regiment of the 13th Panzer Division. His commander recommended that he receive the *Ritterkreuz des Eisernen Kreuzes* on 21 October 1944.[485] For some unknown reason, this was not permitted. However, Pichlmaier received the decoration *Ehrenblattspange des Deutschen Heeres* on 15 December 1944. The award was in connection with his brave and endeavouring conduct in the armoured combat at the Battle at Debrecen. On 10 October 1944, his company went into action against an advancing Soviet armoured group east of Püspökladány, and Pichlmaier knocked out a number of Soviet tanks with the 7.5 cm guns mounted on armoured personnel carriers. On 19 October 1944, the 13th Panzer Division, and within that Pichlmaier's company, assaulted a Soviet division advancing towards the northwest of Balmazújváros and completely disrupted its advance; it was only a matter of bad luck that the Germans were not able to capture the Soviet divisional staff. Pichlmaier had advanced as far as the Soviet division's field post office.

Pichlmaier was wounded on 4 November 1944, not far from Vecsés. After he recovered, he took over command of the 3rd Company of *Panzer-Aufklärungs-Abteilung 13* of the 13th Panzer Division, however, was again wounded on 29 December 1944. From this point, it is not possible to determine his fate.

DECORATIONS	RANKS
• *Ehrenblattspange des Deutschen Heeres* 15 December 1944	• Dates of promotions are unknown.

4.

PERSONNEL DECORATED WITH THE *ANERKENNUNGSURKUNDE DES OBERBEFEHLSHABERS DES HEERES FÜR HERVORRAGENDE LEISTUNGEN AUF DEM SCHLACHTFELD* DURING THE SIEGE OF BUDAPEST

BULLE, EDUARD, DR.

Eduard Bulle was born on 6 August 1892 in the village of Montepiano near Florence; his father was born in imperial Germany and worked as a linguistics professor. Bulle attended secondary school in Munich. He served in the First World War between 1915 and 1917; on 7 August 1915, he was captured by the British on the Western Front (he was hit in the hip and pelvis and was seriously wounded). Due to his injuries, he was released in the same year during an exchange of prisoners. Thereafter, he worked in a military hospital in Göttingen.

After taking his university exams, he received his medical certification on 1 March 1920. On 1 May 1933, he joined the *NSDAP* and the SA and worked as the doctor of one of the SA districts. In 1941, he was promoted to *Sturmbannführer* in the SA.

Of his service in the Second World War, we only know that he started his service in the II Battalion of 19th Infantry Regiment of the 7th Infantry Division. He took part in the Polish and French campaigns as a doctor; however, during this time, he received both the *Eisernes Kreuz II. Klasse* and the *Eisernes Kreuz I. Klasse*, which suggests that he was active on the battlefield as well. He was the first doctor to be decorated with the *Deutsches Kreuz in Gold*, on 19 December 1941. Bulle had personally taken part in saving and caring for wounded soldiers under enemy infantry and artillery fire – considering his age and his rank as *SA-Sturmbannführer,* this was an extraordinary undertaking. He was twice wounded during the Second World War.

In Budapest he was the *Divisionsarzt* of Panzergrenadier Division *Feldherrnhalle* in the rank of *Oberstleutnant*. On 7 January 1945, he received the decoration *Anerkennungsurkunde des Oberbefehlshabers des Heeres für hervorragende Leistungen auf dem Schlachtfeld* (approximately "Appreciation Document of the Supreme Commander of the Army for Prominent Achievements on the Battlefield"). During the war, only 1,322 of these documents were awarded. According to *Oberleutnant* Ernst Klose,[486] Bulle shot himself during the breakout attempt.[487]

DECORATIONS	RANKS
• *Eisernes Kreuz II. Klasse* • *Eisernes Kreuz I. Klasse* • *Deutsches Kreuz in Gold* 19 December 1941 • *Anerkennungsurkunde des Oberbefehlshabers des Heeres für hervorragende Leistungen auf dem Schlachtfeld* 7 January 1945	• Dates of promotions are unknown.

5.

THE MILITARY ELITE – AN ATTEMPT AT STATISTICAL ANALYSIS

It is worth comparing the present analysis with the results that can be read in János Rainer M.'s work, *Századosok* ("Captains"*)*. Although Rainer M.'s work is aimed at a similar number of personnel, his group is much more homogenous in its composition. Regarding their age, rank, socialization, and fate after 1945, the "captains" share a number of common features, so it is reasonable to suggest that, in that case, the included personnel constitute a group whose members share similar characteristics, and thus a socio-historical analysis of such a group can lead to telling conclusions.

The same, however, cannot be said of the German military elite in Budapest. This group contained officers, reserve officers and personnel without rank. Their social backgrounds were intensely diverse. In view of their varying ranks, educational levels, and positions in society, they can hardly be considered a homogenous group, and they do not view themselves as a group either. This is in marked contrast to the officers from the Ludovika Academy, where a form of collective identity was shaped during their years at the Academy. In terms of date of birth, again, the group is not homogenous; it includes young soldiers just reaching adulthood and officers, some of whom were more than sixty years old. The only common features shared by the German military elite is that they lived through three months of siege in Budapest and held relatively important positions and/or received high-ranking military decorations. Considering the fact that the German military elite in the siege of Budapest forms such a heterogeneous group suggests they are hardly eligible subjects for research in a socio-historical sense. The only possible focal point of such research would be the German officers' connections to the siege of Budapest and their receipt of the *Ritterkreuz des Eisernen Kreuzes* and the *Deutsches Kreuz in Gold.* The present work does not offer a representative group analysis in this regard.

Despite the above, the author is confident that this work can serve as an aid to answering certain socio-historical questions. The cooperation, or collaboration, of the German military elite with the Nazi regime (or keeping their distance from it); their relationship with, and involvement in, war crimes; and their fate after 1945 are aspects of their lives that are not without moral lessons. A potential subject for further research would be to examine how the fate and career of the related personnel after 1945 were affected and influenced by their military service, which became increasingly performance-oriented during the war and opened the door to upward social mobility for many of these soldiers.

The author has classified 48 personnel as German military elite in a strict sense. Of these, nine had already received the *Ritterkreuz des Eisernen Kreuzes* or the *Eichenlaub* before the siege of Budapest, and thirty-four of them received the decoration during the siege (of the latter, there was no award that was not related to Budapest, and seven *Eichenlaub* decorations were awarded during the siege itself).[488] Of the awards of the *Ritterkreuz des Eisernen Kreuzes* and *Eichenlaub* connected to Budapest, at least seven cases are clearly not connected to the given person's military performance or heroic deeds but were awarded for political reasons or as propaganda.[489] Because losing the war was no longer in doubt, the leaders of important army units received these decorations, regardless of their activity, as a sort of recompense. In other words, even in the case of such high-ranking decorations, at least 20.5 percent of the awards were independent of the recipient's personal military bravery or performance on the battlefield. The percentage is much higher if one considers the group of officers receiving these decorations. During the siege of Budapest, only six recipients of the *Ritterkreuz des Eisernen Kreuzes* were enlisted men (or non-commissioned officers). For this group, at least, it is highly probable that the award of these decorations was not related to the recipient's personal connections or for political reasons. Considering the 24 officers as a base for the calculation, the percentage of awards not related to combat activity now reaches 29 percent. This highlights the need for military historians to closely research the circumstances in which such high-ranking decorations were awarded.

Unfortunately, such a comparison and calculation cannot be executed in the case of the decoration *Deutsches Kreuz in Gold* (or the *Ehrenblattspange des Deutschen Heeres*). These decorations were awarded to soldiers who were mainly in combat on the frontline, and the majority of the recommendations for these awards have not survived. Regarding the 71 *Deutsches Kreuz in Gold* decorations awarded during the siege of Budapest, it is an interesting fact that the commanders of the following units *did not* receive this decoration: the commanders of the I Battalion and II Battalion of *Heeres-Pionier-Brigade 127*; the commander of *Landesschützen-Bataillon 318* (none of the soldiers serving in this unit received this decoration); the commander of the II *Abteilung* of the 4th Panzer Regiment of the 13th Panzer Division and the commander of *Panzer-Pionier-Bataillon 4* of 13th Panzer Division. This essentially suggests that this decoration – precisely because of its much lower prestige value – had not become the subject of higher political consideration. Instances of the misuse of these decorations can usually be traced back to those recommending the awards and not the German High Command itself. For example, only *SS-Hauptsturmführer* Meiert's immediate, higher-ranking superiors could discern what he was doing on Csepel Island on the last days of November 1944, particularly so because, according to the criteria for recommending the *Deutsches Kreuz in Gold*, the related military deeds for which the decoration was awarded should have been of local importance. Only by comparing the German award recommendations with related Soviet sources can any reasonable evaluation be made as to how closely the military deeds recorded in the recommendations relate to the actual military situation at a particular time and place.

It is also worth considering the German military elite in Budapest in terms of their survival and further fate. Summarizing the 125 persons included in the present work (this includes personnel not included in the military elite based on their decorations), the results are as follows:

Interned as a prisoner of war, later released, returned home	18	14.4%
Took part in the breakout attempt and succeeded	14	11.2%
Managed to get out of the city before it was encircled	6	4.9%
Died, the fact of death can be proven, and the approximate location of primary burial is known	21	14%
Died in captivity	1	0.8%
Executed in captivity	1	0.8%
Missing in action	41	26%
No data available	23	18.4%
Total	125	100%

The data in the above table clearly show that only around 30.5 percent of the personnel included in this study survived the siege of Budapest. If one compares this result with the group of Hungarian officers researched by János Rainer M., of whom approximately 20 percent died or went missing during the war, the 69.5 percent loss in the present group is exceptionally high for a single military event (the siege of Budapest).[490] The proportion of those missing in action is especially high, which is related to the fact that the majority of deaths occurred during the breakout attempt itself (only eight persons belonging to the author's selected group died prior to the breakout attempt, typically during the combat actions in November 1944). Those about whom the author has not been able to acquire any data most probably died during this period because, if they had survived, then on returning from Soviet internment – if they lived in West Germany – they would have been eligible for war compensation, and this would have been documented in the archives.

The fact that only eight persons of those included in the present work died between the early phase of the siege and 11 February 1945 does not automatically mean that the remainder of the group spent the entirety of this period in safe command posts. This conclusion is supported by the fact that many of the personnel who took the risk of attempting to break out set off with light or sometimes severe wounds. It is also remarkable that there is almost no information available about personnel who died while imprisoned. This might be connected to the fact that the Soviet Union only registered deaths within the territory of the Soviet Union while – especially in the case of the siege of Budapest – the majority of captives had indeed died between the location of their capture and the Romanian relocation camps (usually Focșani). Their remains are today interred in mass graves without the slightest chance of identification.

It is also interesting to compare the number of decorations awarded to the different military units during the siege of Budapest closely. The majority of the decorations (19 *Deutsches Kreuz in Gold* and 12 *Ritterkreuz des Eisernen Kreuz*) were awarded to personnel serving in the 8th SS Cavalry Division. The personnel serving in the 13th Panzer Division received altogether seven awards of the *Ritterkreuz des Eisernen Kreuz* and 15 of the *Deutsches Kreuz in Gold.* Compared to the above, the personnel serving in the 22nd SS Cavalry Division received only 6 *Ritterkreuz des Eisernen Kreuz* and 10 *Deutsches Kreuz in Gold* awards (it also needs to be noted that a number of the *Ritterkreuz des Eisernen Kreuz* awards are ambiguous). Soldiers serving in Panzer Division *Feldherrnhalle* received altogether 6 *Ritterkreuz des Eisernen Kreuz* awards and 7 instances of the *Deutsches Kreuz in Gold*, and the personnel serving in the 271st *Volks-Grenadier-Division* received altogether one *Ritterkreuz des Eisernen Kreuz* with *Eichenlaub* and five awards of the *Deutsches Kreuz in Gold.* Four awards, namely, for Dörner, Geschke, Jansa and Pfeffer-Wildenbruch are not related to any units. These statistics are, however, misleading as a different number of soldiers belonged to these aforementioned units. It is difficult to provide exact numbers because, at the time of the completion of the encirclement, many units that had been in combat on the outskirts of the city were stuck outside of the encirclement; however, it can be stated that the two SS Cavalry Divisions possessed approximately twice as many soldiers and resources than the armoured units of the Wehrmacht, and only a regiment-sized group of the 271st *Volks-Grenadier-Division* was trapped in Budapest. Looking at the statistics from this angle, the statement voiced by a number of soldiers during the war, namely that the SS *units* had been preferred when awarding decorations, is not entirely correct. The fact that it did seem to be true can be connected to the uneven and disproportionate distribution of the decorations: in particular, during the second week of February 1945, the awards became almost mass events in all categories, and it was undoubtedly true that the SS units were over-represented among those decorated at this time.

It also needs to be discussed why two of the categories of decorations were awarded in such a few cases: only three *Ehrenblattspange des Deutschen Heeres* and only one single *Anerkennungsurkunde des Oberbefehlshabers des Heeres* were awarded in connection with Budapest. However, 4,547 of the former and 1,322 of the latter were awarded throughout the war. The author's research is currently seeking answers as to why the award of these two decorations was under-represented to such a degree during the siege of Budapest while the *Ritterkreuz des Eisernen Kreuz* awards rather show over-representation: of the proven *Ritterkreuz des Eisernen Kreuz* awards made between 1939 and 1945, 0.5 percent of them at the first degree level, and 0.7 percent of them at the second degree (*Eichenlaub*) level, were made in connection with combat activity around Budapest. Of the confirmed awards of the *Deutsches Kreuz in Gold*, 0.26 percent of them were made in connection with Budapest. These numbers would be approximately 30 percent higher if the decorations awarded to *Luftwaffe* and *Kriegsmarine* personnel were not included in the statistics. The Second World War lasted approximately 67 months, therefore the average rate of award of the *Ritterkreuz des Eisernen Kreuze* is 108/month. In this sense, the rate at which this decoration was awarded during the siege of Budapest does not seem to be that low.

The award of decorations more or less followed military actions. This can be discerned most clearly from the award of the *Deutsches Kreuz in Gold*, which was awarded in prominently large numbers for combat actions during the beginning of November 1944 and for the combat actions on Csepel Island. At the same time, there are no data – although, in the absence of the recommendation documents, one can only presume this – to prove decorations had been awarded for combat actions during the first three weeks of December 1944. The complete absence of decorations awarded to personnel serving in certain units is remarkable. No personnel from the police units and the members of the *Landesschützen* units received the *Deutsches Kreuz in Gold*. As opposed to this, the *Heeres-Pionier* units received three, and the *Flak-Artillerie* units received five *Deutsches Kreuz in*

Gold decorations. In the case of the *Deutsches Kreuz in Gold*, the ratio of those in enlisted ranks receiving it is especially high: of the 69 decorated personnel, 19 were non-commissioned officers or enlisted ranks.

This leads to the supposition that, from January 1945 onwards, the vast majority of recommendations either did not reach Berlin or, if they did, no decision was reached regarding their merit until the end of the siege. The fact that many of these documents remain unsealed is demonstrated by the manuscript of Georg-Wilhelm Schöning. As the author has already mentioned in the introduction to the present work, according to the provisions of the Third Reich, decorations were not permitted to be awarded to personnel presumed to be in captivity. Consequently, one may assume that a number of *Ritterkreuz des Eisernen Kreuzes* recommendations and even more *Deutsches Kreuz in Gold* recommendations had been left pending.

It is almost impossible to make valid assumptions regarding the percentage of the military elite included in the present work being ardent followers of Nazi ideology or, more precisely, being perpetrators of war crimes. In the majority of cases, there are no traces of such activities. In the remaining cases, only a suspicion can be formed because no detailed investigation had been carried out (in most cases, due to the death of the relevant personnel). If we classify as "actively Nazi" that personnel who, apart from being a member of the *NSDAP*, have expressly identified themselves with Nazi ideology and served in important positions within the ideological bureaucracy, we can name fifteen persons – however, this is partial data only.

As the author has already stated in the introduction, decorations are physical tokens of appreciation that are only on paper and are not necessarily connected with real events. Awards are shaded by politics and propaganda, and apart from this, pure luck, as well as the recipient's "proximity to high circles", also play their part. All this warns us, contemporary readers, that in assessing the merits of those who received such awards, we should examine not only the presumed military achievement behind these decorations but also the man himself and the system that sent him to war. This work is an attempt to achieve this aim.

APPENDIX

LIST OF PERSONNEL DECORATED DURING THE SIEGE OF BUDAPEST

The German military elite of the battle for Budapest

Pfeffer-Wildenbruch, Karl
Bartsch, Kurt
Boosfeld, Joachim
Buck, Friedrich
Bunge, Hellmut
Charpentier, Hans-Georg Von
Dallmann, Werner
Dörner, Helmut
Drexler, Walter
Ekesparre, Arthur Carl Johann Von
Erdmann, Otto
Fehrensen, Wilhelm Dr.
Geschke, Hans-Ulrich
Gottstein, Reiner
Hamel, Heinz
Heuer, Alfred
Hitschler, Konrad
Jansa, Ernst
Klett, Albert
Korth, Siegfried
Krauss, Oswald
Krämer, Paul
Kündiger, Herbert
Liebisch, Franz
Lindenau, Daniel
Mainka, Erhard
Maringgele, Hermann
Mitzlaff, Sven Von
Mösslacher, Erhard
Müller, Kurt
Phoenix, Harry
Raeder, Kurt
Reißmann, Paul
Remlinger, Heinrich
Rumohr, Joachim
Schaarschmidt, Herbert
Schack, Hans Von
Schaper, Bodo
Schitthelm, Karl
Schmidhuber, Gerhard
Schöning, Georg-Wilhelm
Soldner, Gustav
Stiegler, Johann
Ulrich, Emil
Weber, Rudolf
Wendrinski, Gustav
Wolff, Helmut
Zehender, August

Military personnel decorated with the *Deutsches Kreuz in Gold* during the siege of Budapest

Bischoff, Helmut
Böglmüller, Josef
Bollack, Helmut
Bresinski, Bruno
Buttkereit, Johannes
Drücker, Bernhard
Eichel, Willi
Findeis, Eugen
Finger, Johannes
Fischer, Ernst
Flügel, Wolfgang
Friedrich, Helmut
Georgs, Heinz
Görcke, Wilhelm
Greger, Friederich
Grossmann, Heinz
Haberstroh, Fritz
Hahn, Fritz
Hasenbein, Erich
Haslehner, Ferdinand
Hehn, Viktor Von
Heller, Hans
Hennig, Hans
Herrmann, Karl
Holz, Ewald
Kammerer, Erich
Keitel, Karl-Heinz
Kerkau, Otto
Klauss, Hans-Heinrich
Kraetzig, Lothar
Krämer, Gabriel
Kreipe, Ernst
Kunz, Josef
Mazurek, Franz
Medla, Henry
Mehles, Günther
Meier, Friedrich
Meiert, Bruno
Meissner, Walter
Metzig, Heinz
Meyer, Claus-Dietrich
Mittelberger, Otto-Eugen Dr.
Möller, Adolf
Münchow, Leopold Von
Otto, Helmut
Paul, Reinhard
Panck, Bernhard
Plänk, Wilhelm
Pleschinger, Karl
Präger, Walter
Reinhard, Karl-Werner
Richter, Herbert
Röschmann, Ernst
Rosenfelder, Fritz
Rothe, Friedrich
Rutzke, Paul
Sander, Friedrich
Schaffner, Ottomar
Schmedding, Ernst
Schonert, Werner
Schrader, Erwin
Sobotta, Karl-Heinz
Stahlberg, Werner
Steinberger, Ernst-Martin
Tappeiner, Josef
Tauer, Herbert
Thoma, Johann
Waller, Karl
Wassersleben, Hermann-Erich
Weber, Willi
Weltner, Andreas
Wernisch, Oskar
Wolf, Heinz
Zick, Helmut

Personnel decorated with the *Ehrenblattspange des Deutschen Heeres* during the siege of Budapest

Büchner, Willy
Kempny, Walter
Pichlmaier, Max

Personnel decorated with the *Anerkennungsurkunde des Oberbefehlshabers des Heeres für hervorragende Leistungen auf dem Schlachtfeld* during the siege of Budapest

Bulle, Eduard, Dr.

WAFFEN-SS AND EQUIVALENT WEHRMACHT RANKS AND THEIR APPROXIMATE BRITISH EQUIVALENTS

Waffen-SS	Wehrmacht	approximate British equivalents (where applicable)
SS-Sturmmann	Gefreiter	Private
SS-Rottenführer	Obergefreiter	Private 1st class
SS-Unterscharführer	Unteroffizier	Corporal
SS-Scharführer	Unterfeldwebel	not applicable
SS-Oberscharführer	Feldwebel	Sergeant
SS-Hauptscharführer	Oberfeldwebel	Battalion master sergeant
SS-Stabsscharführer	Hauptfeldwebel	Company master sergeant
SS-Sturmscharführer	Stabsfeldwebel	Staff sergeant
SS-Untersturmführer	Leutnant	Second lieutenant
SS-Obersturmführer	Oberleutnant	First lieutenant
SS-Hauptsturmführer	Hauptmann/Rittmeister (Kavallerie)	Captain
SS-Sturmbannführer	Major	Major
SS-Obersturmbannführer	Oberstleutnant	Lieutenant colonel
SS-Standartenführer	Oberst	Colonel
SS-Oberführer	not applicable	not applicable
Brigadeführer und Generalmajor der Waffen-SS	Generalmajor	Brigadier/Major general
Gruppenführer und Generalleutnant der Waffen-SS	Generalleutnant	Lieutenant general
Obergruppenführer und General der Waffen-SS	General der Infanterie/Panzertruppe/Artillerie	General (army branch)
Oberst-Gruppenführer und Generaloberst der Waffen-SS	Generaloberst	Colonel general
Reichsführer-SS (Heinrich Himmler)	Generalfeldmarschall	Field marshal

GERMAN MILITARY DECORATIONS

Ritterkreuz des Eisernen Kreuzes mit Eichenlaub und Schwertern	Knight's Cross of the Iron Cross with Oak Leaves and Swords
Ritterkreuz des Eisernen Kreuzes mit Eichenlaub	Knight's Cross of the Iron Cross with Oak Leaves
Ritterkreuz des Eisernen Kreuzes	Knight's Cross of the Iron Cross
Eisernes Kreuz (I. und II. Klasse)	Iron Cross (1st and 2nd Class)
Kriegverdienstkreuz (I. und II. Klasse)	War Merit Cross (1st and 2nd Class)
Deutsches Kreuz (in Gold und Silber)	German Cross (in Gold and Silber)
Nahkampfspange (Gold, Silber, Bronze)	Close Combat Clasp (Gold, Silver, Bronze Classes)
Verwundetenabzeichen (in Gold, Silber, Schwartz)	Wound Badge (in Gold, Silver, Black)
Allgemeines Sturmabzeichen	General Assault Badge
Panzerkampfabzeichen	Panzer Badge
Infanterie-Sturmabzeichen	Infantry Assault Badge
Sonderabzeichen für das Niederkämpfen von Panzerkampfwagen durch Einzelkämpfer (Panzervernichtungsabzeichen)	Special Badge for the Close-Combat, Single-Handed Destruction of a Tank (or other armoured vehicle; Tank Destruction Badge)
Anerkennungsurkunde des Oberbefehlshabers des Heeres für hervorragende Leistungen auf dem Schlachtfeld	Appreciation Document of the Commander in Chief of the Army for excellence on the battlefield
Ehrenblattspange des Deutschen Heeres	Honour Roll Clasp of the German Army
Nennung im Ehrenblatt des Deutschen Heeres	Mentioning in the Honour Roll of the German Army
Ärmelschild Demjansk	Demyansk Shield
Ehrenwinkel der alten Kämpfer	Honour Chevron for the Old Guard

Tapferkeits und Verdienstauszeichnung für Ostvölker (Ostvolkmedaille)	Medal for Gallantry and Merit for Members of the Eastern Peoples (Eastern Medal)
Ehrendegen Reichsführer-SS (RFSS)	A ceremonial short sword of the Reich Leader, a personal gift from Heinrich Himmler
SS-Ehrenring	SS Honour Ring
Julleuchter	A clay candleholder adorned with Germanic symbols

ABBREVIATIONS

AHS	Adolf-Hitler-Schule	Adolf Hitler School
BdS	Befehlshaber der Sicherheitspolizei und des Sicherheitsdienstes	Commander of the Sicherheitspolizei and SD
DNSAP	Deutsche Nationalsozialistische Arbeiter-partei	German National Socialist Workers' Party (National Socialist party in Austria)
Fela	Feldlazarett	Field hospital
HIAG	Hilfsgemeinschaft auf Gegenseitigkeit der Angehörigen der ehemaligen Waffen-SS	Mutual Aid Association of Former Waffen-SS Members
HVPL	Hauptverbandsplatz	Clearing station, dressing station
KdS	Kommando/Kommandeur der Sicherheits-polizei und des Sicherheitsdienstes	Regional headquarters/commander of the Sicherheitspolizei and SD
Korück	Kommandant des rückwärtigen Armeege-bietes	Commandant of the Army Rear Area
NSDAP	Nationalsozialistische Deutsche Arbeiter-partei	National Socialist German Workers' Party
NSFO	Nationalsozialistischer Führungsoffizier	National Socialist Leadership Officer
NSKK	Nationalsozialistisches Kraftfahrkorps	National Socialist Motor Driver Corps
HSSPF	Höherer SS- und Polizeiführer	Higher SS and Police Leader
OdR	Ordensgemeinschaft der Ritterkreuzträger	Association of Knight's Cross Recipients
OKH	Oberkommando des Heeres	High Command of the Army
RAD	Reichsarbeitsdienst	Reich Labour Service
RFSS	Reichsführer-SS	Reich Leader of the SS
RSHA	Reichssicherheitshauptamt	Reich Main Security Office
RuSHA	Rasse- und Siedlungshauptamt	Race and Settlement Main Office
SA	Sturmabteilung	'Storm Division', a paramilitary organization of the Nazi Party
SD	Sicherheitsdienst	Security Police
SS	Schutzstaffel	'Protection Squadron', a paramilitary and military organization of the Nazi Party

SS-VT	SS-Verfügungstruppe	The predecessor of the Waffen-SS between 1934 and 1940
TVPL	Truppenverbandsplatz	Field dressing station
WASt	Wehrmacht-Auskunftsstelle	Information office handling the documents on Wehrmacht casualties
Wfstb	Wehrmachtführungsstab	Headquarters and staff of the Oberkommando der Wehrmacht (OKW)

BIBLIOGRAPHY

ARCHIVAL SOURCES

Állambiztonsági Szolgálatok Történeti Levéltára (ÁBTL; Historical Archives of the State Security Services)

1114 67-46/171-30/1988.

V-80871, Confession of Vilmos Lucska, 31 December 1948. p. 27.

Bundesarchiv Berlin-Lichterfelde (BA-B)

NS 33/368, SS-Auffangsstelle für Budapest-Rückkämpfer 19.02.1945.

R 10–451/32–33 Übersicht über Kräfte der Ordnungspolizei und ihren Einsatz, Stand 15. Juli 1944.

R 20/49, RFSS Chef der Bandenkampfverbände, Bandenlage "Ost" für die Zeit von 15. 7. bis 31. 7. 1943.

R 20/45b.

Berlin Document Center (BDC) personal document files

Rasse und Siedlungshauptamt (RuS) marriage requests and approval documentation

Bundesarchiv-Militärarchiv Freiburg (BA-MA)

B 43/86 Usdai Lindenau an die Ordensgemeinschaft der Ritterkreuzträger 15.06.1960.

N 370/6, The letter of Pfeffer-Wildenbruch to Carl Lutz, dated 31 March 1957.

RH 2 332, 146–147 and BA-B NS 33/368.

RH 7/282, Schreiben OKH PA/P5 26345

RH 7/665 Documentation titled "Summary of staff officers reassigned from the Wehrmacht to the Waffen-SS".

RS 2-9.

Bundesarchiv Berlin-Reinickendorf (former WASt)

Daily combat casualty reports of *Heeresgruppe Süd*

Central files and the documentation thereof of the personnel contained in the present work

Casualty reports and strength reports of the units mentioned in the present work

Bundesbeauftragte für die Unterlagen des Staatssicherheitsdienstes der ehemaligen DDR (BStU)

HA IX/11, ZR 920 A51 Telefonverzeichnis HSSPF Budapest, KdS Budapest, Sondereinsatzkommando Budapest

Budapest Főváros Levéltára (BFL; Archives of Budapest)

VII5e 1950-7587.

XXV-1-a 1945-2462

XXV2b-85706/1949

Diplomatische Dokumente der Schweiz (DODIS)

18860, Report of Harald Feller on 31 October 1946.

18861, Friedrich Born: Bericht an das Internationale Komitee von Roten Kreuz Juni 1945.

Hadtörténelmi Levéltár (HL; Hungarian Military History Archives)

TGY 2829, József Paulits: *Budapest végnapjai.*

I. 89. VKF 1945 306/b, 1945.02.10 Kgl ung Honvédminister an Greiffenberg

Documentation collection of awards and decorations

Hadtörténeti Múzeum (HM-HIM; Hungarian Museum of Military History)

16456/Em war log

National Archives and Records Administration (NARA)

T 77 R1142 F000797-798.

Politikatörténeti Intézet Levéltára (PIL; Archives of the Institute of Political History)

Zseni Várnai–Zoltán Bokody: *A "Várnai" ellenállási csoport rövid vázlata* (Short outline of the activities of "Várnai" resistance group) 274. fond 7/280. storage unit.

682. fond, 1. storage unit, II 23., 305, report 1948. 10. 23.

686. fond, 42 storage unit, the report of Miklós Steinmetz to Mihály Farkas.

Central Archives of the Ministry of Defence of the Russian Federation (TsAMO)

109. Long-Range Guards Artillery Brigade operational logs, 9937 fond 1. storage unit

500. fond: separately published on www.germandocsinrussia.org

12472. sub-fond, documentation of the 6th Army

12480. sub-fond, captured documentation of the Soviet military reconnaissance

Sächsisches Hauptstaatarchiv Dresden (SHD)

13471, NS-Archiv der MfS, ZA I 05422 Akte 6.

Personal collection of the Author

The letter of Győző Benyovszky 25 January 1945.

Bollwerk im Kampfraum Falaise Wie sich Major Kündiger das Ritterkreuz erkämpfte (contemporary newspaper article, a copy owned by the author)

Report of Ernst Schweitzer dated 26 February 1945.

Hans-Otto Wachter: Als die Feuer brannten Band IV (manuscript).

Interviews: Győző Benyovszky, Joachim Boosfeld, Ferenc X. Kovács, Harry Phoenix, Johannes Finger, Aurél Salamon, Ernst Schweitzer, Hans-Otto Wachter, Péter Városy.

Gyula Kokovay: *Budapest védelme.*

Ferenc X. Kovács: *Villanások.*

The letter of Rudolf Raab to Gerhard Emmerich, dated 3 February 1950.

Memories of S Wagner

Manuscript of Aurél Salamon

Memories of Péter Városy

Ferenc Villányi: *Édesapánk naplója 1944 december 9. – 1945 május 17.*

The letter from W Bierwirth, dated 21 August 2001.

PUBLISHED SOURCES

A magyar antifasiszta ellenállás és partizánmozgalom. Kislexikon. Ed. Ervin Liptai. Budapest, Kossuth, 1987.

Anger, Per: *Raoul Wallenberggel Budapesten.* Budapest, Belvárosi, 1999.

B. Stenge, Csaba: *Elfelejtett hősök. A magyar királyi honvéd légierők ászai a második világháborúban.* Nagykovácsi, Puedlo, 2006. [2. revised and extended edition: Budapest, Zrínyi, 2016.]

Balck, Hermann: *Ordnung im Chaos. Erinnerungen 1893–1948.* Osnabrück, Biblio-Verlag, 1981.

Bayer, Hanns: *Die Kavallerie der Waffen-SS.* Gailberg-Heidelberg, 1980.

Bayer, Hanns: *Kavalleriedivisonen der Waffen-SS.* Gailberg-Heidelberg, published by the author, 1980.

Berger, Florian: *Ritterkreuzträger mit Nahkampfspange in Gold.* Wien, published by the author, 2004.

Blanckenburg, Peter von: *Herzschläge. Erinnerungen aus einem bewegten Jahrhundert.* Berlin, Books on Demand, 2001.

Bokor, Péter: *Végjáték a Duna mentén. Interjúk egy filmsorozathoz.* Budapest, RTV-Minerva–Kossuth, 1982.

Bondor, Vilmos: *A Mikó-rejtély. Mikó Zoltán és Raoul Wallenberg kapcsolata a magyar ellenállásban, 1944–1945.* Budapest, Püski, 1995.

Carl, Willi: *Unter dem Schwert des Damokles.* Wickede, Hutters, 1985.

Cesarani, David: *Adolf Eichmann. Bürokrat und Massenmörder.* München, Propyläen, 2004.

Creveld, Martin van: *Fighting Power. German and US-Army Performance, 1939–1945.* Westport, Greenwood, 1982.

Creveld, Martin van: *Kampfkraft. Militärische Organisation und militärische Leistung, 1939–1945.* Einzelschriften zur Militärgeschichte 31. Freiburg, MGFA, 1989.

Curilla, Wolfgang: *Der Judenmord in Polen und die deutsche Ordnungspolizei, 1939–1945.* Paderborn, Ferdinand Schöningh, 2011.

Cüppers, Martin: *Wegbereiter der Shoah. Die Waffen-SS, der Kommandostab Reichsführer-SS und die Judenvernichtung, 1939–1945.* Veröffentlichungen der Forschungsstelle Ludwigsburg der Universität Stuttgart 4. Darmstadt, WBG, 2005.

Csillik, Gábor: *Budapesten harcoltunk.* Budapest, Magvető, 1964.

Dési, János: *Wallenberg-jegyzőkönyv.* Budapest, Ab Ovo, 2014.

Die Wehrmachtberichte 1939–1945. Bd 3. Köln, GLB, 1989.

Dokumentumok a zsidóság üldöztetésének történetéhez. Iratok a Tolna Megyei Levéltárból. Ed Ágnes Ságvári. Budapest, Magyar Auschwitz Alapítvány, 1994.

Dörr, Manfred: *Die Inhaber der Anerkennungsurkunde des Oberbefehlshabers des Heeres, 1941–1945.* Osnabrück, Biblio, 1993.

Erőd a Duna mentén. A Budapestért 1944–45-ben folytatott harcok katonai iratai a Hadtörténelmi Levéltárban. Ed. Norbert Számvéber. Budapest, Petit Real, 1999.

Fellgiebel, Walther-Peer: *Die Träger des Ritterkreuzes des Eisernen Kreuzes, 1939–1945. Die Inhaber der höchsten Auszeichnung des Zweiten Weltkrieges aller Wehrmachtteile.* Friedberg, Podzun-Pallas, 1986 [2006].

Fischer, Ferenc: "Karl Pfeffer-Wildenbruch vezette német rendőrségi misszió titkos közreműködése a chilei csendőrség, a Cuerpo de Carabineros felállításában (1928–1929)". In *Historia est lux veritatis. Szakály Sándor köszöntése 60. születésnapján.* Ed. Endre Marinovich. Budapest, Magyar Napló, 2016, 171–184.

"Freid gemacht". In *Der Spiegel,* 1976. május 24. http:// www.spiegel.de/spiegel/print/d-41213414.html.

Fröhlich Dávid: *Huszárok előre! Magyar sereglovasság a II. világháborúban.* Nagykovácsi, Puedlo, 2012.

Gabori, Georg: *Amikor elszabadult a gonosz.* Budapest, Magyar Világ, 1990 [1991].

Gafke, Mathias: *Heydrichs Ostmärker. Das österreichische Führungspersonal der Sicherheitspolizei und des SD, 1939–1945.* Darmstadt, Wissenschaftliche Buchgesellschaft, 2015.

Gerlach, Christian: *Kalkulierte Morde. Die deutsche Wirtschaftsund Vernichtungspolitik in Weissrussland 1941 bis 1944.* Hamburg, Hamburger Edition, 1999.

Gerwarth, Robert: *Reinhard Heydrich.* München, Siedler, 2011.

Gogun, Alexander: *Stalin's Commandos. Ukrainian Partisan Forces on the Eastern Front.* London, I. B. Tauris, 2016.

Gosztonyi, Péter: "Budapest ostroma 1944–1945-ben". In *Nyugati magyar tanulmányírók antológiája 1987.* Ed. Gyula Borbándi. Bern, EPMSZ, 1987, 85–99.; Digital version: http:// mek.oszk.hu/02900/02929/02929.pdf.

Gosztonyi, Péter: *Légiveszély, Budapest! Szemelvények Magyarország második világháborús történetéből (1939–1945).* Budapest, Népszava, 1989.

Gosztonyi, Péter: *Háború van, háború! Újabb szemelvények Magyarország második világháborús történelméből.* Budapest, Népszava, 1989.

Gosztonyi, Péter: *Vihar Kelet-Európa felett.* Budapest, Népszava, 1990.

Gosztonyi, Péter: *Budapest lángokban, 1944–1945.* Budapest, Móra, 1998.

Győrffy, Sándor – Spáczay, Hedvig: "A IX. SS-hadtestparancsnokság titkos napi jelentései a Budapestért folyó harcokról (1945. január 1–24.)". *Hadtörténelmi Közlemények* 1975/1. 187–209.

Haase, Norbert: "Wehrmachtsangehörige vor dem Kriegsgericht". In Rolf-Dieter Müller – Hans-Erich Volkmann ed.: *Die Wehrmacht. Mythos und Realität.* München, Oldenbourg, 1999, 474–485.

Heiber, Helmut ed.: *Der ganz normale Wahnsinn unterm Hakenkreuz. Triviales und Absonderliches aus den Akten des Dritten Reichs.* München, Herbig, 1996.

Heintz, Daniel: *Zerschlagen und vermisst! Rückkämpfer, Rückkehrer und die Abwicklungsstäbe der Wehrmacht.* Aachen, Helios, 2018.

Hingyi, László: *Budapest ostroma, 1944–1945. Források Budapest ostromának történetéből I.* Budapest, Etalon, 2018.

Husemann, Friedrich: *Die guten Glaubens waren. Geschichte der SS-Polizei-Division (4. SS-Panzergrenadier-Division).* Band I.: *1939–1942.* Osnabrück, Munin-Verlag, 1971 [2. ed.: 1984; 3. ed.: Coburg, Nation Europa Verlag, 1999].

Huss, Jürgen – Sondermann, Heinz-Werner: *Ritterkreuzträger im Mannschaftsstand, 1941–1945. Fotos und Tatberichte der hoch ausgezeichneten Soldaten.* Saarbrücken, VDM, 2009.

Ich Adolf Eichmann. Ein historischer Zeugenbericht. Ed. Rudolf Aschenauer. Leoni am Starnberger See, Druffel, 1980.

Illésfalvi, Péter – Kovács, Vilmos – Maruzs, Roland: *„Vitézségért". A Magyar Tiszti Arany Vitézségi Éremmel kitüntetettek a második világháborúban.* Budapest, Hermanos, 2011.

Jánossy, Dénes: "Budapest ostroma és az Országos Levéltár". *Levéltári Közlemények,* 1946 (26), 1–12.

Jester, Werner: *Im Todessturm von Budapest, 1945.* Landser am Feind 1. Dresden, Winkelried, 2010.

Józsa, Béla: *Egyetemisták az ostromgyűrűben.* Budapest, Történelmi Hagyományőrző és Hadisírgondozó Alapítvány, 1999.

Kádár, Gyula: *A Ludovikától Sopronkőhidáig.* Budapest, Magvető, 1978.

Kalakán, László: *Fejezetek Magyarország egészségügyének történetéből 1920–1945.* Doktori diszszertáció.: https://pea.lib.pte.hu/bitstream/ handle/pea/16132/kalakan-laszlo-phd-2012. pdf.

Kammerer, Anja – Kammerer, Willi ed.: *Narben bleiben. Die Arbeit der Suchdienste. 60 Jahre nach dem Zweiten Weltkrieg.* Deutsche Dienststelle, Berlin, 2008.

Keresztes, Csaba: "Az Országos Levéltár Budapest ostromában és a levéltár helyreállítása". *Levéltári Közlemények* 2015 (86), 87–104.

Kilian, Jürgen: *Wehrmacht und Besatzungsherrschaft im russischen Nordwesten, 1941–1944. Praxis und Alltag im Militärverwaltungsgebiet der Heeresgruppe Nord.* Paderborn–München–Wien, Schöningh, 2012.

Klemp, Stefan: *„Nicht ermittelt". Polizeibataillone und die Nachkriegsjustiz.* Ein Handbuch. Essen, Klartext, 2011.

Klemp, Stefan: *„Rücksichtslos ausgemerzt". Die Ordnungspolizei und das Massaker von Lidice.* Münster, Villa Ten Hompel, 2012.

Kókay, György: "Dokumentumok a Budai Vár 1945. évi ostromáról". In *Tanulmányok Budapest múltjából 26.* (1997). 221–249.

Komisszarov, N. V.: "Harc Budapestért". *Hadtörténelmi Közlemények,* 1980/1. 134–141.

Krätschmer, Ernst-Günther: *Die Ritterkreuzträger der Waffen-SS.* Berlin, Pour le Mérite, 2010.

Kukin, Vasiliy Tikhonovich: *Ot pervogo i do poszlednego vistrela. Parenek iz Mordovii.* Moscow, DOSAAF, 1986.; http://nozdr.ru/militera/prose/russian/kukin_vt/10.html.

Kurschat, Heinrich A.: "Schicksalsstunden für Budapest. Eichanlaub-Dörner verteidigt Ungarns Hauptstadt. Zahllose Sperren und Hindernisse". *Marburger Zeitung,* 1945. január 5.

Landwehr, Richard: *Budapest, the Stalingrad of the Waffen-SS.* Bennington, Merriam Press, 2012.

Lehmann, Hans Georg: "Unternehmen Panzerfaust. Der Putsch der SS in Budapest am 15. Oktober 1944". *Ungarn-Jahrbuch* 5 (1973). 215–231.

Lévai, Jenő: *A pesti gettó csodálatos megmenekülésének hiteles története.* Budapest, Officina, 1946.

Lévai, Jenő: *Raoul Wallenberg regényes élete, hősi küzdelmei, rejtélyes eltűnésének titka.* Budapest, Magyar Téka, 1948.

Luknitskiy, Pavel: *Leningrad deystvuyet.* Kn. 3. Moscow, Sovyetskiy pisatel, 1968.

Magyarország 1944. Üldöztetés – Embermentés. Ed. Szita, Szabolcs. Budapest, Nemzeti Tankönyvkiadó, 1994.

Maruzs, Roland: *Vitéz és önfeláldozó magatartásért. Hősi halált halt és posztumusz kitüntetett katonáink adattára, 1939–1945.* 2. enlarged ed. Nagykovácsi, Puedlo, 2009.

Maruzs, Roland: *Középkereszt, Tisztikereszt, Lovagkereszt. A Magyar Érdemrend hősi halottainak emlékkönyve.* Budapest, Zrínyi, 2013.

Máté, György: *Budapest szabad!* Budapest, Móra, 1980.

Meruk, József – Ungváry, Krisztián: Budapest hídjai a város ostromában. *Archívnet,* 19. 2019/1; http://www.archivnet.hu/budapest-hidjai-a-varos-ostromaban.

Moschanskiy, I. B. – Isayev, A. V.: *Triumfi i tragedii Velikoy voyni.* Moscow, Veche, 2010.

Müller, Klaus-Dieter: *Todesurteile sowjetischer Militärtribunale gegen Deutsche (1944–1947). Eine historisch-biographische Studie.* Göttingen, Vandenhoeck & Ruprecht, 2015.

Nitz, Günther: *Die 292. Infanterie-Division.* Bonn, Bernard & Graefe, 1957.

Pataki, Ferenc: *Vihar a sziget körül.* Ráckeve, Járási Pártbizottság, 1967.

Pogranichniye voyska v gody Velikoy Otechestvennoy voyni, 1941–1945. Sbornik dokumentov. Moscow, Nauka, 1968.

Portugalskiy, R. M. – Domank, A. S. – Kovalenko, A. P.: *Marshal S. K. Timoshenko.* Moscow, Izdatelstvo MOF "Pobjeda – 1945 god", 1994.

Schäfer, Torsten: *„Jedenfalls habe ich auch mitgeschossen". Das NSG-Verfahren gegen Johann Josef Kuhr und andere ehemalige Angehörige des Polizeibataillons 306, der Polizeireiterabteilung 2 und der SD-Dienststelle von Pinsk beim Landgericht Frankfurt am Main 1962–1973. Eine textanalytische Fallstudie zur Mentalitätsgeschichte. Villigst Perspektiven.* Dissertationen des Evangelischen Studienwerks e. V. Villigst, Band 11, Münster, LIT Verlag, 2007.

Scheibert, Horst. *Die Träger des Deutschen Kreuzes in Gold. Das Heer.* Bd. 1. *Kriegsmarine–Luftwaffe–Waffen-SS und des Deutschen Kreuzes in Silber.* Bd. 2. *Heer–Kriegsmarine–Luftwaffe–Waffen-SS.* Friedberg, Podzun-Pallas.

Scherzer, Veit: *Ritterkreuzträger 1939–1945. Die Inhaber des Ritterkreuzes des Eisernen Kreuzes 1939 von Heer, Luftwaffe, Kriegsmarine, Waffen-SS, Volkssturm sowie mit Deutschland verbündeter Streitkräfte nach den Unterlagen des Bundesarchivs.* Jena,

Scherzers Militärverlag, 2006.

Scherzer, Veit: *Himmlers militärischer Elite. Die höchst dekorierten Angehörigen der Waffen-SS.* Bd. 1. *A–Ke.* Bayreuth, Verlag Scherzer, 2014.

Scherzer, Veit: *Das Auszeichnungssystem der Wehrmacht.* Bayreuth, Verlag Veit Scherzer, 2015.

Schmeitzner, Mike: "Unter Ausschluss der Öffentlichkeit? Zur Verfolgung von NS-Verbrechen durch die sowjetische Sonderjustiz". In *NS-Prozesse und deutsche Öffentlichkeit.* Ed. Clemens Vollnhals – Jörg Osterholh. Göttingen, Vandenhoeck & Ruprecht, 2011, 149–166.

Schulz, Andreas – Wegmann, Günter – Zinke, Dieter: *Die Generale der Waffen-SS und der Polizei. Die militärischen Werdegänge der Generäle sowie der Aerzte, Veterinäre, Intendanten, Richter und Ministerialbeamten im Generalsrang.* Bd 2. Bisendorf, Biblio, 2005.

Seres, István: *Solymár története és néprajza.* Solymár, Helytörténeti Alapítvány, 1993.; http://www.solymar.hu/tortenet/1k_001_352.htm.

Steinert, Gyula: *Budapest ostroma egy orvos szemével.* Vigilia, 1995/5, 377–388.

Stockert, Peter: *Die Eichenlaubträger, 1940–1945.* Bd. 1–9. Bad Wimpfen, Verlag Peter Stockert, 1996.

Stockmann, Franz: *Kriegstagebuch Budapest, 1945. Aufzeichnungen eines Truppenarztes.* Engelsbach, Fouqé, 2001.

Szakály, Sándor: *A 2. vkf. osztály.* Budapest, Magyar Napló–Veritas, 2015.

Szakály, Sándor: *A magyar katonai felső vezetés, 1938– 1945. Lexikon és adattár.* Budapest, Ister, 2001 [2. improved edition: 2003].

Számvéber, Norbert: "Adalékok a budapesti hídfőben harcoló magyar alakulatok harcértékéhez az újabban visszatért levéltári források tükrében". In *Ad Acta. A Hadtörténelmi Levéltár Évkönyve 2001.* Budapest, Hadtörténelmi Levéltár, 2001, 73.

Szappanos, István: *Emlékirataim.* Mentor, published by the author, 2013.; http://mek.oszk. hu/18900/18980/18980.pdf.

Szarka Józsefné: *A Budavári Palotában születtem. Visszaemlékezésem a XX. századra.* Budapest, Litea, 2006.

Szekeres, József: *A pesti gettók 1945 januári megmentése.* Budapest, BFL, 1997.

Szita, Szabolcs: *A Gestapo tevékenysége Magyarországon, 1939–1945.* Budapest, Corvina, 2014.

Sokolov, Boris: *Krasnaya Armiya protiv voysk SS.* Moscow, Yauza, 2008.

Sztehlo, Gábor: *Isten kezében.* Budapest, Magyarországi Evangélikus Egyház Sajtóosztálya, 1986.

Thomas, Franz – Wegmann, Günter: *Die Ritterkreuzträger der Deutschen Wehrmacht.* Osnabrück, Biblio, 1985–1994.

Tolubko, V. F.: *Nedelin. Perviy glavkom strategicheskikh.* Moscow, Molodaya Gvardiya, 1979.

Töppel, Roman: "Das Ritterkreuz des Eisernen Kreuzes und der Kampfwert militärischer Verbände". *Zeitschrift für Heereskunde* 76 (2012), 180–190.

Ungváry, Krisztián: *Budapest ostroma.* 7. improved and enlarged ed. Budapest, Corvina, 2015.

Ungváry, Krisztián: *Magyar megszálló csapatok a Szovjetunióban, 1941–1944. Esemény – elbeszélés – utóélet.* Budapest, Osiris, 2015.

Ungváry, Krisztián: Hullarablás a köztévében. https://24.hu/poszt-itt/2019/02/18/ungvary-krisztian-hullarablas-a-kozteveben/.

Wachter, Hans-Otto: *Wir funkten. Geschichte der Funkkompanie Nachrichtenabteilung 8 "Florian Geyer".* Kassel, published by the author, 1980.

Weber, Claudia: „Too Closely Identified with dr. Goebbels". Die Massenerschiessungen von Katyn in der Geschichte des Zweiten Weltkriegs und des Kalten Kriegs. *Zeithistorische Forschungen,* 2011/1; http://www.zeithistorische-forschungen.de/1-2011/id=4747.

Wolter, Markus: "Radolfzell im Nationalsozialismus. Die Heinrich Koeppen-Kaserne als Standort der Waffen-SS". In *Schriften des Vereins für Geschichte des Bodensees und seiner Umgebung.* Sonderdruck aus Heft 129. Ostfildern, Jan Thorbecke Verlag, 2011.

Yerger, Mark C.: German Cross in Gold. *Holders of the SS and Police.* Volume 4. *Cavalry Brigade and Divisions.* San Jose, R. James Bender Publishing, 2009.

Zeidler, Manfred: *Stalinjustiz contra NS-Verbrechen. Die Kriegsverbrecherprozesse gegen deutsche Kriegsgefangene in der UdSSR in den Jahren 1943–1952. Kenntnisstand und Forschungsprobleme.* Berichte und Studien 9. Dresden, HAIT, 1996.

Zeidler, Manfred: "Der Minsker Kriegsverbrecherprozeß vom Januar 1946". *Vierteljahreshefte für Zeitgeschichte* 52 (2004/2), 211–244.

NOTES

1 See https://24.hu/poszt-itt/2019/02/18/ungvary-krisztian-hullarablas-a-kozteveben

2 Martin van Creveld: *Fighting Power. German and US-Army Performance 1939–1945.* Westport, Greenwood, 1982.

3 See https://www.focus.de/magazin/archiv/serie-und150-teil-vi-ans-hakenkreuz-geschlagen_aid_212248.html

4 Martin van Creveld: *Kampfkraft. Militärische Organisation und militärische Leistung 1939– 1945.* (Einzelschriften zur Militärgeschichte 31). Freiburg, MGFA, 1989, p. 203.

5 See Norbert Haase: Wehrmachtsangehörige vor dem Kriegsgericht. In Rolf-Dieter Müller – Hans-Erich Volkmann (ed.): *Die Wehrmacht. Mythos und Realität.* München, Oldenbourg, 1999, pp. 474–485., with further references.

6 BA-MA Pers 15/284 Strafsache Hans Heller. This person is not identical to Hans Heller featured in present work.

7 See Krisztián Ungváry: *Magyar megszálló csapatok a Szovjetunióban 1941–1944. Esemény – elbeszélés – utóélet.* Budapest, Osiris, 2015, pp. 137–148.

8 PIL 686. fond, 42. storage unit., report of Miklós Steinmetz to Mihály Farkas, "1944 szeptemberi beszámoló", p. 9.

9 *Hősök. A Szovjetunió hősei a magyarországi felszabadító harcokban 1944–1945.* Ed. Ervin Liptay – A. I. Babin, Budapest, Zrínyi, 1981.

10 Sándor Szakály: *A magyar katonai felső vezetés, 1938–1945. Lexikon és adattár.* Budapest, Ister, 2001 [2. edition: 2003].

11 Sándor Szakály: *A 2. vkf. osztály.* Budapest, Magyar Napló–Veritas, 2015.

12 Assessment of the Hungarian officers had been processed in different ways: the superiors were to hand in reports on the skills and capabilities of their subordinates at regular intervals and had to include details of subordinates' virtues and deficiencies as well. At the same time, the "combat readiness" of officers was assessed by assigning points on a scale from one to seven.

13 This would have been particularly interesting in the case of the decorations awarded for military merit in the First World War, as these recommendations usually described the actual military deeds in detail and, as opposed to later assessments, had more opinions of superior officers attached – including de-

rogatory opinions. Luckily, these sources are much more readily available for research than later documents.

14 It is known that a large number of officers in the Hungarian military elite were members of the Arrow Cross Party (for example, Lajos Nádas, Dezső László); furthermore, there were others who worked as agents for the German secret services (for example Jenő Ruszkay).

15 Szakály: *A magyar katonai felső vezetés,* p. 7.

16 Roland Maruzs: *Középkereszt, Tisztikereszt, Lovagkereszt. A Magyar Érdemrend hősi halottainak emlékkönyve.* Budapest, Zrínyi, 2013; furthermore, Roland Maruzs: *Vitéz és önfeláldozó magatartásért. Hősi halált halt és posztumusz kitüntetett katonáink adattára 1939–1945.* 2. edition. Nagykovácsi, Puedlo, 2009.

17 Péter Illésfalvi – Vilmos Kovács – Roland Maruzs: *"Vitézségért". A Magyar Tiszti Arany Vitézségi Éremmel kitüntetettek a második világháborúban.* Budapest, Hermanos, 2011.

18 Csaba B. Stenge: *Elfelejtett hősök. A magyar királyi honvéd légierők ászai a második világháborúban.* Nagykovácsi, Puedlo, 2006. [2. extended edition: Budapest, Zrínyi, 2016.]

19 János Rainer M.: *Századosok.* Budapest, Osiris, 2018.

20 Ignác Romsics: *Utak a kommünhöz. Az 1919-es magyar népbiztosok előélete.* In *Heller Ágnes-ünnep/90.* Edited by János Kőbányai. Budapest, Múlt és Jövő, 2019, pp. 243–278.

21 See the website dedicated to the *SZT*-officers (SZT – "szigorúan titkos", Top Secret) (*www.szigoruantitkos.hu*), and the databases (partly edited by me) of the now defunct 1956 Institute available at *www.rev.hu* or on CD-ROM, and the research paper of the author on the leaders of the military intelligence: Krisztián Ungváry: "A magyar katonai elhárító szolgálatok vezetői". In Tamás Drusza (ed.): *A magyar elhárítás fejlődése. Tanulmányok a katonai és polgári nemzetbiztonsági elhárítás múltjáról, jelenéről, jövőjéről.* Budapest, Dialóg Campus, 2019, pp. 13–70.

22 The Állambiztonsági Szolgálatok Történeti Levéltára (Historical Archives of the State Security Services) has published the careers of intelligence officers from department leaders upwards.

23 See the websites and databases maintained by the *Kommunizmuskutató Intézet* (Institute for Research of Communism) and the *Nemzeti Emlékezet Bizottsága* (Committee of National Remembrance), the quality of which may be problematic in certain cases.

24 One needs to mention here the "gallery of perpetrators" that can be seen in the *Terror Háza Múzeum* (Museum of the House of Terror).

25 Walther-Peer Fellgiebel: *Die Träger des Ritterkreuzes des Eisernen Kreuzes 1939–1945 — Die Inhaber der höchsten Auszeichnung des Zweiten Weltkrieges aller Wehrmachtteile.* Friedberg, Podzun-Pallas, 1986 [2006]. Henceforward, the most important literature, relevant to the subject of present work, will be mentioned.

26 Ernst-Günther Krätschmer: *Die Ritterkreuzträger der Waffen-SS.* Berlin, Pour le Mérite, 2010. The first edition was published in 1955.

27 Franz Thomas – Günter Wegmann: *Die Ritterkreuzträger der Deutschen Wehrmacht.* Osnabrück, Biblio, 1985–1994.

28 See Peter Stockert: *Die Eichenlaubträger 1940–1945.* 1–9. volumes. Bad Wimpfen, Verlag Peter Stockert, 1996. [The same in two volumes, third edition: 2018.]

29 Florian Berger: *Ritterkreuzträger mit Nahkampfspange in Gold.* Wien, Author's publication, 2004.

30 Jürgen Huss – Heinz-Werner Sondermann: *Ritterkreuzträger im Mannschafts-stand 1941– 1945. Fotos und Tatberichte der hoch ausgezeichneten Soldaten.* Saarbrücken, VDM, 2009.

31 Mark C. Yerger: *German Cross in Gold. Holders of the SS and Police.* Volume 4: *Cavalry Brigade and Divisions.* San Jose, R. James Bender Publishing, 2009.

32 Horst Scheibert: *Die Träger des Deutschen Kreuzes in Gold. Das Heer.* (Volume 1) *Kriegsmarine–Luftwaffe–Waffen-SS und des Deutschen Kreuzes in Silber. Heer–Kriegsmarine–Luftwaffe–Waffen-SS.* (Volume 2) Friedberg Podzun-Pallas, without date of publication. Scheibert based his research on the documents of the *Bundesarchiv* based at that time in Aachen-Kornelimünster; the documents had been rearranged in the meantime.

33 Veit Scherzer: *Ritterkreuzträger 1939–1945. Die Inhaber des Ritterkreuzes des Eisernen Kreuzes 1939 von Heer, Luftwaffe, Kriegsmarine, Waffen-SS, Volkssturm sowie mit Deutschland verbündeter Streitkräfte nach den Unterlagen des Bundesarchivs.* Jena, Scherzers Militärverlag, 2006. The following work also needs to be mentioned: Veit Scherzer: *Himmlers militärischer Elite. Die höchst dekorierten Angehörigen der Waffen-SS.* Volume 1: *A–Ke.* Bayreuth, Verlag Scherzer, 2014.

34 Quoted by Christian Gerlach: *Kalkulierte Morde. Die deutsche Wirtschaftsund Vernichtungspolitik in Weissrussland 1941 bis 1944.* Hamburg, Hamburger Edition, 1999, p. 560.

35 For details, see Gerlach: *Kalkulierte Morde*, pp. 560–610.

36 Erich von dem Bach-Zelewski (1899–1972) was born in a noble but impoverished family; he was 15 years old when he signed up for military service. He served in the First World War, and his rank was *Leutnant* in 1918. He joined the *NSDAP* in 1930 and the SS in 1931, where he quickly ascended to prominent positions. After the National Socialist political turn in Germany, he was ordered to commit a number of murders. It was he who ordered, in 1940, the establishment of the concentration camp in Auschwitz; after the invasion of the Soviet Union, as the leader of the rear areas of the *Heeresgruppe Mitte*, he was responsible for murdering hundreds of thousands of people. At the beginning of 1942, he suffered a mental breakdown partly due to his experiences during the murders; this played a part in Himmler's decision to seek out methods of mass murders that would not be detrimental to the mental health of the perpetrators. In October 1942, he was assigned the title *Bevollmächtigten des Reichsführers SS für die Bandenbekämpfung* (Chief of Bandit Fighting Operations). In this role, he led the anti-partisan and other mass murder actions in Belarus, as well as the crushing of the Warsaw Uprising in 1944. Thereafter, he organized actions to counter the

armistice attempt by Miklós Horthy. After the war, he was a member of several various far-right organizations. He appeared at the Nuremberg Trials only as a witness and offered an incriminating confession against the defendants. He was released in 1950, and although he was named one of the main war criminals in 1951, he was only sentenced to 10 years in a labour camp. This latter sentence was soon changed to house arrest. From 1954 he worked as a night guard. He was again arrested in 1958, this time for a murder committed in 1934. Other court proceedings had been opened against him as well, and at last, in 1962, he was sentenced to life in prison. At the same time, he was never convicted for his crimes committed during the Holocaust and the partisan-hunting activities.

37 Martin Cüppers: *Wegbereiter der Shoah. Die Waffen-SS, der Kommandostab Reichsführer-SS und die Judenvernichtung 1939–1945* (Veröffentlichungen der Forschungsstelle Ludwigsburg der Universität Stuttgart. 4). Darmstadt, WBG, 2005. Stefan Klemp: "*Nicht ermittelt*". *Polizeibataillone und die Nachkriegsjustiz. Ein Handbuch*. Essen, Klartext, 2011. Stefan Klemp: *"Rücksichtslos ausgemerzt". Die Ordnungspolizei und das Massaker von Lidice*. Münster, Villa Ten Hompel, 2012, p. 65. Also see: an interview with H.-O. Henkel, 20 May 2019.

38 See Roman Töppel: "Das Ritterkreuz des Eisernen Kreuzes und der Kampfwert militärischer Verbände". *Zeitschrift für Heereskunde* 76 (2012), pp. 180–190. Töppel has statistically researched and compared altogether 29 different units regarding the *Ritterkreuz des Eisernen Kreuzes*, the *Deutsches Kreuz in Gold* and other decorations.

39 Of the details, see Krisztián Ungváry: *Magyar megszálló csapatok*.

40 The Soviet writer Aleksandr Bek has written a Stalinist novel of "Bildungsroman" about Panfilov's soldiers, titled *Volokolamsk Highway*.

41 The author has interviewed the following personnel who took part in the breakout attempt and successfully reached the German lines: Joachim Boosfeld, Johannes Finger, Adolf John and Josef Ringhoffer. Of these, only Ringhoffer (who was aged 18 at that time and did not have any kinds of decorations) received an *Eisernes Kreuz II. Klasse* and *Nahkampfspange Bronze*.

42 See Veit Scherzer: *Das Auszeichnungssystem der Wehrmacht*. Bayreuth, Verlag Veit Scherzer, 2015, pp. 36–39.; also Manfred Dörr: *Die Inhaber der Anerkennungsurkunde des Oberbefehlshabers des Heeres 1941–1945*. Osnabrück, Biblio, 1993.

43 Scherzer: *Das Auszeichnungsystem,* p. 38.

44 TSAMO, 500. fond (www.germandocsinrussia.org), 12472. sub-fond., 408. volume, document no. 301.

45 Disclosure of Győző Benyovszky to the author. Copy of the award document owned by the author.

46 See the manuscript of Wilhelm Schöning owned by the author.

47 Elischer's memories are quoted in Béla Józsa: *Egyetemisták az ostromgyűrűben*. Budapest, Történelmi Hagyományőrző és Hadisírgondozó Alapítvány, 1999, p. 62.

48 Józsa: *Egyetemisták,* p. 69.; also Dénes Vass: *Egyetemisták az ostromgyűrűben. Az I. honvéd egyetemi rohamzászlóalj története,* p. 23. Manuscript owned by the author.

[49] Between 1995 and 2000 the author communicated with Dénes Vass on a number of occasions. He proved to be a reliable source of data, did not hide his motivations and inclinations, and neither his descriptions nor his life contained any logical inconsistencies.

[50] Anja Kammerer – Willi Kammerer (eds.): *Narben bleiben. Die Arbeit der Suchdienste 60 Jahre nach dem Zweiten Weltkrieg.* Deutsche Dienststelle, Berlin, 2008, p. 89.

[51] Ferenc Fischer: "Karl Pfeffer-Wildenbruch vezette német rendőrségi misszió titkos közreműködése a chilei csendőrség, a Cuerpo de Carabineros felállításában (1928–1929)". In *Historia est lux veritatis. Szakály Sándor köszöntése 60. születésnapján.* Edited by Endre Marinovich. Budapest, Magyar Napló, 2016, p. 180.

[52] BA-B, SSO 375a, Pfeffer-Wildenbruch, pp. 217–218.

[53] TSAMO, 500. fond (www.germandocsinrussia.org), 12472. sub-fond, 373. volume, document no. 49.

[54] TSAMO, 500. fond (www.germandocsinrussia.org), 12472. sub-fond, 373. volume, document no. 49.

[55] The German army had a special system developed for organizing and commanding the rear area of combat units: this was the system of "Korücke" (*Kommandantur des rückwärtigen Armeegebiets*). The rear areas of the 6th Army was commanded by the *Korück* 593, however this command remained in Budapest during the siege.

[56] Kindly disclosed to the author by Ferenc X. Kovács

[57] TSAMO, 500. fond (www.germandocsinrussia.org), 12472. sub-fond, 410. volume, document no. 0069.

[58] BA- MA MSg 2/4631, Ernst Schweitzer: *Der Kessel von Budapest*, p. 5.

[59] BA–MA, N 647/13.

[60] TSAMO, 500. fond (www.germandocsinrussia.org), 12472. sub-fond, document no. 239. 29 December 1944. Of the events prior to this, see document no. 240, which is dated 26 December 1944.

[61] This is attested to by the surviving documents. The *IX. Waffen-Gebirgskorps* had already reported on 9 January that the Soviets achieved deep incursions on both sides of the Keleti Railway Station. In reality, at that time, the frontline was on the Népliget–Százados Street–Rákosrendező Railway Station line.

[62] Most probably *SS-Sturmbannführer* Ulrich von der Damerau-Dambrowski or *SS-Hauptsturmführer* Hans Lösch.

[63] BA–MA, N 647/13.

[64] Hermann Balck: *Ordnung im Chaos. Erinnerungen 1893–1948.* Osnabrück, Biblio-Verlag, 1981, p. 661.

[65] Péter Gosztonyi: *Vihar Kelet-Európa felett.* Budapest, Népszava, 1990, p. 63.

[66] HL TGY 2829, József Paulits: *Budapest végnapjai*, p. 46.

[67] BA-MA N 370/6, Letter of Pfeffer-Wildenbruch to Carl Lutz, dated 31 March 1957.

68 The report of Ernst Schweitzer, dated 26 February 1945., owned by the author.

69 Helmut Friedrich: *Wanderer, rufst Du uns heim,* pp. 61–62. Manuscript owned by the author.

70 Péter Gosztonyi: *Budapest lángokban 1944–1945.* Budapest, Móra, 1998, p. 149.

71 It was not a full-scale battle; most probably only a few shots were exchanged.

72 The report of the political officer of the 297th Rifle Division is quoted by György Máté: *Budapest szabad!* Budapest, Móra, 1980, p. 180.

73 N. V. Komisszarov: "Harc Budapestért". In *Hadtörténelmi Közlemények,* 1980/1, p. 140.

74 In the Red Army, various units may have received geographical forenames as a form of award after important combat actions.

75 The report is not correct, Lindenau was in the rank of *Oberstleutnant.* According to Soviet terminology, the head of the staff of certain units was called the chief of staff.

76 *Pogranichnye voyska v gody Velikoy Otechestvennoy voyny, 1941–1945 gg. Sbornik dokumentov.* Moscow, Nauka, 1968 [Border patrol forces in the years of the Great Patriotic War 1941–1945. Collection of Documents.] Moscow, Nauka, 1968, pp. 552–553.

77 Kukin, Vasiliy Tikhonovich: "Ot pervogo i do poslednego vystrela". In *Radi zhizni na zemle.* Moskva, DOSAAF, 1986 [From the first shot to the last. See chapter "A lad from the land of the mordvins"]. Can be reached at: http://militera.lib.ru/prose/russian/kukin_vt/10.html. The author wishes to thank József Meruk for finding and translating this document.

78 http://www.coldwar.ru/rvo/112009/medal-za-gorod-budapesht.php.

79 Moshchanskiy, Il'ya Borisovich – Isaev Aleksey Valer'evich: *Triumfy i tragedii velikoy voyny.* Veche, 2010 [Triumphs and tragedies of the great war]. Moscow, Vecse, 2010, pp. 582–591. The author wishes to thank József Meruk for finding and translating this document.

80 Ulrich von Damerau-Dambrowski (1900–1980) served from 1916 to 1931; was discharged as *Hauptmann.* Thereafter, until 1936, he served as the military advisor of the Chinese national government. In 1933 he joined the *NSDAP* and from 1936 worked in the German Foreign Office. From 2 February 1940, he worked as the German consul in Kolozsvár (Cluj); from 20 August 1943, he worked as a consulate councillor in Budapest. On 1 October 1944, he was ordered to serve in the Waffen-SS, and was assigned to the *IX. Waffen-Gebirgskorps.*

81 Gosztonyi: *Budapest lángokban,* p. 149. It is not entirely certain if this data is correct, as the Gosztonyi-fond of the *Osteuropa-Bibliothek* in Bern does not contain Lindenau's correspondence.

82 New St. John Hospital (Új Szent János Kórház). Here, the German units attempting the breakout were mainly hiding in the building dedicated earlier to urology. The building was completely destroyed by the Soviet units.

83 It is not entirely clear whether it belonged to the *Luftwaffe* or the *Flak* (ground) units. The Soviet descriptions usually do not distinguish between the two,

which is understandable, as only the colour of their tab was different: the *Luftwaffe* units wore yellow tabs while the *Flak* (ground) units wore red. In Budapest, the majority of the *Luftwaffe* personnel belonged to the ground units.

84 http://kunstkamera.ru/images/history/65/pdf/novikov.pdf.

85 N. V. Komisszarov: *Harc Budapestért*, p. 140.

86 Sokolov, Boris: *Krasnaya Armiya protiv voysk SS.* Moskva, Yauza, Eksmo, 2008 [The Red Army against the SS forces], p. 79. Sokolov was most probably writing about this story based on a relation of Vladimir Tolubko (from 1972 commander in chief of the strategic rocket force), who, in his 1979 biographical novel about General Nedelin (in the period in question, Nedelin was the artillery commander of the 2nd Ukrainian Front, and later became the commander of the strategic rocket forces) had written about this event in almost the exact same way. Tolubko, Vladimir Fyodorovich: *Nedelin. Pervy glavkom strategicheskikh.* Moscow, Molodaya gvardiya, 1979, p. 27. [Nedelin. The first commander of the strategic rocket forces].

87 Commander of the NKVD battalion 134/I.

88 Kukin: *Ot pervogo i do poslednyego.*

89 Krätschmer: *Die Ritterkreuzträger*, p. 838.; also Stockert: *Die Eichenlaubträger*, volume 2., p. 149.

90 According to Matvey Zaharov, "the route taken through the sewage canal took its toll on him, and before they could even talk to him, they needed to take care of him being cleaned – in the actual sense of the word". Considering that the Devil's Ditch was not a sewage canal but was filled with rainwater, the sentence seems to be more of an overstatement. Regardless of this, it is possible, even plausible, that Pfeffer-Wildenbruch, as a very important captive, was provided with bathing facilities.

91 Péter Gosztonyi states that "as a consequence of a car crash", and this was the data the author has taken over in his earlier works. However, the data in the Bielefeld registrar's office contradict this entirely.

92 BA–MA MSg 2/4631, Ernst Schweitzer: *Der Kessel von Budapest*, p. 6. The delivery of awards and decorations entirely stopped after 10 January 1945, as this was the day when the last courier aircraft landed on the Vérmező.

93 BA-MA RS 2-9, p. 159.

94 https://new.liveauctioneers.com/item/33931264#&gid=1&pid=3.

95 HM HIM *Hadtörténelmi Levéltár* (Budapest) *Kitüntetésadományozások gyűjtő* (Collection of Decorations), 1872/8e-1945.

96 Pfeffer-Wildenbruch, as the commander of the colonial police forces, received this emblem, worn on the left arm as the sign of service in the German Eastern African police forces, from Hermann Göring as a special award for his help in establishing the *Landespolizeigruppe General Göring.*

97 Of his unit, see Friedrich Husemann: *Die guten Glaubens waren. Geschichte der SS-Polizei-Division (4. SS-Panzergrenadier-Division).* Band I: *1939–1942*, Osnabrück, Munin-Verlag, 1971 [2. edition: 1984; 3. edition: Coburg, Nation Europa Verlag, 1999].

[98] HM HIM *Hadtörténelmi Levéltár* (Budapest) *Kitüntetésadományozások gyűjtő* (Collection of Decorations), 1872/8e-1945.

[99] The letter from Gyula Litteráti-Loótz to Péter Gosztonyi, 1973. Copy owned by the author.

[100] Józsa: *Egyetemisták*, p. 160.

[101] Scherzer: *Himmlers militärische Elite,* p. 128., Berger: *Ritterkreuzträger,* pp. 39–43.

[102] The Boosfeld-interview owned by the author.

[103] Schippmann, Friedrich (1917–?) went missing during the breakout attempt. According to hearsay he shot himself.

[104] Of the details, see Daniel Heintz: *Zerschlagen und vermisst! Rückkämpfer, Rückkehrer und die Abwicklungsstäbe der Wehrmacht.* Aachen, Helios, 2018, p. 457.

[105] On the details, see Daniel Heintz: *Zerschlagen und vermisst! Rückkämpfer, Rückkehrer und die Abwicklungsstäbe der Wehrmacht.* Aachen, Helios, 2018, p. 457.

[106] Reinhard Gehlen (1902–1979). From 1942, he was the commander of the *Abteilung Fremde Heere Ost* (Foreign Armies East), a military intelligence organisation of the *OKH*. From 1945, with a couple of his colleagues he was employed by the American military intelligence, and from 1956, he was the leader of the *Bundesnachrichtendienst* (BND), West Germany's intelligence agency.

[107] BA-MA Pers 1/105410 Joachim Boosfeld.

[108] The *Ritterkreuz des Eisernen Kreuzes* that can be seen worn by Buck is the result of a photo manipulation made after 1945.

[109] Richard Landwehr: *Budapest, the Stalingrad of the Waffen-SS*. Bennington, Merriam Press, 2012, p. 29.

[110] Berger: *Ritterkreuzträger*, pp. 47–51.

[111] Freid gmacht. *Der Spiegel*, 1976. május 24. http://www.spiegel.de/spiegel/print/d-41213414.html.

[112] Johannes Göhler (1918–2003) *SS-Sturmbannführer*, according to his last service assignments, was Hitler's adjutant in the *Führerbunker*. After 1945, he was one of the leaders of the *Hilfsgemeinschaft auf Gegenseitigkeit der Angehörigen der ehemaligen Waffen-SS* (*HIAG*, Mutual Aid Association of Former Waffen-SS Members) and remained an ardent National Socialist.

[113] Gustav Lombard (1895–1992) *SS-Brigadeführer*, was responsible for the murdering of more than 11,000 persons during the summer of 1941. His lecture given on 25 September 1941 is very characteristic of him; he stated that "…we might consider the methods by which the Jew can be most effectively wiped out from the territories in our hands, but that we need to finish him [*"er beseitigt werden muss"*], is without question because the Jew is a partisan!" (Cüppers: *Wegbereiter der Shoah*, p. 221.) Although he was sentenced in the Soviet Union, the whole range of crimes he committed was not investigated. After the war, an investigation was launched against him in Germany, but this was terminated on 22 December 1970 with the explanation that it was not possible to prove that his crimes were "aggravated". He, therefore, escaped punishment.

[114] The *Ritterkreuz des Eisernen Kreuzes* that can be seen worn by Bunge is the result of a photo manipulation made after 1945.

115 BA-MA Pers 6/265667 Heinrich Bunge.

116 BA-MA Pers 6/265667 Heinrich Bunge.

117 The memoirs of S. Wagner owned by the author. The author wishes to thank Norbert Számvéber for providing him with the text.

118 TSAMO, 500. fond (www.germandocsinrussia.org), 12742. sub-fond, 409. volume, document no. 0308., 29 January 1945.

119 The author wishes to express his gratitude to Veit Scherzer for the letter from Hellmut Bunge.

120 BA-B R-9361-III/520104 and R-9361-III/26397 Personalakte Charpentier, Beurteilung 17.06.1944.

121 BA-B R-9361-III/520104 and R-9361-III/26397 Personalakte Charpentier, Beurteilung 17.06.1944.

122 BA-B NS 33/368, SS-Auffangsstelle für Budapest-Rückkämpfer 19.02.1945.

123 *WASt*, Akte Hans-Georg von Charpentier, *Heimkehrererklärung* Georg Koch, Fritz Emmerich, Adam Binder.

124 Bruno Streckenbach (1902–1977), as *Befehlshaber der Sicherheitspolizei und des SD (BdS) in Krakau* (the commander of the Security Police in Krakow responsible for Poland) ordered the extermination of at least 8,500 persons and the deportation of at least 88,000 persons. In 1943 he joined the Waffen-SS. For a short period he commanded *SS-Panzerjäger-Abteilung 8*, and the 8th SS Cavalry Division *Florian Geyer* itself. In 1945 he fell into Soviet captivity, and in 1952 was sentenced to 25 years in prison. He was repatriated into West Germany in 1955. Thereafter two criminal investigations were launched against him, but neither went to trial.

125 Ernst Imhof (1901–1982) *SS-Sturmbannführer*, between 1944 and 1945 was commander of the *SS-Feldersatz-Abteilung 8*, and commander of the *SS-Ersatz-Abteilung 37*. He was in Soviet captivity until 1956.

126 BA-MA N 756/154b, Streckenbach's letter to Vopersal.

127 Scherzer: *Himmlers militärische Elite*, p. 192.; also BA-B BDC SSO 134 Personalakte Dallmann.

128 Scherzer: *Himmlers militärische Elite*, p. 192.; also BA-B BDC SSO 134 Personalakte Dallmann.

129 *WASt*, Zentralkartei Dallmann.

130 Gyula Steinert: "Budapest ostroma egy orvos szemével". *Vigilia*, 1995/5, p. 387.

131 Pfeffer-Wildenbruch's letter to Péter Gosztonyi, BA-MA N 370/7.

132 TSAMO, 500. fond (www.germandocsinrussia.org), 12472. sub-fond, 380. volume, 117. and 408. volume, 318.

133 *Erőd a Duna mentén. A Budapestért 1944–45-ben folytatott harcok katonai iratai a Hadtörténelmi Levéltárban.* Edited by Norbert Számvéber. Budapest, Petit Real, 1999, pp. 151–152. Document no. 133.

134 The article begins with the following sentence: "Lately, Moscow radio was forced to call attention to a person in a commentary related to the situation in Budapest; this person is not known to many even in the Hungarian capital, but his name was connected with the resistance to the Bolshevist assault." In reality,

until now, there is no definitive proof that the Soviet news would have been preoccupied with Döner personally.

135 Heinrich A. Kurschat: "Schicksalsstunden für Budapest. Eichenlaub-Dörner verteidigt Ungarns Hauptstadt. Zahllose Sperren und Hindernisse". *Marburger Zeitung*, 5 January 1945. p. 2. Furthermore, a separate article with identical content, but different typography: "Eichenlaub-Dörner verteidigt Budapest". The copy of the magazine article without date and page numbering, owned by the author.

136 Schweitzer report, p. 6.

137 Sándor Győrffy – Hedvig Spáczay: "A IX. SS-hadtestparancsnokság titkos napi jelentései a Budapestért folyó harcokról (1945. január 1–24.)". *Hadtörténelmi Közlemények* 1975/1., p. 196.

138 Hanns Bayer: *Kavalleriedivisonen der Waffen-SS.* Gailberg-Heidelberg, author's edition, 1980, p. 355.

139 According to a sidenote of Ferenc Kovács X., added to the manuscript of József Paulits, first he was taken for interrogation to the corner of Ráth György Street and Greguss Street. Manuscript owned by the author.

140 Ferenc X. Kovács: *Villanások*, p. 8. Manuscript owned by the author.

141 BA-B B0031, Heiratsakte Walter Drexler, 1350.

142 Helmut Heiber (ed.): *Der ganz normale Wahnsinn unterm Hakenkreuz. Triviales und Absonderliches aus den Akten des Dritten Reichs.* München, Herbig, 1996, pp. 138–140., p. 142., p. 154., pp. 156–157., pp. 190–191.

143 Hans-Otto Wachter: *Wir funkten. Geschichte der Funkkompanie Nachrichtenabteilung 8 "Florian Geyer".* Kassel, author's edition, 1980, p. 227.

144 Scherzer: *Himmlers militärische Elite,* p. 234.

145 Bayer: *Kavalleriedivisionen,* p. 351.

146 Although there are several eyewitnesses who attested to Drexler's death noted down in the casualty files, the detailed letters of the witnesses are not available. During the exhumation process conducted in the Kispest Cemetery in 2002, the remains of 182 German soldiers were unearthed. Drexler's identification tag was not found among them.

147 The *Wehrmachtführungsstab (Wfstb.)* was the staff of the *Oberkommando der Wehrmacht (OKW)*, headed by *Generaloberst* Alfred Jodl, during the entire course of the war. The separate army branches had their own general staff. In various operational areas, the *OKW/Wfstb.* was in charge, while in other areas, the *OKH* commanded military operations.

148 BA–MA MSg 2/4631, Ernst Schweitzer: *Der Kessel von Budapest,* p. 2.

149 BA–MA MSg 2/4631, Ernst Schweitzer: *Der Kessel von Budapest,* p. 7.

150 BA–MA MSg 2/4631, Ernst Schweitzer: *Der Kessel von Budapest,* p. 13.

151 BA–MA MSg 2/4631, Ernst Schweitzer: *Der Kessel von Budapest,* p. 15.

152 László Veresváry, commander of the *Budapest Őrzászlóalj* (Budapest Guard Battalion).

153 István Seres: *Solymár története és néprajza.* Solymár, Helytörténeti Alapítvány, 1993. http://www.solymar.hu/tortenet/1k_001_352.htm.

154 László Hingyi: *Budapest ostroma 1944–1945*. Budapest, Etalon, 2018, p. 357. It needs to be noted, however, that the reminiscences of Kárász are not trustworthy. According to him they were marching for eight straight days – which seems to be impossible.

155 BA-MA P 6/269053, Beurteilung 1.2.1944.

156 TSAMO, 500. fond (www.germandocsinrussia.org), 12483. sub-fond, 95. unit, 51.

157 TSAMO, 500. fond (www.germandocsinrussia.org), 12483. sub-fond, 95. unit, 63.

158 BA-B, R-9361-II/226077.

159 BA-B, R-9361-III/523757.

160 We have a relatively large number of sources on what happened in the war hospitals. In addition to Werner Hübner, who will be mentioned later, the nurse E. v. K. and the doctor Miklós Konkoly-Thege also wrote notes, and László Kalakán produced an unpublished PhD thesis on the history of health conditions in Budapest during the Second World War. See: https://pea.lib.pte.hu/bitstream/handle/pea/16132/kalakan-laszlo-phd-2012.pdf.

161 Bericht an das Internationale Komitee vom Roten Kreuz erstattet von Friedrich Born, Delegierter für Ungarn, Juni 1945, p. 14. See: https://dodis.ch/18861.

162 Dénes Jánossy: "Budapest ostroma és az Országos Levéltár". *Levéltári Közlemények* 1946 (26), p. 6.; Furthermore: Csaba Keresztes: "Az Országos Levéltár Budapest ostromában és a levéltár helyreállítása". *Levéltári Közlemények* 2015 (86), p. 90.

163 Werner Hübner dr. (1912–1988) was a doctor and surgeon. He became a general practitioner after the war, was the mayor of Rehburg between 1961 and 1973, and was a member of various civilian associations.

164 Alois Huml Dr. (1911–?), a reserve staff medical officer, went missing during the breakout attempt. In connection with this, see Szarka Józsefné's memories below.

165 Walter Osten (1907–?) reserve medical officer, went missing during the breakout attempt. In connection with this, see Szarka Józsefné's memories below.

166 Refers to an unidentifiable person.

167 BA-MA MSg 2/238, Werner Hübner: *Geschichte der in Ungarn eingesetzte Panzereinheiten,* p. 11.

168 Józsefné Szarka: *A Budavári Palotában születtem. Visszaemlékezésem a XX. századra.* Budapest, Litea, 2006, p. 188.

169 Wilhelm Schöning's notes owned by the author.

170 Robert Gerwarth: *Reinhard Heydrich*. München, Siedler, 2011, p. 345.

171 General governmental administrative command for White Ruthenia, that is, approximately contemporary Belarus.

172 https://www.army.cz/images/id_7001_8000/7419/assassination-en.pdf.

173 Richard Breitman: *Staatsgeheimnisse. Die Verbrechen der Nazis – von den Alliierten toleriert.* München, Karl Blessing Verlag, 1999, p. 128.

174 Grácia Kerényi (1925–1985) poet, philologist, Polish literary translator, antifascist resistance member in 1944, and in the 1980s, one of the members of the Polish *Solidarność* movement.

175 Gyula Kádár: *A Ludovikától Sopronkőhidáig*. Budapest, Magvető, 1978, 2. vol., pp. 679–680.

176 See Péter Bokor: *Végjáték a Duna mentén. Interjúk egy filmsorozathoz*. Budapest, RTV-Minerva–Kossuth, 1982, pp. 189–191.; Szabolcs Szita: *A Gestapo tevékenysége Magyarországon, 1939–1945*. Budapest, Corvina, 2014, p. 113.; David Cesarani: *Adolf Eichmann. Bürokrat und Massenmörder*. München, Propyläen, 2004, pp. 265–266.

177 Szita: *A Gestapo*, p. 72.

178 Lásd ÁBTL 1.11.4. 67-46/171-30/1988 and Szita: *A Gestapo*, pp. 72–74.

179 Szabolcs Szita mistakenly took the number of personnel in each *KdS* group to be approximately 200-300 people. See Szita: *A Gestapo*, p. 72. For the number of personnel, see: Bokor: *Végjáték*, p. 84.

180 Hanna Szenes (1921–1944) was born in Budapest; in 1939 she emigrated to Palestine. He voluntarily joined the British Army, where she was trained in parachute and radio tasks. In March 1944, she was deployed in Yugoslavia, and with her comrades, she crossed the Hungarian border in May. Thereafter, a police officer captured them and handed them over to the *Gestapo*. After the Arrow Cross Party came to power, the court martial sentenced her to death by firing squad, although she was wearing a uniform when she was captured and therefore would have been entitled to the prisoner-of-war status.

181 Szita: *A Gestapo*, p. 188.

182 Péter Gosztonyi: *Légiveszély, Budapest! Szemelvények Magyarország második világháborús történetéből (1939–1945)*. Budapest, Népszava, 1989, p. 101.

183 BA-B R 9361-III/560330.

184 Cesarani: *Adolf Eichmann*, pp. 268–269.

185 Hans Georg Lehmann: Unternehmen Panzerfaust. Der Putsch der SS in Budapest am 15. Oktober 1944. *Ungarn-Jahrbuch* 5 (1973), p. 224.

186 Wilhelm Höttl also refers to this; see Bokor: *Végjáték*, pp. 196–197.

187 See Lehmann: *Unternehmen Panzerfaust*, p. 224.

188 WASt, Z-Kartei Franz Pataschitsch.

189 István Szappanos: *Emlékirataim*. Mentor, author's edition, 2013. http://mek.oszk.hu/18900/18980/18980.pdf

190 Walter Rauff (1906–1984), a National Socialist activist from 1938 employed by the *Reichsicherheitshauptamt* (*RSHA*), developer of the gas trucks, was an accomplice in the death of at least 97,000 persons. From 1943, he was one of the commanders of the German security police forces in Italy. After 1945, he was employed by the intelligence agencies of West Germany and Syria. From 1949 onwards he lived in South America; the Chilean government refused to extradite him.

191 Mathias Gafke: *Heydrichs Ostmärker. Das österreichische Führungspersonal der Sicherheitspolizei und des SD*. Darmstadt, Wissenschaftliche Buchgesellschaft, 2015, p. 281.

192 Scherzer: *Himmlers militärische Elite,* p. 373.

193 The *Nemzeti Számonkérő Szervezet* (National Accountability Organization) was established by Ferenc Szálasi on 1 November 1944.

194 Georg Gabori: *Amikor elszabadult a gonosz.* Budapest, Magyar Világ, 1990 [1991], pp. 121–134.

195 Of the actions of the *KdS* and the *Számonkérő Különítmény* see PIL 682. fond 1. storage unit, II. part nr. 23., protocols of the investigations against the "Red Brigade".

196 Gábor Csillik: *Budapesten harcoltunk.* Budapest, Magvető, 1964.; furthermore: *A magyar antifasiszta ellenállás és partizánmozgalom. Kislexikon.* Ed. Ervin Liptai. Budapest, Kossuth, 1987, p. 214.

197 PIL 274. fond 7/280. storage unit. Zseni Várnai – Zoltán Bokodi: *A "Várnai" ellenállási csoport rövid vázlata.*

198 *A magyar antifasiszta ellenállás,* p. 310.

199 Szalai is quoted by József Szekeres: *A pesti gettók 1945 januári megmentése.* Budapest, BFL, 1997, p. 242.

200 Béla Kubissy (1899–?) was, from 1 February 1944, an adjutant of the Chief Commissioner of Budapest Police, and from 1 January 1945, the commander of the police forces on the Pest side of the city. According to the regulations, his wife could have been classified as a Jew, but this fact was successfully concealed. Later, the people's tribunal sentenced him to 5 years and 6 months in prison. See BFL VII.5.e. 1950-7587 and XXV-1-a 1945-2462.

201 The name cannot be exactly identified according to our present knowledge; however, both Pál Szalai and Vilmos Lucska mentioned "Mummi" or "Mumi" standing trial at the people's tribunal.

202 HL I. 89. VKF 1945 306/b, 1945.02.10. Kgl. ung. Honvédminister an Greiffenberg.

203 Unfortunately the author owns the magazine article only in transcription. The author wishes to express his gratitude to Zsolt Alkay for providing the transcription.

204 During the siege, there were a number of executions taking place in the so-called Arrow Cross houses at 12 and 46 Kapás Street. Theoretically, regarding Hungarian citizens, the German authorities were only eligible to act in cases where the given person was caught in the act; it is, however, questionable to which extent this rule was observed during the siege of the capital.

205 BA-B BDC SSO VBS 286/6400012979 Reiner Gottstein.

206 BA-B BDC SSO VBS 286/6400012979 Reiner Gottstein.

207 *A magyar antifasiszta ellenállás*, pp. 62–63. Today it is impossible to discern who had ordered the executions and who carried them out. Vilmos Bondor: *A Mikó-rejtély. Mikó Zoltán és Raoul Wallenberg kapcsolata a magyar ellenállásban 1944–1945.* Budapest, Püski, 1995, p. 100. Bondor suggests that certain captives of the *Számonkérő Különítmény* (Accountability Detachment) were given over to the *Gestapo.*

208 PIL 682.f.1. storage unit. II. nr. 23., The confession of Imre Nidosi p. 302.

209 PIL 682.f., 1. storage unit., II. nr. 23., 305. Report dated 23 October 1948.

210 Kurt Wegener (1909–?), an officer of the *Reichswehr* from 1927; between 1934–1937, he served in the *Luftwaffe*, and from 1937 he joined the SS. He served in the unit responsible for guarding the concentration camps. In 1941, as a *Rittmeister* of an SS Cavalry Regiment he perpetrated mass murder around the Pripyat' area. He took part in the breakout attempt from Budapest and succeeded in reaching the German lines. After 1945, he worked as a salesperson. In 1962, he was sentenced to five years in prison for his role in the mass murders.

211 Liedtke, Helmut (1925–?) *Grenadier*, his unit cannot be identified.

212 WASt, Z-Karte Reiner Gottstein.

213 *WASt*, Z-Kartei Heinz Hamel and BA-MA RH 7/278, questionnaire.

214 Walter Rosler (1902–?), an officer in the Romanian army, from September 1944, joined the Waffen-SS as *SS-Sturmbannführer*. During the siege of Budapest, he served as regiment commander in the 22nd SS Cavalry Division and *Dritter Generalstabsoffizier (Ic)* in the same division. The author wishes to express his gratitude to the daughter of Walter Rosler, Hildegard Rosler, who was kind enough to provide the author with the document in question.

215 Franz Stockmann: *Kriegstagebuch Budapest 1945. Aufzeichnungen eines Truppenarztes.* Engelsbach, Fouqé, 2001, pp. 34–46.

216 BStU HA IX/11, ZR 920 A.51. Telefonverzeichnis HSSPF Budapest, KdS Budapest, Sondereinsatzkommando Budapest.

217 BA-B R 10-451/32-33 Übersicht über Kräfte der Ordnungspolizei und ihren Einsatz, Stand 15. Juli 1944.

218 The only data the author managed to acquire attests to the actions of the 5th and 7th companies of the 5/II *SS-Polizei-Bataillon*. According to the war log of the battalion these companies served with 10-member detachments for a short time as the guards of the Siklós and Barcs ghettoes. See Wolfgang Curilla: *Der Judenmord in Polen und die deutsche Ordnungspolizei 1939–1945*. Paderborn, Ferdinand Schöningh, 2011, pp. 281–282.

219 NARA T 77 R1142 F000797-798; Szita: *A Gestapo*, p. 80. The unit is mistakenly mentioned as *Einsatzgruppe* "F." Its strength is given as 800 personnel.

220 Gosztonyi refers to the fact that Pfeffer-Wildenbruch stated the following in his interview with him: he had given an order personally to Hitschler to safeguard the ghetto, adding that he was permitted to leave the ghetto only when the Soviets were already standing on the other side of it. See Péter Gosztonyi: "Budapest ostroma 1944–1945-ben". In *Nyugati magyar tanulmányírók antológiája*. Edited by Gyula Borbándi. Bern, EPMSZ, 1987, pp. 85–99. http://mek.oszk.hu/02900/02929/02929.pdf, pp.42–43.

221 György Kókay: "Dokumentumok a Budai Vár 1945. évi ostromáról". In *Tanulmányok Budapest múltjából 26.* (1997), pp. 221–249, the diary of László Szabó, the commander of the Castle, p. 226.

222 The note of Frau E. v. K. dated 18 February 1995., owned by the author.

223 R. M. Portugalsky – A. S. Domank – A. P. Kovalienko: *Marshal S. K. Timoshenko.* Moscow, Izdatelstvo MOF "Pobjeda – 1945 God", 1994.

224 Werner Jester: *Im Todessturm von Budapest 1945.* (Landser am Feind 1.) Dresden, Winkelried, 2010, p. 200.

225 Jester: *Im Todessturm,* p. 201. Jester mentions the *Ritterkreuz des Kriegsverdienstkreuzes.* Hitschler, however, did not possess this decoration, only the *Kriegverdienstkreuz II. Klasse* and the *Kriegverdienstkreuz I. Klasse.*

226 Of Hitschler, see Andreas Schulz – Günter Wegmann – Dieter Zinke: *Die Generale der Waffen-SS und der Polizei. Die militärischen Werdegänge der Generäle sowie der Aerzte, Veterinäre, Intendanten, Richter und Ministerialbeamten im Generalsrang.* Band 2. Bisendorf, Biblio, 2005. pp. 282–285.

227 TSAMO, 500. fond (www.germandocsinrussia.org), 12472. sub-fond, 410. volume, document no. 0292. The last sentence of the text refers to the fact that Jansa was also in talks with Pfeffer-Wildenbruch and was afraid that his similar suggestion would not reach the necessary levels via the usual channels of the SS.

228 https://www.nd-archiv.de/ausgabe/1962-10-08

229 Stockert: *Die Eichenlaubträger,* 8. volume, pp. 65–67.

230 BA-B SSO Albert Klett.

231 Bayer: *Kavalleriedivisionen,* p. 361, p. 370.

232 Szigetter, Fritz (1917–?), was a bank clerk who was most probably a member of the Waffen-SS since 1941. On 1 October 1944, he was promoted to *SS-Untersturmführer.* He is assumed to have been serving in the 52nd SS Cavalry Regiment. During the breakout attempt, he successfully reached the German lines.

233 *WASt,* The letter of Konrad Augustin regarding Albert Klett, 1978.

234 Augustin, Konrad (1919–?) was a member of the SS from either 1939 or 1940. During the siege of Budapest, he was serving as *SS-Untersturmführer* in the 8th SS Artillerie-Regiment of the 8th Cavalry Division. During the breakout attempt, he reached German lines on 14 February 1945. Between 13 May 1945 and 27 September 1953, he was a prisoner of war; thereafter, until the 1990s, he lived in West Germany.

235 Richard Landwehr: *Budapest,* p. 17. In his book (*The German Defeat in the East, 1944–45.* Mechanicsburg, Stackpole, 2007, p. 254.), Samuel Mitcham probably took the incorrect data from here.

236 BA-B VBS 286/6400023300 Siegfried Korth.

237 His name does not appear in the list compiled on the evening of 16 February 1945, which contains the names of those successfully reaching the German lines (the list was most probably compiled based on data from the evening of 15 February 1945). His name appears on the 19 February list. See BA-MA RH 2 332, pp. 146–147. and BA-B NS 33/368.

238 Peter von Blanckenburg: *Herzschläge. Erinnerungen aus einem bewegten Jahrhundert.* Berlin, Books on Demand, 2001, p. 39.

239 BA-B R 9361-III/106087, Personalakte Oswald Krauss.

240 TSAMO, 1428. fond, 1. sub-fond, 3. volume.

241 The letter of Konrad Augustin dated 28 January 1993. to Peter Meier; owned by the author.

242 http://en.ww2awards.com/person/42318.

243 BA-B, NS 33/368, SS-Auffangsstelle für Budapest-Rückkämpfer.

244 Carl Strobel (1895–?) was a representative of the *Reichstag*; most probably he committed suicide on 19 April 1945 in the Leipzig city council.

245 BA-B BDC 1060047157. The author wishes to express his gratitude to Ingo Möbius for providing the document.

246 SHD 13471, NS-Archiv der MfS, ZA I 05422 Akte 6. The author wishes to express his gratitude to Ingo Möbius for providing this document.

247 WASt, Zentralkartei Paul Krämer. Scherzer: *Ritterkreuzträger* provides Érsekújvár as the place of death; however, this is incorrect.

248 "Bollwerk im Kampfraum Falaise. Wie sich Major Kündiger das Ritterkreuz erkämpfte." A copy of a contemporary magazine article owned by the author.

249 BA-MA Pers 6/49865, Herbert Kündiger.

250 Győrffy–Spáczay: *A IX. SS-hadtestparancsnokság*, pp. 195–196.

251 Memories of Péter Városy, written around 1980. p. 26. Owned by the author.

252 The letter of Rudolf Raab dated 3 February 1950 to Gerhard Emmerich. In the possession of the author.

253 Heinrich Fothe (1915–?) was a car mechanic who served as a police officer before 1939. During the siege of Budapest, he was ranked *Leutnant* and served as the commander of the *Feldgendarmerie-Trupp* of the 13th Panzer Division. During the breakout attempt, he was captured on 17 or 18 February (!) 1945 and released on 27 September 1953.

254 *WASt*, the letter of Heinrich Fothe, dated 14 October 1957.

255 The letter of Rudolf Raab dated 3 February 1950 to Gerhard Emmerich. Owned by the author.

256 BA-B R 9361-III/1178715 and R-9361-III/540414 Franz Liebisch.

257 *WASt* The letter of Joachim Boosfeld to the *WASt*, undated (from the 1950s).

258 See Lindenau's letter, dated 15 June 1960, to Gerhard Seemen, chairman of the *OdR*; BA-MA B 43/86 Usdai Lindenau an die Ordensgemeinschaft der Ritterkreuzträger 15.06.1960.

259 BA-MA RH 7/665 Collection titled *"Kimutatás a Wehrmacht kötelékéből a Waffen-SS-hez vezényelt vezérkari tisztekről"* ("Summary of the staff officers reassigned from the Wehrmacht to the Waffen-SS"). 22 of these are detailed with biographies, however, Daniel Lindenau is not contained therein.

260 BA-MA RH 7/282, Schreiben OKH PA/ P5 26.3.45. It needs to be mentioned here that the Association of Knight's Cross Recipients was aware of this document. However, this did not prevent them from honouring Lindenau afterwards.

261 BA-MA B 43/86 Usdau Lindenau an die Ordensgemeinschaft der Ritterkreuzträger 16.11.1959. and 15.06.1960.

262 In the higher units of the Hungarian army, these two functions were separated; at the division-level units, there was a separate chief of staff, whose subordinate was the chief of the operations department. In the German military structure, these two functions were not separated.

263 BA-MA RH 7/665, *WASt*, Erhard Mainka's casualty files.

264 The relevant section of the war log of the Soviet 109th Heavy Artillery Brigade; see in TsAMO 9937. fond, 1. sub-fond, 45. volume, p. 15.

265 Ferenc Dr. Villányi: *Édesapánk naplója 1944. december 9. – 1945. május 17.*, p. 3. Manuscript owned by the author. The text mentions Maringgele as "German lieutenant Maringer". Béla Józsa: *Egyetemisták*, p. 69. most probably also refers to Maringgele.

266 BA-B SSO Personalkarte Hermann Maringgele. According to certain statements, he had already received this rank at the beginning of January 1945. However, no sources confirm this, and the recommendation of the *Ritterkreuz des Eisernen Kreuzes* itself contradicts this, as he is still mentioned as *Hauptscharführer*. In his personal files, the date of 21 February is mentioned, which makes it even more plausible that Maringgele received the *Ritterkreuz des Eisernen Kreuzes* on the same day.

267 BA-B SSO Hermann Maringgele, 2235–2236.

268 BA-MA P-654557, Beurteilung 10.2.1941. Reiter Regiment 2. von Corvin Oberst und Rgts. Kdeur.

269 BA-MA Beurteilung 30.10.1941, von Hülsen, Oberst und Regimentskommandeur.

270 BA-MA RH 7/665. His assignments are often given incorrectly on certain internet forums without any references.

271 https://www.german-racing.com/gr/aktuelles/pressemitteilungen/20140711-sven-von-mitzlaff-siege-waren-sein-leben.php.

272 *Tolna Megyei Levéltár* (Tolna County Archives), alispáni iratok (vicecomes documents) 5820/1944/5657, quoted by *Dokumentumok a zsidóság üldöztetésének történetéhez. Iratok a Tolna Megyei Levéltárból.* Edited by Ágnes Ságvári. Budapest, Magyar Auschwitz Alapítvány, 1994, pp. 19–20.

273 http://www.virtualgrenadier.com/sale_item. php?iid=1375.

274 BA-MA Pers 6/55377.

275 TSAMO, 500. fond (www.germandocsinrussia.org), 12483. sub-fond, 95. volume, pp. 71–72.

276 Schöning manuscript, p. 26. Owned by the author.

277 This information was made kindly available to the author by Hartmut Müller.

278 See his biography at the recipients of *Deutsches Kreuz in Gold*.

279 Rasmussen, Johann (1923–?) *SS-Obersturmführer*, one of the battery commanders of the 8th SS Artillery Regiment, went missing during the breakout attempt.

280 *Major i.G.* Von Mitzlaff.

281 Transcription of the voice recording with Harry Phoenix. Recorded by Mirko Bayerl in 1989. The author wishes to express his gratitude to Bayerl for kindly providing the recording.

282 BA-B SSO Phoenix. The text of the recommendation is partly unintelligible.

283 Berger: *Ritterkreuzträger*, p. 360.

284 See Günther Nitz: *Die 292. Infanterie-Division*. Bonn, Bernard & Graefe, 1957.

285 The author wishes to express his gratitude to Ingo Möbius for sharing his collected data regarding Paul Reißmann.

286 B-MA Pers 6/1767 Heinrich Remlinger, Beurteilung 19.02.1941.

287 B-MA Pers 6/1767 Heinrich Remlinger, Beurteilung 19.02.1941.

288 BA-MA Pers 6/1767, Beurteilung 10.12.1943.

289 TSAMO, 500. fond (www.germandocsinrussia.org), 12472. sub-fond, 380. volume, p. 164.

290 BA-MA Pers 6/1767, Beurteilung 03.12.1944.

291 BStU HA IX/11, ZR 920 A.51.Telefonbuch KdS Budapest.

292 Manfred Zeidler: Stalinjustiz contra NS-Verbrechen. Die Kriegsverbrecherprozesse gegen deutsche Kriegsgefangene in der UsSSR in den Jahren 1943–1952. Kenntnisstand und Forschungsprobleme. (Berichte und Studien 9.) Dresden, HAIT, 1996, p. 25.

293 Klaus-Dieter Müller: *Todesurteile sowjetischer Militärtribunale gegen Deutsche (1944–1947). Eine historisch-biographische Studie.* Göttingen, Vandenhoeck & Ruprecht, 2015.

294 Manfred Zeidler: "Der minsker Kriegsverbrecherprozeß vom Januar 1946". *Vierteljahreshefte für Zeitgeschichte* 52 (2004/2), p. 223.

295 Zeidler: *Der minsker Kriegsverbrecherprozeß,* p. 218.

296 Jürgen Kilian: *Wehrmacht und Besatzungsherrschaft im russischen Nordwesten 1941–1944. Praxis und Alltag im Militärverwaltungsgebiet der Heeresgruppe Nord.* Paderborn–München–Wien, Schöningh, 2012.

297 Arno Diere (1920–?) was sentenced to 15 years of correctional camp labour.

298 Pavel Luknitsky: *Leningrad deystvuet* [Leningrad acts]. Kniga 3. Moscow, Sovietsky pisatel, 1968.

299 Mike Schmeitzner: "Unter Ausschuss der Öffentlichkeit? Zur Verfolgung von NS-Verbrechen durch die sowjetische Sonderjustiz". In *NS-Prozesse und die deutsche Öffentlichkeit.* Ed. Clemens Vollnhals and Jörg Osterholh. Göttingen, Vandenhoeck & Ruprecht, 2011, pp. 149–166, here pp. 159–160.

300 Claudia Weber: "Too closely identified with dr. Goebbels". Die Massenerschiessungen von Katyn in der Geschichte des Zweiten Weltkrieges und des Kalten Kriegs. Zeithistorische Forschungen 2011/1, http://www.zeithistorische-forschungen.de/1-2011/id=4747.

301 Pavel Luknitsky: *Leningrad deystvuyet...*

302 Eduard Sonnenfeld (1911–1946) *Leutnant.*

303 For the transcription of Remlinger's trial documents, the author wishes to express his gratitude to Wolfgang Oleschinski, the director of the *Dokumentations- und Informationszentrum Torgau.*

304 Schuster, Fritz (1894–?) went missing during the breakout attempt.

305 DODIS 18860, report of Harald Feller dated 31 October 1946, p. 3.

306 The German army was called *Reichsheer* until 1933. Then, the denomination was changed to Wehrmacht. Feller most probably coined a third one from these two expressions.

307 DODIS 18860, report of Harald Feller dated 31 October 1946, pp. 3–4.

308 A survivor mentions this in the documentary of János Varga titled *Razzia*.

309 The letter of Gábor Dénes in the author's possession.

310 http://www.hetek.hu/hatter/201505/az_elfeledett_magyar_embermento.

311 The report of Poul Poulsen, Danish royal consul to the Danish Ministry of Foreign Affairs in June 1945 from Istanbul. Copy owned by the author.

312 Ritter Eberhard Ritter und Edler von Oetinger (1892–1945?) *Oberst, Ehrenritter des Johanniter Ordens* (Knight of the German Order of Saint John): from 10 November 1939 the military commander of Hohensalza, western Prussia (today: Inowrocław, Poland); from 6 December 1940 commander of the *Heeresstreifendienst 9* (belonging to the 9th Army) and from 16 January 1943, the commander of the *Wehrmacht-Streifendienst z.b. V. 26.* stationed in Hungary. The circumstances of his death are unclear.

313 http://www.germandocsinrussia.org/de/nodes/2106-akte-311-akte-nr-7-der-aufklarungsabteilung-des-stabes-der-2-ukrainischen-front-ubersetzungen-deutscher-beutedokumente#page/131/mode/inspect/zoom/6.

314 Dénes Kövendi (1923–2011) student in the Eötvös-college, secondary school teacher, from 1968 a librarian, and a leading figure of the Hungarian librarian community.

315 The notes of Dénes Kövendi, dated 14 January 1945, owned by the author.

316 Pavel Luknitsky: *Leningrad deystvuet...*

317 According to Luknitsky's report, the court made Remlinger account for his decorations as well. During this process, Remlinger mentioned a decoration awarded to him in Budapest, which was, however, not awarded because of his frontline service. He was most probably referring to some kind of Hungarian medal, as he was not among the recipients of *Deutsches Kreuz in Silber*, the only German decoration for which he would have been eligible based on his position.

318 http://radolfzell-ns-geschichte.von-unten.org/ns-ehrenmal. Also see Markus Wolter: "Radolfzell im Nationalsozialismus. Die Heinrich Koeppen-Kaserne als Standort der Waffen-SS". In *Schriften des Vereins für Geschichte des Bodensees und seiner Umgebung.* Sonderdruck aus Heft 129., Ostfildern, Jan Thorbecke Verlag, 2011, pp. 16–22.

319 BA-B R 20/49, RFSS Chef der Bandenkampfverbände, Bandenlage "Ost" für die Zeit von 15. 7. bis 31. 7. 1943. Also, Tagebuch des Chefs des Stabes SS zur Partisanenbekämpfung von dem Bach-Zelewski, Eintrag vom 23.07.1943, BA-B R 20/45b. 81.

320 For the details, see Alexander Gogun: *Stalin's Commandos. Ukrainian Partisan Forces on the Eastern Front.* London, I. B. Tauris, 2016.

321 Helmut Friedrich: *Was ist aus uns geworden*, p. 61. Manuscript owned by the author.

322 Hans-Otto Wachter: *Als die Feuer brannten Band IV.*, p. 108. Manuscript owned by the author.

323 *WASt*, Z-Karte Joachim Rumohr.

324 The letter of Endre Fazekas to Krisztián Ungváry, dated 3 March 1998.

325 *WASt*, Z-Karte Joachim Rumohr.

326 http://www.degob.hu/index.php?showarticle=15.

327 http://beszelo.c3.hu/cikkek/az-%E2%80%9Eorok-vamzer%E2%80%9D.

328 Sztehlo later heard about him that he was reassigned to the frontline section near the Keleti Railway Station, where he was wounded and thereafter airlifted out of the encirclement. Others who were saved mention him by the name "Major Voight". The person has not yet been identified.

329 Gábor Sztehlo: *Isten kezében*. Budapest, Magyarországi Evangélikus Egyház Sajtóosztálya, 1984, p. 133.

330 Ein Besuch in Ungarn. *Der Freiwillige*, 1977, p. 11. Copy owned by the author.

331 TSAMO, 9937. fond, 1. sub-fond, 45. volume, 61.

332 Gyula Takátsy (1892–1957), deputy commander of the Prónay Detachment, as well as serving in the Hungarian I Corps during the siege of Budapest.

333 Rudolf Schindler (1910–?) in 1944 *Zweiter Generalstabsoffizier (Ib)* of the 13th Panzer Division. During the siege of Budapest, an officer of the *IX. Waffen-Gebirgskorps*. There is no data regarding him after he was taken captive; most probably, he died before reaching the main camp.

334 TSAMO, 9937. fond, 1. sub-fond, 45. volume, 15. The other "staff major" was most probably *Major i. G.* Erhard Mainka.

335 TSAMO, 9937. fond, 1. sub-fond, 1. volume.

336 Willi Carl: *Unter dem Schwert des Damokles*. Wickede, Hutters, 1985, p. 337.

337 BA-MA P 6/62279.

338 BA-MA Pers 1/, Lebenslauf Bernhard Panck, 12.4.1953 (Panck was the subordinate of Schack).

339 Norbert Számvéber: "Adalékok a budapesti hídfőben harcoló magyar alakulatok harcértékéhez az újabban visszatért levéltári források tükrében". In *Ad Acta. A Hadtörténelmi Levéltár Évkönyve 2001*. Budapest, Hadtörténelmi Levéltár, 2001, p. 73. (The article mistakenly attributes an SS rank to Schack.)

340 BA-MA, N 370, a magazine cut-out in the personal files of Pfeffer-Wildenbruch.

341 BA-MA, N 370, a telegram, undated (between 15 January and 20 January 1945) in the personal files of Pfeffer-Wildenbruch.

342 Andreas Thies auction April 2008, pp. 328–330., item no. 359.

343 BA-MA Pers 6/62491.

344 BA-MA RH 7/665.

345 Schöning-manuscript. Owned by the author.

346 The author wishes to express his gratitude to Heinz-Werner Sondermann for providing photography and additional documents regarding Schitthelm.

347 Some of the German imperial infantry regiments were numbered in a double manner. In addition to the original numbering of the states, they received "common" numbers as well, similar to the Hungarian K.u.K. (*kaiserlich und königlich*, "imperial and royal") system. The common number of the 12th Royal Saxon Regiment was 177.

348 Joachim-Gerhard Schmidhuber (1924–?), assigned as *Leutnant* to the 36th Panzer Regiment on 1 December 1943. Wolfgang Schmidhuber (1922–1944),

Oberleutnant at the 150th Panzer Brigade, died during *Operation "Greif"* near Malmédy when a grenade splinter hit him in the chest. (the 150th Panzer Brigade received American equipment to deceive the American troops in the Battle of the Ardennes. However, the action failed.)

349 BA-MA P 6/1863. Beurteilung von 15.2.1934.

350 BA-MA P 6/1863, 14. Schützen Brigade Vorschlag zur bevorzugten Beförderung.

351 The author wishes to express his gratitude to Zsolt Dávid for providing him with the assessment files.

352 BA-MA P 6/1863, Beurteilungsbeitrag über Oberst Schmidhuber 1. August 1944.

353 The letter of Miklós Nagy Miklós. Owned by the author.

354 The kind disclosure of Győző Benyovszky to the author in December 1997.

355 *Die Wehrmachtberichte.* 1939–1945. Band 3. Köln, GLB, 1989, p. 373.

356 Only a fraction of the strength of *Panzergrenadier-Division Feldherrnhalle* came from the SA. Initially, the personnel of the III battalion of the 271st Infantry Regiment of the 93rd Infantry Division came from the *SA-Standarte "Feldherrnhalle"*. On 9 August 1942, the regiment received the designation *"Feldherrnhalle"*. In February 1943, the 271st Infantry Regiment of the 93rd Infantry Division was incorporated into the 60th Infantry Division. In May 1943, the 60th Infantry Division was renamed *Panzergrenadier-Division Feldherrnhalle.*

357 Ernst Fischer, Paul Krämer, Ernst Röschmann and Gustav Soldner.

358 Only one veteran soldier remembered the sewing of the armbands. Willibald Bierwirth, serving in the *Instandsetzungsdienst* of the II *Abteilung* of the 4th Panzer Regiment. See the letter of Bierwirth dated 21 August 2001, in the possession of the author.

359 Schmidhuber referred to the fact that the Hungarian army was much less preoccupied with the resting of the soldiers, as well as the post office and healthcare services and the catering to the soldiers as the Wehrmacht.

360 TSAMO, 500. fond (www.germandocsinrussia.org), 12472. sub-fond, file 380., 47–50.

361 Ilona "Csibe" Elek (1907–1988) Olympic fencing champion in 1936 and 1948. She got acquaintanced with Sédey in the field of sports, as he was one of the leaders of the Hungarian Fencing Association.

362 Vilmos Lucska (1919–1949) became a hairdresser's assistant, having completed six years of elementary school. He joined the Arrow Cross Party in 1944. His membership was suspended because of his theft and forgery of official documents. After the Arrow Cross coup, he worked in the Majestic Hotel (*Majestic Szálló*) at the *KdS* high command as an "intern" (during his trial, the details thereof were not questioned). After the encirclement of Budapest was complete, he became one of the commanders of the Arrow Cross detachments of the Royal Hotel. At the end of the siege, he went into hiding and, until his arrest in 1948, he lived in Várpalota as János Lantos. He was sentenced to death and executed.

363 The confession is quoted in Szekeres: *A pesti gettók*, p. 184.

364 Szekeres: *A pesti gettók*, p. 28.

365 Miksa Domonkos (1890–1954) mechanical engineer, reserve captain, one of the leaders of the Pest ghetto; between 1945 and 1950, general secretary of the Pest Jewish Religious Community in Budapest. In 1953, he was arrested as one of the main suspects in a planned Zionist show trial. The aim of the trial was, among other issues, to demonstrate that Jewish people murdered Raoul Wallenberg. Due to Stalin's death, the trial was eventually not organised. Domonkos was released on 13 November 1953 but died shortly afterwards as a result of the torture he had suffered in detention.

366 Szekeres: *A pesti gettók*, p. 234.

367 Szekeres: *A pesti gettók,* p. 238. Also ÁBTL V-80871, Pál Szalai's confession in the Vilmos Lucska trial, 22 December 1948. pp. 36–37.

368 ÁBTL V-80871, confession of Vilmos Lucska, 31 December 1948., p. 27.

369 BFL XXV.2.b-85706/1949, Imre Nidosi and his accomplices, the confession of Imre Nidosi, 3 March 1948, p. 54.

370 BFL XXV.2.b-85706/1949, Imre Nidosi and his accomplices, the confession of Ferenc Perjési, undated, p. 43.

371 BFL VII.5.e. 1950-7587, the confession of Béla Kubissy, 6 March 1945, p. 29.

372 Jenő Lévai: *A pesti gettó csodálatos megmenekülésének hiteles története.* Budapest, Officina, 1946, p. 133. Also, Jenő Lévai: *Raoul Wallenberg regényes élete, hősi küzdelmei, rejtélyes eltűnésének titka.* Budapest, Magyar Téka, 1948, p. 251. In the literature on the persecution of the Jews, the issue was dealt with on the basis of Lévai's report and Szalai's testimony, without researching the details of the case or taking into account Kubissy's testimony. See *Magyarország 1944. Üldöztetés – Embermentés.* Ed. Szabolcs Szita. Budapest, Nemzeti Tankönyvkiadó, 1994, p. 101.

373 BFL XXV.2.b-85706/1949, Imre Nidosi and his accomplices, the confession of Károly Szabó, undated; p. 33.

374 Statement of Tamás Szabó to the author, 1 February 2015.

375 Lajos Kósa (1924–?). Interview owned by the author.

376 Per Anger: *Raoul Wallenberggel Budapesten.* Budapest, Belvárosi, 1999, p. 86.

377 Per Anger: *Raoul Wallenberggel Budapesten.* Budapest, Belvárosi, 1999, p. 86.

378 See János Dési: *Wallenberg-jegyzőkönyv.* Budapest. Ab Ovo, 2014. See also the interview with the United States Holocaust Memorial Museum in Washington, which János Dési kindly disclosed to the author.

379 János Dési: *Wallenberg-jegyzőkönyv.* Budapest, Ab Ovo, 2014, p. 53.

380 BA–MA MSg 2/4631, Ernst Schweitzer: *Der Kessel von Budapest,* p. 6.

381 ÁBTL V-80871, 13–14., the confession of Lajos Pollok, 31 December 1948.

382 https://nepszava.hu/1152958_karsai-laszlo-a-gettomentok-mitosza.

383 Péter Sipos: "Egy régi legenda újrafelfedezése". *História,* December 2006., pp. 32–33.

384 Artillery Colonel Lajos Lehoczky, in this time period, was the appointed commander of the Division.

385 Staff Captain Ferenc Irmay.
386 Today, the location belongs to the Hungarian Army Military Reconnaissance Office (Katonai Felderítő Hivatal); earlier, it had served as the seat of the *Országos Légvédelmi Parancsnokság* (Territorial Air Defence Command).
387 The exact name of the decoration is not known.
388 The letter of Győző Benyovszky, dated 25 January 1945. p. 7. Owned by the author.
389 Ernst Schweitzer: Bericht über die Kämpfe der 13. Panzerdivision Budapest und mein Ausbruch am 11.2.1945. (Feldlazarett 2/542, 26.2.1945), p. 4. Copy owned by the author.
390 Helmut Friedrich: *Was ist aus uns geworden*, p. 67.
391 In the summer of 1940, the 244th Infantry Regiment was refitted to become a motorised unit. On 15 September 1940, it received a new unit number; thus, it became 120th Infantry Regiment in subordination to the 60th Infantry Division.
392 https://ro.wikipedia.org/wiki/Ordinul_Militar_de_R%C4%83z-boi_%E2%80%9EMihai_Viteazul%E2%80%9D
393 BA-MA P 6/83624 The personal files of Wilhelm Schöning.
394 BA-MA P 6/83624 The personal files of Wilhelm Schöning.
395 Manuscript by Aurél Salamon, p. 34. Owned by the author.
396 Schöning-bequest, 1152/Pk. Billnitzer-group 45.I.30. num. Copy owned by the author.
397 Schöning-bequest, manuscript, p. 39.
398 Gerhard Stolley, commander of the 10th (heavy infantry gun) Company of the 66th Panzergrenadier Regiment of the 13th Panzer Division.
399 Wilhelm Fehrensen.
400 Dr. Bernhard Seeger (1909–2006), from November 1944 was the *Hauptartzt* of the 13th Panzer Division, ranked *Major der Reserve.*
401 The letter of Schöning to Schirmler (between 1960 and 1964) owned by the author.
402 It is not known where and when the article was published; it was found in Schöning's bequest in his own handwriting. The title was: *Kameradschaft stärker als der Tod.*
403 The author wishes to express his gratitude to Tibor Sugár for providing him with the bequest of Schöning.
404 Hans-Hermann Büllersbach (1923–?) officer of the 6th Company of the II Battalion of the 93rd Panzergrenadier Regiment of the 13th Panzer Division, successfully reached the German lines after the breakout attempt. He was still alive in 1995.
405 "…aus seinem Leben aus der Kampfzeit" – most probably a reference to his past as a party activist before 1933.
406 Pessel, *leitender Divisionsintendant* of the 13. Panzer Division, his name and date of birth are unknown.
407 Johann Sauer (1915–1944), legendary *Bataillonskommandeur* of the I Battalion

of the 93rd Panzergrenadier Regiment (13th Panzer Division). On 15 May 1944 he was decorated with the *Ritterkreuz des Eisernen Kreuzes*; in the summer of 1944, he died of his sustained wounds.

[408] *WASt* Zentralkartei Soldner.

[409] Számvéber: *Páncélos hadviselés a budapesti csatában,* pp. 143–172.

[410] Számvéber: *Páncélos hadviselés a budapesti csatában,* p. 355.

[411] TSAMO, 500. fond (*www.germandocsinrussia.org*), 12742. sub-fond, 409. volume, document no. 0308., 29 January 1945.

[412] The author wishes to express his gratitude to Ingo Möbius for the data.

[413] https://www.emedals.com/germany-heer-a-preliminary-award-document-for-the-knight-s-cross-of-the-iron-cross-to-unteroffizier-emil-ulrich.

[414] BA-B, R-9361-III/494291, Personalakte Wendrinski.

[415] HM HIM 16456/Em war log, p. 26. The diary ends with this fragmented page.

[416] BA-MA Pers 1/31177 and Pers 1/81629.

[417] BA-MA Pers 6/81629.

[418] BA-MA Pers 6/81629.

[419] The deployment area of Wolff's unit from the end of December 1944 was in District XIII, and after 18 January 1945, it was relocated to the middle and southern sectors of the Buda defensive ring.

[420] BA-MA Pers 1/31177, Pers 1/81629.

[421] BA-B R-9361/232080, Personalakte Zehender.

[422] BA-B R-9361/232080, 1935.11.08.

[423] BA-B R-9361/232080,1937.03.30.

[424] BA-B R-9361/232080, 1937.05.01.

[425] He signed all his documents as "m. d. F. b.", that is, *"mit der Führung beauftragt".* The author wishes to express his gratitude to Roland Pfeiffer for this information.

[426] Hans Bayer: *Die Kavallerie der Waffen-SS.* Gailberg-Heidelberg, author's edition, 1980, pp. 263–264.

[427] David Cesarani: *Adolf Eichmann,* p. 266.

[428] David Cesarani: *Adolf Eichmann,* p. 268.; see also *Ich Adolf Eichmann. Ein historischer Zeugenbericht.* Edited by Rudolf Aschenauer. Leoni am Starnberger See, Druffel, 1980, pp. 386–388.

[429] BA-B R-9361/232080, 06.09.1944.

[430] Fritz Landauer (1919–?) born in Nagyszeben (Hermannstadt/Sibiu). Until 1942, he was a reserve officer in the Romanian army; from November 1944, he was one of the company commanders of the *SS-Aufklärungs-Abteilung 8.* He was captured on 17 (!) February 1945 and released on 21 December 1949.

[431] *WASt,* Vermißtenmeldung Zehender.

[432] Scherzer: Himmlers militärische Elite, p. 118.

[433] *WASt,* Z-Kartei Helmut Bischoff, also HKE Fritz Landauer.

[434] Scheibert: *Die Träger,* 1. volume, p. 283. The name was incorrectly written as Pollack.

[435] Scherzer: *Himmlers militärische Elite,* p. 559.

436 *WASt,* Z-Kartei Johannes Buttkereit, also BA-B, R 9361-III/519947, the letters of Adolf John owned by the author.
437 BA-MA Pers 6/283861, Art. Stab z.b.V. mot 959 Beurteilung.
438 3rd Cavalry Brigade.
439 The letter of Johannes Finger to the author, dated 15 October 1994.
440 Jürgen Flügel's kind disclosure to the author.
441 Dénes Vass: *Egyetemisták az ostromgyűrűben*, p. 24. Manuscript owned by the author.
442 The letter of Gyula Kokovay, dated 21 November 1994, p. 7.
443 Gyula Kokovay: *Budapest védelme*, p. 12. Manuscript owned by the author.
444 The Regiment was renamed *Panzer-Artillerie-Regiment 13* in 1942.
445 *WASt,* Eidesstattliche Erklärung von Garola Göttler 1946.08.21.
446 BA-B, SSO Personalakte Friedrich Greger.
447 The unit was initially subordinated to the 13th Infantry Division. In 1940, the Division was reclassified as 13th Panzer Division. *Artillerie-Regiment 13* was renamed in 1942 as *Panzer-Artillerie-Regiment 13*.
448 Hans Kiesewetter (1906–?) originally served in the Wehrmacht as *Zugführer*; from 1936, he was a member of the Waffen-SS, but he did not join the *NSDAP*.
449 *WASt* Z-Kartei Fritz Hahn.
450 BA-MA Pers 6/275279 Vorschlag zur vorzugsweisen Beförderung 3.1.1943.
451 According to the work of Schreiber, on 16 January 1945.
452 BA-B R 9361-III/529307.
453 BA-B R-9361-III/529723, Posen, 26 May 1941.
454 *WASt,* Abwicklungsakten 13. Panzerdivision, Vernehmung Maikath 27.02.1945.; see also Z-Kartei Heller.
455 *WASt,* the letter of Heinrich Schumacher, dated 3 July 1962.
456 *WASt,* Abwicklungsakte 36. Beob.Abt.(mot.).
457 The person who wrote the recommendation over-interpreted the roles and possibilities of the Soviet troops. The combat task of the 23rd Rifle Corps was not to occupy Budapest from the march but to continue the encirclement of the city.
458 BA-B, SSO Karl-Heinz Keitel.
459 *WASt,* Z-karte Ernst Kreipe.
460 According to the *Deutsches Kreuz in Gold* volume, he was the *Schwadron-Chef* of the 5th *Schwadron* of the 18th SS Cavalry Regiment; however, according to the opinion of the author, this is incorrect.
461 BA-B SSO Bruno Meiert.
462 Torsten Schäfer: *„Jedenfalls habe ich auch mitgeschossen". Das NSG-Verfahren gegen Johann Josef Kuhr und andere ehemalige Angehörige des Polizeibataillons 306, der Polizeireiterabteilung 2 und der SD-Dienststelle von Pinsk beim Landgericht Frankfurt am Main 1962–1973. Eine textanalytische Fallstudie zur Mentalitätsgeschichte. Villigst Perspektiven.* Dissertationen des Evangelischen Studienwerks e. V. Villigst, Band 11, Münster, LIT Verlag, 2007.

463 *WASt,* Z-Karte Claus-Dietrich Meyer.

464 BA-B R-9361/II-715997 Personalakte Mittelberger.

465 Dávid Fröhlich: *Huszárok előre! Magyar sereglovasság a II. világháborúban.* Nagykovácsi, Puedlo, 2012, p. 152.

466 BA-B R 9361-III/543839.

467 Ferenc Pataki: *Vihar a sziget körül.* Ráckeve, Járási Pártbizottság, 1967, pp. 43–60.

468 The banner of the *Jungsturm* was blue-white-blue. Until 1909, the organisation was called the Blue-White-Blue Union.

469 TSAMO, 500. fond (*www.germandocsinrussia.org*), 12472. sub-fond, 387. volume, p. 375.

470 See Scheibert: *Die Träger,* 1. volume, p. 258.

471 http://kolberg-koerlin.de/familienforschung/totentafel/.

472 BA-B R-9361-III/551209.

473 BA-MA Pers 6/62049.

474 TSAMO, 401. fond, 95111. sub-fond, 541. lot.

475 BA-B SSO Ottomar Schaffner.

476 BA-B, R 601/1691 and VBS 2866400039506.

477 Schöning-manuscript, p. 26, p. 31.

478 BA-MA P 6/64756, Beurteilung 26.3.1943.

479 BA-B R 9361-III/195116, 557102.

480 Of this question, see József Meruk – Krisztián Ungváry: "Budapest hídjai a város ostromában". *Archívnet,* 19. (2019) 1. issue. http://www.archivnet.hu/budapest-hidjai-a-varos-ostromaban

481 *Bericht für Nachrichten der Burschenschaft Primislavia,* pp. 50–53.

482 BA-B R 9361-III/197992.

483 *WASt,* the letter of Willy Eberz, dated 14 February 1945. Eberz was most probably able to get out of Budapest at the beginning of January 1945 due to his injuries.

484 BA-MA Personalakte Willy Büchner.

485 Schöning-manuscript, p. 20.

486 Ernst Klose (1900–?) an observer officer of the *Panzer-Artillerie-Regiment "Feldherrnhalle 1"* captured during the breakout attempt. He was released on 8 December 1947.

487 *WASt,* Z-Kartei Eduard Bulle.

488 Dörner, Jansa, Pfeffer-Wildenbruch, Rumohr, Schmidhuber, Schöning and Zehender.

489 Pfeffer-Wildenbruch (*Ritterkreuz des Eisernen Kreuzes* and *Eichenlaub* as well), Dörner, Gottstein, Rumohr, Schmidhuber and Zehender.

490 See Rainer: *Századosok,* pp. 74.